In this book, Anthony Jenkins examines seven Victorian playwrights who, despite their own ideals and prejudices and the theatre's conservatism, tried to come to terms with such momentous subjects as womanliness, honour, and money. The opening chapter sets a frame of reference that briefly describes the social transformation of theatre during the century and the increasing respectability of actors and playhouses. Subsequent chapters deal with the drama of Edward Bulwer, Tom Robertson, W.S. Gilbert, H.A. Jones, Arthur Pinero, Oscar Wilde, and Bernard Shaw. The plays are examined within the social and political context of the Reform Bills, the Revolution of 1848, the Great Exhibition, royal patronage, censorship and copyright, and, above all, the 'Woman Question'. Jenkins combines politics and theatrical history with literary criticism to shed provocative light on the struggle to relate the London theatre to the realities of Victorian England.

The Making of Victorian Drama

The Making of
Victorian Drama

ANTHONY JENKINS

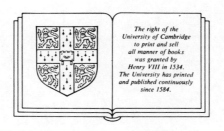

The right of the
University of Cambridge
to print and sell
all manner of books
was granted by
Henry VIII in 1534.
The University has printed
and published continuously
since 1584.

CAMBRIDGE UNIVERSITY PRESS

Cambridge

New York   Port Chester   Melbourne   Sydney

Published by the Press Syndicate of the University of Cambridge
The Pitt Building, Trumpington Street, Cambridge CB2 1RP
40 West 20th Street, New York, NY 10011, USA
10 Stamford Road, Oakleigh, Melbourne 3166, Australia

First published 1991

Printed in Great Britain at the University Press, Cambridge

British Library cataloguing in publication data

Jenkins, Anthony *1936*–
The making of Victorian drama
1. Drama in English, 1837–1900–Critical studies
I. Title
822.809

Library of Congress cataloguing in publication data

Jenkins, Anthony. 1936–
The making of Victorian drama / Anthony Jenkins.
p. cm.
Includes bibliographical references (p.   ) and index.
ISBN 0-521-40205-0 (hardback)
1. English drama–19th century–History and criticism.
2. Literature and society–Great Britain–History–19th century.
3. Theater–Great Britain–History–19th century.   4. Social
problems in literature.   I. Title.
PR734.S5J46   1991
822'.809355–dc20   90–2687   CIP

ISBN 0 521 40205 0 hardback

Contents

Illustrations

Acknowledgements

This book could not have been completed without the skill and energy of Diana Rutherford who coped patiently with a thousand and one revisions over several years. I am also indebted to William Benzie, Michael Booth, Ann Saddlemyer, Reginald Terry, and Doreen Thompson, for their suggestions and encouragement, and to Sarah Stanton, of Cambridge University Press, who spurred things on at a crucial stage in the book's development. Corinna Gilliland researched the political and social background, discovered a wealth of interesting illustrations, and helped create the index; her assistance has been of fundamental importance. The University of Victoria has generously supported this project from its beginnings, and my research has been facilitated at every turn by the expertise and courtesy of the staff at the University Library, particularly Special Collections and Interlibrary Loans, at the Theatre Museum, Covent Garden, and at the Royal Archives, Windsor Castle. Excerpts from Queen Victoria's journals are quoted by the gracious permission of Her Majesty Queen Elizabeth II.

Victoria, B.C.

CHAPTER I

Breaking through the darkness

The time has come when a change may be produced in the destinies of the stage as complete as that in a nation bursting from slavery to freedom. The patronage of the drama by HER MAJESTY at Court was the first streak of welcome light breaking through the darkness of the dramatic horizon. The bright dawn is already advancing; and if the profession be but true to itself, we may live to see the sun of prosperity shedding its noon-tide glories on the British Stage.
The Court Theatre and Royal Dramatic Record of Performances at Windsor (1849)

The attempt to rescue British Drama from the theatre's rowdy spectacle began a few months before Princess Victoria became Queen. By the time the Empress died, the theatre itself had grown respectable and a drama of ideas, adapted (more or less) to middle-class taste, had its place in that respectability. For without the approbation of the box-office, no dramatist, however independent and open-minded, could make his mark. Until theatre buildings and actor-managers became fashionable enough to attract the sort of audience which might, for whatever reason, support a serious drama, 'the worst and deadliest enemy of the English drama [was] – the English theatre'.[1] Even by the mid nineties, when theatres had become safely domestic and actors were gentlemen and ladies, a mind like Shaw's was prisoner to a manager's idea of popular taste. Richard Mansfield, who had won success with *Arms and the Man* and would make Shaw's reputation in America with *The Devil's Disciple*, rejected *Candida* because it was all talk and anti-heroics. Mansfield wanted an ideal:

The stage is for romance and love and truth and honor. To make men
better and nobler. To cheer them on the way –
Life is real. Life is earnest. And the grave is not its goal.
. . .
Be a hero in the fight! . . . Candida *is* beautiful . . .
There are fine things here – but – we are paid – alas – Shaw – we are paid to *act*.[2]

The Victorian theatre was rich in romance. Ideas which possessed an entire century, like the status of women, a hero's idea of chivalric

I

service, money's allure (which gaudy billboards might have alliter-
ated as WOMEN, WAR, and WEALTH), could not be examined
seriously until the theatre learned to be serious about itself. So, to
understand the playwright's struggle, this account of Victorian
Drama begins with that theatrical context and with the monarch
whose conventional taste, like that of her son, mirrored the romantic
sentiments of the audience at large. Royal patronage did nothing to
'improve' serious drama nor did it directly affect the dramatists'
prestige: Gilbert and Pinero received their knighthoods after 1901.
But the Queen's fascination with the theatre, her affection for
particular actors, and the political decision she and Prince Albert
came to in the revolutionary year of 1848 affected 'the destinies' of
actors, playhouses, and playgoers. Then, governed by their own
personalities, certain playwrights tried, at Matthew Arnold's urging,
to 'organize' the drama within the limits of that hard-won dignity.

At Victoria's accession, fashionable society favoured the Opera,
though, as the Queen's own theatregoing proves, not as exclusively as
is sometimes suggested. Drury Lane and Covent Garden, the two
patent theatres, had been remodelled at the turn of the century into
huge caverns that could each seat over 3,500 people. The 'town' still
came. At Mrs Siddons's farewell performance in June 1812 as Lady
Macbeth, Covent Garden 'was crowded in an extraordinary manner
in every part. Persons of high distinction were in the uppermost
Boxes – Ladies as well as gentlemen',[3] and two years later they flocked
to see Edmund Kean at Drury Lane. But in order to fill those vast
spaces on more ordinary occasions, managers were pushed ever closer
to the spectacular entertainments offered by the non-patent theatres.
Stunning processions, acrobats and clowns, performing animals were
added to the bills; as the proprietor of Astley's Amphitheatre
protested, 'Why do they take my horses? I never tried to engage Mrs
Siddons.'[4] An evening of Shakespeare followed by a ballet and a
pantomime might last from seven till after midnight and, since
admission was at half-price after eight-thirty, spectators not uncom-
monly came for part of a play and its afterpiece, though without the
distraction which attended the Queen's arrival 'just after the
beginning of the last act' of *The Lady of Lyons* (Covent Garden,
March 1838). However, she dispatched an equerry to assure
Macready she 'would come to see the whole play on Tuesday'.[5]

Though they tried to be all things to all people, the two 'major'
houses could not ward off the challenge from the 'minor' establish-

ments. The King's Theatre (Her Majesty's after 1837) in the Haymarket had been the sanctioned home of opera and ballet since Queen Anne's day. Across the road, the Little Theatre had been licensed since 1766 to perform legitimate plays during the summer, a privilege which was later extended to the Lyceum after having housed the Drury Lane company whose theatre burnt down in 1809. The Olympic and the Sans Pareil (Adelphi) were built in 1806, the Strand in 1832, and the St James's three years later. On the South bank, Astley's was joined by the Royal Circus (1782) which, in 1810, became the Surrey Theatre. The Coburg (later to be the Royal Victoria and later still the Old Vic) opened in 1816. These 'minor' theatres were forbidden legitimate drama but were able to circumvent that restriction by interpolating songs into a play and calling it a burletta, though what that term exactly meant not even the Lord Chamberlain's Office knew. 'In the 1830s the inclusion of five songs per act was held to redeem any amount of spoken dialogue, and by the early 1840s an occasional chord on the piano seems to have been all that was required.'[6] Under this convenient vagary, Madame Vestris at the Olympic could present tastefully translated French comedies and fairy-tale extravaganzas. By 1842, the prestige of the Haymarket's ever expanding 'summer' season earned a year-round patent. The twin-citadel had been breached and, in 1843, parliament at last repealed the Patent Acts and so gave way to the scramble for entertainment in a metropolis whose population had doubled since the turn of the century. In 1850 Leigh Hunt looked back in his *Autobiography* to a time before drama had succumbed to diversions of all sorts:

forty or fifty years ago people of all times of life were much greater playgoers than they are now. They dined earlier, they had not so many newspapers, clubs, and pianofortes; the French Revolution . . . had not yet opened a thousand new channels of thought and interest, nor had railroads conspired to carry people, bodily as well as mentally, into as many analogous directions. Everything was more concentrated, and the various classes of society felt a greater concern in the same amusements. Nobility, gentry, citizens, princes – all were frequenters of theatres, and even more or less acquainted personally with the performers. Nobility intermarried with them; gentry, and citizens too, wrote for them; princes conversed and lived with them.[7]

Troubled by his bustling times, Hunt exaggerates the performers' fall from society. Helen Faucit, Macready's leading lady, was to become Lady Martin and the Queen's friend. Macready, upon his retirement, received a personal message from Prince Albert commending 'the

efforts made by him for the purification and elevation of the stage'.[8]
The Prince could not accept the invitation to chair that testimonial
dinner, but he and the Queen certainly conversed with actors, if they
did not actually mix with them socially, and their patronage became
immensely important.

From her earliest visit to Drury Lane (1828), the young Victoria
was fascinated by performers as individuals. To mark the Princess's
sixteenth birthday, a concert was arranged at Kensington Palace;
afterwards she was able to meet Giulia Grisi, the soprano she
idolized: 'Grisi is *quite beautiful* off the stage . . . She is very quiet,
ladylike and unaffected in her manners. I spoke to her, and she
answered in a very pleasing manner.'[9] But though she loved opera
with a passion – for twenty years she studied singing with the bass-
baritone, Luigi Lablache – and thrilled to the ballet, a visit to the
Olympic in 1836 drew her attention to Charles Mathews: 'not good-
looking, but very clever and pleasing; he has a very slight, pretty
figure, with very small feet, and is very graceful and immensely
active'.[10] Here she writes as a connoisseur of the dance. After seeing
him and his vibrant partner, Madame Vestris, again in the following
April, she made pen-and-ink sketches of both, and they remained
favourites over the years. As an expert in voice production, she
reacted to other performers in a decisive if changeable way: 'Miss
Faucit is plain and thin, and her voice is much against her . . . she rants
and screams too much also, but as she is very young, they say she may
become a good actress.'[11] In *The Lady of Lyons* 'she was *quite detestable*
and *ranted, screamed*, and I may say ROARED to disgust every one',[12]
but in *Richelieu* 'Miss Faucit . . . surprised me agreeably'.[13] Charles
Kemble earned a severe critique on all counts: 'his voice is not
pleasant to me; he makes terrible faces also which spoils his
countenance and he looks old and does not carry himself well'.[14]
Nevertheless, the Princess and her mother were amongst the throng
at Covent Garden to witness Kemble's farewell a few months later.
She was so impressed by his Benedick that, immediately after her
marriage, she requested the actor to return to the stage for a few
nights so that her consort might share in her pleasurable memories.
So the 64-year-old Kemble returned for four performances – Don
Felix in *The Wonder*, Mercutio, Benedick, Hamlet. On the first night
(24 March 1840) it seemed, said a writer in *John Bull*, 'as if by a
vigorous effect of the will he had shaken forty years off his back, and
bounded before us in all the vigour, elasticity, and fervid enthusiasm

of youth. Oh! when will our young men learn to be and move the lover like him!' The Queen echoed that praise; as Hamlet he 'acted most beautifully and looked very well and quite young'.[15] Four years later, Kemble was asked to read *Cymbeline* at Buckingham Palace; he had to decline a second invitation in 1848 because of his deafness.

As Princess, Victoria was able to pursue her enthusiasm, in a way which as Queen and then as wife and mother she could not. In 1833, she had crossed the river to the Royal Victoria and had also seen the horseback heroics of Ducrow at Astley's in *St George and the Dragon*; but as Queen she upheld the dignity of the two patent theatres and, on occasions, the Haymarket under Webster's enterprising management. But once the opera season opened in the Spring, she would go nowhere else. Her theatregoing in 1838 was typical of those early years: three visits to Drury Lane to see Charles Kean as Hamlet and (twice) as Richard III; two to Covent Garden where she caught the last Act of *The Lady of Lyons* and two afterpieces, then returned three days later to see the whole of Bulwer's play; three to the Lyceum's winter season of opera; twenty-eight visits to opera at Her Majesty's between the end of March and the middle of August. However, ardour and duty coincided when, in the following year, she attended the pantomime at Drury Lane and saw that 'miracle of a performance', Van Amburgh's lions: '[he] makes them roar, and lies upon them after enraging them. It's quite beautiful to see, and makes me wish I could do the same!'[16] The Queen saw them six more times in as many weeks. Macready, then manager of the rival house, was not happy. He would have been still less so had he read his sovereign's diary once she again graced Covent Garden: 'I was much more amused at Drury Lane . . . *those Lions* knock Rob Roy and everything else of that sort to the ground.'[17] After her marriage, Victoria visited the circus only once (Astley's 1846) but, even before the repeal of the Patent Acts, she and the Prince found mutual pleasure at the St James's which, for six months or so each year, became the 'Théâtre Français à Londres'.

In 1848, a year of revolution throughout Europe, Alexander Dumas brought his Théâtre Historique from embattled Paris to Drury Lane. This French invasion of a theatre still regarded as a British institution touched off a furious protest. On the opening night (12 June), the boos and shouts of demonstrators waving placards and umbrellas disrupted the entire performance. In the press, letters of dismay over that mob scene jostled others which complained about this foreign intrusion and the parlous state of British drama as a whole, since so many plays on the London stage were 'adapted from the French'. Dumas's actors struggled on through a second riotous night and then retreated to the St James's. A fortnight later, their majesties interrupted their opera-going for a command performance by the Keans in *Money* and *The Wonder* at the Haymarket and, a week later, for the sake of English Drama, they gave a similar accolade to Macready whose *Henry VIII* had hurriedly replaced the French at Drury Lane. Ben Webster, proprietor of the Haymarket, writing to a friend, complained of the monarch's favour to one whose vanity would only draw distinction upon himself instead of the whole profession:

Is it not too bad that Her Majesty should have been humbugged into a Command [performance of *Henry VIII*] at Drury Lane for Macready's *exclusive* benefit and under the idea that by such patronage she is serving the English Drama? You know as well as I do that the exorbitant terms of this lump of egotism and his only condescending to act in plays when *he* only has a chance – written by his *particular* friends, has been the bane of the profession.[18]

Then, in a conscious effort to raise the theatre in society's eyes, the Prince instructed his private secretary to ask Charles Kean to organize 'English performances once a week at Windsor Castle, commencing after Christmas – for six weeks'. Kean realized at once that this 'grand business . . . will be of the utmost service to me',[19] but the royal intent was to shed 'welcome light' on the entire profession and to educate the nation:

From time immemorial mankind has delegated to the affluent, the educated and the powerful the province of directing taste and opinion on all subjects connected with happiness and mental improvement . . . in the SOVEREIGN LADY of these realms the people of England happily possess an example which their own approval . . . must ever incline them to follow . . . By all ranks it was esteemed a graceful and becoming act in the Ruler of a civilised and intellectual people to set the example of patronising a class of entertainments that, when directed to the improvement of the heart and mind, becomes a valuable adjunct to education in its highest aims, and only when neglected sinks into a coarse and demoralising amusement.[20]

To those same ends, Macready was honoured by the royal presence, when as King Lear (February 1851) he retired from the Haymarket, and by the Prince's approbation of a career which had so 'elevated' the British stage.

Important as the annual Windsor performances were as a social symbol, they also deepened that loyalty to individual performers which had always coloured Victoria's attitude to the stage. It was evident even before the Windsor venture, for when Charles Mathews and Madame Vestris assumed the management of the Lyceum that theatre became immediately acceptable. After the first Windsor season, although the St James's French plays retained their undiminished attraction until their quality fell away in the mid fifties, those theatres which were associated with actors who played at Windsor began to appear on the royal calendar. When Webster moved to the Adelphi the royals went too, and John Buckstone, the next manager at the Haymarket and a particular favourite of the whole royal family, received their increasing patronage as did Alfred Wigan when he took over at the Olympic. But it was Charles Kean and his wife, Ellen Tree, who received especial favour, first under Webster's management in Shakespeare at the Haymarket and then at their own theatre in Oxford Street, the Princess's.

Royal patronage brought social cachet to an expanding circle of actors and theatres but it did not provoke new plays which might add to the 'mental improvement . . . of a civilised and intellectual people'. The plays selected for Windsor were either those of Shakespeare, scaled down to the particularities of the Rubens room or St George's Hall, or farces and sentimental comedies. In town, the royal family found pleasure in the same fare presented more spectacularly. At the Haymarket, Webster moved and delighted them with *Masks and Faces* – Tom Taylor and Charles Reade's play about Peg Woffington and other actors of a former age – or Buckstone sent them into fits of laughter as his quirky self in burlesques like *Mr Buckstone's Ascent of Mount Parnassus*. At the Lyceum there were such magical extravaganzas as *The King of the Peacocks* and at the Olympic they saw Frederick Robson as *The Yellow Dwarf*.

The Queen loved strong emotional contrasts and spectacular effects, and in Kean's grand-opera productions of Shakespeare she could indulge that appetite in the assurance that Mr Kean's researches at the British Museum, as pointed out in his programme notes, meant that each gorgeous tableau was scrupulously faithful to historical TRUTH. If the soul of Catherine of Aragon was not in fact transported by angels to heaven then it surely ought to have been. Also at the Princess's were genteel comedies like *Love in a Maze* which the Queen saw twice and pronounced 'full of wit – and with an excellent moral, particularly for young ladies'.[21] There, too – oh, shades of Van Amburgh's lions – were gentlemanly melodramas such

7

as *Pauline* ('one quite held one's breath, and was quite trembling when the Play came to an end'[22]) and the sensational *Corsican Brothers* which ran for sixty-six nights in 1852 and which the Queen saw five times, sketching a scene from it in her journal. Yet she was not uncritical. That same season she attended a benefit for the Keans and saw, as an afterpiece, *The Vampire*, a 'phantasm' in three 'dramas' which carried the tale across the centuries from 1660 to 1860. Dion Boucicault who had concocted this story (and those other successes) from French sources impressed the Queen so much in the title role that she commissioned a watercolour of him as Sir Alan Raby: 'I can never forget his livid face and fixed look, in the two first Dramas. It quite haunts me.'[23] But the play itself, when she returned the following week, did 'not bear seeing a second time, and is, in fact, very trashy'.[24]

It was Boucicault who evoked her very last tears, smiles, and tingles of excitement in a public theatre. Nine years later, this time at the Adelphi, she saw *The Colleen Bawn*: 'went with Albert and the two girls . . . to see the celebrated melodrama . . . D. Boucicault and his wife (former Miss Robertson, whom I remember some years ago at the Princess's) acted admirably as the ragged Irish peasant and the Colleen Bawn. The scenery was very pretty, and the whole piece very characteristic and thrilling.'[25] Two days after a third visit, her mother, the Duchess of Kent, died and Victoria plunged into unconsolable grief. In December, the Prince Consort succumbed to typhoid and the Queen commenced her own long-running drama as widow to Albert the Good.

Within two years of that cataclysm, the Prince of Wales married Princess Alexandra and the young couple entered upon a whirl of amusements, much to the Queen's displeasure. Yet their gaiety had at first a certain innocence. Private visits to the Haymarket retained something of the domestic jollity that characterized those of former times when the Queen and her consort struggled to keep straight faces as Buckstone, 'lighting' them to their box, tripped over the stairs as he backed before them or when she and the Princess Royal rode away in tears of laughter because the deaf old manager, his eyes watering after quickly removing his makeup, had thought the Queen, in complimenting him, had asked if he had a cold: 'No, Ma'am, no. It's soap.'[26] When the Prince brought his bride to see *Mr Buckstone at Home*, Mrs Keeley (a favourite since the early days at the Princess's) sang a song about fairy-tale princes and princesses. Pointing to the Royal Box, she improvised a reference to the royal pair who sat invisibly behind their attendants. The audience caught the allusion and stopped the show until the couple came forward to acknowledge the cheers.

The Queen kept that box till Buckstone retired, although she would not see his management's big successes, *Our American Cousin* (with E.A. Sothern as Lord Dundreary) and its sequels (*Lord Dundreary Married and Done For* and *Brother Sam*), which maintained the style and tone of the comedies she had delighted in. Nor would the 'revolution' worked by Marie Wilton at the newly named Prince of Wales's in 1865 have bewildered the Queen: the company's acting was as subtle as that of any troupe at the old Théâtre Français à Londres, the meticulous sets and costumes carried on the traditions of Madame Vestris, and the success of their repertoire, particularly Tom Robertson's *School*, a transparently simple Cinderella story, can be explained by one of Victoria's most frequent words of praise – it was 'charming'. Robertson's plays continued to be the company's staple money-makers when Marie and her husband, Squire Bancroft, moved to the Haymarket in 1880 though they began their tenancy with *Money*, a perennial since 1840.

Melodrama also continued to maintain its hold over a public whose desire for sensational effects grew ever more voracious. Boucicault's *Formosa* at Drury Lane (1869) culminated in a realistic staging of the Oxford and Cambridge boat race; it also included a different sort of sensationalism by presenting several women of ill repute. They aroused fierce protest as did the thought that an Oxford stroke could approach his big day in 'the very vortex of dissipation',[27] but the play ran for over one hundred nights. And when Henry Irving, who had played the villain in *Formosa*, assumed control at the Lyceum, that temple of English Drama offered spectacular Shakespeare and melodrama with all the sumptuous theatricality, if not the pomposity, of a Charles Kean. Appropriately, the two actors who were knighted by the end of the century, Irving and Bancroft, represented a continuity which lasted, especially in the provinces, until the First World War.

Yet within that continuing tradition there occurred a distinctive change. By the late eighties women began to rebel against man's stifling patronage. Onto the stage came ladies whose pasts were decidedly shady, and even respectable women were seen to be capable of untruths; officers and gentlemen might be rotters; money could perhaps buy a person out of awkward situations. Yet although Paula

9

Tanqueray and her saintly step-daughter are worlds away from the heroines of the forties, *The Second Mrs Tanqueray* might well appear concurrently with an old favourite like *The Lady of Lyons*. Both were acceptable and, like Marlborough House and Windsor Castle, both typifed the values of the century's final decade.

This had not been so before the eighties. As stories began to circulate about the Prince's habits, his gambling, his eye for the ladies, his rich and raffish friends, life at Marlborough House became a symbol to the sixties of disintegrating social standards and raised fears of a return to the extravagances of George III's feckless sons. Allowed no official authority by his mother, 'poor foolish Bertie' hurtled from theatre to club, yacht to spa, race-course to baccarat table; and certain elements of society followed his lead. A public outcry followed the disclosure that Sir Charles Mordaunt had cited the Prince among others in his impending divorce case. The Prince maintained his innocence but was brought into court in February 1870 as a witness for Lady Mordaunt. The Princess of Wales was pitied but had to endure the boos that greeted their appearance at the Olympic a week after the Prince's day in court. 'To speak in rude and general terms,' said Gladstone to the Foreign Secretary, 'the Queen is invisible and the Prince of Wales is not respected.'[28] Republican feeling grew in many quarters and then, exactly a decade after his father's death, the Prince also fell victim to typhoid and all England trembled. Slowly he recovered, and by February 1872 London was alive with bunting and shouts of 'God bless the Prince of Wales' as he and the Queen, in public again at last, rode in an open carriage to a service of national thanksgiving at St Paul's. Love and loyalty returned, and there began a period of adjustment as continuing disapproval of the Prince's lifestyle gave way to a growing appreciation of his charm and the value of his energetic sociability to the nation.

An episode from the Prince's tour of India in 1875–6 exemplifies those conflicting attitudes. Even at its outset, the tour raised doubts from the more radical members of parliament, but reports of the Prince's triumphant reception allayed this criticism. Yet under that enthusiasm were ripples of displeasure. In Calcutta, where the white Raj were more English than the English, society had fought for a place at Lady Clarke's dinner party to honour HRH. The Prince did not consider this an official function and, learning that Charles Mathews was appearing at the city's theatre, asked that he and his second wife

(Madame Vestris had died in 1856) might join the assembly after dinner. Mathews broke off *My Awful Dad* in mid performance, announcing the royal command, and hastened to Lady Clarke's whereupon the Prince took the pretty Mrs Mathews 'to the verandah and sat there chaffing and smoking cigarettes from directly after dinner until 2 a.m. – the official Indignants kicking their feet in impatient and envious rage, not thinking it respectful to go before the Prince. Calcutta was furious at this.'[29]

The Prince came home to further trouble. Gossip had it that he had implicated himself with Lady Aylesford, but when he and the Princess appeared together at Covent Garden on the night of his return, 'the shouts, the cheers, the "bravos" were as vociferous and long-continued as they were hearty and spontaneous. The whole assembly rose; and it seemed as if the demonstrations of welcome would never cease.'[30] Provided the Prince's rumoured relationships did not become an open scandal, the public was now prepared to applaud him.

This was particularly true after Lillie Langtry caught the royal eye in 1877. Although their intimate friendship was soon common knowledge, it remained just talk and, besides, the lady was ravishingly beautiful. People stood up on their chairs to catch a glimpse of her as she rode in the park, her photograph graced the smartest shop windows, she was presented to the Queen and received by the Princess. In 1881, when the birth of her daughter (by Prince Louis of Battenburg) and the threat of a divorce endangered that respectable veneer, the Prince and Princess lent their support to her debut as Kate Hardcastle at a special charity matinée of *She Stoops to Conquer* at the Haymarket. Society flocked to this aptly titled occasion; it was in a good cause, and Mrs Langtry, having been coached by the actress Henrietta Hodson, gave a performance that was creditable enough for the Bancrofts to offer her a contract. The Royal Box was tactfully empty on her first night as a professional; no one seems to have thought it an anomaly for her to play the sweetly virginal Blanche Hay in the company's revival of Robertson's *Ours*. The Prince later saw her performance three times and, exactly a month into the run of the play, gave a dinner at Marlborough House at which Bancroft, Irving, and several other actor-managers mingled with the aristocratic guests. Some years later, Mrs Langtry herself went into management. When she returned to the Haymarket in 1898 to present Sydney Grundy's *The Degenerates*, there was much talk about whether the play was based on her own life, but this only increased the box-office receipts.

Outward beauty and pleasing opulence covered over less comforting realities. On stage, in elegantly upholstered drawing-rooms, glistening actors and actresses displayed their charm and grace. By 1883, Lillie Langtry was ordering her stage costumes from Worth of Paris; in the nineties, George Alexander invented the modern collar and tie, setting the fashion for off-stage gentlemen. By then it was quite usual for notices about what the performers wore to be printed side by side with the first-night reviews. W.S. Gilbert or Oscar Wilde might scratch at this veneer, but since their satire was deceptively cosy or so assertively unserious, audiences laughed yet held on to the Victorian illusion. The direct attacks of Ibsen and Shaw met, for the most part, with angry resistance or blinkered indifference.

A need for entertainment drew audiences in ever-increasing numbers. Theatres multiplied: the Comedy (1881), the Savoy (1882), the Garrick (1889), Wyndham's (1899) extended London's pleasure grounds from Drury Lane westward to Mayfair and beyond. The Prince went everywhere. Trapped at Sandringham by fog on the opening night at the Bancrofts' remodelled Haymarket, he was there for their tumultuous farewell and turned first nights at Irving's Lyceum or Tree's Her Majesty's into glittering occasions. That patronage 'made the theatre fashionable and respected'.[31] He preferred society pieces to Shakespeare but once admitted that 'the play that impressed me most was *The Corsican Brothers*'.[32] Under his aegis, burlesque evolved into the elegantly satirical Savoy operas of Gilbert and Sullivan, and the old burlettas were transformed into the romantic musical comedies presented by George Edwardes at the Gaiety. The gas-lit world of the early Victorian theatre burgeoned into the electric lavishness of the Prince's realm whose spangled centrepiece was Leicester Square where the minarets of the Alhambra, the operettas at Daly's, and the variety stars at the Empire entranced both the diamond-studded and the drab.

Although these pleasure palaces were almost as spacious as the old patent theatres, the century had witnessed the transformation of those auditoria and their methods of presentation. When John Philip Kemble raised Covent Garden from its ashes in 1809, he acknowledged the debasement of the once-fashionable pit benches on the theatre's main floor by creating a third tier of boxes for the opulent and by raising pit prices in order to discourage undesirables. He thus brought on himself the OP (Old Prices) riots when, for sixty-seven nights, the actors could scarcely be heard. Forced to capitulate, Kemble nonetheless continued to strive for scenic magnificence. A generation before, Garrick's designer, de Loutherbourg, had modified the standard system of backdrops and side wings that slid forward in fixed grooves by creating irregular cut-out flats and transparencies lit by battens of oil lamps. But essentially these scenic effects were confined to the shallow space behind the main arch as a background to the actors on the forestage who entered through doors on either side of the proscenium. Spectacular processions eventually pushed the action behind the proscenium arch; the forestage was about to disappear, and in those new conditions Kemble sought a balance between theatrical effectiveness and realistic accuracy. Even for a pantomime pageant he would instruct his artisans to 'observe there are no arms borne in England before Richard I, and then I give every king his arms and motto on shields of shapes proper to the times'.[33] Such heraldic opportunities explain the odd popularity of Shakespeare's *King John* in the years to come. Kemble's own production drew plaudits for its historical richness: 'their wardrobe is curious, extensive, and well assorted; their armoury is polished, and plentiful, and their scenery is descriptive of every thing remarkable on land or water'.[34] Under the regime of his brother Charles, the management issued a booklet on *Dramatic Costume* in which James Planché explained his antiquarian researches for the play's 1823 revival. Suitably instructed, the audience showed its appreciation:

When the curtain rose, and discovered King John dressed as his effigy appears in Worcester Cathedral, surrounded by his barons sheathed in mail, with cylindrical helmets and correct armorial shields, and his courtiers in the long tunics and mantles of the thirteenth century, there was a roar of approbation, accompanied by four distinct rounds of applause, so general and so hearty, that the actors were astonished.[35]

Planché brought a similar authenticity to Madame Vestris's non-patent Olympic. Exercising her considerable charms on Lord Adolphus FitzClarence, one of William IV and Dorothy Jordan's illegitimate sons, Vestris secured royal permission to copy Lely's gallery of beauties at Hampton Court for Planché's *The Court Beauties* (1835); these reproductions were hung on genuine seventeenth-century tapestries and hidden by material exactly copied from their actual covers until they were unveiled to admiring audiences. On a less splendid level, that management's *petites comédies* showed the same tasteful realism:

The Olympic . . . introduced for the first time in England that reform in all theatrical matters which has since been adopted in every theatre in the kingdom. Drawing-rooms were fitted up like drawing-rooms, and furnished with care and taste. Two chairs no longer indicated that two persons were to be seated, the two chairs being removed indicating that the two persons were not to be seated. A claret-coloured coat, salmon-coloured trowsers with a broad black stripe, a sky-blue neckcloth with large paste brooch, and a cut-steel eye-glass with a pink ribbon no longer marked the 'light comedy gentleman', and the public at once recognized and appreciated the change.[36]

In their revival of *The Old and Young Stager* (1836), the floor of the stage was covered with suitable carpets instead of the traditional green baize cloth. The auditorium was also redecorated with an understated elegance: painted garlands and floral medallions graced the front of each tier of boxes and the walls were in subtle pastel colours. To appeal further to smart audiences, Madame Vestris shortened the Olympic's play-bill and, when she assumed control of the Lyceum (1847), abolished half-price admissions.

In 1839, Vestris and Mathews became managers of Covent Garden where, for three years, they fought a losing battle against vulgar show. 'Glutted with farces', Mathews wanted 'a good five-act comedy of modern life.'[37] He found one by the unknown Boucicault. The script was adjusted and shaped under Mathews's experienced eye; actors' individual personalities were adapted even to the smallest roles, and in March 1841 *London Assurance* opened to considerable success. Much of that was due to the care and expense that the Vestris management had given to the sets and costumes. The scenery alone was reported to have cost £600 at a time when new productions often made do with bits and pieces taken from stock. The exterior of Oak Hall had been realized in minutest detail; its warm Tudor brick was something 'they don't make . . . now'.[38] Folding glass doors afforded a view of a richly furnished interior 'displayed in the most chaste and costly style'.[39] Act Three's morning-room conveyed the same realistic substantiality: 'It was really the first time that the perfection of the modern boxed-in scenery was displayed to the public',[40] though the records are unclear as to whether that box set included a closed-in ceiling. The actors themselves were dressed in the same meticulous style, echoing the latest Bond Street fashions.

Macready, too, had fought to improve production standards at the patent theatres. Often forced by economics to rely on stock pieces, he nonetheless aimed at a unified stage picture. His Drury Lane revival of *King John* (1842) brought a new coherence to the antiquarian tradition of the Kembles to present

an animated picture of those Gothic times which are so splendidly illustrated by the drama. The stage is thronged with the stalwart form of the middle ages, the clang of battle sounds behind the scenes, massive fortresses bound the horizon. The grouping is admirably managed. The mailed figures now sink into stern tranquility; now, when the martial fire touches them, they rouse from their lethargy and thirst for action. The sudden interruption in the third act to the temporary peace between John and Philip Augustus was a fine instance of the power of making the stage a living picture.[41]

Looking back over his management at both patent houses, Macready took pride in his determined policy of harmonious design and, in his retirement, he fulminated against Charles Kean, whom he detested, for making historical detail and pictorial display ends in themselves, so reducing Shakespeare's text to 'a running commentary upon the spectacles exhibited'.[42] The thought of Shakespeare at the Princess's filled him with horror:

the public is willing to have the magnificence without the tragedy, and the poet is swallowed up in display. When I read such a description as this of the production of a great drama, I am touched with a feeling something like remorse. Is it possible, I ask myself. Did *I* hold the torch? Did *I* point out the path?[43]

But, in the years after the Great Exhibition of 1851, the public saw more than magnificence at the Princess's. Kean's historical researches and manipulation of scenic effects were satisfyingly scientific and exhibited the wondrous ingenuity of machines. The Queen's reaction to *The Corsican Brothers* demonstrates the deep impression they made:

The effect of the ghost in the Ist act, with its wonderful management and entire noiselessness, was quite alarming. The tableau of the Duel, which Fabien witnesses, almost immediately after the vanishing of the ghost, was beautifully grouped and quite touching. The whole, lit by blue light and dimned with gauze, had an unearthly effect, and was most impressive and creepy . . . We both, and indeed everyone, was in admiration at the whole performance and much struck by it.[44]

The ghost's silent walk as he gradually materialized through the stage floor was achieved by a specially constructed long, multileaved trapdoor. Soon other theatres had installed their own Corsican Traps and Vampire Traps, which enabled actors to walk through walls, or Star

Traps, which catapulted them noiselessly up to the stage. In addition, as the duel scene shows, Kean was peculiarly alive to the emotive power of light. Gas had replaced candles in the two major theatres by the twenties and Macready had experimented with ways of concentrating light upon a particular object or person on stage.[45] A stick of lime burning in a gas-jet threw out an intense shaft of light, and, directed through coloured glass on to gauze transparencies, that limelight added to the extraordinary illusions at the Princess's.

The Great Exhibition had provided a showcase for the latest domestic comforts also, and the smaller theatres in particular responded to those improvements. Webster at the Haymarket did not install gas-light till 1843, and Macready, never the most gracious of guests, considered the place 'a dog-hole'. By 1853, however, Webster looked back upon 'the extensive alterations' that had occurred during his tenancy. The boxes now ranged in graceful curves instead of a three-sided square; the front seats had become stalls; backs had been affixed to the pit benches which could now hold their own '– for respectability – against any pit in London'. The proscenium had been widened, the lighting had cost 'the fee of £500 a year and the presentation of the centre chandelier to the proprietors; and behind the curtain money has not been spared to render the stage as perfect for dramatic representation as its limited means will furnish'.[46]

A more sudden and radical change happened when Marie Wilton leased 'The Dust Hole' off Tottenham Court Road in 1865 and sank most of her available capital into turning the house into a smart home-away-from-home. The floors were carpeted, the chairs in the boxes were upholstered with chintz, and the productions on stage reflected that careful domesticity. And, since their prospective audiences now dined at five, instead of at three, the management eventually offered one item only on the programme. During the building boom of the seventies and eighties, the Prince of Wales's, with its 800 seats and creature comforts, became the model for the new theatres.

Before the Bancrofts themselves moved to the Haymarket in 1880, they completely refurbished its interior to accord with the now-respectable audience's image of itself: on the main floor, rows of well-upholstered seats faced an enormous golden frame. That the proscenium arch should have become a picture-frame was but the culmination of the detailed realism of the Bancrofts' past productions. To complete the pictorial effect, the carpenters devised a system whereby the footlights rose behind the frame when the curtain went up. However, the rows of stalls for well-dressed, well-fed, well-behaved people caused a furore on opening night. The pit had already disappeared from the St James's and the Opera Comique, and Bancroft had publicly advertised the fact that, to meet 'the present expenses of a first-class theatre', it would have to be abolished at the Haymarket. In its place he offered a new upper tier, 'the second circle', with a raised ceiling, stone staircase, refreshment room, and an unobstructed view.[47] But, as Webster had cheerfully proclaimed, the Haymarket pit had always been special, so the curtain rose to jeers and catcalls from the new balcony: 'Give us the pit, Bancroft! . . . Where's the pit?' Although it must have seemed that the OP riots had come again, the anger of a politer age subsided after twenty minutes or so. Another pit was gone. Soon the management was introducing matinées, an innovation first tried at the Gaiety.

Seven years later, the Haymarket was again redecorated. Other theatres, like the St James's under Hare and the Kendals, had become equally elegant, so the new manager, Herbert Beerbohm Tree, widened the circles by removing some old-fashioned boxes. He also installed electric light. To allay public fear, the management took 'the highly practical and sensible course of stationing a fireman with a hose attached to a hydrant in the "flies" during every performance'.[48] But the new opulence reached its apotheosis in 1897, the Queen's Diamond Jubilee year, when Tree's own theatre arose on the site of the bygone opera house across the road. The foyer glowed with mahogany and gilt; a full-length portrait of Tree as King John dominated the grand staircase; a circular retiring room in cream and white gave access to the Royal Box; the auditorium was decorated in the style of Louis XV in muted scarlet, blue, and gold. The orchestra played discreetly behind palm fronds; programmes were free and contained no advertising. For the first time in any Victorian theatre, the stage was flat – instead of raked – to facilitate the machinery on which the company's lavish productions depended. Behind the scenes, Tree had his own palatial dressing-room suite, while high up in the dome were spacious offices and an enormous reception room. Shaw called it 'quite the handsomest theatre in London, . . . a place where high scenes are to be enacted and dignified things to be done', but went on to prick the bubble of first-night celebration: 'Our unique English loyalty – consisting in a cool, resolute determination to get the last inch of advertisement out of the Royal Family – has seldom been better pushed.'[49] That thought also struck the Prince of

Wales who took exception to the footmen who flanked his arrival on that opening night: their liveries were like those at Buckingham Palace.[50]

As lord of all that magnificence, Tree seems eras away from the 'low pantomime actor' of just seventy years before whom Dickens described as, 'like many people of his class, an habitual drunkard'.[51] For centuries, actors had been considered rogues and vagabonds. Yet Edmund Kean, a drunkard and a womanizer who struggled through bitter poverty as an itinerant acrobat and performer to blaze across the London stage in the first quarter of the century, was not typical of his contemporaries. Dorothy Jordan might seem to have shared his roaring reputation, but throughout her long association with the Duke of Clarence she was a faithful, good-humoured and, eventually, pitiful victim of circumstance. The Kembles were born to parents who played up and down the Hereford circuit, but Mrs Siddons became a paradigm of domestic virtue, despite a flutter or two in middle age, while her brothers, John Philip and Charles, were both schooled at the Catholic seminary in Douai, and that respectability governed their careers on the stage. John Philip was the first of those actor-managers who, throughout the century, laboured to 'elevate' the English Drama. His productions went into print as the Kemble Shakespeare, a series of acting editions whose authority outlasted him. Macready, also the son of a provincial circuit manager, loathed the theatre, despised actors, and was never happier than on the day he could at last retire. That attitude did not endear him to his peers, yet he drove himself as fiercely as he lashed out at others and, though he did not publish his own versions of Shakespeare, he did much to rescue the texts from two centuries of theatrical 'improvement'. In addition, his diaries reveal him as a new type of actor in that, before the emergence of directors, he tried to drill his company into some semblance of a unit which would serve the play and he strove to take on the personality of each character he played. Ben Webster was no vagabond either. His relationship with his business partner, Madame Céleste, remained a matter of discreet conjecture even amongst his family; he grew wealthy enough to own quarries in Wales from which he donated the stone for the oddly named Royal Dramatic College, a retirement home for poor and elderly actors which received the Queen's own blessing. Begun in 1860, the institution eventually foundered, but even Webster's critics admitted that 'no man has been a more loyal friend to the "poor player"'.[52] His tenure at the

THE SOCIAL POSITION OF THE ACTOR HAS IMPROVED OF LATE YEARS, BUT STILL
LEAVES MUCH TO BE DESIRED.

Walter Lissom (the Jeune Premier of the Parthenon). "I ASK YOU ALL, LADIES, HAS AN ACTOR EVER YET BEEN MADE A KNIGHT OF
THE GARTER, OR EVEN HAD THE REFUSAL OF A PEERAGE! *NEVER!*"
Chorus of adoring Duchesses, Marchionesses, and Countesses. "SHAME!"

1   The social position of the actor

Haymarket established that theatre as the last remaining bulwark of
legitimate drama in the years immediately following the abolition of
the patents.

But no career better exemplifies the actor's changing status and
lifestyle than that of Madame Vestris. She made her debut in 1815 at
the Italian Opera in days when the dress circle of that fashionable
venue was 'filled with extraordinary-looking people who suck
oranges or munch apples between the parts . . . women in [the] boxes
are exposed to much that is unpleasant unless they are actually
hemmed in by their male friends',[53] and town 'swells' ogled and
chaffed the assembly from Fops' Alley in the pit. As wife to the
company's leading dancer, she went off to Paris where reportedly she
had a number of sexual escapades before returning to become the
cynosure of every male eye as the Don in *Giovanni in London* at Drury
Lane in 1820. She was so much the rage of the season that other
theatres produced the Don according to their own established
recipes: the Adelphi, home of melodrama, presented *Giovanni
Vampire* while Astley's displayed *Giovanni on Horseback*.[54] Long

since deserted by her roving spouse, the lady bargained her way between opera engagements and britches parts in which her petite beauty and Italianate vivacity earned further compensation from a string of fashionable lovers. Throughout the twenties, Madame Vestris's exploits became the subject of admiring broadsheets; models of her famous legs were much in demand. Then, in a transformation worthy of Planché's fairy-tale extravaganzas, Madame Vestris leased the Olympic where, by the mid thirties, she not only attracted the Princess Victoria but the refined taste of Charles Mathews. The son of an 'eccentric' comedian, Mathews had wanted to become an architect and so travelled to Italy as courier to aristocrats on the Grand Tour. At Florence he dabbled in theatricals with his exalted clients; then, deciding to take to the stage, he determined – 'without a moment's hesitation' – on the Olympic as the only place where he could pursue a 'lighter phase of comedy, representing the more natural and less laboured school of modern life, and holding the mirror up to nature without regard to the conventionalities of the theatre'.[55] So began a partnership which took them onwards to Covent Garden and the Lyceum. And though Macready grumbled to his diary at the invasion of this low pair, from their Olympic days onwards they impressed high society by their air of good breeding so that the Princess was not only drawn to Mathews's 'pretty figure' and 'very small feet': 'He is *so* natural and amusing, and never vulgar but always very gentlemanlike.'[56]

It was that lack of vulgarity which surprised the Queen when, fifty years later, actors came once more to the royal residences. The Prince of Wales persuaded her to attend a performance at Abergeldie Castle by Edgar Bruce's company: 'strange to say, most of the actors are gentlemen by birth, who have taken to the stage as a profession'.[57] She had always been charmed by the manners of her adored opera singers even when, as in *Carmen*, the person depicted was 'really not very nice'.[58] Mlle de Lussan, the first of two Carmens who performed at Windsor, 'acted admirably, full of byplay, and with a "coquetterie" and impudence, accompanied by grace, so that it was never vulgar'. The elegance of the Comédie Française was also as expected: 'M. Coquelin recited and gave some most amusing monologues, so clever and witty, without the least vulgarity. There is nothing like the French for doing that kind of thing.'[59] That their British counterparts were now equally polished occasioned repeated comment. After a performance at Sandringham she 'waited a moment in the Drawing room, to speak to Irving and Ellen Terry. He is very gentlemanlike, and she, very pleasing and handsome.' After other performances, John Hare was pronounced 'a very small, spare, gentlemanlike man, and is a gentleman, as so many are nowadays' and George Alexander of the St James's company was 'an excellent actor, a gentleman'.[60]

The Queen's long absence from the theatre made her suddenly aware of the gentility which had gradually permeated the entire acting profession. Charles Kean had spent several terms at Eton and, in reaction to his father's self-destruction, ran the Princess's like a middle-class *pater familias*, making up for his limitations as an actor by wielding his authority as Fellow of the Society of Antiquaries. In the same spirit of respectability, his more talented wife clung to her crinolines under costumes of whatever period. Marie Wilton, like Madame Vestris, began as a singing soubrette but evolved into an impeccable matron whose silvery laugh and generous smile proved as engaging as her aged sovereign's. After twenty years of management, she and Squire Bancroft were wealthy enough to retire from the stage to a social and professional eminence that raised no eyebrow when Bancroft was knighted along with lord mayors and captains of industry in Diamond Jubilee year or when he was made administrator of the new Academy of Dramatic Art at the turn of the century.

By then the census of 1901 showed that the profession had swelled to three times the number recorded in 1881, and many actors and actresses now came from the upper middle class.[61] Accustomed to actual drawing-rooms, they stepped easily into their mirror-images on stage. Like Charles Hawtrey (Eton) and Cyril Maude (Charterhouse), many actors were the product of élite schools: they talked beautifully and were used to well-cut clothes. Long before, in 1831, the Garrick Club had been founded as a place 'in which actors and men of education and refinement might meet on equal terms'. Though the Prince of Wales became a member in 1867 and associated with the profession socially as well as sexually, in 1880 only thirteen actors were members; by 1900 there were thirty-eight.[62] 'Five-and-twenty years ago a gentleman . . . was rare on the stage. Nowadays', wrote Seymour Hicks in 1910, 'gentlemen hover round it as thick as May-flies on a Hampshire stream.'[63]

Less concerned with gentility than with the status of his profession, Henry Irving said 'no' to suggestions of a knighthood in 1883: 'He thinks that it would be very *ill* taken . . . he wishes before all things to stand well with his profession & not seem to be put over them.'[64] At that time he did stand alone or at least supreme among lesser colleagues. After his hypnotic performance as Mathias in *The Bells* (1871), his acting brought to the Lyceum an eminence it would not otherwise have achieved under Colonel Bateman's management. When Irving assumed the lease in 1878, he made the Lyceum into the shrine of the nation's drama with himself as guardian of its mysteries. Ironically, no 'gentleman' could have had a more ungainly manner and peculiar speech. Yet Irving overcame his many detractors and enthralled his admirers with the force of his own idea of the Lyceum and with the power of his personal mystique as actor and manager. When his productions went on tour after the London season, Irving met with civic dignitaries, lectured on British Drama and the Lyceum's place in that tradition, and, as a quasi-royal figure, was always 'on stage'. At the Lyceum itself, each production was the result of years of thought and intensive preparation. Sets, costumes, music, lights, and the grouping of actors were all shaped by his extraordinary instinct for the theatrically effective. His own image was orchestrated with the same care and instinct. An entirely black proscenium and a darkened auditorium (not then the norm) isolated the on-stage picture; a splash of colour against a co-ordinated background of contrasted costumes lured the audience towards that face, those hands. Their mystical quality was further enhanced by gas-light: 'The effect was to persuade the Lyceum audience that they were witnesses to "another world", an impression that contributed enormously to the acceptance of Irving's Lyceum as a Temple of Theatrical Art, in a different category from rival establishments.'[65]

By 1883, Irving embarked on his company's first tour of America with all the authority of Ambassador Extraordinary. His departure was heralded by two official banquets and a personal interview with the Prime Minister, Mr Gladstone. On arrival in New York, he was greeted by a private yacht on which, after chicken and champagne, he addressed America's press. After six triumphal weeks, the company set out for Philadelphia in a private train 'of eight coaches, two boxcars, and an immense open "gondola", all packed with poles and rigging, 150 stage baskets full of costumes and small props, and a fold-away wonderland of palaces, parapets, churches, gardens, balustrades, stairways, and snowy landscapes'.[66] Their train to Chicago was provided by the president of the Erie Railroad; in Washington, Irving and Ellen Terry dined at the White House with the President of the Republic. Irving was more than 'a gentleman'.

His prestige in society and his aura of saintly suffering and haunted evil on stage created for his critics an insurmountable phenomenon and for his worshippers a god. However, by 1895, other actors with important theatres and regal tours of their own were enthroned on the upper reaches of Parnassus, and Irving, as lord of that pantheon, accepted knighthood for himself and his profession.

But, as Irving's dominance at the Lyceum also illustrates, the last to win respect and independence were the playwrights. The Victorian theatre appealed to the eye rather than the ear. However much he purported to encourage new writers and uplift the nation's drama, an actor-manager was apt to judge a script in theatrical terms: as opportunity for display. On the crudest level, he might, like Vincent Crummles, urge aspirants to 'write us a piece to bring out the whole strength of the company . . . peculiar resources of this establishment – new and splendid scenery – you must manage to introduce a real pump and two washing-tubs'.[67] More insidiously, he might, like Macready, complain to his diary about the way his role was written: 'In the last scene [of *Money*] Miss Faucit, as I had anticipated, had quite the advantage over me.'[68] Not surprisingly, writers of stature shied away from the theatre even when, like Dickens, they loved the stage. In monthly instalments, they captured the undivided attention of a larger and wider audience whose emotions were theirs alone to command.

Audiences went to the theatre to cheer the actor's rousing crescendos or thrilling silences, to wonder at his telling 'points', to laugh at his physical dexterity, to applaud the scenery; so the playwright had to supply melodious fustian, melodramatic *coups de théâtre*, and farcical situations on which the actor could work his magic. When Ben Webster offered a prize for the best new comedy of British life and manners, the winner out of ninety-eight scripts failed lamentably in the theatre. The experiment cost him £500 whereas, in the absence of copyright laws, he could buy a translation of a proven success from Paris for £50. So French adaptations continued to occupy the London stage. Mrs Gore, the novelist who won that competition, attributed her failure to an audience who demanded 'a very different species of entertainment, for whose diversion, exaggeration in writing and acting is as essential, as daubing to the art of the scene-painter'.[69] But even when theatres became smaller and the acting more delicate, audiences came prepared to listen harder but were not yet prepared to think.

23

Dion Boucicault, whose career spanned most of Victoria's reign, set out to redress the balance between writers and actors by 'raising my profession to the only standard which the English mind applies to everything – the standard of money'.[70] Experience had taught him early that a major success and a constant succession of other plays had not made him the performers' equal. Flushed with the triumph of *London Assurance*, he blamed the actors' inadequacies for the failure of his second play and so joined Webster at the Haymarket where, after a number of hits and misses, he drew the town to *Used Up* (1844) which, like his first success at Covent Garden, owed much to Mathews's collaboration. However, at the rehearsals of *Old Heads and Young Hearts* he balked at the way Mathews and Vestris wanted to alter their own and others' parts. He was convinced that he now knew as much about stagecraft as they did and so told Mathews that 'I want no one's opinions but my own as to the *consistency* of the characters I draw – *your* business is to utter what *I* create'. The Mathewses reacted indignantly to 'this inflated view of the relative positions of actor and dramatist',[71] and returned their scripts. Webster soothed things over but was soon to teach Boucicault another lesson-for-writers. The manager offered him £100 for a new script; Boucicault refused, since even his first play had sold for £300; Webster promptly explained how cheaply he could order up a trans-lation of a guaranteed success: 'The argument was unanswerable and the result inevitable. I sold a work for £100 that took me six months' hard work to compose and accepted a commission to translate three French plays at £50 apiece. This work afforded me child's play for a fortnight.'[72] So he churned out a stream of adaptations and the occasional original script which might, if it ran long enough, earn him an added fee. A short foray as manager of the Dumas company's disastrous appearance at Drury Lane confirmed his chosen course and, as a French copyist, he became house-writer for Kean at the Princess's where he learned yet another lesson. Engaged for each season at a flat fee, he gained nothing when his adaptation of *The Corsican Brothers* brought the management a small fortune, and he earned twice as much for playing the lead in *The Vampire* as he did for concocting the script.

Accordingly he determined to use his skills as an actor to further his fortunes as a writer. Settling in New York after the discovery of his affair with Kean's ward, Agnes Robertson, led to banishment from the Princess's, he married the lady and set about his double career. In addition, he created *The Young Actress* (1853) to show off his wife's talents as singer, dancer, and player in five different roles. New York was enraptured, and in Boston 'special trains were run to bring thousands to witness this exquisite actress'.[73] Boston also witnessed his own debut (in *Used Up*), and for the next two years the Boucicaults toured from city to city in his expanding repertoire of plays. He then leased a theatre in New Orleans and prepared, as manager, to pocket more of the profits. He could also drill his company to perform his plays as he wanted them, a control he was always to retain after his Gaiety Theatre quickly failed and he joined other managements. To deal better with those businessmen, he threw his energies into the campaign for a Dramatic Authors' Bill which, when passed in 1856, gave dramatists sole rights to their scripts, rights which this adeptest of adapters defended ever afterwards in the courts of law.

But Boucicault had no delusions of genius. In his view, a playwright had 'to be practical, utilitarian, . . . in sympathetic accord with the minds of the people. He must not consider anything too deeply; his audience cannot follow him. He must not soar; their prosaic minds, heavy with facts, cannot rise.'[74] In 1857 he discovered the path to that 'sympathetic accord'. *The Poor of New York* reflected, in the faintest way, a financial panic which had just swept the city; within that situation, he created a conventional romance whose misunderstandings were resolved when the villain staggered from his burning house with a document which revealed all. That scene created a sensation as the engulfing flames (carefully organized by Boucicault himself) were tamed by a *real* fire-engine. Here was the magic formula, and Boucicault quickly presented other contemporary problems which would elicit astounding climaxes without troubling the audience as to the pros and cons of those problems. Even *The Octoroon* (1859) steered a middle course between North and South at a time of heated passions over the Slave Question. What really stirred audiences was the spectacle of a burning Mississippi river boat and the novelty of a murderer's 'exposure' by a camera: 'A photographic plate. What's this, eh? two forms! the child – 'tis he! dead – and above him – Ah! ah! Jacob M'Closky – 'twas you murdered that boy!'[75]

Excruciating as that snatch of dialogue now sounds, these sensation dramas cannot be dismissed out of hand. Boucicault knew precisely what the public wanted and professed himself happy to oblige: 'I can spin out these rough-and-tumble dramas as a hen lays eggs. It's a degrading occupation, but more money has been made out of guano than out of poetry'.[76] The complacent statement scarcely hides his self-contempt. Too much the businessman to resist easy money, he had become too skilled a craftsman to deliver shoddy goods. Seizing the public interest, he produced *Jessie Brown* within weeks of the news of the relief of Lucknow (the play's sub-title) and built his plot from an eye-witness report of the way the besieged garrison gained courage from a young Scots girl who, in fevered exhaustion, screamed out to the men that she could hear the pipers of the relieving Highlanders. The characters are one-dimensional stereotypes and gauged exactly to the audience's taste. Jessie herself is a rural saint: modest, kind-hearted, loving, she tirelessly comforts the women and children and keeps up the defenders' spirits. Randal is the sort of hero to whom a bullet wound is but a scratch: 'Tut! we have other things to do.'[77] The villainous Nana Sahib wants Mrs Campbell for his harem, hates the white heathen dogs, and sneers at their code of honour. In real life no one has ever talked in the way his characters do, but their declamatory idealism creates a lyric flow which sweeps from one crescendo to the next.

However cynically Boucicault had mined the golden vein of sensationalism – the metaphor is his – money bought power and, abandoning the newsworthy for a brand of charming roguery which as an Irishman and as Mr Dion Boucicault he understood more deeply than chivalric platitude, he returned to London in 1860 with *The Colleen Bawn*. Ben Webster at the Adelphi had fallen on hard times and Boucicault, the toast of New York, brought off a momentous bargain. In addition to the fees Agnes and he received as the fair-haired maiden and Myles-na-Coppaleen, the good-hearted poacher and distiller of illegal potcheen, Boucicault demanded one pound per Act per night for the play his audience clamoured to see. And though other managements fought this precedent for the next twenty years, that nightly royalty opened the way to the future. Night after night – 230 in all – audiences flocked to the Adelphi to cheer Myles's breathtaking, headlong dive into yards of gauze to rescue Eily as she rose from the waves for the third time, and Boucicault saw an added opportunity to assert himself as a writer. Refusing to allow provincial managers the rights to his play, he organized first one, then two companies to tour Britain's remotest theatrical corners; he received one half of the weekly profits. Coincidentally, the play's unparalleled success was to alter the situation for all actors; seasons of one-night attractions – with their successes and failures – gave way to engagements in a single, long-running play.

As an actor, Boucicault continued to attract audiences who came to see Shaun the Post in *Arrah-na-Pogue* (Arrah of the Kiss: 1864) and Conn, the vagabond (*The Shaughraun*: 1874), but as a playwright he gradually lost touch with his public until, at his death in 1890, he had become the grand old man of a former age. In the eighties, a more sophisticated audience abandoned rustic love for the urban charms of *The Great Divorce Case* and *Hot Water* at Charles Wyndham's Criterion Theatre. Yet, by the time melodrama and farce evolved into the society pieces of Jones and Pinero and, subversively, the iconoclasm of Wilde and Shaw, Boucicault's career had proved that a man could earn his living as a playwright and nothing else. Moreover, despite the strictures of the Lord Chamberlain's Office, which lagged but a small step behind the anathemas of a self-satisfied public, a playwright could stretch the boundaries of accepted thought on the printed page, protected by copyright laws for which Boucicault had fought.

The printed text also gave rise to a new school of critics whose judgement mapped the way to a 'serious' drama for audiences, actors, and writers. Critics of the old school, trained in the sixties, tended to write about actors and about moments of particular beauty or terror even when they were furnished with a privately printed script. They worshipped theatricality and loathed those who sought to wrest the theatre from the average thrill-seeker. Clement Scott, the *doyen* of that group, thought the drawing-room plays of the nineties were 'the outcome of an age that allows Society to rule the stage and not the people'. Paula Tanqueray and her ilk would 'rest in the cemetery of the dead drama', whereas delightful Lavender would 'perfume the stage of tomorrow' because '*Sweet Lavender* is, as its happy little title implies, a wholesome, pure, refreshing, and a charming play'.[78] The new critics, impatient of the theatre's histrionics, goaded writers into taking their craft seriously by analysing moments in their texts. Years before the general availability of playscripts, William Archer's *English Dramatists of To-day* (1882) set down a page or two from a phenomenally popular comedy and ridiculed its emptiness.[79] In the year of Victoria's Diamond Jubilee, Archer derived hope from those writers who 'have gone straight to life for their material, have observed sincerely and reproduced thoughtfully' and from those

27

managers who 'are following, more or less consistently, a progressive policy'. His concern arose now from the theatre's economics: 'there is practically no middle course between a huge success and a disastrous failure. Unless such a middle course can be discovered or devised, our Victorian Drama will come to little enough.'[80]

But amidst these uneasy alliances with actors, audiences, and critics, and despite the imponderabilities of theatrical production, copyright laws, and box-office receipts, the responsibility for a vital drama lay with the writers themselves. Most Victorian playwrights could not look piercingly at life, for even those who consciously set out to enliven the stage often shaped their plays to the patterns of drama's golden age or resorted to the formulaic language of the contemporary theatre. They failed, as Pinero noted, 'to realize that the art of drama is not stationary, but progressive'.[81] In consequence they imitated the blank verse of Shakespeare and the comic types of Sheridan or they adapted the twopence-coloured scenarios of the early Victorian theatre whose wooden characters and rhetoric ('dolls and declamation') had, by the end of the century, come to typify the 'transpontine' tastes of the working masses south of the Thames or east of St Paul's. Those writers who did master the theatre, to use it for their own ends, were ensnared to some degree by 'the high Victorian standard of bashfulness',[82] and either compromised their own vision in order to placate audiences or were themselves blinkered by the moral conventions they hoped to question. And so, very little Victorian Drama lives on into the twentieth century except for a shimmer of farces and overtly theatrical comedies whose deliberate artifice allowed playwright and playgoer a holiday from everyday morality.

Farces like *The Magistrate*, *Charley's Aunt*, and *The Importance of Being Earnest*, that 'trivial play for serious people', retain their place in the national repertory, although in their own day they seemed insignificant to the dramatists' bid for independence. Shaw's plays also made little impact on the Victorian theatre; only one, *Arms and the Man*, was produced by the establishment. But because Shaw used the theatre's 'trivial' mechanics as a means to inform and disturb 'serious people', his comedies represent the drama's one decisive victory. Independent of the playgoers' restricting sensibilities, he won an audience for his printed texts and their stimulating prefaces. And, as a theatre critic in the nineties, he attacked outworn conventions, sniped at his fumbling cohorts, and cleared the territory he would occupy in the new century. The other leaders fought with less abandon, constrained by the community they worked for or by their own temperament. Yet with all their limitations, the plays of Bulwer, Robertson, Gilbert, Jones, Pinero, and Wilde illustrate, in vivid ways, the differing conditions each writer sought to overcome. Each responded to the world he lived in and each subscribed to the theatre's dominant theme: love was the complicating factor in comedy, 'strong' drama, satire, and farce. That common topic and the politics of each decade – particularly as they touched the Woman Question – create a continuous sub-plot which vivifies each writer's struggle to come to terms with conventional or idiosyncratic ideals that barred the way to a drama of ideas.

CHAPTER 2

The grandeur of Nature

There are two sources from which we should now seek the tragic influence, . . .
the Simple . . . Tales of a household nature, that find their echo in the hearts of
the people . . . Another and totally distinct source of modern tragedy may be
sought in the MAGNIFICENT. True art never rejects the materials which are
within its reach. The Stage has gained a vast acquisition in pomp and show –
utterly unknown to any period of its former history.

Edward Bulwer, *England and the English* (1833)

As a reflector of contemporary values, the theatre creates its own
distorting filters which derive from the day-to-day compromises that
the transmission of a text to an on-stage performance imposes: the
talent and physique of the actors, the management's estimate of what
will 'go' with the public, the personality of the prime-mover (chief
actor, actor-manager, or modern director) which colours that
estimate. This was particularly the case in the mid 1830s when those
who thought at all seriously about the drama's power to comment on
real life saw themselves as a noble rear-guard ranged bravely against
the commercial savvy of a man like Alfred Bunn, manager of Covent
Garden. And no occasion more sharply illumines the social and
stylistic limits within which a playwright had to work than the
moment when William Charles Macready entered the fashionable
portals of Edward Bulwer's chambers in the Albany on 23 February
1836.

Macready had encountered the eminent novelist while driving
through Dublin two years before and, at a dinner party that October,
had found a man 'whom I liked very much'.[1] He urged Bulwer to
write a play and was interested to learn that the novelist had already
contemplated something on the death of Cromwell. Later, John
Forster, the critic for the *Examiner*, who knew everybody, brought
them together at another dinner party, but nothing more ensued until
that summons to the Albany where Bulwer announced he had written
a script designed for, and dedicated to the only upholder of British
Drama.

Macready, whose character was stubbornly democratic, felt ill at ease before this creature from another world who was 'dressed, or rather *déshabillé*, in the most lamentable style of foppery – a hookah in his mouth, his hair, whiskers, tuft, etc., all grievously cared for. I felt deep regret to see a man of such noble and profound thought yield for a moment to pettiness so unworthy of him. His manner was frank, manly, and cordial in the extreme – so contradictory of his appearance.'[2] Nevertheless, homage from so great a personage reduced Macready to tears and he was still more impressed by the script itself: 'What talent he possesses!' Then, with the deference befitting an actor who wished to impress his own gentility upon a member of parliament and social luminary, Macready praised 'the picture of manners it presents, the variety of its characters, the charm of its language and its truth of passion' and professed himself at a loss to know how a plot of 'so lively an interest' might be better arranged for the stage: 'I have never in any previous instance so distrusted myself.' Those courtesies over, Macready embarked on an acute critique which outlined ways in which Bulwer's plot could be made to work more effectively upon an audience's feelings.

And so began a relationship which, over the next five years, saw the transmutation of an established novelist into a playwright whose initial falterings led to three plays which held the stage for the rest of the century. Neither collaborator considered the intricacy and consistency of human character as a major point of discussion: Macready always concentrated on the effect of each scene, how it linked to the next episode and how that interest might be sustained from beginning to end; Bulwer aimed at an ideal truth which, whatever the manners and history of the past, might stand for all time.

Macready's advice came from long experience in huge theatres before audiences whose perceptions were attuned to the big dramatic moment. Each episode had to make its effect through large brush-strokes and generalized colours; each character had to present himself in an overt, enunciatory way. To make those broad effects still clearer, characters should balance and contrast each other in order to point a moral rather than illumine the subtleties of human behaviour. Possessing no interior lives, they were all outward show.

For example, in Bulwer's first play, *The Duchess de la Vallière*, Bragelone stands for an ancient nobility whose integrity lies beyond the perquisites of favour at the new Versailles of Louis XIV. Responding to Macready's suggestion that the transition between La

Vallière's farewell to her rural home and her arrival at Versailles was too abrupt, Bulwer inserted an episode between Bragelone and his family's aged armourer which specifically – and, to modern taste, crudely – illustrates the honour of the old aristocracy:

> BERTRAND (*the armourer*): They tell me, that to serve one's king for nothing,
>   To deem one's country worthier than one's self,
>   To hold one's honour not a phrase to swear by. –
>   They tell me, now, all *this* is out of fashion.
>   Come, take the sword, my Lord! – you have your father's
>   Stout arm and lordly heart: they're out of fashion,
>   And yet you keep the one – come, take the other.   (I, 3, pp. 13–14)[3]

Later, at Versailles, Lauzun, the fashionable breed of aristocrat, announces his position in the same overt way, and his battle metaphor emphatically presents him as the antithesis of worthy Bragelone:

> The times are changed! – 'twas by the sword and spear
> Our fathers bought ambition – vulgar butchers!
> But now our wit's our spear – intrigue our armour;
> The antechamber is our field of battle;
> And the best hero is – the cleverest rogue?   (I, 4, p. 19)

Macready also knew that action and gesture create meaning on a stage. Accordingly, his first critique to Bulwer recommended 'some token' which would emphasize in a concrete way the tacit engagement between La Vallière and Bragelone. Then, with an eye to maintaining interest and creating a telling effect, he went on to suggest that this token 'would add to his motives for seeking her in the fourth act, and heighten the pathos of that scene, where he might return it to her'. Consequently, Bulwer arranged for La Vallière to bind her scarf about the departing warrior's hauberk, a token which he returns later, much to the remorse of the corrupted Duchess:

> Give it me! – let me bathe it with my tears!
> Memorial of my guilt –   (IV, 3, p. 74)

Simplistic though these methods were, Macready's theatricalism conveyed a sort of reality, heightened and arranged to emotional effect but nonetheless credible within the context of the whole, because – as a contemporary critic explained – that mode created a 'sense of the *optique du théâtre* which demanded a more elevated style than would have suited the familiarity of daily intercourse. He knew he was there to act, ... to impress an idealised image on the spectator's mind, and he could not succeed by the naturalness of his own manner.'[4] Lifelike it was not, yet this stylized truth-to-life persuaded audiences that Macready, like David Garrick or Sarah Siddons before him, was a 'natural' actor who plumbed the essence of life itself. Such electric theatricality has, until quite recently, been lost to the modern stage which documents the minutiae of surface appearances, but it once had power to convince even so confirmed a realist as William Archer who was apt to view the nineteenth century as an evolutionary journey to an actual mirroring of everyday manners. Recalling one of Bulwer's own plays, he saw *Richelieu* as 'stagey and . . . adroit' yet could 'never forget the effect produced by that great actor, Edwin Booth . . . It was thrilling, startling, electrifying, beyond anything dreamt of on our humdrum realistic stage. It was not imitation – it was passion incarnate.'[5]

Bulwer also aimed at reality: 'No matter in what department, the essence of the drama is still the faithful representation of life.'[6] In the preface to his collected plays (1841), he saw in his costume dramas an elemental portrait of the individual as the repository of a nation's spirit and believed his Bragelone to be 'the highest and the completest delineation of ideal character which I have yet accomplished either in the drama or romance'.[7] To a romantic novelist, this ideal suggested human values which, refined to their essence, represented a continuum which ran through all the ages of man. Yet though the characters of his novels might be just as representative of lasting traits, in developing the intimate relationship between reader and writer, Bulwer had time and space to shade those figures and endow them with an apparent complexity which was foreign to the moment-to-moment scheme of the contemporary theatre. If drama was action and quickly sketched character, the novel depended on analysis, however superficial that might be.

For instance, in Bulwer's novel, *The Last Days of Pompeii* (1834), Ione, the paragon of beauty, is distinguished from her rivals in Pompeii by a Greek heritage whose details add a spiritual radiance to her bodily attractions. Glaucus, a Latin playboy, is also individualized and set apart by the details of his past life. And though the novel moves from one dramatic high point to the next, a moment like the scene in the cave of the witch-prophetess on the foothills of Vesuvius seems to have larger dimensions than its theatrical equivalent. Partly this results from the narrative's power of suggestion which allows the unspoken to activate the imagination in more powerful ways than mere words can do. Glaucus and Ione, threatened by the evil power of

Arbaces, 'that dark Egyptian, with his gloomy brow and icy smiles', look out towards the mountain on whose summit hangs an ominous cloud: 'A sudden and unaccountable gloom came over each as they thus gazed; and in that sympathy which love had already taught them, and which bade them, in the slightest shadows of emotion, the faintest presentiment of evil, turn for refuge to each other . . . What need had they of words to say they loved?'[8] Under Macready's tutelage, Bulwer had to learn that *statement* counted in the Victorian theatre and that a voice, a physical gesture, and the impact of a stage property (like La Vallière's 'token') were all adjuncts to the art of the actor and the scene-painter in creating a totality over which a writer had no ultimate control.

Bulwer and Macready were, however, in total accord in their attitude to the fallen state of drama in the patent theatres. At the time of their interview, Macready was engaged at Covent Garden and smarting under the sharp practices of his manager, Alfred Bunn, who had stumbled on to a good thing with the public by presenting menagerie acts, operatic spectacles, and colourful panoramas like Planché's *The Jewess* and *Chevy Chase* and Auber's *The Bronze Horseman*. None too happy at having to pay Macready a weekly retainer when he could pack the theatre with his technicolour extravaganzas, Bunn forced the actor's hand by insisting he perform a cut-down version of Sheridan Knowles's *William Tell* as an after-piece to Maria Malibran's performance in the opera, *Zampa*. Macready swallowed his bile and did as he was ordered. Meanwhile Bulwer, in the innocence of his reputation as a novelist, expected Bunn to pay, sight unseen, for a script which bore his prestigious name, just as his publishers would have done. The manager naturally balked at this, and *The Duchess de la Vallière* would probably have returned to the closet had it not been for the explosive events of 29 April. On that evening, Bunn required Macready to play the first three Acts of *Richard III* as a curtain-raiser to what the half-price customers would afterwards crowd in to see: the first Act of the *Jewess* and the whole of *Chevy Chase* which even Macready acknowledged as 'the most gorgeous pageant I have ever seen on an English stage'.[9] It was a calculated insult to Macready's standing as an actor and epitomized the wretched conditions of the national theatre, but Macready would not give in to Bunn's tactics by resigning. However, after his performance, on the way back to his dressing-room, Macready happened to pass the manager's open door, and the sight of him sitting there proved too much for the actor's volatile temper. An enraged Richard III set upon the hateful Bunn who gave as good as he got until the two were forced apart. Bunn sued for assault, but no fine could assuage Macready's own sense of shame at having behaved so uncivilly.

This fracas, which became the talk of London, nicely illustrates the accidents of play-production in that Bulwer's script was then performed at Drury Lane after Macready fled there. It also accounts for the style of an entire group of playwrights who saw Macready as the champion of legitimate drama. In this fight between mutilated Shakespeare and gorgeous frippery, they allied themselves with the Bard's high seriousness and so adopted a neo-Elizabethan grandeur. High-sounding rhetoric resounds through *The Duchess de la Vallière*: Bulwer already knew what made drama 'serious'. But when Macready himself became manager of Covent Garden (in the year Victoria assumed her own royal mantle), Bulwer consciously aligned his plays to the cause of 'Dramatic Art'. Refusing payment for *The Lady of Lyons*, he told Macready that 'our compact was not of an ordinary nature, and on consideration, you will see that it is impossible to lower it into a pecuniary arrangement. It was a compact based upon feelings worthy of the Art, which in our several lines we desired to serve – let me add that it was worthy of ourselves . . . Neither money nor *any other kind of remuneration which money purchases*, can I accept – or you propose. My guerdon is the boast to have served, not as a Mercenary but a volunteer, in an enterprise that will long be memorable in the Literary History of my time. I will not sell my Waterloo Medal.'[10]

The weapons for that battle were to be of high-tempered metal. For his third play, *Richelieu*, Bulwer originally intended that long sequences which furthered the action should be 'left plain and simple, prosaic in words – in order to throw the whole vividness of contrast and light upon those passages, where thought or passion, as in real life, burst spontaneously into poetry'. But on hearing Macready read a version that had been cut for performance, he was mortified to find that the poetry had been 'struck out, as not essential to the business', and so determined to re-write what remained in order to recover 'all the bloom and *purpureum lumen* of the Poetry that it once possessed'. In pursuit of 'the Grandeur of Nature', he turned to the example of 'more experienced Dramatists – Knowles and Talfourd – [who] have studiously sought it – I say, when a Door is to be shut, "Shut the

Door." Knowles would say . . . "Let the room be airless." Probably
he is right.'[11]

Unfortunately, the plays themselves are 'airless' and empty now
that the exigencies of the nineteenth-century theatre and its idea of
natural acting and high art (to which they were shaped) have also
crumbled to dust. Yet though their sound and fury have little to say,
these plays live on to present an animated gallery of nineteenth-
century standards and assumptions in ways their author never
intended. *The Duchess de la Vallière* died a quick death in its own day,
not because of its posturing rhetoric but because certain actors were
miscast, the performance lasted till well after eleven o'clock, its
author's politics were anathema to the Tory critic of *The Times*. Freed
from those imponderabilities, the play now offers a crudely drawn,
and therefore especially vivid picture of early Victorian values while
purporting to show life at the Sun King's court.

Louise de la Vallière was Louis XIV's first mistress. One might not
realize that after seeing Bulwer's play, and his reticence is as revealing
of his own times as any flippant, racy account by a modern historian is
of ours. Nancy Mitford's thumbnail sketch is mischievously ironic
about teary-eyed, country simplicity:

Modest Louise, who blushed to be a mistress, a mother, a duchess, was now
brought into the glare of public life; it did not suit her. She was a woman to be
kept hidden away, visited by moonlight ... or encountered as by chance in some
forest glade while the hunt went crashing by – a simple country girl, an excellent
rider, puzzled and perplexed in the Byzantine atmosphere of the Court, though
by no means averse from the financial benefits to be picked up there. She is
supposed to have been responsible for more *placets* . . . on all of which she took a
comfortable percentage, than any of the other mistresses.[12]

Bulwer's Louise is a bride of heaven, an angel who falls yet who
somehow remains unsullied; she is Dickens's Little Em'ly or
Gounod's Marguerite whose prototype is the Gretchen of early Faust
stories. And the fact that in history (and in Madame de Genlis's novel
on which the play is based), Louise ended her life in a convent justifies
that portrait. Like his audience, Bulwer felt the attraction of
penitence.

To prepare for that, the play opens on a scene of quiet domesticity
whose details are as evocative as those in a Victorian genre painting of
A Mother's Last Farewell! Beyond an old château whose 'every stone
. . . speaks eloquent of happy years', vineyards and woods lead to a
river lit by the setting sun. Soon the 'vesper bell' tolls from the tower

of a distant Carmelite convent reminding Louise, who loves her childhood's Eden, to lift that love to God. A 'spotless . . . dove', a 'soft plant' whose delicate leaves 'shrink / From vice by instinct', she is 'kind / To the poor cotters in the wood' and, each winter, feeds the forest birds from her hand. Her mother has a Wordsworthian faith in the power of thought to protect her daughter across the miles that will separate them, and Louise assures her that 'amidst the court / My childhood's images shall rise'. Her reasons for leaving that childhood retreat remain vague, but she has been much affected by a recurring dream of godlike beauty, 'a royal vision' of the king she has never seen but whom her dead father taught her 'in thy cradle yet' to worship:

> to lisp
> Thy sovereign's name in prayer – and still together,
> In thy first infant creed, were link'd the lessons
> 'TO HONOUR GOD AND LOVE THE KING'; it was
> A part of that old knightly faith of France
> Which made it half religion to be loyal.   (I, I, p. 7)

Such loyalty depicts the stalwart values of the old aristocracy but it also represents a timeless ideal, a disembodied spirituality which palpitates through her mother's words: 'prayer . . . creed . . . honour . . . love . . . faith . . . religion . . . loyal'.

Louise demonstrates what Bulwer's prologue calls 'Nature's deep fountain – woman's silent heart'. That heart tells her, despite her maiden innocence, that her affectionate regard for Bragelone, to whom she was betrothed in childhood, differs from the sort of ardour he professes nor can it match the pure flame of her own nightly dreams. Too kind and feeling to mislead or disappoint the man she will always associate with home and honour, she has no answer to his mature and manly passion: 'love! – methinks / It is a word that –'. But her heart is also her undoing. At Louis's court, her religious adoration of the king draws snickers from the other maids-in-waiting and gives her beauty an added allure for the young ruler. Yet though she becomes his favourite and though stories of the way she has been showered with diamonds reach Bragelone who arrives at Versailles to castigate her fall, Louise's love is 'virgin' still. In fact, the play's second Act flounders upon this has-she-or-hasn't-she until Bragelone spirits her away to the nuns: 'Joy! – I have saved thee' (II, 2, p. 33). In 1837, this frisson was tiresome enough to provide ammunition for Bulwer's political enemies who sneered at 'the pathos of the stews'.[13]

Even well-wishers must have felt the ambiguity of Louise's

religious fervour when, like Alexander Pope's Eloise, she kneels in the cloisters at night, as thunder and lightning whirl about her, and cannot pray (in the 'tempest' of her own 'weak and erring heart') to forget her adored Louis (II, 4). When the king invades the convent to demand her return, she rushes towards him but, in the nick of time, pulls back and cries to God: 'Protect me from his arms – protect me from myself.' Bulwer's critics had a field day: 'It is in the worst taste of the worst school, the school of the modern French romance. We have all but an enforcement under the crucifix ... This may pass in Paris, where jaded roués and faded demireps require the stimulus of blasphemy to rouse their exhausted passions; but in England the public mind is, thank God, yet too healthy to demand such abominable incentives.'

These accusations shed a particularly interesting light on the way Bulwer circles round the fact of Louise's fall from grace. The king snatches her from the convent by promising to 'nurse no dream / Thy spotless soul itself shall blush to cherish!' However, as Act Three begins, Louise has become a duchess with her own mansion, yet her actual seduction has been pushed off-stage and she continues to be 'meek' and impervious to those who seek an avenue to the king's favour: not for her the *placets* of history. Nor is there mention of the children the actual Louise had by Louis. As if her seduction had never happened, Louise's purity remains unaltered save for her remorseful tears which Louis finds unflattering and which drive him to the happier charms of Madame de Montespan. Even in the courtiers' eyes, Louise has been 'betray'd by love, and not by sin, / Nor low ambition', and she continues to trust in the king until, at a public fête, he offers his devotion to Montespan and Bragelone returns, having taken holy orders, to chide the duchess back to her own true God.

Louise's shining image eventually causes Louis to tire of his latest mistress and to breach her spiritual refuge for a second time. But Bragelone guards the threshold – 'Descendant of Saint Louis, / Move – and the avalanche falls!' – and Louise, in her 'gorgeous attire' as the bride of Christ, needs now no champion: 'my soul is my protector'. Realizing that Louis still loves her, and 'in the knowledge of my weakness, strong', she turns to the world for one last time before taking the veil, happy that she can unite both King and God once more:

> Bear witness, Heaven! I never loved this man
> So well as now! and never seem'd *his* love
> Built on so sure a rock! Upon thine altar

I lay the offering. I revoke the past;
For Louis, Heaven was left – and now I leave
Louis, when tenfold more beloved, for Heaven!   (v, 5, p. 99)

Bulwer had consciously developed the parallel between Louise's devotion to her king and her love of God, but his letters to Macready give no indication as to whether he recognized his own sleight-of-hand in turning her past sin into heroic self-sacrifice as she lays that treasured offering on the altar. In 'revoking' the past, she does not offer remorse but a lover, ten times *more* beloved. Having turned dross into gold, she happily leaves the world and is welcomed into bliss by a joyous choir of singing nuns. The play ends as grand opera, and its spectacle makes Louise's sacrifice emotionally convincing even though Bulwer's grandiose word-music jangles on the modern ear.

However he managed it, Bulwer was persuaded that this seventeenth-century story showed 'woman's silent heart' in all its timeless glory. No man could possibly 'feel as woman feels', and yet her sensibilities exposed a 'weakness' which no man could 'sound' (II, 2, p. 33). Paradoxically, this tremulous spirituality which makes her so vulnerable glows like a saving beacon for the men who love her. Even Louis, whom the play characterizes as a thoughtless youth, finds himself dissatisfied with the latest pretty face and, as Louise slips from his grasp, discovers that her 'angel voice / But tells me what a sun of heavenly beauty / Glides from the earth'. Her loss leaves him in 'darkness . . . unmann'd . . . I – I – I choke!' (v, 5, p. 100). For dour and upright Bragelone, the very thought Louise might love him 'speaks / Of home and rest after a stormy sea'. Her virgin purity has been his 'life's IDEAL, / Breathing through earth the Lovely and the Holy'. Yet that spiritual light seems strangely entangled in flesh so that, when court rumours convince him she has been the king's 'kind mistress', he brands her tears a 'harlot's trick' and can not retrieve the ideal he worships after the lady's bodily ruin has robbed him of 'all hope, all confidence, of virtue' (II, 2, pp. 29–31). But when he returns as a friar to hurl down shame upon her, Bragelone sees in her sorrow proof that 'the angel hath not left her! – if the plumes / Have lost the whiteness of their younger glory, / The wings have still the instinct of the skies' (IV, 3, pp. 77). She becomes a dove again, 'weary . . . / And sullied with dust', and so seeks rest and refuge at the convent near her childhood home. Virginity regained, she goes as a bride, a soul freed from earth, to meet 'celestial destinies'.

If the feminine ideal is tenderness and feeling, the masculine heart is 'sterner' and warlike. And just as love is disembodied, so war becomes an amalgam of noble abstractions – courage, glory, decisiveness – which forbid all thought of battle's realities. Wounds are decorative badges: a dented sword commemorates the time when Bragelone 'clove through the helmet' of a Dutchman and saved the king. Battles soothe a disappointed heart, and famous deeds will surely win a lady's love at last. On leaving for the wars, Bragelone likens himself to a knight of 'old romance', and Louise's mother urges her to present 'the banner of her colours' like some maiden of yore. Medievalism was already dear to the nineteenth century. Nurtured on the Gothic and the romantic poems and novels of Sir Walter Scott, the city warrior also braved the 'din' of commerce to bring back glories to his lady. Consequently, a man had to be worldly and his passions fierce. After Louise has fallen, Bragelone assumes she has 'learnt, betimes, the truth, that man's wild passion / Makes but its sport of virtue, peace, affection; / And breaks the plaything when the game is done' (IV, 3, p. 75). And herein lies the pathos of the masculine ideal: honour vies with natural roughness, just as womanly feeling strives with weakness.

Bragelone is older (more experienced) than Louise and, in pressing her to say she loves him, protests that should his 'soul's divine excess' offend her timid innocence he will instantly be silent. But when she shies away, he finds his 'soul is less heroic than [he] deem'd it' and soldiers on, begging her to let him love whether she will or no. That struggle intensifies after the noble warrior has taken holy orders. Beneath the dispassionate ardour of the father and counsellor burns a love which grows wilder as the penitent becomes more tearful. Though he insists that 'the holier part of love' has risen from the clay of his dead passion and will guide her to redemption, his feelings burst through his disguise, for when Louise recognizes him she swoons into his arms. Now he might proffer a chaste kiss, but honour beats down base desire:

> She does not breathe;
>   . . . poor child! One kiss!
> It is a brother's kiss – it has no guilt;
> Kind Heaven, it has no guilt. – I have survived
> All earthlier thoughts: her crime, my vows, effaced them.
> A brother's kiss! – Away! I'm human still;
> I thought I had been stronger; God forgive me! (v, 2, p. 89)

After Louise pledges herself to the veil, he is left with thoughts of easeful death until he chances upon a glove she has inadvertently dropped. The spiritual and the fleshly again collide in that 'single relic' which he stoops to kiss: 'And this hath touch'd her hand'. The dilemma is as old as romantic love itself, and this new Lancelot quickly drops the glove – ' 'Tis sinful!' – and sublimates his rougher nature despite one last trial as he watches his 'morning star' prepare to fade into the dark cloister. He too will enter a gloomy cell beside the convent walls and spend his life in prayer which 'shall join our souls in heaven'. A hope which may prove disconcerting since Louise has convinced herself that 'in Heaven at last / My soul, unsinning, may unite with Louis'.

This is not the least of the absurdities which surround the struggle for the 'ideal', a separation between spirit and body which is scarcely less healthy than the morbid pleasure audiences derived from watching it. Far more attractive is the way Bulwer's ideal hero challenges a world of luxury and shallow pleasure with a reformist's zeal. Partly this derives from his wish to warn Louise against the flatteries of court, but its energy suggests Bulwer's own liberal aspirations and results in one scene of magnificent rage. Like a dark avenging angel, Bragelone stands before Louis to bar his way. In his double role of friar and disguised knight, he reminds him that a king is first a man like any other and that his rank has destroyed the humanity of his subjects and himself. He has rewarded loyalty and virtue by 'rais[ing] a maiden to a duchess'.

The euphemism works well here to launch the irony which fires the rest of the attack. The King's great victories were bought by a million soldiers' blood and 'a million peasants starved to build Versailles'. Priests and poets extol his glory; painters depict him as Jove; but to the friar he is simply the king who betrayed a people's trust. Appealing to Louis's conscience, this Gaunt figure, new inspired, conjures up 'dark warnings' of another haughty king, his flattering priests and courtiers: 'behold the scaffold' of Charles I. He ends in thunderous prophecy. 'A heartless court and breadless people' may bring his descendants to the same fate: 'Beware, proud King! the Present cries aloud!' (IV, 4, pp. 78–81). For Bulwer, the past extravagance of George IV and the present intransigence of William IV to his Whig ministers – 'No, my Lord, I will not have that word, strike out "conciliatory", strike out "liberal" '[14] – loom out of the friar's diatribe, a resonance Macready would be happy to articulate.

The Duchess de la Vallière is neither well written nor thoughtful. Except for that one energetic outburst, Bulwer's attitude to a vain world comes from other plays rather than from his own experience or the facts of history. The actual Madame de Montespan lived quite happily with the mistress she had supplanted; in the play, she goes down to defeat because her rival's essential virtue makes her ugly in her own as well as Louis's eyes. She and Lauzun often talk like Iago and share his self-hatred when faced with another's 'daily beauty'. But this lack of original thought lays bare a number of basic social assumptions; ideas which are never so plain and simple in Bulwer's more characteristic and theatrically important plays. A woman's 'silent heart' offers a boundless source of strength to others, yet that strength does not save her from the dangers of a corrupt society. In the shelter of home, she is both protected and protector. But out in the world she is by nature susceptible and needs the strength of a manly guardian. However, that stern, loving guide (Bragelone, the friar) is himself susceptible to his own rough nature and (like Bragelone, the warrior) needs the inspiring power of a virtuous woman. In romance, the way to break that circle is to shun the world and pray for reunion in heaven. In life, that heaven shone with increasing brightness from the Victorian hearth.

One of the reasons this and the majority of nineteenth-century plays contain so few ideas is that actors and audiences regarded drama as narrative: a sequence of episodes each of which was designed to provoke an immediate and emotional response. There lay the theatre's challenge to the novelist accustomed to a looser, wide-ranging narrative through which his authorial presence could guide his readers and, on occasion, instruct them how to think. Accordingly, when Bulwer started his second play for Macready, he felt he had 'the most both to learn and *un*learn' about dramatic structure:

it was to the development of the plot and the arrangement of the incidents that I directed my chief attention; – and I sought to throw whatever belongs to poetry less into the diction and the 'felicity of words' than into the construction of the story, the creation of the characters, and the spirit of the pervading sentiment.[15]

He saw the articulation of 'the story' as a sort of poetry, but said nothing about the thoughts behind that 'pervading sentiment'. Yet *The Lady of Lyons* (1838) has within it an idea which he expressed most directly and astringently in his book on *England and the English* five years before:

A notorious characteristic of English society is the universal marketing of our unmarried women; – a marketing peculiar to ourselves in Europe, and only rivalled by the slave-merchants of the East. We are a matchmaking nation . . . We boast that in our country, young people not being affianced to each other by their parents, there are more marriages in which the heart is engaged than there are abroad. Very possibly; but, in good society, the heart is remarkably prudent, and seldom falls violently in love without a sufficient settlement: where the heart is, *there* will the *treasure* be also![16]

For purposes of sentiment, he turned this marriage market into a romantic and uplifting story.

Pauline Deschappelles, the beautiful daughter of a Lyonnese merchant, is displayed in a series of vignettes: at her dressing-table, pampered by her maid and flattered by her silly mother; rejecting the wealthy Beauseant because he has no title; reacting coldly to cousin Damas when he criticizes her high pretensions. Bulwer does not intend to illustrate the effect her upbringing has had on her character except in the most generalized way. She is given little to say in Act One and, significantly, her least attractive behaviour takes place off-stage. We only *hear* how the love poem of Claude Melnotte, a gardener's son, passed 'from lackey to lackey' to the lady who 'never [was] so insulted' and returned it by a servant who threw it into the mud and struck Claude's messenger. By Act Two, Pauline behaves enchantingly to the man she takes to be the Prince of Como and, although her vivacity is so obviously in response to Como's ancestry that even Melnotte (the 'Prince') accuses her of loving his rank rather than himself, it rapidly appears that her heart does indeed warm to her suitor's high ideals and tender words.

So her pride, which must be punished, is sketched with the lightest of brush-strokes and Pauline soon becomes another Louise. The play's last three Acts build entirely from that conflict between woman's weak nature and her inspiring purity. The idea of the merchant's daughter selling herself to the highest bidder fades behind the romantic dream. Yet in real life Bulwer had found his own love-match a nightmare; the lady for whom he risked his own fortune turned out to be the mindless product of the marriage mart after all:

The ambition of women absorbed in these petty intrigues, and debased to this paltry level, possesses but little sympathy with the great objects of a masculine and noble intellect. They have, in general, a frigid conception of public virtue: they affect not to understand politics, and measure a man's genius by his success *in getting on*.[17]

The essential Pauline has none of that vapidity. Bulwer saw her as 'charming tho' I say it', and wanted her 'to be played by a Lady light in hand – something like Vestris only with more feeling'. He made do with Helen Faucit (she 'freezes me'), although he begged Macready to teach her 'to speak more clearly . . . For she was perfectly inaudible in Cordelia. It is a great pity.'[18] But whatever the personal mannerisms of the actresses who played her, Pauline charmed Victorian audiences because her predicament roused such strong feelings about home and all it stood for.

She leaves her father's house as wife to the supposed Prince. But before the couple reach his humble dwelling, Bulwer shows them at the Golden Lion where the servants, who know Melnotte, giggle at Pauline's airs and where the accommodations are as slovenly as the food. In this way, Bulwer enables the audience to feel that Melnotte's cottage is a refuge even while Pauline, having discovered she has married the man she despised, regards the place as a hovel. There Melnotte protects her from the taunts of the outside world and there she is pitied and cared for by his widowed mother. Next day, Pauline – 'pure and virgin as this morn' – awakens to the power of that influence. Though she still feels the house is loathsome, 'yet the place seems still more desolate' without the husband who has spent the night downstairs guarding her like 'some marble saint / Niched in cathedral aisles . . . / From the rude hand of sacrilegious wrong'. There then follows a scene which brilliantly manipulates the domestic idyll.

The repentant Melnotte has left to arrange Pauline's return to her father's house, and Beauseant, who still has vengeful designs of his own, pushes past the widow and enters the cottage. He tries to be rid of the old woman by saying her son needs her in the village. Pauline begs her to stay and then remembers her wifely duty: 'Go, madam, if your son wishes it; I will not contradict his commands whilst, at least, he has still the right to be obeyed.' She expects Beauseant to revel in her present humiliation, but he wishes only to carry her off from 'the arms of a base-born peasant': his 'carriage waits without' to take her to a life of 'wealth, luxury, station'. To these temptations the guardian of the hearth responds in fury:

Sir! leave this house – it is humble: but a husband's roof, however lowly, is, in the eyes of God and man, the temple of a wife's honour! Know that I would rather starve – yes – with him who has betrayed me, than accept your lawful hand, even were you the prince whose name he bore!

Undaunted, Beauseant suggests she look more closely at the poverty around her and compare it to 'the refinement, the luxury, the pomp' he offers. Feeling alone and a stranger, Pauline begs him to respect the

weakness of 'a betrayed, injured, miserable woman'. The way now
lies open to the evils of the world. Beauseant prepares to force his
consolations on her while Pauline helplessly calls her absent husband:
'Have I no protector?' Whereupon Melnotte leaps in to the rescue,
'*dashing* [Beauseant] *to the other end of the stage*', heedless of his
enemy's pistol since a 'coward' who has 'outraged the laws' would
never dare to fire it. But Pauline has fainted in Melnotte's arms and,
when the villain leaves with threats of future vengeance, Bulwer
screws his audience's emotions to the sticking point. As a husband,
Melnotte takes one 'last embrace . . . Soft – soft! one kiss' which, as a
repentant betrayer, must ever more be lost to him (IV, 1, pp. 152–4).
Like Bragelone, he hovers between the hallowed and the forbidden.

Act Five offers a variant of this motif which was to have a
particularly lively career in the century's melodramas. Over two years
have passed since Pauline returned to her father and Melnotte went
off to cleanse his name or die in the wars. Now, by one of those
convenient strokes of fate, Damas, general of the Republic, returns
with a mysterious Colonel Morier on the very day Pauline will pledge
herself to Beauseant. Damas has said it would be a miracle to find one
constant woman in Lyons, and news of his cousin's intentions leads
him into soliloquy upon the follies men commit for women's sake. But
Morier–Melnotte, whose 'world is crumbled at [his] feet', checks his
impulse to curse her frailty: she has no reason to stay faithful to one
who betrayed her. In his desire for 'one last look more' before death,
he accompanies the general to witness the bill of divorcement and her
betrothal to Beauseant. Having played upon female weakness,
Bulwer then reveals the truth. Monsieur Deschappelles stands at the
brink of ruin, and Pauline, torn between love and duty, will save the
good name of her 'honour'd father, – / You, who so loved, so cherish'd
me, whose lips / Never knew one harsh word!' Beauseant will pay the
family's debts the moment Pauline contracts herself to him. She
readies herself for 'The loathsome prostitution of a hand / Without a
heart', but at the crucial moment Melnotte rips up the document and
gives her father twice the sum. Beauseant retreats with 'Curses on ye
both!':

PAULINE: Oh!
 My father, you are saved, – and by my husband!
 Ah, blessed hour?
MELNOTTE: Yet you weep still, Pauline!
PAULINE: But on thy breast! – *these* tears are sweet and holy!   (V, 2, p. 175)

45

A pure daughter willing to 'give all' to save her father's name made a poignant paradox. Mary Shelley, writing to congratulate Bulwer, noted this 'charm of nature and high feeling'. She also thought he had 'left the beaten road of old romance, so worn by modern dramatists, and *idealised the present*'.[19] Nothing shows that better than the 'token' he selected to picture Melnotte's devotion. His mother offers Pauline breakfast: 'I will get out Claude's coffee-cup – it is of real Sèvres; he saved up all his money to buy it three years ago, because the name of *Pauline* was inscribed on it' (IV, I, p. 151).

Domestic sentiment vibrates round Melnotte too. As Prince of Como he invents a palace fit for Pauline's ambitions but, as he loads every rift with ore, the dream of marble walls and alabaster lamps is less substantial than the idea of two soul-mates, 'shut out . . . from the rude world', in a paradise where orange groves sigh and fountains murmur amongst roses:

> We'd have no friends
> That were not lovers; no ambition, save
> To excel them all in love; we'd read no books
> That were not tales of love – that we might smile
> To think how poorly eloquence of words
> Translates the poetry of hearts like ours! (II, I, p. 131)

The speech seems to have made a powerful impression in the theatre. G.H. Lewes remembered 'the youthfulness of Macready in that part; you lost all sense of his sixty years in the fervour and resilient buoyancy of his manner; and when he paced up and down before the footlights, describing to the charming Pauline . . . the home where love should be, his voice, look, and bearing had an indescribable effect'.[20] Yet the *written* dialogue is unconvincing and the movement between semi-colloquial prose and heightened blank verse generally infelicitous, as are the violent shifts of tone: it is hard to know how to take Damas's 'I'll be hanged if I am not going to blubber!' at the moment when Pauline has realized she loves Melnotte in spite of his poverty. None of this mattered. Pauline's charm and Melnotte's youthful idealism invested ordinary life with such nobility that even a sophisticated and intelligent observer liked Lady Blessington 'felt the charm of the high-souled and beautiful sentiments, and the eloquent words in which they are dressed'.[21]

Bulwer set his play in the turbulent years following the French Revolution in order to justify Melnotte's egalitarian ambition and rapid rise in the army. However, that spirit of optimism and

2 *The Lady of Lyons* at the Haymarket Theatre: *Claude Melnotte* (Mr Anderson), pretending to be the Prince of Como, is speaking to *Pauline* (Miss Helen Faucit) of his imaginary Palace

aspiration also made him a hero of the 1830s. Elsewhere, Bulwer had described England after the Reform Bill of 1832: 'the action, the vividness, the *life* of these times . . . the great prevailing characteristic of the present intellectual spirit is one most encouraging to human hopes'.[22] It was this that stirred audiences both for and against the play. Macready told his diary that he had acted the part 'pretty well' on the first night but added that 'the audience felt it very much, and were carried away by it'. The more conservative were less pleased.

The *Morning Post* complained that 'a manly peasant would never talk, about his natural equality, and so on, with persons of family'. In the following week, Macready stepped before the curtain to point out that the 'political allusions' were necessary 'to the working of the story' and that the Lord Chamberlain *had* licensed the performance. Fighting as he was for English Drama, his claim that 'art and literature have no politics' may not have been totally disingenuous despite the fact that, given the political attacks on Bulwer's first play, he had agreed to withhold the author's identity until the new play established itself. When Bulwer's name did appear on the playbills, *The Times* rumbled against 'such morbid sentimentality, such turbid sansculottism' from the school of contemporary French scribblers.[23] But the play's success was already assured and, in the years to come, many a clerk or shop-assistant recognized in Melnotte the mirror of his own aspirations: 'Wealth to the mind – wealth to the heart – high thoughts – bright dreams — the hope of fame.'

Yet this individuality lies buried under a superstructure of conventional heroics. In making Melnotte the only playboy of his particular western world, Bulwer endows him with noble gifts: he knows Latin, sings, plays the guitar, dances, paints, writes poetry, and fences magnificently. When we first hear of him, he has just won a shooting-match and the local lads bear home 'the Prince' in triumph. The gardener's boy has achieved all this since the day he first saw Pauline. When he lays those glories at her feet and she rejects them, he falls victim to what Bulwer's preface calls 'his unsettled principles': his manliness has not yet subdued his masculine roughness. However, just as in Pauline's case, Bulwer shows the dark side of that conflict as briefly as possible.

Pauline's 'heartless insolence' not only hurts his pride and his messenger's body; those blows challenge the honour of all citizen peasants. So he agrees to join Beauseant (who has also been insulted) and becomes a prince in name as well as in deeds. This pact does not take place on stage and, when he next appears, his manly sensibility soon reasserts itself so that he becomes an unwilling participant in the final move to ensnare Pauline. Bound by oath to go through with the wedding, and fearing Pauline would marry Beauseant in 'resentment' were he to reveal his true identity, this most innocent of betrayers tries to persuade Pauline to refuse 'this hasty union'; he declines any dowry and – interestingly – appeals to the bride's own natural fears. But when the chastened Lady eventually acknowledges her peasant husband's true worth, Melnotte no longer sees that worth in himself and tears himself from her now willing embrace. Brave deeds must restore the name of Melnotte and prove him a fitting husband. In exile as Morier, the warrior's every act is always for Pauline. Returning home, he learns 'the nature of [her] sacrifice' and hears her pray 'that we shall meet again in Heaven'. But this hero and heroine achieve an earthly bliss – and the satisfaction of wealth and position amongst the good citizens of Lyons.

Romantic patterns continued to possess Bulwer's mind as he again thought of writing for the theatre. Macready urged him to 'persist in your adherence to the mixed plot' which makes an audience laugh and cry and provides a continuing flow of sentiment. Searching for a subject, Bulwer had been attracted to historical accounts of the Marques de la Ensenada. However, the story of a noble Spanish statesman whose attempts 'to revive the ancient grandeur of his country' ended in his banishment could not, he thought, be popular. The comedy of such a subject would have to evolve from the machinations of the statesman's enemies, a court satire which would be 'too subtle' for English audiences. They might also object to the necessary 'politics' and could not be expected to tolerate 'the want of poetic justice' in such a tale of defeated nobility; 'besides where is the domestic interest?' In consequence, his first draft for what is now *Richelieu* was shaped by his excited reaction to a recent French novel, *A Mistress to Louis XIII*, which promised familiar territory. His hero was to be 'the wittiest & bravest gentleman' whose 'extravagant valour' led him into difficulties especially in regard to a lady who, on their wedding night, learns that the king intends her as his mistress. She, of course, is chaste and true despite the natural weakness of her sex, but the chevalier does not discover that until the play's last moments. Across this tale of a wronged and valorous husband would loom the shadow of Cardinal Richelieu. But which of Covent Garden's actors could play him? If Macready 'took Richelieu, there would be two acts without you, which will never do, & the principal intent of the plot would not fall on you. Tell me what is to be done. Must we give up this idea?'[24]

Macready found the proposed outline too packed with incident, but in the next months, under the actor's tutelage, Bulwer came to see that Richelieu was in fact his central character and, for the first time in his plays, there emerged a figure in whom the noble and the base contend on *equal* terms. The comedy would arise from the Cardinal's mordant humour and 'brilliant charlatanism', much in the manner of Richard III as restored by Macready from Cibber's pasteboard version. The court intrigue would be made 'familiar' by the tribulations of the two lovers, de Mauprat and Julie. Since Richelieu had the legendary aura of a 'Henry 8th or Queen Mary – or almost of Cromwell, viz: a Notion not to be found in books', audiences might accept 'the necessity for politics' especially since this statesman's labours for his country's glory did not suffer defeat. The overriding problem was how 'some Home interest might link itself with the Historical'. Here the actor's personality, rather than his advice on tone and structure, gave Bulwer his solution. Through each revision he strengthened the Cardinal's fondness for his ward: 'the clinging of Julie to Richelieu, the protection he gives her, will have, I imagine, the physical effect of making the audience forget whether he is her father or not. There they are before you, flesh & blood – the old man and the young Bride involved in the same fate & creating the sympathy of a Domestic relation.'[25]

This picture-from-life was exactly the effect Macready aimed for in his own acting. A master of the grandiose, he could at times seem artificial so that, almost fifty years later, the Queen noted how Irving, in *The Bells*, 'though a mannerist of the Macready type, acted wonderfully'.[26] But to his contemporaries he spoke the language of ordinary men, a Wordsworth to Edmund Kean's Byron. Despite his temper and brittle nerves, Macready was the very model of domestic gentility. He chose a wife many years his junior and, to make her worthy of himself and his sister, instructed her in moral philosophy for a year before their marriage. The trio settled in Pinner Wood, some fifteen miles from the patent houses, whither the actor would retreat between performances to become lord and master of a respectable, middle-class household. Later he leased Elm Place, a nine-acre farmstead in Elstree, and devoted himself to his sister, wife, and growing family.

Though he never allowed the theatre to invade his home, he brought a tender domesticity to the stage. Even as a bachelor, struggling to shine while Kean flashed lightning, he had made such tenderness his own particular sphere. In 1820, an untried Sheridan Knowles presented him with *Virginius*, a fable which goes back in English to Chaucer's *Canterbury Tales*. At Covent Garden, Macready's Virginius was a timeless figure whose supreme love for his daughter, Virginia, reached out to the heartstrings and susceptibilities of unheroic audiences. When Appius persuades his minion, Claudius, to say that Virginia is a slavegirl who was stolen from him, Virginius hastens to the Forum to defend his family before all Rome. Suddenly, amidst the public furore, the father turns to the daughter he has raised from childhood: 'I never saw you look so like your mother / In all my life.' Such startling ordinariness could not have been more human and true.

Macready's idiosyncratic style attracted a number of young writers with ambitions to restore the English Drama – Knowles, Thomas Talfourd, Browning, Mary Mitford among them. To test the effectiveness of their scripts, the actor consulted, or read them to, his friends – Forster, Stanfield, Landor, Serle, Dickens, and several lesser lights – who were artists but never 'fellow artists'. These circumstances gave birth to Bulwer's *Richelieu*, and almost ruined a friendship when Forster fell asleep during one reading of the play's many revisions.

In several ways, *Richelieu* is like *King John*, that other Victorian perennial, and the Cardinal gathers to himself most of the aspects which made Shakespeare's play so appealing: the cunning of King John; the mocking bravado of Faulconbridge; the pathos of little prince Arthur and Hubert, his unwilling torturer; the anguish of Constance, grieving wife and mother. Both plays have a double centre of interest, but whereas Shakespeare uses both the King and the Bastard to comment on the nature of the body politic, Bulwer focusses his two stories on love, that aspect of 'history' which gave such pleasure to the Victorians. The de Mauprat/Julie episodes present this vividly and conventionally: nobility and purity come under attack, are further shaken by misunderstandings and misperceptions, only to shine the brighter at play's end. The Cardinal also soldiers honourably in the name of his heart's chaste mistress: France. However, because that honour is sometimes difficult to perceive, Bulwer creates a more complex (and believable) hero than the standard warrior who, even at moments when he seems to falter, remains a transparently idealized figure. Treating history's detail with a playwright's licence, Bulwer depicts a crafty autocrat and then pushes beyond that image to present a schemer whose aspirations are more truly disinterested than those of the usual romantic hero. In *Richelieu*, the 'unsettled principles' of the masculine psyche allow the Cardinal to make a convenience of the hate and sordid ambition of underlings in what is ultimately a praiseworthy quest.

Bulwer knew that even the dullest of audiences would bring to the play a preconceived idea of the Cardinal. In consequence, a larger-than-life figure of immense power and wealth rears up behind the initial conspiracy between Baradas, the play's outright villain, and his dupes, de Beringhen and the Duke of Orleans. Their agent, the Chevalier de Mauprat, has from his youth suffered the first minister's enmity and peculiar mercy when, as a traitor to the State, he was told either to seek death in battle for France or die on the scaffold. Our sympathies therefore lie with the Chevalier and his co-conspirators, despite the unattractive 'jealous demon' that love for Julie rouses amongst them. De Mauprat is arrested on the Cardinal's orders: 'the tiger's played / Long enough with his prey'. The second scene shows Richelieu savouring his reputation as 'the old fox', as he stalks his palace with Brother Joseph. Yet the pleasure-loving king is weak; the courtiers and churchmen are grasping sycophants; only the Cardinal sees that de Mauprat, 'a humorous dare-devil', can become the instrument of France's good. Rather than behead him, he will marry him to Julie so that the king, despite himself, may be saved from those who would use de Mauprat for their own greed and their country's destruction. Richelieu may be a tiger and a fox, but his heart is a lion's:

> I have shed blood – but I have had no foes
> Save those the State had – if my wrath was deadly,
> 'Tis that I felt my country in my veins,
> And smote her sons as Brutus smote his own. (III, 1, p. 239)

Soon, even the Chevalier's single-minded heroics seem childlike – a charge to be laid at many a Victorian hero's feet – when compared to the Cardinal's calculating policy. Like his enemies, Richelieu lusts after power: 'Ambition has no rest!' Like Marlowe's Faustus he flings aside the books of moralists: 'Philosophy, thou liest! / Quick – the despatch! Power – Empire!' (III, 1, pp. 241–2). Yet unlike theirs, his ambition and pride are not entirely self-serving. This villainous hero speaks to something deep within the nineteenth-century consciousness; his duality goes far beyond man's struggle to tame his base nature. The Cardinal raises questions about the aspiring spirit of the age by showing how little separates the scrupulous from the unscrupulous.

The force of this idea probably escaped most audiences since the play repeatedly assures them of Richelieu's altruism and diverts them with an excessively complicated plot – the play's subtitle is 'The

Conspiracy' – which turns upon the recovery of a package which will prove Baradas the enemy of France. In addition, Bulwer's methods bring the Cardinal safely within the purlieus of an audience's theatrical expectations by picturing him in a series of exciting *coups de théâtre*. Act Three finds Richelieu cornered in his own apartments. De Mauprat storms into his presence, eager for revenge against the man who has married him off to a woman intended for the king. But learning that Richelieu had actually relied on his tender honour to prevent the king's plans for Julie, the Chevalier changes allegiance and fends off the conspirators by telling them he has murdered the Cardinal who now lies dead. Act Four begins with congratulations to the king on becoming his own master. Growing ever more confident, the courtiers defame the dead minister, and Baradas, wanting Julie for himself, persuades the king to imprison de Mauprat. As the guards seize him, the doors swing open to admit the 'dead' Cardinal, to the consternation of his enemies. Act Five's grandest 'effect' involves an equally sudden reversal of Richelieu's fortunes. Having tasted independence, the king prefers to choose new councillors and Richelieu falls ill, partly as a ruse but also because strength fails him now he no longer guides his country. A shadow of his former self, he enters the royal palace supported by Brother Joseph and accompanied by secretaries bearing bundle after bundle of state papers. He sits by weakly as the king and his advisors try to cope with the country's business, a task which obviously defeats them. But though the king begins to regret his actions, the Cardinal dare not make his move until a package is safely in his hand. At last it reaches him and, with what appears to be his dying breath, he delivers it to the king who, faced with the treachery of those around him, begs Richelieu to 'live! / If not for me – for France!' At that name, the Cardinal becomes himself once more. He arrests Baradas and instantly takes up the reins of power:

> for in one moment there did pass
> Into this wither'd frame the might of France! –
> My own dear France – I have thee yet – I have saved thee!
> I clasp thee still! – it was thy voice that call'd me
> Back from the tomb! What mistress like our country?
>
> (v, 3, pp. 296–7)

The speech places this devious figure within the recognizable conventions of romance; the Cardinal could indeed be talking of an actual lady's inspiring power. It links him to Julie who has also assumed a more-than-ordinary strength in love's cause:

> Child no more;
> I love, and I am woman! Hope and suffer –
> Love, suffering, hope, – what else doth make the strength
> And majesty of woman? – Where is Adrien? . . .
> Answer me but one word – I am a wife –
> I ask thee for my *home* – my FATE – my ALL!
> Where is my *husband*? (IV, 2, pp. 273–4)

And through constant emphasis upon the affection that also unites the Cardinal and his ward, Bulwer further ensures that, however surprising or cruel Richelieu's actions are, he will remain 'familiar' and sympathetic.

In illustrating that fatherly care for Julie, daughter of a long-dead friend, Bulwer endows his Cardinal with one of the qualities often reserved for the lover whose devotion to his lady contains large amounts of paternal feeling. When *Richelieu* was in rehearsal, Bulwer was always on the lookout for ways to increase that bond. He was particularly anxious about a scene in which Julie clings to her protector when messengers command her to go to the king. With all the tact he could muster, he lectured Macready about this effect:

Tell me . . . if my alterations generally meet your suggestion, which was a masterpiece in conception. Why the deuce were you not author as well as actor? I am now going to retaliate, and (mark my modesty) suggest how I meant a line to be said by you. In Act IV., when you say, 'And sheltered by the wings of sacred Rome', I want you *actually* to shelter her with the priestly robe, and to cower over her like an old eagle. When I wrote this I had in my mind a dim recollection of an action of yours, somewhere, I think, as Lear with Cordelia. I *think* it was Lear; but I remember that, wherever it was, it was thoroughly grand and tender in its *protectiveness*.

Macready took the advice with laconic patience: 'I will try and realise your notion of the "dove-like brooding over" – Miss Faucit.'[27]

Such moments as this between Julie and the Cardinal raise both the 'tender' and the 'grand' to a higher, idealized reality. As she clings to him, Julie begs Richelieu to remember 'my dead father! – / Think, how, an infant, clinging to your knees, / And looking to your eyes, the wrinkled care / Fled from your brow before the smile of childhood.' The tenderness of that image appeals to the statesman's humanity but, in its domestic sweetness, also encourages the audience to see how an innocent appeal from any young child smooths away a father's weariness. The ordinary, or what the audience would like to feel was ordinary, is then transmuted by a huge and magnificent gesture as the Cardinal resolutely stands his ground and enfolds the suppliant figure within his red robes. The image now takes on the force of a holy father protecting his helpless 'daughter', 'couch'd upon this heart, as at an altar, / And shelter'd by the wings of sacred Rome!' (IV, 2, pp. 275–6). Thus the picture is lifelike and larger than life, moving yet terrible, and that combination opens the audience to 'the Grandeur of Nature'.

This resonant interplay of word and gesture fascinated Bulwer. Three weeks after *Richelieu* opened, he told Macready he had 'almost finished' another play and thought it 'most powerful'. When Macready threw in the managerial towel at Covent Garden in the Spring of 1839 and arranged to join the Haymarket Company for their six-month season, Bulwer offered the play to Webster: '[its] very strong domestic interest . . . I think will suit the Haymarket well'. However, when Macready read the completed script, he 'was much struck with the *effect* of the two last acts' but found the whole play 'far too melodramatic'. After much revision, *The Sea-Captain* opened that October and pleased neither the critics nor the public. At the same time, the indefatigable Bulwer had been working on 'a sentimental Modern Comedy' in case his romantic drama should fail.[28] The Haymarket actors were predominantly comedians, and the relative intimacy of the auditorium also prompted that new direction. In addition he may have remembered Macready's earlier comment about satirical comedy which 'affords great scope for touching on those unhealthy parts of our social system, which you have the power of taking advantage of for real good'.[29]

By June 1840 he had thought of a new comedy which developed an idea that had been implied, but never fully dramatized in *Richelieu*: 'My proposed title is "Appearances", the idea a genteel Comedy of the present day – the Moral, a satire on the way appearances of all kinds impose on the public, . . .' Macready disliked the excerpts Bulwer read to him and nothing further came of the project. Yet, within weeks, Bulwer had still another script under way: 'I fancy it is comedy & so far in a new genre that it certainly admits stronger & more real grave passions than the comedy of the last century . . . All we act more in earnest than our grandfathers.'[30] The result was *Money*, the one play of Bulwer's which still belongs in the national repertoire.

Freed from the pseudo-Elizabethan verse and inflated prose of the 'serious' style, ideas which had formerly been pictorialized for 'effect' now evolved from the interchange of rational dialogue. A sequence (I, 4, p. 314) between Alfred Evelyn, the sardonic hero, and the equally perceptive Clara Douglas illustrates this change. Evelyn has been angered by Sir Frederick Blount's insolent behaviour: were Clara rich, her beauty and virtue would merit respect, but since she is 'poor – dependent – solitary – walking the world defenceless', those same qualities become fair game for 'fops' and 'libertines'. This irony adds point to the vocabulary of female vulnerability, but Evelyn grows less detached as he laments his inability to defend her. He can 'mock' those who insult his own poverty but is tortured at having 'no shield to protect' a lady 'so delicately framed and nurtured' from similar slights. With the simplest of replies, Clara cuts through that romantic agony: 'But I, too, have pride of my own – I, too, can smile at the pointless insolence –.' Weak though she may be, a woman of sense and philosophic humour can also brave the world, though Evelyn, launched upon the drama of his own sufferings, is incapable of understanding that. Macready was not far wrong in dismissing the hero as 'a damned walking gentleman': he could see he had 'nothing great or striking in situation, character, humour, or passion to develop'.[31] On the other hand, all three women in the play have a surprising individuality which tests many of the assumptions that prop up the Victorian ideal.

They themselves generally subscribe to what men would have them be and do. Georgina happily allows her father to sell her to the highest bidder even though she has an independent wit and a genuine fondness for Sir Frederick Blount. Her aunt, Lady Franklin, has no illusions about that: 'she is handsome and accomplished – but her father's worldliness has spoilt her nature'. Clara would rather view her cousin as an unformed girl who only needs the guidance of the right man. Her own adoration of Evelyn persuades her that he can reform Georgina: 'Once removed from the worldly atmosphere of her father's counsels, and you will form and raise her to your own level. She is so young yet – she has beauty, cheerfulness, and temper; – the rest you will give, if you will but yet do justice to your own nature.' Subsequent events show what an impossible picture this is. Georgina is so little affected by Evelyn's worth that she continues to trick that new-made Croesus after their engagement, prefers to spend her mornings with Blount and, once her father warns her of Evelyn's approaching bankruptcy, takes the first opportunity to elope with Blount to Scotland. Her aunt 'chanced on them by the Park just in time to dissuade and save her'. Georgina is no wicked villainess; 'to do her justice, a hint of [her father's] displeasure was sufficient' to halt the elopement. But her story suggests that a thoughtless, good-hearted girl is as likely to gravitate to a cheerfully careless man as to an upright mentor. When she marries Blount, this 'frail one' will simply find wider scope for folly.

In one crucial instance, Clara is also the victim of the way men would like to see her. Evelyn, who begins the play as a penniless dependant on his relatives' self-serving charity, cannot find £10 to pay the rent of a dying woman 'who was my nurse and my mother's last friend'. Clara secretly uses her 'little all' to provide the money while rejecting Evelyn's proposal of marriage. By Act Two, he has been left a fortune so that Clara feels even less inclined to explain her refusal. Again Lady Franklin holds to the realities of the situation: 'My dear child, happiness is too rare to be sacrificed to a scruple.' But Clara has a firm view of womanly propriety and a romantic conviction that Evelyn should be able to 'read my heart'. Lady Franklin does not, however, counsel immodesty, merely good sense: 'let me only tell him that you . . . sent that money to his old nurse . . . He will then know, at least, if avarice be your sin.' Clara believes he should have 'guessed' who the donor was and describes the force of her own love which can turn a girl who trembles at the smallest spider into someone who 'would lay this hand upon the block . . . to save Alfred Evelyn one moment's pain'. Lady Franklin has already pointed out that marriage to Georgina would bring Evelyn pain, but she can only give way to Clara's fierce idealism and speak her own thoughts about that high-minded attitude in private: 'What fools these girls are! – they take as much pains to lose a husband as a poor widow does to get one!' (II, 4, pp. 335–6).

Lady Franklin is a *rich* widow, blessed also with a wealth of common sense and good humour. If her half-brother's carriage-horse falls lame, then that saves her from 'making a great many tedious visits'. If her maid has accidentally ruined her new turban, she finds she looks 'best, after all, in the black hat and feathers' and tells Clara that the best 'turban' a woman can wear is a sweet temper: 'Think of that when you marry.' She never pretends to false feeling and can see precisely how money governs all her brother's affections or how 'there is something noble' beneath Evelyn's outward scorn. Handsome and young (Bulwer told Forster she was twenty-eight), she represents an alternative ideal, but one available only to women of sufficient means and character. She is free from the marriage-market and from attendance on a man's 'choice' – 'that humiliating word', as

Clara calls it. She can make her own choice and then jolly the man along to make him think he has done the choosing. Yet she plays that game as frankly as her name suggests when she chivvies 'Mr Graves who is always in black – always lamenting his ill-fortune and his sainted Maria, who led him the life of a dog . . . I always liked him: he made an excellent husband.' She understands his devotion to his lost Maria better than he does himself: 'it's the way with widowers; that is, whenever they mean to marry again'. Wit, intelligence, good humour and – not least – a healthy exchequer allow this woman to dance past the snares of the world.

And Clara, snagged on the womanly ideal, also has a saving intelligence. She adores Evelyn with all the dedication of her 'silent' heart but she knows only too well what poverty does to love. Evelyn thinks she refused him because he was poor, whereas she did so to save their love. Her final explanation, despite its high-flying sentimentality creates one of the most original and realistic moments on the early Victorian stage. Clara's parents had married for love, only to discover that poverty wore away their romantic idyll. Had Clara said 'yes' to Evelyn she would have condemned him to the misery her father suffered: 'I saw that ambition wither to despair! – I saw the struggle – the humiliation – the proud man's agony – the bitter life – the early death!' No house-angel can save a man from that internal destruction:

In marriages like this, the wife cannot share the burden; it is he – the husband – to provide, to scheme, to work, to endure – to grind out his strong heart at the miserable wheel! The wife, alas! cannot share the struggle – she can but witness the despair! And therefore, Alfred, I rejected you.   (v, 4, pp. 398–9)

Alfred, alas, dreams on. To him, her words prove the unfathomable power of virtuous woman: 'Fair angel, too excellent for man's harder nature to understand! – at least it is permitted me to revere.'

Bulwer has endowed Clara with a human past which dictates her present course of action. Georgina's behaviour has been formed by her father's pecuniary education just as Lady Franklin's values have been shaped by her experience of men and marriage, but the effect of those connections is unconscious. Clara makes a decisive and painful decision *because* of the past, and it also tells her that money, however unromantic a commodity, is indispensable. Bulwer knew the force of that experience, having forfeited his mother's financial support by marrying for love; in his case, the disaster was compounded by his wife's slapdash intellect and insane whims. Yet he managed to hide all personal bitterness. Writing to a friend, he would only admit 'I am . . . peculiarly glad that you like Clara. I own I had an object in her delineation. It is so common for a young woman of a generous and romantic temper to think that there is something very noble in an imprudent marriage, that I wished to show that there were two sides to think of.'[32]

However, Bulwer sometimes undermines Clara's character by making her the puppet of a scene's comic balance. For instance, her behaviour is unbelievably silly when she sees Evelyn's attentions to Georgina and retaliates by encouraging Blount's overtures. This matters less with the other three characters. Bulwer intends Georgina and Blount to *be* silly and has not been able to imagine Evelyn with the same objectivity and depth. Evelyn's past creates attitudes, not decisions. His widowed mother had scrimped for his education. At the height of his academic success he was sent down from Cambridge for thrashing a young aristocrat while the lord who first picked that quarrel went scot free. He is as sensitive to insult as Claude Melnotte and, since experience has only taught him hearts are 'cold and souls as vile', just as romantic in his defiance of the world. His education as a poor sizar may have been less a fairy-tale than that of the gardener's boy, but it has not shown him more of life's realities. When he falls in love with Clara, he seems to forget what his past drudgery entailed, for 'with you to toil for – your step to support – your path to smooth – and I – I poor Alfred Evelyn – promise at last to win for you even fame and fortune'.

Nevertheless, this attitudinizing opens the way for the play's satire on wealth and position. As Sir John Vesey's poor relation, Evelyn can only comment at first from the sidelines. 'The drudge of fools', he must submit to being Georgina's errand boy or 'Stingy Jack's' unpaid secretary. His patron has spent a lifetime making much out of very little. 'There are two rules in life – FIRST, Men are valued not for what they *are*, but what they *seem* to be. SECONDLY, If you have no merit or money of your own, you must trade on the merits and money of other people.' Eager to trade on the money Georgina will surely inherit from her uncle Mordaunt's will, he tells her that Blount is not as 'charming' as he once was: 'an heiress such as you will be should look out for a duke'. Bulwer is much more specific about Georgina's education than he was about Pauline Deschappelles's. Sir John grooms his daughter for 'show'. On the strength of his own supposed riches, she has always passed as someone with Great Expectations.

To make her still more attractive, he ensures that her 'merits' include drawing – which she does prettily but unskilfully – singing, dancing, and deportment. Furnished thus, she is her father's 'pride' (for intellectual and moral qualities have no marketable value) and a 'blessing' for any husband. Evelyn would agree, since Blount, 'a fine puss gentleman that's all perfume', appears to be the only bidder.

Things change once Evelyn turns out to be Mordaunt's heir. Hurt by Clara's rejection when he was poor, he seeks revenge by surrounding himself with luxuries she must have thought he could never provide. Like a new Timon, he is besieged by painter and architect, silversmith and tailor. Money has made him an arbiter of taste; the poem he once could not sell for £5 will now fetch ten times as much. But Clara remains unimpressed, and he begins to see Georgina's greed, so he takes up with Captain Smooth, a celebrated gambler, and pretends to lose his fortune. Whereupon the tradesmen scurry to collect whatever they still can, and Sir John thinks Georgina should break off her engagement: 'a daughter's like any other capital – transfer the stock in hand to t'other speculation'. The one thing Evelyn seeks to hold on to as his financial bubble supposedly bursts is the Groginhole estate. In a speculating world, land represents stability. It creates an instant pedigree for Lord Glossmore, 'whose grandfather kept a pawnbroker's shop', and gives credence to his stance as county gentleman, despite whispers of 'Trade' behind his back. It becomes the crucial test of Georgina's sincerity, for Evelyn asks to borrow her settlement of £10,000 so that he might complete his purchase of the property whose rents would eventually restore his fortune.

To a society which worships land, gambling is the worst of sins. It is the one immorality in Sir John's worldly creed, for a gambler not only risks money and property but the social 'consequence' which depends entirely on others' belief, however unfounded, in his financial solidity. So Bulwer makes Dudley Smooth into a figure of sinister charm who seems to have hypnotic power over Evelyn's breakneck plunge to ruin. He becomes a metaphor of the way society estimates a man's worth. Under such an influence, Evelyn, who three days before 'was universally respected', finds himself 'singularly infamous. Yet I'm the same man.' Had his losses to 'Deadly' Smooth been less public or had he ruined his opponent instead of himself, society would have congratulated him.[33] Evelyn puts that neatly – he can afford to, since his 'ruin' was a charade: 'Cant! it was not criminal to gamble – it was criminal to lose . . . The Vices and the Virtues are written in a language the world cannot construe; it reads them in a vile translation, and the translators are – FAILURE and SUCCESS!' (v, 3, p. 394).

For Clara, Evelyn's success can only be measured by the 'noble and bright career' that opens to a man of means and by the way he wields such power. After she talks to him 'as a sister – herself weak, inexperienced, ignorant, nothing – *might* speak to a brother, in whose career she felt the ambition of a man', Evelyn is moved to do battle for her sake, even if she cannot be his wife. Amongst the 'friends' and hangers-on who clamour for his money and favour are two men who beg him to use his influence, as prospective owner of Groginhole, in the local parliamentary by-election. Hopkins 'can't live another month', so Mr Stout, the political economist, would have the patriotic Popkins represent the borough and urges Evelyn to 'turn every man out of his house who votes against enlightenment and Popkins!' Lord Glossmore supports young Lord Cipher who would never act 'without considering beforehand how people of £50,000 a year will be affected'. Bulwer pokes fun at Whig and Tory slogans,[34] but he also has Evelyn realize that, since landowners have authority as well as 'influence', one way to gain Clara's approval would be to stand for parliament himself. So the man who called for 'purity of election – independence of votes' and saw 'Both sides alike! Money *versus* Man' now uses his own money and his 'consequence' as the district's biggest landowner to secure his election. The gossips suggest he does this to attain parliamentary privilege and so escape his creditors. Bulwer sees Clara's regard as sufficient motive and does not seem to recognize the dubious morality of Evelyn's decision since he gives him no belief or plan to further as member for Groginhole.

Given the sensitivities of his audience, Bulwer could not help but soften his barbs against contemporary values. His policy appears to have been to hit with one hand and stroke with the other. He satirizes electoral influence then lets his hero use his local prestige to win the borough. He exposes a society whose god is Mammon but allows Evelyn to keep his fortune. He is also careful to point out that, though virtue is too frequently a synonym for success, true moral virtue cannot work effectively, cannot *survive* without money. The play ends as Evelyn hails 'the everlasting holiness of truth and love' which Clara has shown him and which reconciles him 'to the world and to mankind'. But, as Graves adds, truth and love do not by themselves ensure happiness. At the final curtain, each major character adds another ingredient to the recipe for well-being, and the last is Evelyn's 'plenty of Money!' That wish may be devastatingly frank, but it is also comfortably reassuring.

Among the congratulatory letters Bulwer received after *Money* opened at the Haymarket was one from Charles Dickens who thought it 'so full of real, distinct, genuine character'.[35] Some ten years later,[36] Dickens led a group of distinguished friends in a private performance of Bulwer's *Not So Bad As We Seem* at the Duke of Devonshire's London mansion. The Queen felt he acted 'admirably' and the play was 'full of cleverness though rather too long'.[37] An odd combination of Jacobean city comedy and Victorian melodrama, the play actually takes place in the reign of Queen Anne. Its central idea that there are many different sides to a character points to a concern with appearances which runs through all Bulwer's plays. La Vallière is not the 'kind mistress' she might seem to be; Pauline discovers a true worth in her peasant husband; Richelieu and Baradas present two aspects of the same burning ambition. Appearances were to dominate the Victorian age for, in a volatile society dedicated to making money, first impressions were vital, yet they could also mask moral or financial deceptions[38] and, as the century grew older, hide sexual and psychopathic secrets.[39]

CHAPTER 3

Domestic and commonplace

These works are thoroughly characteristic of Mr Robertson's method in art. They are simple almost to baldness in plot, and altogether free from improbable incident or melodramatic situation. Their hold upon an audience is due to three gifts . . . power of characterization, smartness of dialogue, and a cleverness in investing with romantic associations commonplace details of life . . . In all there is a scene of lovemaking, the effect of which is heightened by surrounding selfishness and cynicism. Love is the diamond in the play[s], worldliness its setting.

The Athenaeum, 23 January 1869

Tom Robertson lived and breathed the theatre from his cradle. Even his comedies-in-miniature at the Prince of Wales's, regarded by his contemporaries as so astonishingly natural, gave priority to the stage picture, elevating easy feeling above truth to life. Away from the Bancrofts' theatre, when he could not control the intimate style of each production, he felt compelled to explain his intentions in warning notes. For *Dreams* which opened at the Gaiety in March 1869, 'The Author requests that this Drama may be played after the style and manner of Comedy, and not after the manner of Melodrama.'[1] Yet the play is melodrama for much of the time and bears a striking resemblance – on a less grand scale – to Bulwer's romantic dramas of thirty years before.[2] That similarity suggests a continuity of manner in the Victorian playhouse, but it also reveals how earlier values had, by Robertson's time, become entrenched or had undergone an interesting shift of emphasis.

By the fifth Act, Lina, a seamstress and lady's maid, has determined to take the veil after Rudolf, whom she loved faithfully but silently, has recovered from his passion for Lady Clara. Frau Harfthal knows that her son now returns Lina's love, but the girl has seen how his once ungovernable feelings for Clara have been 'worn away by time'. Frau Harfthal appeals, as wife and mother, to Lina's new-found determination to shun transient love:

LINA: . . . Now I am a woman with a mission in life, and that mission is a holy one.

63

FRAU: No mission is more holy than that of a wife – and mother!

LINA: But earthly love is perishable, and is worn away by time, as snow melts before the sun.

FRAU: Is a mother's love so perishable?

LINA: That, even death cannot destroy! (*kissing her*) I can love Rudolf though I shall not be his wife.

FRAU: No woman can love a man as a wife can love her husband. (v, p. 228)

Hearth and home have become such a magnificent combination that no womanly estate could be higher or more pure. Whereas La Vallière slipped away from Bragelone's anguished eyes into the saving darkness of the convent, Lina finally gives herself to the holy cause of Victorian marriage while female voices hymn praises from the convent and Rudolf claims his childhood companion, the 'kind nurse' to his past sorrow:

RUDOLF: ... By the tender memories of our childhood – by my gratitude to my kind nurse – leave this holy garb for the still holier duties of a loving wife! (*as he speaks he draws her down to him*) Let not the envious scissors cut the fair golden tresses I shall be so proud of. Remove this livery of sorrow, of suffering, of restraint (*unloosing her fair hair*), and let the voice of your elected husband bid you welcome to the world again! LINA, *her hair falling over her shoulders, sinks into his arms.* RUDOLF *unfastens her cloak.* FRAU *has taken a light shawl from box, which she throws over* LINA. LINA's *appearance entirely changed – the hymn ceases.* (v, p. 230)

This coronation of an innocent, nurturing wife owes much to the lighting which haloes Lina's shining hair, as it tumbles over her shoulders, and to the shawl, a touchingly simple equivalent of a peeress's mantle, which dignifies the domestic image. Heaven, by the sixties, was very much on earth; there Lina would join her 'elected' bridegroom. These holy rites reach their apotheosis in the play's final tableau when Lady Clara and Mount-Forestcourt emerge from the wedding chapel attended by bridesmaids and groomsmen to form a glorifying background to Rudolf and Lina. In addition, tenants, country people, and Lady Clara's household cluster in groups on either side of the wedding-procession, and this domestic festival is augmented by charity boys and village girls who scatter flowers before the bridal pair but, in effect, enshrine the betrothed hero and heroine within the Victorian pantheon.

Although marriage had become still more sacred, other values had changed since the thirties. Robertson loosely developed *Dreams* from an idea in Tennyson's 'Lady Clara Vere de Vere', written in 1833 and printed in 1842. That poem reflects the egalitarianism which followed hard upon the French Revolution and, more particularly, the 1832 Reform Bill. Accordingly, Lady Clara's yeoman admirer proclaims his equality before God, just as Adam and Eve, 'The grand old gardener and his wife / Smile at the claims of long descent.' The poem's driving theme suggests that the human heart offers a far better indication of worth than any aristocratic bloodline: 'Kind hearts are more than coronets / And simple faith than Norman blood.'[3] But Tennyson drew back from sansculottism in the final hope that Clara would 'Pray heaven for a human heart / And let the foolish yeoman go.' Bulwer had resorted to a similar compromise. In *England and the English* (1833) he criticized the debilitating influence of the aristocracy, yet Claude Melnotte, having trained himself to be Pauline's equal, eventually showers her with wealth and social respectability. However, by the late sixties, Bulwer's youthful, Benthamite ideals had suffered a sea-change: 'popular liberty, would be to elevate the masses, in character and feeling, to that standard which Conservatism seeks in aristocracy – in other words, to aristocratise the community'.[4]

Robertson's *Dreams* reflects that Conservatism. Pictorially, the wedding tableau 'aristocratises' Rudolf and Lina for the play's last few moments, but the shawl reminds us that they know their place. Rudolf has confessed that his dreams of Lady Clara were 'wild', and for that he has 'suffered much'. Having 'seen my folly and my blindness' (p. 229), Rudolf offers his bride the modest life to which they have both 'been reared'; as a kappelmeister, he will never again fall to the dazzlement of 'worldly gifts and worldly splendour'.

In 1867, a second Reform Bill extended the franchise to the manufacturing classes, and *Dreams* reflects their growing importance. As befits a musician and tutor to the aristocracy, Rudolf's ambitions are conventionally and romantically unworldly, though his bitterness at being passed over by his employers in England, who 'make it a rule never to give the world anything written by a man under fifty-five years old' (II, 1, p. 197), undoubtedly derives from Robertson's own long travail in the financial wilderness. However, John Hibbs, 'the commercial man' with whom Rudolf travels to England, is decidedly a sign of the times. He goes to Germany twice a year to further the connections of Triggs, Puddock and Co. Utterly devoid of culture, his dream of glory is to be 'Lord Mayor! and to be able to ask a bishop to tea'. After the bustle of London, he finds Germany a trifle slow and prefers the music-hall's 'Champagne Charlie' ('lots of tune, you know – lots of sound') to Rudolf's compositions for the opera house. In contrasting these two young men, Robertson sides with the artist and offers up Hibbs's crass mercantilism to the patronizing laughter of less-sullied audiences who might, like Hibbs, be just as newly moneyed but whose middle-class gentility showed none of the man's 'push'. That brashness, rather than his money and energy, marks him as someone to sneer at, for the Gaiety's clientele were just as much a part of London's burgeoning success: 'Rare place London . . . Look at me: I started as errand-boy, swept out the offices, put up the shutters. I'm not ashamed of it – I'm proud of it. Now I'm the senior commercial representative of the firm – may perhaps some day be a partner' (I, I, pp. 193–4). Thirty years before, Bulwer had satirized the trade in marriageable daughters and the bubble, reputation, which sustained a 'wealthy' man in society. By the sixties, a successful breed of philistines – and proud of it – was clamouring at the drawing-room doors, and Robertson's own brand of Conservatism responds with contempt. Yet that exaggerates his social consciousness, for Hibbs is above all else a theatrical 'character', contrived as Rudolf's opposite: a well-meaning dolt who admires Lina enough to offer 'a small floral token of my – esteem' whereas the sensitive and tempestuous composer no longer appreciates his childhood companion.

Tom Robertson was not a deep thinker, and his plays typify the sixties because of that. The eldest son of a large family of provincial actors, he knew instinctively what worked on stage, but, as his own father once wrote, 'The most painful penalty of an actor's social position results in its isolation from every community of interest.'[5] He was five when he played the hero's son in *Rob Roy* for a benefit night, and he then acted other child-roles up and down the Lincoln circuit, graduating to the youthful François for Macready's Richelieu during one of that eminence's country tours. His schooling was fitful. In his teens, as part of the family troupe, he studied when he could, and his French was to aid him, years later, when he became a hack adapter of Parisian successes for Lacy's, the drama publishers. In his early twenties he worked for a time as prompter at the Lyceum during the Vestris/Mathews 1854 season when he might have noted the management's refined manner and attention to detail, qualities which were to stamp his own productions some twelve years later at the Prince of Wales's. This prolonged apprenticeship in all aspects of the stage meant that he saw the world through a theatrical filter and drew from the repertory of acting types (first walking-gentleman, low

66

comedian *et al.*) as much as from life, shaping his plots, in the well-made pattern of Eugène Scribe and his tribe, for their maximum effect upon an audience's emotion.

Not surprisingly, his eventual success in London came when an established actor perceived the *theatrical* possibilities of one of his scripts. In 1863 he wrote a novel, derived oddly enough from a French play, about a supposed incident in the life of David Garrick. The play which was then carved from the book came to the notice of E.A. Sothern who asked to read out the script to his manager, John Buckstone:

[Sothern] frequently interrupted himself with such remarks as 'Capital!' 'First-rate!' 'Strong situation!' and 'I like that!' But when he came to the party scene, in which David acts like a madman, Sothern became so excited that he began to smash the glasses and upset the furniture. 'I think *that* will do, Bucky?' he said to his manager. 'Yes, it will do,' replied Buckstone, 'and I rather like that fellow Chevy.'[6]

Dick Chivy, who so attracted Buckstone, offers an inane caricature of the huntin'-shootin'-fishin' squire and owes more to Tony Lumpkin than to anything in nature. The play's knockabout childishness epitomizes the Haymarket's well-meaning simplicities which allowed star actors to impose their personalities on to highly coloured routines. The big scene in *David Garrick* involved Sothern in a 'drunken' slapstick at the command of Simon Ingot, a director of the East India Company, whose daughter has formed what he considers an unfortunate attachment for the actor. Within those limits, this play also shows Robertson's scorn for the pretensions of city parvenus, Smith, Jones, and Brown, and their equally self-satisfied ladies.

As a man of the theatre, Robertson directs his critique at the uncultivated tastes of city folk who represent contemporary manners rather than those of Garrick's day. And little Davy becomes the spokesman for the social aspirations of all Victorian actors. Years before, Macready had gibed at the irony of Bulwer's borrowing a stage costume in order to attend a court masquerade to which the actor himself could not be invited. Robertson's Garrick has more breeding than the merchants or Squire Chivy who expects to inherit a peerage. Having pledged his word to disillusion Ingot's daughter, he goes through with his drunken charade although he recognizes her as the lady whose sensitivity had captured his heart. Even Ingot, who constantly questions the wisdom of inviting a player to sit down at dinner, is impressed by Garrick's proud independence. Whereas

Chivy is exposed as a self-indulgent fortune hunter, the actor personifies the natural aristocrat. Remembering his own beloved mother whom he angered 'when I adopted my profession' and who did not live to see him 'applauded, feasted, marvelled at', Davy reminds Ada of her 'obedience to duty, to filial love' and returns her to her father. But now Ingot would readily forget his puritan fears: 'I'll go the play-house every night that Garrick plays, and the Corporation may go to the devil!' (III, pp. 183–4). Since Garrick has said he would never marry unless the lady's father 'comes to me, hat in hand, to beg the honour of my alliance', the play ends as Ingot humbly, though smilingly requests that *honour*.

A similar self-respect drove Marie Wilton into management in the spring of 1865. She too had travelled the provinces from infancy, dancing the hornpipe 'as a wee sailor, in little white trousers and blue jacket', and reciting scenes from Shakespeare or Collins's *Ode to the Passions* at the prompting of her parents in the wings.[7] On one such occasion, she was fussed over by the parish ladies until they discovered the little prodigy was an actor's daughter and speedily withdrew their favours: 'The bags were closed with a cold relentless click, and the owners muttered between their teeth (for fear, doubtless, of breathing the same air as myself), "Oh, gracious!" "Horrid!" "Oh dear!" "Unfortunate child!" and drew back from me as if plague-stricken.' As a juvenile at Bristol, she impressed Charles Dillon who soon afterwards, as manager of the Lyceum, sent for her to play his son in *Belphegor*, but real success came in travesty parts at the Strand Theatre. Dickens saw her in *The Maid and the Magpie*, and his letter to John Forster exhibits the peculiarly ambiguous effect of such performances on the Victorian male:

There is the strangest thing in it that ever I have seen on the stage – the boy Pippo, by Miss Wilton. While it is astonishingly impudent (must be, or it couldn't be done at all), it is so stupendously like a boy, and unlike a woman, that it is perfectly free from offence . . . wonderfully clever – which, in the audacity of its thorough-going, is surprising. A thing that you *cannot* imagine a woman's doing at all; and yet the manner, the appearance, the levity, impulse and spirits of it, are so exactly like a boy, that you cannot think of anything like her sex in association with it.[8]

That Marie's Pippo *did* draw continuous attention to her actual gender could not be plainer, yet her 'levity' was so convincing and so provokingly unfeminine. This anomaly also disturbed Miss Wilton who, as the toast of London, found that managers would only cast her in parts which worked against her own sense of self.

Robertson described what lay behind the enticing versatility of a burlesque actress in one of a series on theatrical types that he wrote for the *Illustrated Times*. As an insider, he understood – and sentimentalized – the woman beyond the footlights:

The men at the clubs go mad about her ... Half Aldershot comes nightly up by train. She is a power in London, and theatrical managers drive up to her door ... Fortunate folks who see her in the daytime complain 'that she dresses plainly' – 'almost shabbily'; but, then, they are not aware that she has to keep half a dozen fatherless brothers and sisters and an invalid mother out of her salary ... Here is a household fairy who can polk, paint, make puddings, sew on buttons, turn heads and old bonnets, wear cleaned gloves, whistle, weep, laugh, and perhaps love.[9]

To escape her own invidious public image, Marie joined forces with H.J. Byron (who wrote burlesques!) and leased the Queen's Theatre off Tottenham Court Road. She could not know that within a year or two Robertson would write comedies which drew upon the contrasting sides of her personality to show her gaily whistling and teasing while she made puddings on stage. Before that could happen, the 'household fairy' had magic to do at 'The Dust Hole': 'It was a well-conducted, clean little house, but oh, the audience! My heart sank!'[10]

Determined to attract the genteel, the proprietress re-fitted the theatre as prettily as her limited funds allowed. There were carpets and curtains, rose-bud chintz in the boxes, and upholstered stalls in blue leather with 'white lace antimacassars over them. This was the first time such things had ever been seen in a theatre.' As further enticement, Byron applied for permission to call the theatre after the Prince of Wales. When fashionable carriages miraculously appeared on the first night, the good fairy 'was standing on a high stool in a private box nailing up the last lace curtain'. And the stage curtain went up on a short piece prophetically entitled *A Winning Hazard* to be followed by Byron's operatic burlesque, *La! Sonnambula! or, the Supper, the Sleeper, and the Merry Swiss Boy*, with Miss Wilton in familiar guise. The evening ended with *Vandyke Brown*, a light-hearted farce. By the autumn, the 'dear wee manageress' – as the Dowager Countess of Harrington (once Maria Foote, the actress) called her – no longer appeared in burlesque. Byron complained that her refusal would damage both their careers by depriving the theatre of its main attraction; in consequence, their partnership was soon dissolved, but not before Byron had introduced his friend, Tom Robertson, whose new script had failed to satisfy the Haymarket company for whom it had been devised.

Following the success of *David Garrick*, Robertson had furnished

Sothern with another drunk scene and had intended John Chodd Senior, an uneducated money-bags, as a contrast to the puppy-dog oafishness of Buckstone's Squire Chivy. But Buckstone would have none of it, and other managers shied away from certain aspects of the script which came from the author's own experience rather than from his response to the talents of particular actors. The two scenes at the Owl's Roost broke away from the Scribe-like climaxes and stereo-types of the rest of the play and brought to the stage the Bohemian club-life Robertson shared with other struggling journalists and playwrights. These scenes demanded an unusual level of ensemble acting from minor characters, and the dialogue and setting were undisguisedly taken from the life of many of the reviewers whose opinion could make or mar the performance. Marie Wilton was prepared to risk that and, after a trial run in Liverpool, *Society* opened at the Prince of Wales's in November 1865.

The play spreads wider than those which were to be specifically tailored for the little theatre, and Maud Hetherington, a colourless stage-heroine, does not reflect Miss Wilton's personality; she reacts to the plot's coincidental 'discoveries' with a subservience that belies the independent spirit she supposedly has. Years later, Bancroft attributed the play's success to the way it followed 'Nature', though that is hard to recognize at moments like the hero's sudden and stagey revelation to Lady Ptarmigant that his little ward is actually the child of her only son whose death at Balaclava broke the heart of the 'poor and humble girl' whom he married – 'Like a brave fellow, a true gentleman' – on the day his regiment left for the Crimea. Another of Bancroft's remarks is apter than he perhaps intended: *Society* proved 'that the refined and educated classes were as ready as ever to crowd the playhouses, provided only that the entertainment . . . was suited to their sympathies and tastes'.[11]

Robertson again appeals to the refined and educated by ridiculing the confident pretensions of a certain type of rich boor. John Chodd is not entirely contemptible for he makes no attempt to hide his origins, and his roughness has a certain innocence. However, his thick accent brands him as 'common' and he has not worked for his money: 'My brother Joe made the fortune in Australey, by gold digging and then spec'lating; which he then died, and left all to me.'[12] He takes a perverse pride in the fact that he will never be a gentleman but can afford to make his son one. That and a lack of loyalty to his employees lead to his downfall. Having decided to create a new daily newspaper in order to ensure that his son will 'cut a figure in the world

– get into Parliament', he treats Tom Stylus, his principal advisor, as a menial, and Stylus avenges that slight by writing a leader against the Chodds in their own paper when he substitutes for their ailing editor. John Junior, or 'Johnny' as his father still calls him, does pass for a gentleman and that makes him dangerous and nasty. He can barter his way into good society, but no cheque-book can buy him the feelings of a true gentleman: 'Honour means not being a bankrupt. I know nothing at all about chivalry, and I don't want to' (I, 1, p. 45). In his contempt for those with less 'brass', he will stoop to any means of getting what he wants. Robertson effects his come-uppance by making a farce of his proposal to Maud. Out of his depth in a situation that requires fine feeling, he cannot comprehend the plain terms of her acceptance. So their interview becomes ludicrous as Chodd proclaims his unswerving love while wondering how things are progressing at the hustings, and his rival's election speech (off-stage) keeps colliding with his own appeal to Maud and reminds her what she has lost in Sidney Daryl. Finally Chodd's pretensions are simply brushed aside. He loses both the lady and the election to Daryl when Lady Ptarmigant, his former ally, rides roughshod over his claim to her niece: 'The impertinence of the lower classes in trying to ally themselves with us!' (III, 1, p. 83).

Not that Robertson condones such snobbery, though he allows his audience to enjoy it fleetingly as a means to young Chodd's destruction. Lady Ptarmigant may have a title, but her behaviour degrades her class and sex. A cartoon termagant, she is hard to take seriously as a character. But through this comic puppet, Robertson suggests that social acceptance in no way guarantees human worth. According to her, 'Money can do anything', but her niece would rather slave as a seamstress or a governess than submit to the 'dreadful temper, which is an equal affliction to you as to those within your reach' (III, 2, p. 71). Robertson weakens that by allowing Lady Ptarmigant a momentary sympathy for the girl's courageous spirit and then manoeuvring her through an obvious volte face when she learns that Daryl has inherited his brother's estate. Like Lord Ptarmigant, who exists only to fall asleep or, as a worm which turns, to assert his natural affection for his unknown grandchild and the man who protected her, Lady Ptarmigant is a victim of the genre. Nevertheless, Robertson does hint at some past betrayal which has led her to sacrifice her womanly feeling in pursuing money, power, society.

As they leaned back against their antimacassars, playgoers could take comfort from the sentiments of Sidney Daryl whose innate nobility prefigures his final assumption of the family title. In his penury, Daryl represents everything Johnny Chodd would like to buy with his brass, and Maud responds to the self-sacrifice which led him to give up a fortune in order to preserve his brother's reputation after the latter had 'squandered everything at the gaming table'. At one point, Daryl also wanders into that forbidden territory by cutting cards and daring Chodd to double and re-double the stakes. His hysteria resembles Alfredo's in *La Traviata* when he hurls insults at his supposed betrayer, to the horror of the assembled company – 'shameless girl, much as I once loved you, and adored, I now despise and hate you' (II, 2, p. 66) – and the Act ends on a crash of music as Maud staggers across the stage and Daryl reels through the crowded ballroom. Maud's consequent insistence on her honour and Daryl's shock when she assumes that he too has acted dishonourably by fathering his 'ward' lead to a tiresome round of misunderstanding and prickly reaction, yet the two are meant to voice an adult critique of a money-ridden society. Robertson owes more than his election scene to Bulwer's *Money* as Daryl castigates the marriage market:

Feeling! Why, man, this is a market where the match-making mammas and chattering old chaperons – those women with the red cheeks and roman noses – have no more sense of feeling than cattle drovers driving their beasts to Smithfield – the girls no more sentiment than sheep, and the best man is the highest bidder; that is, the biggest fool with the longest purse.

(II, 2, p. 63)

In the intervening years, the growth of commerce had injected new energy and colour into this idea. Like Alfred Evelyn, Daryl stands against bought votes, though his lineage gives him an advantage over Chodd, 'that digesting cheque-book [who would] represent the town that my family have held their own for centuries!' (III, 1, p. 69). As scions of true breeding, he and Maud provide a lesson to moneyed upstarts so that, when Lady Ptarmigant offers to find Johnny another blue-blooded lady, Chodd would 'rather have it the natural colour' (III, 3, p. 83).

But Robertson's chief concern lay with each scene's general effect. If the play's ideas and characters were long in the tooth, Miss Wilton's company was refreshingly youthful. She and Bancroft looked their parts while an even younger John Hare submerged himself into Lord Ptarmigant. Clement Scott, who would eventually become the most reactionary of critics, remembered that first night when he and other members of the up-and-coming 'light brigade' stood at the rear of the dress circle:

A little delightful old gentleman came upon the stage, dressed in a long, beautifully cut frock coat, bright-eyed, intelligent, with white hair that seemed to grow naturally on the head – no common clumsy wig with a black forehead-line – and with a voice so refined, so aristocratic, that it was music to our ears . . . All he had to do was to say nothing, and to go perpetually to sleep. But how well he did nothing! How naturally he went to sleep! . . . Had *Society* been accepted at the Haymarket – which luckily for Tom Robertson, it was not – the part of Lord Ptarmigant would have been played by old Rogers, or Braid, or Cullenford, – Chippendale and Howe would certainly have refused it as a very bad old man.[13]

Scott romanticizes that night's perfection; other writers noted the production's skimpiness: 'one does not expect to find . . . the elegance which Madame Vestris exhibited at the Lyceum; but we may reasonably expect to see a fashionable drawing-room . . . furnished with more than one chair and with a carpet of visible proportions, . . .'[14] Yet all cavil gave way to the actors' naturalness, particularly in the crowded conviviality of the Owl's Roost and in the halting, understated duet between Maud and Daryl (1, 2, p. 48) which seemed like 'an idyll, evolving amidst the trees of a London square . . . youthful, tender, tremulous love – in the very heart of this city of mud, fog, and smoke! Love, so near that you might touch his wings.'[15] Robertson was just as pictorial as his predecessors, but he now began to create mood and atmosphere out of the ordinary, urban life around him. The scene in the West End square has exactly the appeal of the twilight farewell between La Vallière and her mother, but instead of Gothic chiaroscuro, convent bells, or childhood haunts, the setting sun catches the windows of the houses which enclose the little park and, as the inconsequential, low-key dialogue floats through the gathering dusk, the street lamps glow brighter to persuade the audience that this is indeed love and reality.

The success of these scenes taught Robertson how to write for Wilton's company. *Ours* (1866), the first play designed specifically for the Prince of Wales's, unfurls one random, familiar miniature after another, and the charm of these episodes evolves from an ordinariness spiced now and then by the tang of world-weary experience. Atmosphere is everything, so that without the actors and scenery the plays seem flat and the ideas banal or childish. The characters remain theatrical types – men of honour, maids of virtue, haughty dowagers, comic and simple working men – but their muted dialogue allows the actors scope for invention and psychological surprise as together they recreate a seemingly accidental and everyday flow within the old fabric of climactic tableaux, dramatic confrontations, and thunderous revelations.

The first Act opens on a vista of trees amongst which the characters will gather in varied groups to sit on stumps, play bowls, or shelter from a storm. These unimportant rhythms are immediately established by a solitary figure on stage who lies dozing with a handkerchief over his face. When the action begins, two minor characters enter simply to talk about themselves rather than to unravel the preliminaries of the plot, so that though Sergeant Jones is the standard low comedian he seems more individualized. A passing gamekeeper bids him 'good morning' and is surprised when the soldier warmly shakes him by the hand. The Sergeant has just become the father of twins and needs to talk about them, whereupon the keeper responds admiringly and the two walk off 'to drink to this here joyful double-barrelled event' (p. 87). Hugh Chalcot rouses himself, lights his pipe, 'looks round moodily', then settles back under his handkerchief. A further pause, and two young ladies with baskets thread their way through the trees to begin a new duo from which we learn that Blanche Haye is a rich heiress and Mary Netley loathes her subservient position as Lady Shendryn's companion: 'I don't receive wages, which the cook does. But then she's respected – she's not in a false position. I wish I hadn't been born a lady' (p. 88). The Act builds on these delicate contrasts and is bound together by a prevailing camaraderie beneath which Hugh and Mary's banter and the bitterness between Sir Alex and Lady Shendryn run in counterpoint. But all those moods are painted with the prettiness of the autumn leaves which punctuate the action as they flutter from the trees.

Under the conventions of the Victorian stage, these pictures must tell a story – Robertson is no Chekhov – and that narrative is propelled by weary clichés. The ladies take up a collection for Sergeant Jones's twins. Chalcot who (according to Mary) is an ill-humoured loafer, refuses to contribute although he owns a fortune. Prince Perovsky, on the other hand, exhibits an old-world courtesy by suggesting that Blanche should name whatever sum she pleases, and the lady modestly writes out a figure to which he instantly agrees: 'Charmingly chivalric!' Mary's prejudices seem to be confirmed – 'What a difference!' – until Chalcot finds himself alone with the Sergeant. Hugh is acutely embarrassed by his money since, if he gave as

generously as he would like to, people would extol his openhanded-
ness. Nevertheless, as he talks to Jones, he feels more and more like
giving him £50, 'If I were only sure he wouldn't mention it' (p. 98).
The episode manipulates that comic tension and then ends with a
theatrical flourish as Jones looks at the note and calls after his
departing benefactor: 'I beg your pardon, sir, for calling you back;
but you've made a mistake; you meant to give me a five-pun' note –
and many thanks, sir; but this here's for fifty' (p. 99). In this way,
Robertson reveals Hugh's good heart and neatly places the amusing,
honest Sergeant as one of the deserving poor.

Viewed from that angle, the play's ideas appear contrived: Hugh is
really a fine chap and Jones is loyal and true because both belong
(eventually) to 'Ours', Shendryn's highland regiment, and so could
not be other than stalwart. Yet this contrivance relies on certain
revealing assumptions. Hugh's modesty distinguishes him from
someone like Johnny Chodd. He feels a victim of the 'metallic refuse'
he has inherited, for wealth has made him into a great catch, 'a prize
pig tethered in a golden sty' (p. 96), and he can never be sure he is
loved for himself. Yet though he despises it, money threatens his
manly fibre. To please Shendryn, 'who thought the two properties
would go well together', he drifted into asking Blanche to marry him
and was relieved when she declined. The same lassitude makes him
'moody' and aimless since he has never had to work for anything. He
is saved by work – for glory, *not* for money. In a patriotic glow, as he
watches the regiment march off to war, he enlists in 'Ours' and finds
himself roughing it in the Crimea: 'Everything has improved since
I've had something to do – and a bayonet in the calf of my leg' (III,
p. 126). The ideal, then, is to be energetic, brave, and rich.

But more frequently in Victorian romance, chivalry and wealth (or
the lack of it) collide. Shendryn goes to what now seem ridiculous
stratagems to preserve his honour under financial strain. As a soldier
and a gentleman, he will not involve his wife in the sordid forgeries
regularly perpetrated by her brother. He prefers to endure her
insulting accusations that the money he has used to save her name
from dishonour has gone to some mistress, although those suspicions
make him hate her. This ludicrous situation shows the hypnotic
power of that code of honour and how persuasively it masked a lack of
frankness and trust between husbands and wives. When Lady
Shendryn discovers the truth, she is overwhelmed by her husband's
'noble nature'; it did not occur to Robertson that she ought to have

been furious. Chivalry also erects a barrier between Angus MacAlister and Blanche, since he is 'poor as a rat' and to marry for money is 'not the way with the MacAlisters' (I, p. 94). Like so many Victorian heroes, he only wishes to be able to shower his beloved with 'proofs of his affection', so he thinks of going to India to seek his fortune. Though he cannot declare his feelings, they are transparent enough for the pair to reach a delicate understanding through the verses he gives her before going to war with his honour intact.

Paradoxically, no chivalrous gentleman enjoys his wealth, yet without wealth he cannot enjoy his chivalry. In the same way, a 'noble nature' shines most brightly in war yet, as Chalcot aptly says, 'they never do get killed in "Ours"' (III, p. 130). They suffer a wound or two – 'It is but a scratch' – which merely stiffens the upper lip or becomes an occasion for jokes and flirtation, as when Mary accidentally knocks against Chalcot's bayoneted leg:

MARY: I have hurt your wound! – Pray, forgive me!
CHALCOT: It's nothing. Do it again. I like it.
MARY: I'm very, very sorry.
CHALCOT: Don't mention it – hurt me again! But speak in that tone – and look in that way again! (p. 128)

As such moments show, Robertson prettifies war along with so much else. He gives to Sergeant Jones a hearty respectable simplicity which panders to the legend of 'the thin red line': the fact that he and his large family exist on one-and-tenpence a day adds another worthy detail to that picturesque image. In the Crimea, as part of the play's happy ending, Chalcot rewards Jones for saving his life by promising to buy the boy-twin a commission when the child is old enough. For a second or two, reality breaks across Jones's comic enthusiasm: 'I'll have him taught reading and writing directly.' But up till then, nothing in Jones's manner suggests the swearing, drinking, degraded life of the ordinary British bulldog. Instead, Robertson gives his middle-class audiences what they want to hear and see. The finale of the second Act apparently had them in raptures: band music plays in the distance, off-stage, and cheers ring out as the troops march to their country's call. The presence of the Russian Prince, now an enemy officer, makes for some embarrassment, but the on-stage enthusiasm mounts as the bands play 'The Girl I Left Behind Me' and Shendryn calls his regiment to order. Even the Prince is stirred by those 'Fine fellows'. Robertson orchestrates this excitement by having Mary and Hugh rush to the balcony window where they wave farewell to the

3   Scene from the new play, *Ours*, at the Prince of Wales's Theatre

soldiers while the band crashes out the National Anthem. He then surrounds that glory with pathos: Lady Shendryn struggles to contain her grief (at centre stage) and Blanche, overcome by her fears for Angus, '*totters down stage and falls fainting at her feet*' (p. 114).

Act Three, in the Crimea, is just as painterly. The realism of the free-standing hut, within a few feet of those comfortable seats in the stalls, presents a superficial picture of war's surface. Built from boulders and mud, the shack stands against the cold with a cosy resilience. Straw and rags litter the floor and jam the cracks of makeshift walls; the furniture is made from barrels, crates, and tubs; horse-cloths divide the sleeping quarters from the living space; and – wonder of wonders – each time the door opens, snow blows in. But, like Angus and the Sergeant, Hugh regards the Crimea as a *Boy's Own* adventure in which the officer next door *will* keep borrowing supplies or ruining 'our own private and particular gridiron', and those who go off to battle load their wounded, stay-at-home friend with last testaments for the girls they left behind them. When those ladies appear at the hut-door, Robertson allows his audiences some moments' wonder before turning their incredulity aside with Chalcot's 'By Jove! If this were put in a play, people would say it was improbable' (p. 122). Whereupon, Lady Shendryn and Blanche request to attend what they think will only be a parade, thus leaving the stage to Hugh, Mary, and Victorian domesticity.

Robertson leads up to that through the comparisons Hugh draws between present conditions and life back home as he invites the ladies to admire an armchair (made from a tub) or to dine on onions before the Opera (*Cannonade, distant*). Alone with Chalcot, the houseproud fairy – Marie Wilton played Mary – organizes dinner. Robertson plays her feminine adaptability against Chalcot's helplessness and the supposed hardship of life at the front: 'A roly-poly pudding in the Crimea! It's a fairy-tale!' (p. 127). Miss Wilton's tomboy exuberance, made safe by the dress which now hid her legs, gives the episode a provocative edge. The ladies arrived at the hut to find no one at home, but there was a sword stuck to a leg of lamb and a box of cigars on the mantelpiece. So Blanche pretends to be a 'swell' until Mary takes up that imitation with more panache. Then the girls decide to 'play at soldiers'. Mary picks up a gun and, with a satisfying show of feminine terror, charges down upon her friend. This cloying make-believe prepares us for the roly-poly and Chalcot's patronizing description of the little woman who, as she explains, learned to cook while acting as her clergyman-father's housekeeper: 'What an accomplished creature it is!' (p. 126).

Although Marie Wilton's personality projected a welcome sprightliness into those scenes, Robertson 'writes down' to the feminine principle. Capturing that leisured world, he lays it open to the enervating rule of the Little Miss who, as an unformed 'creature', cannot be expected to have an idea in her head. Consequently, *Ours* resounds with girlish baby-talk. The young ladies march up and down the hut, whisper to each other about the mysterious note pinned to the leg of lamb, and, when the men return, giggle about 'the horrors of war' and thus subvert the hardships that the men of 'Ours' supposedly endure. The entire play, from the Shendryns' stately park to the rude and cosy hut in the Crimea, transforms reality into the comforting nursery-games of the Victorian house-angel. To match that tone, the men, when they talk between themselves, can admit that marriage and love are something of a battle – and naughty Mary would agree to that – but their chat always obeys the 'rules of the game'. The play does not explore Mary's uncomfortable position as Lady Shendryn's unpaid companion any more than it investigates the rivalry between Angus and the Prince. For a moment, Blanche worries about her attachment to a man who must shortly become her enemy, but the Prince finally loses because of his advancing years: 'Oh, Youth! Inestimable, priceless treasure!' (p. 131).

Such idealized triviality was still more apparent away from the Prince of Wales's and Miss Wilton's redeeming hoydenism. Just before Robertson's death, *War* was produced at the St James's in January 1871. At the time, France was preparing to surrender to Prussia and a play about that conflict proved too strong a morsel for the public palate even though its pathos followed a well-tried recipe. No other play of Robertson's so clearly illustrates his reliance on emotional tableaux for, in *War*, his pastel tones explode into the high colours of opera.

The first scene, a picture-book villa and garden near Sevenoaks, begins with an extended sequence of innocent chatter. Blanche and Jessie run on to the sunlit lawn. Each has a parcel behind her back and each refuses to reveal its contents unless her friend swears to keep it secret. After some by-play as to who will tell first, a third girl runs on with yet another parcel and the busy whisperings begin all over again. Then Katie enters, but, as the smallest and youngest, she has no parcel. The other three wonder about that but eventually unwrap the gifts they have bought for the betrothal of their friend, Lotte. The presents – a sachet, a lace handkerchief, a bridal wreath – are sentimental and increasingly magnificent so that Katie bursts into tears. Running towards the shrubbery, she is suddenly startled '*and gives a little scream*':

BLANCHE: What is it – caterpillars? (*Katie shakes her head*)
AGNES: Snails? (*Katie shakes her head*)
JESSIE: A big bumble-bee?
KATIE: (*shakes her head emphatically*) No.
BLANCHE: ⎤
JESSIE: ⎥ What then?
AGNES: ⎦
KATIE: (*her finger on her lips, turning to the* GIRLS) Sweethearts!
JESSIE: (*approaching* AGNES) Pretty things: don't disturb them, they might run away.
KATIE: 'Tis Lotte and the Captain.
BLANCHE: His arm is round her waist.
AGNES: Oh, how wrong.
BLANCHE: Oh, how right![16]

The four run giggling into the house, 'They mustn't see us', and their schoolgirl idyll transmutes into a romantic genre piece between the two lovers, posed beneath an arbour. They rhapsodize about wedding rings and their forthcoming marriage until taps from the quartet at the garden window disrupt their dream.

This long prologue is entirely atmospheric, a world whose radiance diminishes as the Act continues. Robertson requests that Oscar's father, Colonel de Rochevannes, should not be played as a stage Frenchman; he should have 'a *slight* French accent'. Lotte's German father and English godfather are also required to be lifelike and gentlemanly. But although they mention rumblings of war in the daily papers and trust to diplomacy, no one really discusses the politics and the personal impact of that conflict. Despite the touches of realism, Robertson's methods are a showman's. He artfully groups his characters at an *al fresco* luncheon party and uses the godfather's wedding present to symbolize the union between Germany and France. He then develops that theme through effective counterpoint. Each father sings a national song; then, as the girls take up the last chorus, the stage suddenly darkens and a servant enters with letters for the Colonel and his son so that the singers' gaiety seems obtrusive and discordant. War has been declared. The innocent garden is invaded by letters, telegrams, and personal strife. The French Colonel extols the glory of his profession; the German merchant calls it 'an accursed trade'; the English sea captain, when appealed to, remains neutral because the fight will be on land. But all further thought about the rights and wrongs of war gives way to the skilfully staged pathos of Lotte's 'blighted' marriage. The four girls hurry away; a peal of thunder ushers in the quarrelling fathers; Lotte faints, and the Colonel prevents Oscar from helping her. France and honour call: the lovers cannot reach across that barrier.

The rest of the play offers an astonishing example of Victorian doublethink. War means broken dreams and grieving widows; it also means glory, courage, and national pride. In the second Act, Robertson uses all his stagecraft to colour those two images. At one side of the darkened stage, a shattered church and heaps of rubble shelter the fallen figure of Oscar and his wounded father: the tableau reproduces Vernet's painting, 'The Retreat from Moscow'. Emotive lighting and scenery, and a group of nuns who cross to the church with supplies for the wounded, prepare for the entrance of Lotte's father who, as a volunteer in the Ambulance Corps, tends friend and foe alike. Lotte enters with a lamp: her black-and-white travelling dress implies the womanly role she now adopts when she recognizes her fallen lover. The pathos builds as she bathes his wounds, and organ music, from the ruined church, accompanies the dialogue. Oscar's last wish is to marry Lotte with the ring he has worn next to his heart since the day they parted. He is carried to the church while his father, maddened by the pain of a head-wound, imagines himself back on the battlefield to defend the wives and infants of his native land. Herr Hartmann takes up that war-cry with an enthusiasm which is less frenzied *'but as deep and as earnest'* as the Colonel's: fight for the Fatherland, then honour the fallen heroes. As the new day dawns, an equally radiant Oscar comes with his bride from the church:

His head falls upon his father's chest. Distant cannonade. Trumpets sound nearer. At the sound of the trumpet OSCAR *raises his head, cries,* 'Vive la France!' *and falls.* LOTTE *and his father over him . . . The coloured light from the stained-glass windows strikes upon the picture; at the same moment female voices are heard singing hymn in church (only female voices, and without accompaniment).* (p. 773)

But Robertson does not try to resolve or examine these conflicting emotions. In the third Act, he indulges his audience with the picture of Lotte, in deepest mourning, reading and being read to from Tennyson's 'In Memoriam' as her four friends, also dressed in sober colours, gather around her in the garden to work on 'various things for the sick and wounded'. The poet's words seem to fall like tears, as if his lines were printed in 'black silk velvet'. In her unending grief, Lotte accepts that the world's rulers are 'too cold and too proud to think of silly, weeping women', and her soliloquy makes much of those 'silly' tears from a maiden-widow whose life has emptied before she is one and twenty: 'The demand for glory must be satisfied, the desire for conquest must be sated, and it is we who pay the costs!' (p. 775). Why glory and conquest should be satisfied is never a question, despite the insanities of the Franco-Prussian War. The playwright shies away from the realities which still rocked Europe and resorts to abstracts like courage and grief. His characters are similarly generalized as children, lovers, parents, or as representatives of England, France, and Germany. So the Colonel stands for all fathers who have lost a hero-son and rejoice in that honour while lamenting that loss. Robertson, whose brother was a soldier, revels in the idealism of war and he marshals his stage pictures as witnesses to the nobility of loss and sacrifice. Then, having worked those tears for widow and father, he brings Oscar back from the dead to effect a joyous reunion.

Within that ludicrous denouement, two ideas point back to *Caste*, his most enduring play and his third production for the Prince of Wales's. Worrying how to tell Lotte about Oscar's miraculous recovery, the three gentlemen assume that as a woman, and tubercular to boot, she must be protected. Their first strategy is characteristically Victorian for they automatically know they must lie to her for her own good. Her godfather, as an upright Englishman, detests all falsehood but immediately acknowledges that to deceive a woman 'does make a difference' (p. 785). Whether Robertson approves of that notion is never entirely clear for, though their lies result in ridiculous complexities which increase Lotte's anxiety, he does not allow her to express her irritation. The second idea reveals one of the author's own idiosyncrasies when the protective trio wonder whether the joyful news might be too much to bear. Here Robertson contradicts 'those men of science' who maintain that an excess of joy can prove fatal: 'my child, the human heart is large enough to contain any quantity of happiness!' (p. 787). So Lotte survives her husband's return, and the curtain falls as the Colonel places her in Oscar's arms. The three seniors shake hands, and Lotte's four friends cluster around to complete the picture as timid little Katie buries her head in Agnes's skirts.

The affecting irrelevance of that concluding still-life seems a far cry from *Caste* (1867), yet the two plays share many of the same ideas and, in essence, depend for their effect on the playwright's magnetic use of the stage. The difference, especially in *Caste*'s first two Acts, lies in Robertson's approach to his story. He first wrote about the Eccles sisters for a collection organized by his friend and Owl's Roost bohemian, Tom Hood, to illustrate the theme of rates and taxes. Robertson seems to have started with a detailed idea of how the economics of life create human character. In consequence, each element of the sisters' little house in Stangate and, more precisely, the manners of those who enter that setting are signposts to the adjustments each individual has made within the class to which he or she was born. The exterior realism, which earned these plays their cup-and-saucer soubriquet, probes inwards and tells more than the falling autumn leaves of *Ours* or the mud-splattered rags of the wounded in *War*.

Act One's living-room immediately establishes the sisters' genteel poverty by means of its shabby wallpaper, plain chairs, and scrap of worn carpet, or through the fact that the main door gives on to a minute vestibule before emerging directly out to the street. Apart from the usual bric-à-brac, other details localize the sisters' place in the class structure. Under a bookshelf on the back wall hang a number of playbills (to be distributed for a benefit night) and, beneath those, a ballet-shoe and skirt have been flung onto a small table. Despite all the plainness, the room is full of feminine touches and scrupulously clean. When George D'Alroy enters with his friend, Captain Hawtree, their immaculate, expensive clothes mark them as strangers before either of them has spoken a word. But when they do speak, Robertson gives them a particular kind of slang which denotes their easy friendship and their casual elegance, and he makes Hawtree satirize their excursion 'over the water' to the unfashionable South bank. Their behaviour draws attention to the distinctions between the ballet dancer and the two swells. At one point, Hawtree pulls out his cigar case, and D'Alroy asks him not to smoke. Hawtree assumes that a chorus girl would not mind the smell of tobacco, but D'Alroy's 'I should' speaks volumes. It accepts the fact that, as a woman and as someone from the lower orders, Esther could not herself express her objections and it pinpoints D'Alroy's own respect for her since he wants his friend to behave as he naturally would in the presence of ladies. Another such incident occurs on Esther's arrival. In the slight pause which follows her polite greeting to D'Alroy, Hawtree is impressed enough to remove his hat.

The Bancrofts' company (Marie had become Mrs Bancroft) responded to these novel subtleties under the direction of the author himself. John Hare, who played Sam Gerridge, has recorded his impressions of Robertson as a 'stage-manager':

He had a gift peculiar to himself, and which I have never seen in any other author, of conveying by some rapid and almost electrical suggestion to the actor an insight into the character assigned to him. As nature was the basis of his own work, so he sought to make actors understand it should be theirs. He thus founded a school of natural acting which completely revolutionized the then existing methods . . .[17]

Marie Bancroft called the rehearsals 'a labour of love'. Her husband's comments show how rigid and stylized the previous methods were. As Hawtree, the languid man-about-town, he would have been expected to have fair hair and bristling whiskers whereas D'Alroy, 'the sentimental hero', should have had dark hair: 'I believe . . . I was by more than one person thought to be mad for venturing to clothe what was supposed to be, more or less, a comic part in the quietest of fashionable clothes, and to appear as a pale-faced man with short, straight black hair.'[18] That novelty corresponded to the way Robertson moved the character in and out of the stock type. His conversational chaff and his assumption that his friend could surely come to some arrangement with the little dancer, rather than commit the unforgivable by marrying her, belong to the predictable dandy. As such, he has a ready list of remedies for the sort of affair he thinks his friend involved in and an unswerving belief in 'the inexorable law of caste!' In fact, much of the first scene's comedy erupts from the interplay between that haughty assurance and the chirpy disrespect of Esther's independent sister, Polly. However, even in this confrontation, other less typified aspects appear. His humour has a warmth which makes him more than the detached satirist. Revealed gradually in his jousts with Polly, to whom he first responds as he would to any attractive minx, his genuine good-nature eventually extends to Sam, her working-class beau, and justifies his benevolence and sensitivity in Act Three.

Robertson's unorthodox characterization of Sam Gerridge does not work so smoothly. The traditional antics of the low comedian and the theatre's habitually patronizing attitude to the working class threaten the logic of the inner personality Robertson dares to reveal. Consequently it is not altogether clear how Sam fits D'Alroy's ultimate verdict on the class structure:

> Oh, caste's all right. Caste is a good thing if it's not carried too far. It shuts the door on the pretentious and the vulgar: but it should open the door very wide for exceptional merit. Let brains break through its barriers, and what brains can break through love may leap over. (III, p. 183)

For much of the time, Sam's vulgarity is held up to ridicule and his knockabout routines subvert his good sense and energetic practicality. Sam does have brains, but theatrical custom also makes him a clownish buffoon. So he keeps stumbling into Hawtree, in the first Act, and works himself into a jerky fury at Polly's saucy attentions to the Captain. About to leave in a huff, he finds Polly has locked the door, so he jumps through the window only to have the blind pulled down in his face when he peers back into the room. The slapstick continues in Act Three whenever his bad manners cause Hawtree to stare disapprovingly through his monocle. That extended comic business makes the Captain's final discovery of the 'little cad's' true worth seem unconvincingly sudden and sentimental.

Nevertheless, Sam is an original creation. Proud of his paper cap and overalls, he too believes in the class system which he describes with characteristic forthrightness:

Life's a railway journey, and Mankind's a passenger – first class, second class, third class. Any person found riding in a superior class to that for which he has taken his ticket will be removed at the first station stopped at, according to the bye-laws of the company. (I, p. 146)

This makes him suspicious of the two swells who 'don't come 'ere after any good', and his own notions of caste lead to worries about what the neighbours will say. Like his superiors, he automatically associates life on the stage with wicked ways. Although he drinks tea from a saucer and has excruciating taste in wallpaper, 'the door' opens to Sam because of his honesty, kindness, and – above all – his readiness to work to improve himself. By Act Three, he has taken over the plumbing and decorating business of the late Mr Binks. Enraptured by the jargon of commerce, he knows the importance of advertising and of flattering his customers in his circulars; 'Well, there ain't many of the nobility and gentry as lives in the Borough-road, but it pleases the inhabitants to make 'em believe yer think so' (p. 161). It is precisely his 'constant attention to business, and . . . 'is constant study to deserve' that rouses him against Mr Eccles whose feckless ways give the 'workin' classes' a bad name. However, he is too good-natured and too 'gone' on Polly not to indulge the old man's habits, although he shudders at the thought of his future father-in-law sitting with his 'spirituous liquours' in his shop's back-parlour. Under the farcical rigmarole, Sam exhibits an ideal self-reliance and, although that too is presented patronizingly, he also has the individual dignity of a social 'nobody' which confirms D'Alroy's view that 'Nobody's nobody! Everybody's somebody!'

'What are circ'lars compared to a father's feelings?' laments Mr Eccles, and, as this marvellous one-liner indicates, his character is an entirely theatrical comic-turn. This works well since Eccles, like all Dickensian hypocrites, acts out the drama of his own righteousness. Contemporary melodrama has a place in his battery of effects as do the sentimental songs he sings 'at 'Armonic Meetin's at taverns'. He exists to exemplify Hawtree's warning about the impediments of a misalliance:

My dear Dal, all those marriages of people with common people are all very well in novels and in plays on the stage, because the real people don't exist, and have

85

no relatives who exist, and no connections, and so no harm's done, and it's rather interesting to look at; but in real life with real relations, . . . it's absolute bosh.
(I, pp. 138–9)

Yet, despite that claim, Eccles is not 'real': even his darker side, as when he steals the coral from his grandson's cradle, is lightened by the same comic heroics. Robertson has too high a regard for filial duty ever to explore the uncompromising realities of life with father. He does allow Esther a surprising contempt, but only after she has dutifully handed him her marriage settlement (when she must have known what he would do with it). At the cradle, however, maternal wrath proves stronger than daughterly obedience. Her fierce protectiveness is conventional, yet her show of independence is unusually hard-hitting:

I am no longer your little drudge – your frightened servant. When mother died . . . and I was so high, I tended you, and worked for you – and you beat me. That time is past. I am a woman – I am a wife – a widow – a *mother*! Do you think I will let you outrage *him*? (*pointing to cradle*) *Touch me if you dare!* (III, p. 166)

Polly, who is not a widowed mother, capitulates to a father's sacred name. She refuses to face the fact that he gambled away Esther's money and, though she is often distressed by his behaviour, she always manages to find proof 'that though father had his faults, his heart was in the right place'.

Despite these conventional patterns, the two sisters have more vitality than other Robertsonian heroines. Superficially they resemble Blanche Haye and Mary Netley, but neither sister has her predecessor's insouciance, and *Caste* is all the better for that. The difference lies in the fact that unlike Robertson's other innocents or, for that matter his little seamstresses and unpaid companions, Esther and Polly work for a living. Moreover, he knows their way of life through and through. Rehearsals, small salaries, letters from admirers, victimizing managers are all a natural part of their everyday conversation, and D'Alroy proposes to Esther because, were he to hesitate any longer, she would be off in Manchester playing Columbine in the pantomime for a princely £4 a week. That they can mention money to gentlemen illustrates the ambience of their position, an aura of impropriety which Esther knowingly hurls back at D'Alroy's aristocratic mother in answer to that lady's disrespect. Declining to be intimidated by the Marquise's refusal to know her, Esther returns the insult: 'I am Mrs George D'Alroy . . . Who are you?' (III, p. 168). The lady wants her grandson and assumes that a mere actress can be bought off; whereupon the outraged Esther snatches up her ballet dress, and the Marquise retreats in horror: 'You are insolent – you forget that I am a lady.' Polly is just as horrified when the Marquise calls her 'a woman': 'I'm in the ballet at the Theatre Royal, Lambeth. So was Esther. We're not ashamed of what we are! We have no cause to be' (II, p. 158).

Accordingly, though Esther (like Lotte after her) changes from girl to woman during the course of the play, she behaves with womanly composure before she actually becomes Mrs D'Alroy. This is only partly due to Robertson's desire to raise actors in the eyes of the public, for he understands how the responsibilities and pressures of life weigh on Esther and, incidentally, how they give her a wider vocabulary and a busier mind than those of her maiden counterparts: 'I make the bread here, and it's hard to make sometimes. I've been mistress of this place, and forced to think ever since my mother died, and I was eight years old' (I, p. 144). Yet despite her spirited nature, Robertson treats her like other idealized wives and mothers. D'Alroy cannot tell her that his regiment must leave for India: that would spoil the 'Awfully jolly dream' of their six months' marriage. With an absurd paternalism, Robertson ignores Esther's tough past to make D'Alroy – who once joked that the 'fairy' in her Stangate 'bower' *could* walk, talk, eat and drink[19] – into the guardian of his ethereal bride: 'What angels women are!' Similarly, when D'Alroy's death is reported six days after his son has been born, the doctor advises Polly that the news would kill her sister. After Dal returns from the dead, Polly and Sam act out a living-room version of a favourite ballet, 'Jeanne la Folle, or, the Return of the Soldier', to protect her from the sudden joy of seeing her husband alive.

Polly goes on with the performance even though Esther is intelligent enough to have guessed its meaning. Robertson sees no irony in that. He intends to wring the pathos of Esther's prolonged rapture and to build Polly's burlesque into one of the play's big moments. Robertson always allowed Marie Bancroft to develop her own comic business, but Polly represents his most brilliant response to her talent and personality:

I loved the part of Polly for the innate fine qualities of her nature; her devotion to her dissolute, worthless father; her filial desire to screen him; her love for her sister; her real goodness with a rough exterior; the under-current of mischief and keen appreciation of humour. I enjoyed the boundless love of fun, the brisk gaiety of Polly's happy nature, and I felt, acutely, the pathos of her serious scenes.[20]

That 'rough exterior' saves her from the arch playfulness of a Mary Netley. Polly is not a lady, though Mrs Bancroft would not admit that. She has a coarse cheekiness so that she reacts to D'Alroy's glamorous entry in uniform with cockney humour: 'Oh! Here's a beautiful brother-in-law. Why didn't you come in on horseback, as they do at Astley's? – gallop in and say (*imitating soldier on horseback and prancing up and down stage during the piece*) "Soldiers of France! The eyes of Europe are a-looking at you!"' (II, p. 153). Yet her blushes at Sam's advances and the way she embodies the bright little woman who will inspire him to work 'like fifty men' make her a sympathetic and acceptable figure. As she bustles about at the stove, teaching Hawtree how to deal with a kettle, or inspects the pieces of furniture Sam has brought for her approval, she seems like an emblem of the audiences' own materialistic instincts.[21]

But *Caste* is not all bright hopes and bread and butter. Dion Boucicault was right to equate the play with his own *Colleen Bawn* and *Arrah-na-Pogue*: 'Robertson differs from me, not fundamentally, but scenically; his action takes place in lodgings or drawing-rooms – mine has a more romantic scope.'[22] The last two Acts, especially, are grounded on sentimental tableaux, framed by endearing comedy. The 'Jeanne la Folle' episode is the most imposing of such pictures, but audiences also responded to the miniature delicacy of D'Alroy's departure for India. He asks his wife to 'fetch me my sword, and buckle my belt around me' (II, p. 158). The brave uniform, the image of ancient chivalry, the wife's struggle to act worthily are captured without words through the grouping of the figures and on the face of Esther: 'The effort was made with a breaking heart . . . The audience saw and understood this and, as Esther fell fainting into the arms of those who loved her, rose to the situation with prolonged applause.'[23]

Robertson's work presents a gallery of Academy genre paintings, less windswept than Boucicault's, but just as conducive to tears and gentle laughter. *School* (1869), the most popular of all his plays at the Prince of Wales's, is (like *War*) entirely pictorial, its chocolate-box prettiness made animate by the schoolgirl brightness of Naomi Tighe. She was Mrs Bancroft's favourite gamine, the essence of nineteenth-century maidenhood. Marie's description speaks for itself:

– dear 'Nummy!' . . . The artless simplicity and sunny nature of 'Nummy', the utter ignorance of the existence of any sadness in the whole world except what school discipline enforces, her fearless and open avowal of her romantic adoration for Jack Poyntz, make her a lovable thing. She is one big slice of sunshine, and she had no drunken father! It was a delight to act Naomi Tighe; she is as fresh as country butter, and every word she utters breathes the unladen atmosphere of a bright, green spot 'far from the madding crowd'.[24]

Other plays show vistas of the jostling crowd, but only *Caste* allows an occasional foray into that scramble for survival.

However, during his final illness, Robertson had begun to move in new directions. *M.P.* (1870) was the last of his plays for the Bancrofts; it ran for over one hundred and fifty nights, but it was never revived and has been underestimated ever since. Admittedly, it contains a major flaw at its very centre, a vulgar caricature of a Quaker Miss whose 'thee's' and 'thou's' invite smug titters and whose transformation into a woman of fashion appeals to the basest of acquisitive dreams: 'drab discarded for ever, you will outshine us all, making a Swan and Edgar-like end, fading in muslin' (IV, p. 374).

Most of its themes and characters are from Robertson's usual stock-in-trade but they are delivered with a freer hand. For example, in Isaac Skoome, a much broader version of John Chodd Senior, the satire is harsher, cruder, and more cruel:

> He is hardly a man. He is a money-bag with a dialect – one of those rough brutes who pleases plebeians because he talks to them in their own bad English. An old ruffian, who, because he is rich, people persist in calling a rough diamond. Diamond! It is but a lump of the commonest clay who has never been moulded or burnt into a brick.
>
> (I, p. 329)

Yet this unfeeling monstrosity, who views everything and everyone in terms of 'br-a-a-ss', accords nicely with the play's cartoon style. Robertson always drew types: 'a name, a profession, a ruling passion, . . . With these words he thought he had summed up the ordinary conventional man, as nature had formed him, and society had reformed or deformed him.'[25] Here he exaggerates each type. His aristocrats are more ineffectual, his political sycophants more unscrupulous, and even his lovers have hard edges. *M.P.* contains very little sentiment and no affecting pictures. The sets are still decorative and minutely realized, but they do not speak to the emotions nor do they comment, except in a general way, upon the characters' social standing. Act Three does end with a typical interchange of action when an off-stage voice auctions away the family heirlooms (a portrait of an ancestor at nine years old) and that pathos is enacted on stage as all fight to master their feelings and the voice shouts 'Going – going – gone!' But Robertson appends a warning: 'No tragedy, no tears, or pocket-handkerchief' (p. 365). Scenes like this are reduced to theatrical coups: in the boat episode that ends Act Two, Cecilia lets her hood fall back and Chudleigh discovers he has mistaken his partner while their lovers watch from the shore in bewilderment. This style itself is somewhat different, but the play's most arresting novelties are its brittle, aphoristic dialogue and its portrait of a 'new' woman.

In *M.P.* one hears the voices of Gilbert and Wilde just around the corner. Robertson's contemporaries always detected the bitter-sweet of his plays; some called him cynical. But whereas the acid used to come from peripheral characters, like Sir Alex and Lady Shendryn, and had never lasted long, it now moves to stage centre and works corrosively through the whole play. The first episode introduces that acidity in Dunscombe's unruffled assessment of his impending ruin: 'Pleasant day, and I haven't been served with a copy of a writ these four-and-twenty hours' (pp. 323–4). His brisk, elliptical statements to his son mock the century's household gods – work, money, and marriage: 'When a young man has but a small amount of energy – as is your case – and but a small amount of ability – as is your case – he ought to retire on a girl with money.' His view of women is just as cynical: 'One man is as good as another from a girl's point of view . . . coat, trousers, cigar, and swagger. They have no discernment, – and a very good thing they haven't.' Chudleigh is a languid replica of his father: pleasant enough, but empty of feeling and earnest about one thing only, burlesque. When he meets Ruth, the orphaned Quaker girl, he is neither head over heels in love nor impressed by her money: he is simply drawn moonishly towards the object of his favourite theatre tune, 'a blonde most beautiful to see'. Everything else in the play has the same hollow ring. Skoome's enormous greed has no humanity behind it. He mouths a mechanical set of platitudes whenever he offers his hand in greeting: 'It is rough, but it is clean; it is hard, but it is manly. It never closed, save in the grip of friendship, or to cement a good bargain. It never opened but to melting charity' (p. 332). The political agents who manage the Bramlingdon election build a fine and airy web of words, but the seat will be won by the candidate who hands them the most bribe-money. Although Talbot Piers will have none of that, his friends think him an idealistic dreamer, and he wins, not by some romantic miracle, but because Cecilia can outspend Skoome and is willing to sell kisses for votes: 'Why should not you get into Parliament like anybody else?' She is a realist, rather than a cynic or a hypocrite, but she stands firmly at the play's centre: unsentimental, self-mocking, intelligent, and brave. Enter The Girl of the Period.

Mrs Bancroft liked Cecilia Dunscombe 'immensely', listing her as third favourite after Nummy and Polly. Yet she also considered her an eccentric ' "good fellow" sort of woman':

> She was written as a type of a 'girl of the period', who, if not carefully handled, might on the stage become offensive . . . I was careful to preserve all the points the author intended . . . but I worked to make the audience like her, by giving an amusing, but, at the same time, a feminine rendering of her character.[26]

Cecilia is cooler than that, but it undoubtedly needed the Bancroft treatment to make her palatable. She first enters 'dragging' a pram, and Robertson plays up the naughtiness of that image. It later turns out to be her means of transporting the £2,000 she needs to secure Piers's election. She has, as Dunscombe says, an *'esprit moquer'*, so when her fiancé assumes the pram must contain 'a present from some married friend', she smilingly agrees: 'What clever creatures you men are!' (p. 328). She has, in fact, just learned that her guardian has accepted Piers's proposal, and reacts with the dry thought that Dunscombe is no doubt glad to be rid of her. Alone (at last) with her lover, she 'leans pensively' against the perambulator (her mind on its contents), and though she 'never tire[s] of hearing' him say how much he loves her, it is a pity 'that courtship ends in marriage . . . It would be much better if marriage ended in courtship' (p. 330). She has gone into 'training' for married bliss: her textbook, *The Subjection of Women*, recommends 'a principle of perfect equality, admitting no power or privilege on the one side, nor disabilty on the other' (p. 331). As Mrs Bancroft says, it would have been tempting in 1870 to make Cecilia ridiculous. But she is not one of the play's cartoons. Her book has been written by a man (not, as Piers supposes, by some unnatural virago)[27] and her comments on it are either clever or unemotional: 'I never can argue when I've been travelling by rail.' Piers is far more rattled, but, when he pushes off the pram after a sarcastic apology 'for being the more muscular', Cecilia suddenly sees how funny they both are. Alone on the stage, she looks off in his direction: 'the Subjection of – Men'.

She only becomes angry when she learns that Piers suspects her guardian has used her money to support his political opponent, though even here she may be satirizing her own outrage since her phrasing oozes melodrama:

I permit no doubt of my conduct – past, present, or future! You have your pride; I have mine. (*Working herself up despite herself*) You have courage; I have endurance! You have strength; I have truth! Reconciliation is impossible! All is over! Good day. (III, pp. 357–8)

However, instead of two further Acts of conventional (and foolish) misunderstanding, Cecilia visits Piers in his election chambers and simply asks him to forgive her 'Because I have been wrong – because I am a woman – (*changing her tone*) – and because I am Cecilia' (IV, p. 367). The first statement takes courage. The second could, in a different context, sound cloying, but she does not mean that she is weak; cleverly, she appeals to his chivalry! In the third, she relies on the fact that he loves her. All along she has really been angry with herself, having discovered she had accidentally delivered the money to his opponent. In that circumstance, too, she acts intelligently and independently. Having 'cried my eyes out of my head', she telegraphs her lawyer who recovers over half of the cash; she supplies the rest herself. Piers is insulted by her interference, especially since she knows his attitude to electioneering. While she, and not for the last time, wonders how men can be so short-sighted: 'And these are the sort of things they send to Parliament, and keep us out for!' (p. 373). Robertson explores no farther: to investigate the pros and cons of that or the implications behind Cecilia's 'When I have an end in view I don't care much about the means' (p. 368) would have been another story.[28]

This last, tantalizing experiment might not have led to anything more had Robertson lived. His other plays look backward across thirty-five years of *moving* pictures and heroic idealism. Robertson's lasting reputation rests on *Caste*, whose characters do occasionally behave as they might in the southern suburbs, and on his revolutionary influence upon the actors and actresses of his day. He helped them break free of the theatre's own conventions and the star system, opened them to new ways of looking at character, and taught them how much of a play's meaning lay between the lines of dialogue. Ellen Terry, who acted Blanche Haye at the Prince of Wales's in the 1876 revival of *Ours*, remembered the precision and subtlety of the ensemble:

I have never, even in Paris, seen anything more admirable than the ensemble playing of the Bancroft productions. Every part in the domestic comedies, the presentation of which, up to 1875, they had made their policy, was played with such point and finish that the more rough, uneven, and emotional acting of the present day has not produced anything so good in the same line. The Prince of Wales's Theatre was the most fashionable in London, and there seemed no reason why the triumph of Robertson should not go on for ever.[29]

In *M.P.* the central relationship between Cecilia and Ruth belongs to the sentimental style of the other plays, yet the detached mockery of the surrounding elements points on to *Engaged* and *The Importance of Being Earnest,* and Cecilia herself unties the Victorian corset.

CHAPTER 4

Critics of the hearth

There is a great demand made now for more work for woman, and wider fields for her labour. We confess we should feel a deeper interest in the question if we saw more energy and conscience put into the work lying to her hand at home, . . . What we want to insist on now is the pitiable ignorance and shiftless indolence of most middle-class housekeepers; and we would urge on woman the value of a better system of life at home, before laying claim to the discharge of extra-domestic duties abroad.

Elizabeth Lynn Linton, 'What is Woman's Work?' (1868)

By the early 1870s, the sort of girl suggested by Robertson's Cecilia Dunscombe had roused flurries of dismay. As defined by Elizabeth Lynn Linton in a series of unsigned articles for the *Saturday Review* (1868), 'The Girl of the Period' personified the fallen standards of an acquisitive, pleasure-mad society and challenged the feminine ideal, 'neither bold in bearing nor masculine in mind; a girl who, when she married, would be her husband's friend and companion, but never his rival, . . . a tender mother, an industrious housekeeper, a judicious mistress'.[1] Mrs Linton spoke for all women 'of home birth and breeding' when she castigated the modern type who cared little for maidenly duty, indulged in 'slang, bold talk, and fastness', pursued money instead of love and happiness and, when *she* married, was bored by her domestic confines: 'Love in a cottage, that seductive dream . . . is now a myth of past ages.' The dreams that now seduced the girls of Belgravia and Bayswater seemed alarmingly like those of their fallen sisters, the queens of St John's Wood:

The girl of the period is a creature who dyes her hair and paints her face, as the first articles of her personal religion; whose sole idea of life is plenty of fun and luxury; and whose dress is the object of such thought and intellect as she possesses. Her main endeavour in this is to outvie her neighbours in the extravagance of fashion . . . Nothing is too extraordinary and nothing too exaggerated for her vitiated taste; . . . With purity of taste she has lost also that far more precious purity and delicacy of perception which sometimes mean more than appears on the surface. What the *demi-monde* does in its frantic efforts to excite attention, she also does in imitation . . . and then wonders that men

94

sometimes mistake her for her prototype, or that mothers of girls not quite so far gone as herself refuse her as a companion for their daughters.

Mrs Linton did see that much was wrong with the traditional ways of preparing young ladies for wedlock. She detested the marriage-market and urged parents to pay heed to their daughters' minds as well as their physical attractiveness, but always on the assumption that no sensible husband would choose a mannish intellectual as his life's partner any more than he would want a thoughtless fool. She also assumed that, until anything better emerged to prove her wrong, marriage was woman's one true destiny and proper sphere of influence. Consequently, her satirical thrusts against interfering mothers, managing wives, careless daughters were all intended to reform and strengthen the domestic fortress from within so that English girls might again be 'content to be what God and nature had made them'. In this, she voiced the conservative reaction to demands – grown ever louder since the late forties – for woman's rights and freedom. In the year before those *Saturday Review* essays, London saw its first Society for Women's Suffrage and this rapidly expanded into a National Union. Two years onward, the Municipal and Corporations Elections Act gave the vote to any person who had resided in a municipality for more than one year, except (it was later deemed) all married women since their opinions would naturally be those of their husbands. The Girl of the Period represented such political aspirations, too. Not all the sisterhood were pleasure-loving hoydens, and some had acquired a more than duty-bound education at London University or Cheltenham Ladies College (since the fifties) and, in 1869, were about to invade Cambridge.

Both Houses of Parliament, the pulpits, the daily and weekly papers answered that challenge in tones which ran the gamut from thunderous horror to jocular incredulity. Contemplating the fact that students from the Hitchin Ladies College had sat for examinations at Cambridge, *Punch* found it 'gratifying . . . that out of all those flowers of loveliness, not one was plucked. Bachelors of Arts are likely to be made to look to their laurels by these Spinsters, and Masters . . . [risk being] eclipsed by Mistresses.'[2] Mr Punch also suggested that 'asking a lady what her accomplishments are, is generally speaking, harmless enough. Still, in these days it might in some cases cause embarrass-ment to put the question, "Do you paint?" '[3] The magazine's chief rival, *Fun*, included a '*Girl of the Period*' *Almanac for 1870*, a series of cartoons that envisioned women at the Stock Exchange, the Law

Courts, or 'The Ladies' Own Club'. But though the popularity of the catch-phrase led to Girl of the Period waltzes and galops, in the theatre she merely prompted sneering burlesques or topical jokes at pantomime season. As Mrs Bancroft knew, to present the type seriously 'might on the stage become offensive'.

Instead, Robertson's contemporaries and successors either rallied to the cause of the traditional Miss, in the pastel colours of *School*, or satirized the *nouveau riche* while treating the unruly manners of the younger generation with good-natured mildness. James Albery, whose *Two Roses* caught the public's fancy in the same year as *M.P.*, was for a time the principal exponent of Robertsonian sweetness although his other plays, *Two Thorns*, *Apple Blossoms*, *Forgiven*, met with diminishing success. Seeking to enliven his characters' empty-headed chit-chat with polished epigrams, he made them sound self-conscious and mawkish: 'Flowers are made by angels and smell of their fingers.'[4] The satirists, if less blatantly sentimental, were equally content to skim across the surface of contemporary issues. H.J. Byron, arch-punster of burlesque, having 'tired of being termed "a droll"', turned his attention to the malaise of the middle-class housewife in *Cyril's Success* (1868). Act One presents the boredom of Mrs Cyril Cuthbert whose husband neglects her for his career and – she suspects – another woman. But the rest of the play shies away from further analysis of that marriage and resorts to theatrical contrivance and mistaken identities in order to arrive at a reassuring finale:

We will make it a home of happiness again. We will stay there, and make our dear old friends come to *us* . . . And when the past floats away before us, we will look into one another's eyes and seeing the love light glowing there, say that we have a gladness in our hearts beyond the best we ever knew, in what the world called *Cyril's Success. (Hides her face on CUTHBERT's breast.)*[5]

Byron, the founding editor of *Fun*, was not prepared to shake theatre audiences' faith in the virtues of domestic bliss. Although the chaff in a comic weekly might prod readers into a few minutes' serious thought, those middle-class patrons were not yet willing to spend an evening watching unattractive characters with disagreeable problems. A playwright had to deliver what customers would pay for at the box-office.

In 1875, Byron provided exactly what they wanted: *Our Boys* ran at the Vaudeville Theatre for more than four years, a record which would not be matched until Brandon Thomas's *Charley's Aunt* (1892). *Our Boys* is contrived and flimsy; its characters are broadly contrasted types animated by 'a succession of sparkling jests and brilliant repartees'.[6] All discomforting facts from the outside world have been reshaped into complacent and flattering generalities. The transparent snobbery of Sir Geoffry Champneys, a minor landowner, runs counter to the ill-educated struttings of Mr Perkyn Middlewick who, having amassed a fortune in the grocery trade, can 'buy up any 'arf a dozen nobs in the county' (II, p. 132). The pretensions of both these men are laughable yet, set beside Sir Geoffry's empty civilities, Middlewick's good heart appears in the right place even when his 'h's' do not. And though each man decides to play 'the Roman father', the pair react with endearing horror upon seeing the poverty to which their sons' recalcitrance has led. In the same way, the behaviour of the younger generation invites both ridicule and sympathy. Talbot Champneys' modern dandyism, his ludicrous drawl, and philistine enthusiasm, is countered by an attractive sense of his own inadequacies. Charles Middlewick, determined to strike out alone despite what his parent might say, loves his father nonetheless; although he winces at his pater's every vulgarism, he is hurt by the scorn they produce in his adored Violet.

She and her cousin Mary exemplify the way Byron tames and domesticates the unruly. Mrs Linton would have deemed them 'fast', for Violet, though gentler than her cousin, has a satirical wit and a will of her own, and Mary is decidedly mannish:

VIOLET: . . . Mary, don't make remarks.
MARY: Why not? I *like* to make remarks.
VIOLET: Yes, you like to do a great many things you *shouldn't* do.
MARY: So does everyone. If one's always to do what's proper and correct, life might as well be all rice puddings and toast and water. I hate them *both*, they're so dreadfully wholesome.   (I, p. 127)

Yet this pertness, which serves the dialogue's tumbling puns, never makes them unlikeable, and their spirited intelligence fades away in Act Three when they react like conventional ninnies on discovering a lady's hat in the garret of their (romantically) starving boys. When all is explained, they succumb charmingly to the men's embraces. In this manner, Byron encourages his audience to feel superior to the gentry and to trade. Allowing them a frown or two at the new generation, he then manipulates their sympathetic reaction to such filial disobedience from so charming and essentially dutiful young people. This comic formula assures a cosy sense of well being, of live and let live, between classes and generations as the final curtain falls:

SIR GEOFFRY: ... We haven't understood each other, borne with each other, we haven't shown sufficient of the glorious old principle of 'Give and take' ... hot tempers, hasty judgements, extreme crotchets, thick-skinned prejudice, theory and rule run rampant, ignoring the imperfections of poor human nature – these henceforth, we throw overboard and rise to brighter realms, even as the aspiring aeronaut flings away his heavy ballast and floats serenely through the cloudless sky.   (III, p. 158)

Notwithstanding 'the aspiring aeronaut' or references to 'Cook's Excursions' to the Continent, 'Atlantic cables and other curious things' (I, p. 123), the basic recipe for this 'merry dish' (as one reviewer called the play) had been handed down through the century.

Yet the drama of the seventies and eighties was not totally escapist. For decades, the comic journals had mocked the Victorian Dream by showing that women were not all ethereal paragons, that men were rarely unflinching heroes, and that money dictated the ways of humankind. This satirical breeze finally blew into the theatre with the plays of William Schwenck Gilbert who, in many ways, epitomized the bourgeois establishment but whose sense of the absurd would not lie quiet.

The anomalies surrounding his personality seem prefigured in an incident which occurred when his parents took their infant son to Naples. Their respectable lives were turned suddenly upside down when Baby William's nurse, not the most intelligent of creatures, handed him over to two strangers who told her they had instructions to return the boy to his parents forthwith. These brigands then fled to the mountains and ransomed the child for £25, an adventure which turned up later in *The Pirates of Penzance*. At school, Gilbert developed a talent for drawing and rhyming; once he presented himself at the Princess's Theatre requesting employment, but Charles Kean knew his father and packed the boy back home. His career at King's College, London, was distinguished by his converting the Scientific Society into a Dramatic one. Having taken his degree, he determined on a commission in the Royal Artillery, but while he was cramming for those exams the Crimean War ground to a halt; 'I had no taste for a line regiment, so I obtained, by competitive examination, an assistant clerkship in the Education Department of the Privy Council Office, in which ill-organized and ill-governed office I spent four uncomfortable years.'[7] To relieve the tedium, he studied law and doodled away at comic drawings and verses some of which he sent to H.J. Byron, at the newly established *Fun*, who liked them enough to want more. In the following year, 1862, an aunt left a legacy that enabled him to leave his 'detestable thraldom', to sit for the Bar (for which he proved eminently unsuited), and to eke out a living at his chambers in Clement's Inn by writing theatre reviews and satirical essays.

A stickler for propriety and truth, Gilbert could not help but see that those two qualities rarely went together and, in the cause of truth, attacked sham propriety: 'I am always in the habit of saying what I think, and when I think I have said too much, I am in the habit of saying *that*.'[8] Associates who failed to meet his exacting standards fell victim to those forthright critiques or found themselves suspected of treachery, and Gilbert was slow to forgive. Yet he was also generous, fun-loving, and conscious of his own irascible temper. In the sixties, long before the Savoy Operas brought him a suburban estate, luxurious yachts, and the professional eminence that made him still more vulnerable to imagined slights, Gilbert gleefully unmasked the pretensions of the world around him.

In the pages of *Fun*, after Tom Hood assumed the editorship, Gilbert began to sign his spindly drawings with the name Bab, a relic from his nursery days, and there emerged a persona who, like the child in Hans Andersen, proclaimed that the Emperor had no clothes. Adults could hardly take offence at such innocence, even though in actual fact Bab's knowing ways resembled those of 'The Precocious Baby' in Gilbert's 'very true tale' who, born to a father of almost seventy-three, entered the world with 'a weed in his mouth and a glass in his eye' to accuse his desiccated parent of amorous yearning for the heroines of Nursery Rhymes:

> 'There's Jill and White Cat' (said the bold little brat,
> With his loud, 'Ha, ha!')
> ''Oo sly ickle pa!
> Wiz 'oo Beauty, Bo-Peep, and 'oo Mrs Jack Sprat!
> I've noticed 'oo pat
> *My* pretty White Cat –
> I sink dear mamma ought to know about dat!'[9]

This particular little nuisance 'died an enfeebled old dotard at five', but Bab continued to point his merciless finger at wilting maidens

4   *The Bab Ballads*: a miscellany

The Precocious Baby

He'd a weed in his mouth and a glass in his eye,
A hat all awry –
An octagon tie,
And a miniature – miniature glass in his eye.

Fun, 6 (23 November 1867), 113

The Reverend Micah Sowls

He saw a dreary person on the stage,
Who mouthed and mugged in simulated rage,
Who growled and spluttered in a mode absurd,
And spoke an English SOWLS had never heard.

Fun, 7 (18 April 1868), 65

First Love

Though sterner memories might fade,
    You never could forget
The child-form of that baby-maid,
    The Village Violet!

A simple frightened loveliness,
    Whose sacred spirit-part
Shrank timidly from worldly stress,
    And nestled in your heart.

Fun, 8 (27 February 1869), 248

whose only sincere passion was for cash, at gentlemen who were nothing of the sort, and (since Gilbert was also the paper's drama critic) at the theatre's tawdry substitute for reality.

The monstrous cruelty and self-interest of middle-class society finds exaggerated expression in the posturings of the comic figures who illustrate *The Bab Ballads,* yet they cavort across the page in costumes whose accurate detail is disturbingly realistic. The attractive, jingling verses and Bab's wide-eyed innocence then invite the reader into tales which grow so peculiar that all outward respectability falls away to leave these little grotesques naked for all to see. Ellen of 'First Love' (pp. 238–9), who admires the Reverend Bernard Powles 'In maidenly simplicity', does not look like 'The Village Violet' she purports to be. In the drawings, the way she shrinks 'timidly from worldly stress' is transparently coy and self-satisfied. As she turns away from a grandiloquent Bernard, the restraining hand behind her back appears to urge him on. Those gestures and her aging charms suggest the 'real' Ellen, whereas the mob-cap and nightgown, buttoned up to her double chin, in which she listens to her serenading swain impose a decorous surface, as does Bab's congratulatory tone: 'how blest she was to own / The wealth of POWLES'S love'. The truth beneath this romantic idyll rises to the surface as the balladeer muses over Ellen's love for the wily Bernard who can afford to hire the Grenadiers and 'The Covent Garden band' to play beneath her window. What could possibly attract her to someone 'cursed with acres fat / . . . And gold'?

> For calculated he was *not*
>   To please a woman's whim.

> He wasn't good, despite the air
>   An M.B. waistcoat gives;
> Indeed, his dearest friends declare
>   No greater humbug lives.

Still more amazing is her respectful but cold reaction to her other suitor, old Aaron Wood, whose own serenades at two o'clock in the morning on 'His plain harmonium' exhort the lady to a life of busy toil. Having exposed Ellen's 'simplicity' in this innocently approving way, Bab allows her to re-erect a genteel façade: 'the admirable maid' refuses the penniless curate very politely, invents a prior commitment, and assures him (and herself) that she has only agreed to marry Bernard in order 'To rectify his life' whereas the saintly Aaron would need no such helpmeet.

> She wished him happiness and health,
> And flew on lightning wings
> To BERNARD with his dangerous wealth
> And all the woes it brings.

Other ladies in *The Bab Ballads* show the same concern for their fellow mortals, whenever it suits their own interests, and many of the men share Bernard's hollow eloquence. Not all the ballads are as exaggeratedly eccentric as 'First Love', but each tears at the veil of conventional romance, and though the characters can sometimes escape with their illusions and vanity intact, the reader cannot. Romance may simply be a quixotic dream, like that of the troubadour who determines to rescue an imprisoned maid from a villainous dungeon only to discover that 'Two years this lady's got / For collaring a wotch' and that the castle perilous is actually Pentonville Prison (pp. 111–12). But usually such deception is less innocent and, even if rewarding in the short term, eventually loses its glitter. The caddish officer in 'Tempora Mutantur' used to curse the postman whenever he failed to deliver a love-letter, but 'Quarters in a place like Dover / Tend to make a man forget' (p. 58), and tradesmen's bills, missives from lawyers, creditors' demands are far more pressing than the envelope with the roses on it – 'Ah, I know what that's about' – which lies unopened in their midst:

> And unopened it's remaining!
> I can read her gentle hope –
> Her entreaties, uncomplaining
> (She was always uncomplaining),
> Her devotion never waning –
> Through the little envelope!

Bab also taunts the sanctimonious whose pious horror of life's pleasures in general tends to concentrate upon the theatre in particular. It was no pleasure-house to Gilbert. Having reviewed a succession of first-nights and endured the way several of his own scripts had been mangled, he knew the theatre's drudgery and shoddy incompetence. Accordingly, Bab tells how the Reverend Micah Sowls's usual tirade against the Stage becomes especially fiery in the presence of his bishop since it might earn him one of the 'fatter livings in that see' (p. 160). After the service, the bishop asks if he has ever seen a play; if not, how can he know what he preaches against? Handing him a token for Drury Lane, 'The Bishop took his leave, / Rejoicing in his sleeve' (p. 161) at having condemned Sowls to unendurable boredom:

He saw a dreary person on the stage,
Who mouthed and mugged in simulated rage,
Who growled and spluttered in a mode absurd,
And spoke an English SOWLS had never heard . . .

For hours and hours that dismal actor walked,
And talked, and talked, and talked, and talked, and talked,
Till lethargy upon the parson crept,
And sleepy MICAH SOWLS serenely slept.

The experience teaches him to see the theatre as a penitential hell.

'Only a Dancing Girl' presents two other hell-holes. Tom Robertson, writing about a similar character in his piece for the *Illustrated Times*, had set the glamour and talent of the burlesque dancer against the busy anonymity of her home life. Bab–Gilbert pierces directly to the 'unromantic style' of the dancer's dyed hair, uneducated voice, and mechanical acting:

No airy fairy she,
    As she hangs in arsenic green,
From a highly impossible tree,
    In a highly impossible scene
    (Herself not over clean).
For fays don't suffer, I'm told,
From bunions, coughs, or cold.   (p. 88)

He then turns this tinselled, but all too human drab against the artificial style and impertinent manners of 'stately dames' in the stalls who pronounce the painted creature 'No better than she should be. / . . . Ah, matron, which of us is?' However, away from the theatre's 'palpable lie' and the matrons' disapproving stares, the dancer becomes genuinely magical. Dressed in 'coarse merino', she artfully humours her drunken father amidst the ugliness of her squalid home; 'She's a fairy truly, then.'

So even wicked Bab could turn sentimental at the thought of true worth, but generally that persona gave Gilbert licence to expose hypocrisies and to declare his disillusion with the theatre's illusions. Yet, like many of his journalist and lawyer friends, he wanted to write successful plays and, with a living to earn, was prepared to compromise. Of his many early scripts, a domestic comedy called *Uncle Baby* was accepted in 1863, but the chance to establish himself came three years later when Robertson recommended him to the St James's. *Dulcamara; or, the Little Duck and the Great Quack*, a burlesque of Donizetti's opera, *L'Elisir D'Amore*, was put together in ten days and rehearsed in seven. Loaded with awful puns, even in the cast list where Gianetta is described as 'the pretty *paysanne*, to whom Tomaso *pays an* overwhelming amount of attention', the piece ran throughout the Christmas season to provide mindless fun and a spectacular finale: A GRAND ALLEGORICAL TABLEAU OF LOVE'S DEVICES! Over the next two years, Gilbert consolidated that success with other burlesques so that John Hollingshead chose his version of *Robert the Devil* to open the new Gaiety Theatre. Though Gilbert did have novel ideas about improving the popular theatre,[10] these scripts were exactly like the made-to-order entertainments by the groups of friends who wined and dined in his chambers every Saturday night. Most of them also wrote for *Fun* and were ready contributors to Tom Hood's other projects like *Warne's Christmas Annual* (1866) which includes yet another of Gilbert's burlesques, *Ruy Blas*, whose silliness exemplifies the style of that particular Owl's Roost:

QUEEN: Unhappy Queen – unhappy maiden, I!
  In vain to get a wink of sleep I try;
  But wander, dressing-gowny and night-cappy,
  I seldom get a nap – I'm so un-nappy![11]

Gilbert knew that 'the public are possessed of no critical power whatever'[12] and that managers regarded a script as so many opportunities for star turns and scenic wonderments. Nevertheless, by 1871 he felt secure enough to bring new form and intellectual bite to the Gaiety's Christmas burlesque. *Thespis; or, the Gods Grown Old* was not a travesty opera, set to the tunes of the day, but an original fable with original music (by Arthur Sullivan!). A group of Thessalian actors, out for a picnic on Mount Olympus, offers to change places with the classical gods. But the gods have grown old and powerless and the modern players botch their new roles, so both parties finally return to their own spheres. Within that framework, Gilbert depicted such peculiar reversals as that which befell the Chairman of the North South East West Diddelsex Railway whose singular devotion to his employees led to financial disaster:

Each Christmas Day he gave each stoker
A silver shovel and a golden poker,
He'd button-hole flowers for the ticket sorters,
And rich Bath-buns for the outside porters.
He'd mount the clerks on his first-class hunters,
And he built little villas for the road-side shunters,
And if any were fond of pigeon shooting,
He'd ask them down to his place at Tooting.[13]

Alas, such novel fare bewildered holiday audiences, and the performers at the Gaiety resisted Gilbert's attempts to mould them to his overall design: 'Really, Mr Gilbert, why should I stand here? I am not a chorus girl!' – 'No, madam, your voice isn't strong enough or you would be.'[14] Years later, Gilbert published a comic article about 'Actors, Authors, and Audiences' in which the author of a failed, but original play stands trial before his irate audience, and the unsympathetic actors unintentionally reveal their egotistic intransigence:

MISS JESSIE JESSAMINE: . . . The part I played was that of a simple-minded young governess in a country rectory, who is secretly in love with the Home Secretary . . . I see no reason why a broken-hearted governess should not endeavour to raise her spirits by dancing an occasional 'breakdown' . . . I wore short petticoats because the audience expected it of me. I see no reason why a governess in a country vicarage should not wear short petticoats if she has good legs. I did not charge extra for wearing short petticoats. I wore them entirely in the author's interests. Besides that, I expect to have at least one song and dance in every part I play. I expect this because I possess both accomplishments, and it is essential that I should display them to the public as often as possible.[15]

Nevertheless, Gilbert had already found a discerning audience and less troublesome actors at the Gallery of Illustration on Lower Regent Street. Under the management of Thomas German Reed and his wife, Priscilla Horton, this unpromising hall attracted many who would never venture into a *theatre*; they came prepared to listen and to think. In addition, the limited scale of each production encouraged inventiveness and, shaping his ideas for six or seven performers who often had to assume different identities, Gilbert discovered another mask behind which he could pit truth against illusion and make his satire palatable. After *No Cards* (1869), *Ages Ago* (1869), and *Our Island Home* (1870) for the German Reeds, he accepted Buckstone's invitation to create a blank-verse comedy from a story by Madame de Genlis. *The Palace of Truth* opened at the Haymarket in 1870, and so began the 'fairy' plays which, under the guise of make-believe, 'show up human nature as it is'.

Blank-verse in itself removes the play from ordinary life, but the opening sequence emphasizes this artifice through 'the very affected manner' in which King Phanor recites his latest octave to the strains of a mandolin. The praises of his flattering courtiers sound even more florid, but when Phanor proudly repeats his poem, the bombast of 'pitch-encrusted night' lurches into the bathos of 'scorpions vomit forth their poisonous scum'.[16] The effect of words becomes an important theme in the rest of the play since high-sounding rhetoric gilds the tongues of lovers as well as sycophants and poetasters. So Phanor's bad verse opens the way to other plunges from high to low style that expose the characters' pomposities. Admittedly some of the false eloquence may be Gilbert's own; however, his intentions are unequivocal in regard to Prince Philamir whose articulate passion contrasts with Princess Zeolide's silent heart. His daughter's reticence persuades the King to remove his court to the Palace of Truth, enchanted ground which makes each person speak truly, though 'strange to say, while publishing the truth / He's no idea that he is doing so' (I, p. 37). There Philamir's words present him plainly, despite his external postures, when he admits that the Princess is 'not nearly as attractive as / Five hundred other ladies I could name' (II, p. 46) and that her cold response to his well-practised wooing was at first a novelty until his 'pride was nettled, and I persevered / Until I made you tell me of your love' (II, p. 47). The Prince's passionate manner collides farcically with these unloving truths, and the effect is heightened by his complete amazement over the fact that his intended compliments mortify the Princess. But Gilbert makes Philamir a type, rather than an individual, whose 'very fairest flowers . . . of metaphor' satirize men's amorous posturings. This protects the audience from the full severity of the critique since the Prince's cardboard personality allows them to recognize a caricature, onto whom they can deflect Gilbert's barbs.

Nearly all the men in the play are liars, cheats, and schemers. However, with exotic names like Chrysal and Zoram and with stereotyped roles to play, they and their vanities remain at a safe distance from the front-row stalls. In that way, Gilbert lances at pretension without affronting his patrons. King Phanor, for instance, is a cartoon philanderer. Worried that his wife will find him out once they enter the enchanted palace, he takes along a crystal box which will protect him from that power. When he hints to his trusted counsellor about the rovings of his eighteen married years, his rhythms and vocabulary become colloquial and contemporary but his words also generalize him into the type of husband we all recognize but which none of us is:

> I'm a good husband – as good husbands go.
> I love my wife – but still – you understand –
> Boys will be boys! There *is* a point or two –
> Say two, as being nearer to the mark –
> On which I do not altogether care

To stand examination by my wife.
Perhaps I may have given out that I've
Been dining *here* – when I've been dining *there* –
I may have said 'with A' – when 'twas with B –
I may have said 'with *him*' – when 'twas with *her* –
Distinctions such as these, good Gélanor,
Though strangely unimportant in themselves,
Still have a value, which the female mind's
Particularly quick to apprehend.   (I, p. 40)

Presented vaguely like this, Phanor's naughty secrets and his alarm at what might ensue evoke sympathetic laughter, especially since another of his worries concerns the Queen whom he regards as a model wife and mother: 'I do not care / To run the risk of being undeceived' (I, p. 38). Though not 'perfect', Queen Altemire is entirely faithful, and the play subscribes comfortably to double standards. Accordingly, since 'perfect spotlessness / Is apt to smack of insipidity' (I, p. 41), the women's faults are those which Victorian society would generally allow them. Altemire admits her own quick temper and jealousy, but these flaws are as nothing to her supreme worth as 'wife':

I am a woman, with a woman's faults.
But, being woman, Phanor, I'm a wife;
And, in that I am one, I need not blush.   (I, p. 38)

But in order to achieve that happy status, blushing young girls must behave with demure propriety. Given that expectation, Gilbert introduces Azèma into the Palace of Truth. Her actions are exaggeratedly demure and shy, but her words expose each calculated attempt to snare the Prince:

PHILAMIR: I beg your pardon, but the furniture
Has caught your dress.
AZEMA: (*rearranging her dress hastily*) Oh, I arranged it so,
That you might see how truly beautiful
My foot and ankle are (*as if much shocked at the exposé*).
PHILAMIR: I saw them well;
They're very neat.
AZEMA: I now remove my glove
That you may note the whiteness of my hand.
I place it there in order that you may
Be tempted to enclose it in your own.
PHILAMIR: To that temptation I at once succumb (*taking her hand – she affects to withdraw it angrily*).
AZEMA: (*with affected indignation*) Go on! If you had any enterprise,
You'd gently place your arm around my waist
And kiss me (*struggling to release herself*).
(II, p. 50)

Unable to awaken Philamir's vanity with such brazen artifice, Azèma seizes the next titled bachelor she meets and, with wilting tones and gestures, leads him triumphantly away.

Essentially good-natured, this satire is further qualified by the genuine modesty of Princess Zeolide, a second Cordelia, who cannot speak love and so appears unfeeling. When enchantment frees her inward thoughts, she explains that words would only set limits on her boundless emotion, but the Prince, having extracted the confession of love he so desires, no longer finds her interesting. In her confusion and hurt, Zeolide shows a courage and inner strength denied to any of the male characters. Her confidante, Mirza, exhibits similar depths of feeling; however, her fine words lead to dangerous territory in that her willingness to renounce the Prince, whom she loves, sounds genuine but is actually made possible by the crystal box. After Philamir discovers this hypocrisy, Gilbert quickly sidesteps the fact that women are liars too. Had he explored the reasons behind Mirza's 'goodly show of purity, / And such unequalled treachery of heart', he would have had to examine the social 'policy' which allows a prince to make love to 'a humble waiting lady' though he could never marry her. To maintain the buoyant spirit of the play, he simply removes the lady from the scene (III, pp. 64–9).

Nevertheless, the geniality of *The Palace of Truth* hides one scathing comment about middle-class complacency. Faced with masculine deception, the ladies derive peculiar comfort from the thought that 'When men are over head and ears in love, / They cannot tell the truth – they must deceive' (II, p. 55). As for Philamir's unfeeling vanity, it is, according to the Queen, a 'veneer' under which lies 'sterling stuff'. Her lady-in-waiting adds the consoling thought that Zeolide knows Philamir likes her, even if he does not love her: 'How many maidens when they wed a man / Have reason to be sure of half as much!' (III, p. 63). As lovers, men, it appears, are naturally deceptive and vain. Having shown that, Gilbert then persuades his audience that Philamir's true character 'is honest gold', by giving him the opportunity to deceive the Princess anew. Now, though, with manly fortitude, Philamir relinquishes the crystal box that might protect him:

> Yet I would rather live without that love –
> A life of self-reproach without that love –
> Repentant and alone without that love –
> Than stoop to gain it by such treachery.

> Here is the talisman. (ZEOLIDE *takes it.*) No longer armed
> Against the sacred influence of Truth,
> I tell you of my sorrow and my love
> With all the warmth of a repentant heart!
>   (*He presses* ZEOLIDE *to his heart and kisses her*)   (III, p. 71)

So the play ends happily, but only for those who, like the characters themselves, willingly clutch at appearances rather than know what lurks beneath. Yet the enchanted palace, gone forever once the talisman is shattered, has ridiculed all social polish, and the entire play has mocked at the way its characters compromise themselves by readily ignoring the uncomfortable truths beneath that pleasant veneer:

> GELANOR: When Zoram said that he considered you
> A systematic liar, mean, poor, base,
> Selfish, and sordid, cruel, tyrannical,
> 'Twas what he *thought* – not what he would have *said*!
> CHRYSAL: I see – if that was only what he *thought*,
> It makes a difference.   (III, p. 60)

Without his fairy mask, Gilbert himself made compromises. *Sweethearts,* the brief two-act play he wrote for Marie Bancroft in 1874, offers a realistic picture of a girl's coquetry and her admirer's passion. The action begins with Wilcox, the family's devoted gardener whose own wry sympathy for love's comedy ensures an affectionate response. 'Miss Jenny ain't a job to be hurried over, bless her',[17] so he doubts that young Mr Spreadbrow will be able to reach an understanding before leaving for India that very evening. Yet Jenny's enthusiasm for a newly arrived sapling cut from 'the old sycamore on the lawn' at Hampstead immediately reveals her deep regard for Henry Spreadbrow. Under that parent tree, he and she 'used to sit and learn our lessons years ago', and she appreciates the effort it must have taken to request a cutting from the present owners: 'It was an awkward thing for a nervous young gentleman to do.' But although she continually betrays herself, Jenny will not admit her feelings, partly because society demands a maiden's modesty but also because artifice adds spirit to the game of love. Accordingly when Wilcox warms to the subject of Mr Spreadbrow who only last Tuesday made some excuse to sing the praises of Miss Northcott, the lady herself, after listening to the entire story, is suddenly affronted: 'He had no right to talk about me to a servant' (I, p. 76). And the news that Henry must leave three months earlier than expected rouses her pique: she tells herself he could not go 'if he really, really liked me!' He should at least have let her know immediately his plans changed, and though she might leave him (if the game required that) – 'but then that's different' – why *must* he go to India?

Those thoughts dictate her behaviour once Henry arrives. At first she pretends a cool farewell, and when her unsuppressible emotions lead him on she instantly cloaks them in social platitude; then, under that protective gauze, she toys with the young man's feelings by dangling the name of Captain Dampier, her next-door neighbour, and by seeming not to understand why Henry should so want Wilcox to leave their part of the garden. Bound by conventions which allow them to touch hands only when planting a little sycamore or when saying goodbye, Henry will not ask for more than her signals tell him to. Each hesitant move forward leads to a half-step backward until, summoning up courage to offer her the rose from his lapel, he notices the careless way she lays it aside. His disappointment drives him to a last despairing bid for 'one kind word'. But she wants him to tell her what to say, and he feels the word should come from her heart, so they both have played to a standstill.

Gilbert's gentle comedy exploits the style of the Prince of Wales's ensemble whose tones and gestures weave a delicate web of manners around the two lovers yet whose discipline maintains a balance between sentiment and pathos until the final moments of Act One when pathos predominates. Henry fights back his grief and, wishing Jenny every happiness, hopes she will one day 'marry a good fellow who will – who will – who will – Goodbye!' (I, p. 81). As he rushes away, the strains of 'Goodbye, Sweetheart' rise from the orchestra, but Jenny, alone in the garden, seems utterly carefree or perhaps she believes he must come dashing back. Humming a bright little tune, she eventually notices the rose, plays with it, falters, and then gives way, *'laying her head on the table over the flower he has given her, and sobbing violently'*.

The beginning of Act Two builds on that pathos. Thirty years have passed. The railway has supplanted the stagecoach so that Jenny's garden, once a country retreat, now looks out onto 'picturesque semi-detached villas' and a distant town. The little sycamore has grown into a large tree, and the autumnal colours of the creeper which envelops the house echo the tones of Jenny herself, now a plump and 'pleasant-looking middle-aged lady' (II, p. 82). In a second domestic prelude, she sits beneath the tree, winding cotton from the skein her maid holds out for her. She has grown wiser as well as older so she upbraids the servant-girl for taking 'foolish pleasure in playing fast and loose with poor Tom'. The maid's peevish self-justifications, so like the young Jenny's on a lower scale, prepare for the appearance of Sir Henry Spreadbrow, retired from India's law courts, and for a jolting reversal as Gilbert begins to sprinkle acid over the play's sentimental surface.

Sir Henry gallantly protests that Jenny has not changed, though he needed her promptings and his spectacles to recognize her at all. He is especially gallant in regretting that she never married:

> I am very sorry to hear that. I am really more sorry and disappointed than I can tell you. (*She looks surprised and rather hurt.*) You'd have made an admirable wife, Jane, and an admirable mother. I can't tell you how sorry I am to find that you are still Jane Northbrook – I should say, Northcott. (II, p. 84)

Jenny's name is not the only thing which has faded from his mind. He recalls their childhood friendship, but learns to his astonishment that he once let her know he felt more. The frankness of these revelations is made possible by conventions that befit the couple's advancing years. It is now Henry who assumes a role, as bluff old Indian civil-servant, from which he can laugh at his green and salad days; he does not realize the hurt he causes by treating Jenny as a dear old friend who must surely feel just as satirical towards youthful folly:

> I told you that I adored you, didn't I? – that you were as essential to me as the air I breathed – that it was impossible to support existence without you – that your name should be the most hallowed of earthly words, and so forth. Ha, ha! My dear Jane, before I'd been a week on board I was saying the same thing to a middle-aged governess whose name has entirely escaped me . . . What fools we make of ourselves! (II, p. 86)

And, this time around, it is Jenny's tenderness which finds no response when Henry starts to lecture her for allowing a large sycamore to block out the view and restrict the air from a house that has been carefully planned and dearly paid for. Eventually he does recall the sapling and, to cover his *faux pas*, laughingly remembers how planting it together gave him an excuse to take her hand – though now, as a dear old friend, he can do so openly. But Jenny's companionable laughter verges on tears and ceases altogether when Sir Henry insists that the flower he gave her at parting was a camellia, not a rose:

> Nonsense, Jane – come, come, you hardly looked at it, miserable little flirt that you were; and you pretend, after thirty years, to stake your recollection of the circumstance against mine? No, no, Jane, take my word for it, it was a camellia.
> JENNY: I'm sure it was a rose!

SPREADBROW: No, I'm sure it was a camellia
JENNY: (*in tears*) Indeed – indeed, it was a rose. (*Produces a withered rose from a pocket-book – he is very much impressed – looks at it and at her, and seems much affected.*) (II, p. 87)

Having shown the comic deceptiveness of social behaviour, in that Henry's passion faded quickly while young Jenny's careless manner hid a lasting love, Gilbert dared not end their interview on the emptiness to which the action naturally leads. After Jenny's final self-discovery, 'We were both acting parts – but the play is over, and there's an end of it', he restores the sentimental picture and allows his audience to recover their illusions. In an instant, he returns Sir Henry from man-of-the-world to arch-romantic and, with a sugared vision of devoted old age (for nothing can turn back the years), removes his comedy's bitter aftertaste:

SPREADBROW: No, no, Janet, the play is *not* over – we will talk of nothing else – the play is not nearly over. (*Music in orchestra, 'John Anderson my Jo'.*) My dear Jane – (*rising and taking her hand*) my very dear Jane – believe me, for I speak from my hardened old heart, so far from the play being over, the serious interest is only just beginning. (*He kisses her hand – they walk towards the house.*) (II, p. 88)

This sentimental volte face converts irony into a pleasing frisson, just as the fairy mask of *The Palace of Truth* turns callow humanity into acceptably amusing cartoons. But on at least one occasion Gilbert donned another of his fantastical guises only to discover that many in his audience took the grotesque for the real. That miscalculation says much about the taste of the time, for though Gilbert himself had long been painfully aware of the way the Victorian theatre falsified life, the majority of theatregoers saw life there as they wanted it to be. Consequently when Gilbert set out to satirize the theatre's posturings in *Engaged* (1877), many did not recognize them *as* postures and so balked at his unmasked cynicism:

From beginning to end of this nauseous play not one of the characters ever says a single word or does a single action that is not inseparable from the lowest moral degradation; while, much to the delight of that portion of the audience who believe that to scoff at what is pure and noble is the surest sign of intellectual pre-eminence, speeches in which the language ordinarily employed by true feeling is used for the purpose of deriding every virtue which any honest man reverences, even if he does not possess, are tediously reiterated by actresses whom one would wish to associate only with what is pure and modest . . . To answer that 'all this is a burlesque' seems to us but a poor defence; the characters are dressed in the ordinary costume of the present day; the language, as we have said, is precisely that which would be employed in serious drama; there are few if any of those amusing exaggerations which, in true burlesque, dispel, almost before it has time to form, any idea that the speaker is really in earnest.[18]

Like the characters in *The Palace of Truth*, this reviewer cheerfully accepts the fact that people ought to revere virtues they do not actually possess: fine words are better than naked truths! Naturally, then, the theatre's idealized sentiments are, for him, indistinguishable from all that is 'pure and noble' in life and so he fails to see what Gilbert intends to burlesque.

Nevertheless, despite its contemporary setting, *Engaged* opens with a clear signal as to the fantasy ahead. Gilbert's Scottish cottagers live in exaggerated and picturesque comfort. Their supposedly humble dwelling extends to two storeys behind its wee façade. A pleasing group of trees and a rustic bridge across a purling stream frame a background of gently rolling hills; in the garden, Maggie MacFarlane sings at her spinning-wheel: '*The whole scene is suggestive of rustic prosperity and content.*'[19] A handsome, clean peasant, Angus MacAlister, enters at the back, spies his bonnie Meg, tiptoes down to her, and places his hands over her eyes. When lad and lassie begin to speak in the thickest of brogues, their pretty flutterings ought to explode into farce, at least for those who recognize Gilbert's skilful parody (of plays like Boucicault's *The Colleen Bawn*) when the pure and beautiful rural maid gives her 'true and tender little hairt' into the keeping of the 'tall, and fair, and brave' laddie who has loved her 'honestly these fifteen years, but never plucked up the hairt to tell her so until noo'. As a badge of that honesty, Angus's 'bonnie blue een' fill with tears at the mere thought of Meg's bright beauty, and though Mrs MacFarlane is surprised to find him kissing her daughter she soon gives him her widow's blessing:

Angus, say nae mair. My hairt is sair at losing my only bairn; but I'm nae fasht wi' 'ee. Thou'rt a gude lad, and it's been the hope of my widowed auld heart to see you twain one. Thou'lt treat her kindly – I ken that weel. Thou'rt a prosperous, kirk-going man, and my Mag should be a happy lass indeed. Bless thee, Angus; bless thee!

(I, pp. 138–9)

Such bucolic absurdity was clearly meant to move the audience away from reality into a never-never-land of theatrical romance and melodrama: Gilbert's revenge upon the hardly less ridiculous claptrap he had witnessed since his days as drama critic.[20] But many in the audience failed to make that adjustment. For them, peasants did live in a picture-book world, 'farmin' a bit land, and gillieing odd times', or mouthing sentiments that were equally as pretty. But though 'a bit o' poachin' now and again' and brewing 'illicit whusky' might sound like rural innocence, Angus adds to his happy substance by 'throwin' trains off the line, that the poor distracted passengers may come to my cot. I've mair ways than one of making an honest living – and I'll work them a' nicht and day for my bonnie Meg!' For those who could not see this comic mask, the real now became too real and (what was worse) an impudent attack against a sacred institution:

you do not naturally expect good taste from Mr Gilbert, for grapes do not grow on briars; but the sort of man who attempts to extract humour from the subject of wilful attempts to upset railway trains may well be left to enjoy his funereal fancies . . . For heartless, coldblooded, brutal cynicism, the play has perhaps never been equalled.[21]

In a world less enamoured of the railway, *Engaged* still seems to lack human warmth simply because the theatrical excesses Gilbert parodies are, for the most part, blessedly dead. Whereas many of his contemporaries mistook the play for 'a very laborious and prolix' social satire, modern audiences cannot appreciate its accurate burlesque of the Victorian theatre. The characters are empty automatons in a plot whose extravagance has little to do with actual human experience, and that, after all, was the point Gilbert sought to make about the drama of his time.

A gentleman of property, Cheviot Hill, derailed on the border of Scotland, makes instant love to any woman he meets: 'She is my whole life, my whole soul and body, my Past, my Present, and my To Come' (I, p. 143). When Angus finds that his darling Meg 'is loved by anither', that discovery 'seems to drive a' the bluid back into [his] hairt'. Obeying the dictates of romance, he knows she is far too good for a lad like himself; he would make any sacrifice for her sake, though he does balk at Cheviot's offer of financial recompense. 'The gold is na coined that can set us twain asunder' until his soul's treasure insists that 'a poor little mousie' could hardly compete with 'twa pound' and he briskly pockets the kind gentleman's offer 'wi' a sair and broken hairt' (I, pp. 145–6). Cheviot next encounters Belinda Treherne who, startled to find 'a complete stranger', nonetheless listens to his praise of her beauty and modesty. She has, alas, already pledged herself to Cheviot's friend, Belvawney, 'with a devotion that enthralls my very soul' (p. 148), except for one 'difficulty': Belvawney will lose his entire income on the day Cheviot marries. So Belinda appeals to Cheviot's finer feelings: 'You say that you love me? Then, for my sake, remain single for ever.' But the forces of destiny close in as the first Act ends. Belvawney, forced to wear dark glasses because of an eye infection, can no longer work his 'all but supernatural influence' over Cheviot's susceptibility, and the recklessly jealous Major McGillicuddy, whom Belinda had left at the altar, has followed her on the next train to Gretna and now enters with pistols, two friends, and a singularly large wedding cake. When Belinda cries out 'Save me!', Cheviot proclaims her 'my wife'; the lady confirms that and, as the curtain descends, 'MCGILLICUDDY *falls sobbing on seat*: BELVAWNEY *tears his hair in despair*; MAGGIE *sobs on* ANGUS's *shoulder*' (p. 150).

The complications of the next two Acts derive from this ludicrous tableau. If Mrs MacFarlane's garden lies on the Scottish side of the border, Belinda and Cheviot's words before witnesses have made them man and wife, and Belvawney will lose his income to Cheviot's Uncle Symperson who already has a way to his nephew's fortune in the person of Minnie, his daughter and yet another 'tree upon which the fruit of [Cheviot's] heart is growing'. The grief-torn Belinda arrives in London on Minnie's wedding day to munch a festive tart or two and regale her long-lost friend with the awful tale of marriage to a stranger she has not seen since:

MISS TRE: ... horror – distraction – chaos! I am rent with conflicting doubts! Perhaps he was already married; in that case, I am a bigamist. Maybe he is dead; in that case, I am a widow. Maybe he is alive; in that case, I am a wife. What am I? Am I single? Am I married? Am I a widow? Can I marry? Have I married? May I marry? Who am I? Where am I? What am I? – What is my name? What is my condition in life? If I am married, to whom am I married? If I am a widow, how came I to be a widow, and whose widow came I to be? Why am I his widow? What did he die of? Did he leave me anything? If anything, how much, and is it saddled with conditions? – Can I marry again without forfeiting it? Have I a mother-in-law? Have I a family of step-children, and if so, how many, and what are their ages, sexes, sizes, names and dispositions? These are questions that rack me night and day, and until they are settled, peace and I are not on terms!
MINNIE: Poor dear thing!
MISS TRE: But enough of my selfish sorrows. (*Goes up to table and takes a tart.* MINNIE *is annoyed at this.*) Tell me about the noble boy who is about to make you his. Has he any dross?   (II, pp. 152–3)

This sequence typifies the way the characters mouth the rhetoric and sentiment of romance yet remain grounded in self-serving calculation. In this Palace of Lies, the Victorian theatre, there can be no true feeling, so Gilbert moves his mindless puppets from one conventional situation to another. Were they actually motivated by the greed and vanity they often show, their tangled rivalries could not possibly end in universal happiness; but, given the impossibilities of the stage as he saw it, Gilbert deliberately imposes a final tableau in which all the characters, Mrs MacFarlane included, pair off in blissful disregard for either the mercenary attitudes or the romantic rapture they have proclaimed throughout the play. Divorced from those conventions which gave the play its wit and delicacy, *Engaged* now seems barren and over extended, despite some outrageously funny moments, but it still retains an historic importance in that it gave Oscar Wilde a stand-point and several major incidents for *The Importance of Being Earnest* in which the characters *are* driven by greed and rapture while maintaining a decorous or carefree façade.[22]

There is, however, one sequence in *Engaged* where the theatrical burlesque hits out also at a treasured illusion of Victorian life. On and off stage, the relationship between father and daughter epitomized all that was purest between the sexes. In Gilbert's parody, Symperson girds himself, with suitable pathos, to endure the nuptial sacrifice of his 'little lamb': 'Well, well, it's for her good. I must try and bear it – I must try and bear it' (II, p. 150). But, as Minnie, his 'little dickey-bird', explains, since 'dear old papa comes into £1,000 a year by it, I hope he won't allow it to distress him too much'. And dear papa will find added consolation in brandy, billiards, and betting which, he says, are 'simple pleasures [that] would certainly tend to smooth [a] poor old father's declining years'. Having danced past those cardinal sins with Dickensian playfulness,[23] his little 'wren' accepts the fact that she 'has not done badly either'. Cheviot 'is the very soul of honour . . . fine, noble, manly, spirited', but he is 'very, oh very, *very* stingy', and so Minnie has her own artless way of persuading him to provide her with an eventual settlement:

Papa, dear, Cheviot is an all but perfect character, the very type of knightly chivalry; but he *has* faults, and among other things he's one of the worst tempered men I ever met in all my little life. Poor, simple, little Minnie thought the matter over very carefully in her silly childish way, and she came to the conclusion, in her foolish little noddle, that, on the whole, perhaps she could work it better after marriage, than before. (pp. 150–1)

Continuing the game when alone with Cheviot, she coos with pleasure at the delightful economies he envisions for his child bride:

You shall be the clever little jobbing tailor, and I'll be the particular customer who brings his own materials to be made up . . . Then there's another little fireside game which is great fun. We each take a bit of paper and a pencil and try who can jot down the nicest dinner for ninepence, and the next day we have it.

(p. 156)

But, as for all the women in the play (if we could take them seriously for more than a moment), 'business is business', and when it appears that Cheviot has lost his fortune, Minnie's reaction is wickedly up-to-date:

Dear papa, . . . unless your tom-tit is very much mistaken, the Indestructible [Bank] was not registered under the Joint-Stock Companies Act of Sixty-two, and in that case the shareholders are jointly and severally liable to the whole extent of their available capital. Poor little Minnie don't pretend to have a business head; but she's not *quite* such a little donkey as *that*, dear papa.

(III, p. 165)

The one play of Gilbert's that ought to be revived – *Foggerty's Fairy* – opened at the Criterion Theatre in December 1881. At that time, the overwhelming success of his collaboration with Arthur Sullivan, from *Trial by Jury* (1875) to *Patience* (April 1881), must have made his 'Fairy Extravaganza' seem comparatively slight. Yet in this spirited domestic farce, Gilbert blends the supernatural and the satirical into a harmony he never quite achieved elsewhere. Confident of his own craftsmanship[24] and less nervous of giving offence, he abandons the protective mask of fantasy or sentiment and aims straight at the rapacity and dishonest pretensions of middle-class life. The plot moves rapidly, exploding into frenzy by the end of the first Act when Freddy Foggerty's past catches up with him, and the characters are sufficiently caricatured so that 'nothing what ever . . . could shock the sensibilities of the most fastidious'.[25] But the message beneath this glittering comedy remains clear: the men's sole passion is themselves and the women are either foolish idealists or so down-to-earth that marriage becomes a matter of business.

These unromantic notions come into immediate focus as the curtain rises on a drawing-room full of lugubrious wedding guests, all wearing favours and all sighing in gloomy unison. Uncle Fogle speaks for everyone when he tells Mr Talbot, a Wholesale Cheesemonger, that he 'can't help thinking, that, with her attractions, Jenny might have looked a little higher. You understand, I don't *say* it – I confine myself to *thinking* it' (I, p. 21). Talbot has done more than think those

119

thoughts, but his daughter 'has, somehow, got a ridiculous idea into her head that she could never love any man who had ever loved before, [and] . . . has found this monstrosity in Foggerty' (p. 22). That Jenny's ideal is so evidently 'ridiculous' and the thought of a man's purity, wild oats aside, so amusingly monstrous demonstrates the audiences' increased sophistication, and Gilbert feels no need to exaggerate other facets of Jenny's character to ensure the comic point. She seems, in fact, supremely ordinary when she enters in tears because her wedding-dress has not yet arrived from the fitter's and the bridesmaids, fluttering around her in sympathy, do not share her improbable dream, though 'it's possible, dear, of course' (p. 23). Actually, the Cheesemonger's acquaintances include no such Galahad. Jenny's first attachment to 'poor, broken-hearted Walkinshaw' foundered on the discovery that he was engaged already, and though Foggerty still passes as love's paragon, his behaviour, when alone with Walkinshaw, reveals a complacent rogue. Not that Talbot would mind, since ethics matter less than money. But, faced with his daughter's impracticality, he urges those guests who 'can't bear up . . . [to] shed some tears in the garden'; the rest should remember 'this is really and truly a festive occasion' and keep up appearances. '*All smile grimly*' (p. 22).

Into this matter-of-fact world steps the Fairy Rebecca, a somewhat self-conscious creature in an age of 'frockcoats and trousers' (p. 29). Proud of her faded powers, she enters to slow music as a wall opens and she '*is discovered standing in front of a revolving star*', an effect Foggerty puts down to 'a confounded German band outside, with the clarionet out of tune, as usual' (p. 28). Gilbert then emphasizes these colliding realities through Foggerty's embarrassment over the thought that, in his most private moments, he has been watched over by a female guardian. To those same ends, Gilbert also reduces the fairy's magic to everyday mechanics by making her a flustered chorine ('I've got to dance second in a ballet in a fairy glen in half an hour') who gaily explains how she manages to 'hover' over her mortal charge and is not quite sure where to find the trap-door that will take her back behind the wall:

Where's my vampire? (*Looking around.*) Oh! – I see
– thank you.
(*Placing herself opposite Vampire.*) All right. Go!
(*Vampire opens. She steps into it, it closes, and
she disappears. Hurried music.*)   (p. 32)

The illusions of the Victorian stage, when exposed like this as mechanical trickery, become a metaphor which undercuts the characters' own dreams of moneyed respectability, impossible purity, or romantic magic. Their pretensions crumble away entirely at the arrival of Delia Spiff, a downright harpy from Down Under.[26] In Melbourne, she had once seemed attractive to Foggerty: 'absolutely rolling in bank notes and sound securities . . . What was I to do?' (p. 27). But even those charms dimmed rapidly; Freddy sped to England, and his terror upon hearing that a ship has arrived in Liverpool with Spiff aboard leads to Rebecca's offer of protection since his engagement to the ridiculous harridan has long been 'a standing joke up in Fairyland' (p. 30). Confident he can get Jenny to the church before his philandering becomes public, Freddy declines the fairy's aid, and the wedding-party is just about to leave when Aunt Spiff's entrance stops the proceedings with evidence of a prior engagement, in 'black and white' (p. 34). Unlike the others, Delia has no illusions. In fact she is eager to take Jenny's place at the altar though she knows Foggerty is a mere fortune hunter, and so, seizing her bargain by the collar, she bids him 'Come to joy!' To her that makes 'common sense' because, like Talbot, she too is 'in trade':

> Mine's charms. It's a small business. There ain't many of them, and what there ain't much to speak of. The stock's damaged, isn't it? . . . Not the sort of goods that one can get off one's hands every day in the week?
> TALBOT: Oh, I don't say that. I can quite understand, for instance, that a snug, elderly gentleman, with a comfortable independence, would –
> MISS SPIFF (*abruptly*): Will *you* have me?
> TALBOT (*taken aback*): God bless me, no!
> MISS SPIFF: Of course you wouldn't, and you're right. *I* wouldn't if I was you. Well, I've had a bid from that ridiculous young man. I knocked myself down to him and he fled.   (pp. 35–6)

And there Freddy would have floundered had he not remembered Rebecca's fairy potion which, when swallowed, will ensure 'that my acquaintance with Miss Spiff, and all its consequences, may henceforward be blotted out of my existence!' (p. 37).

Magic remedies pop up constantly in Gilbert's scripts,[27] and in his mature work they provide the means of contrast between a romantic simplicity and the less attractive realities of a complex, unmagical world. Rebecca has already warned Freddy that to blot out the past might not be as simple as it appears and, as she stands over her stunned and prostrate charge at the beginning of Act Two, she predicts 'he won't know whether he's on his head or his heels' after he wakes to the potion's consequences. But Gilbert's satire also depends on Foggerty's modern character so that, in all the confusion of his new surroundings and circumstances, Freddy continues to cheat and lie his way to success. However, since he knows nothing about his altered life, his frantic urge to survive at all costs leads to still greater confusion. Finding himself in a 'handsomely furnished back draw-ing-room in Harley Street', he presumes he has married Jenny and is mildly annoyed that he might now have 'got tired of her' without having experienced their earlier bliss; indeed, a letter in his pocket seems to confirm 'the fact that I've been going it' (p. 40). When friends repeatedly refer to 'this day of all others', he wonders 'if it's a boy or a girl! It would be ridiculous to ask' (p. 41) but, after that minor tangle, he discovers they mean Jenny's wedding day and, he assumes, his own. It is therefore with some consternation that he receives a note from a lady who calls him 'her dearest friend' and, when Malvina de Vere arrives to press her claim, he extemporizes madly, as he later does with Jenny and Walkinshaw (who turns out to be the intended bridegroom), until he can twist and turn no longer. Leaping from the balcony window, he races through the London streets with Malvina in furious pursuit.

In creating this 'Romantic Old Lady', Gilbert underscores the difference between the theatre's false poses and the motives that debase actual life. Outwardly, Malvina behaves like a tragedy-queen whose generalized histrionics make her a figure of fun, even in the present century. Only Jenny can enter that world, responding to Malvina's turgid prose and doom-laden gestures with the sugared sentiment of a bad novelette:

JENNY: Nay, but I'll not consign you to the mercies of the inhospitable street. This is *my* house, or shortly will be so; pray rest you here, and when the solemn ceremony is over, we pray you join our merry-making, and in wild delirium of the breakfast forget the harrowing trouble at your heart.
MISS DE V: I thank you, maiden, for your sympathy. I'll not refuse the shelter that you proffer.
JENNY: You'll find my boudoir on the two-pair-back. So, for the nonce, farewell! May justice pour her balm upon your heart!   (II, p. 46)

Jenny, too, has 'loved, but vainly' and, in pledging herself to Walkinshaw, she remains true to type: 'For you, my Theodore, I have no love, nor have I ever told you that I had; but I esteem you, Theodore, I respect you' (p. 46). Yet despite her borrowed phrasing, Jenny is as candid as Aunt Spiff, whereas Malvina acts the genteel

heroine while relying on men's 'heartless and systematic treachery' so
that she can sue the cads for breach of promise:

Eighteen times I offered up my bleeding heart a sacrifice at Themis' sympathetic
shrine. Eighteen times did I lay bare its holiest workings, and call on all to come
and gaze upon its palpitating pulp. And in each case I recovered substantial
damages. (p. 45)

At the beginning of Act Three, Freddy returns from his epic flight:
'. . . Hackney, Old Ford, Bow, Whitechapel, London Bridge,
Southwark. At Southwark my horse fainted; so did Malvina's. I
jumped out – got another cab. So did Malvina. Off again' (p. 58).
Malvina is not far behind. As the two recover their breath they drop
their pretences and, in one of the play's funniest episodes, present a
hard-headed version of life in the eighties.[28] The lady puts the
question direct, 'Going to marry me?', and the gentleman refuses.
The lady then delivers 'a writ of summons', and the two settle down to
the business of damages: 'it would be altogether more delicate if we
could arrive at an estimate by a friendly calculation' (p. 60). But as he
haggles for a suitable arrangement, Foggerty realizes that Jenny
would not marry him anyway, since he has all too evidently 'loved'
before. So he decides to take the 'Splendid Ruin' and save himself 'six
hundred pounds and costs' if she will only promise to explain 'who I
am, what I am, where I am, and who and what everybody else is – and,
in short, enable me to hold my position before the world without
making an infernal fool of myself' (p. 62). With these questions,
Gilbert forces the more perceptive of his audience to look beyond the
transparent reality of Freddy or Malvina and to judge the true nature
of 'everybody else' in the seemingly respectable world outside. For
the frenzied action of the play suggests that only a shared code of
manners, agreed upon by those in the know, disguises a person's
actual folly. Freddy has no such protection, and the Talbots think
him mad when, struggling to fit in with their lives, he invents an
extraordinary story, out of the clichés of melodrama, about having
helped murder Walkinshaw's Aunt Sarah. But Walkinshaw has no
aunt – 'some mistake somewhere' – and Malvina, who has not had
time to explain the past, recoils in horror from 'a murderer and a
madman! And woe is me, it is to such men as these that I have handed
over my unsuspecting heart!' (p. 70).

Neither Walkinshaw nor Foggerty is a murderer or a madman, and
Malvina's heart, if she has one at all, is hardly 'unsuspecting'. The
three are more ordinary and shabby than that. Aunt Spiff's 'common

sense' may achieve more than their mannered trickery or Jenny's naïveté, but it too is essentially self-serving and, to someone like Talbot (faced with his daughter's bad match), sensible behaviour often means respectable show. The sensible way the whole farce ends contains a similar ambiguity. With mayhem all around him, Freddy summons the Fairy Rebecca who is 'extremely busy', annoyed at the interruption, and unwilling to help. But just as she exits, this time through a floor-trap, Freddy delivers his logical coup:

> ... if I had never known Spiff I should never have got into a difficulty on account of Spiff, and if I had never got into that difficulty I should never have applied to you to get me out of it, and if I had never applied to you to get me out of it you would never have given me that infernal draught, which has been the cause of all the miseries with which I'm threatened. (p. 71)

Rebecca sees the truth of that and, with a wave of her wand, the scene changes back to the morning of Act One. Jenny and her bridesmaids enter, and Foggerty can honestly (?) say he has 'never, never loved before!' Malvina embraces Walkinshaw and, though we know the latter is 'not a very nice man' (p. 57) who has thought of poisoning the wedding breakfast (p. 28), the lady has 'an excellent constitution' (p. 73). So all the characters pair off and '*move towards entrance, laughing heartily*'. Whereupon Gilbert reveals the hollowness behind this sensibly respectable façade as the '*Scene opens at back*' and a troupe of fairies, also laughing gaily, fills the stage. While they wave their wands, Rebecca mounts a stool to their rear, and laughs – perhaps in sympathy with the humans' festivity, perhaps in mockery at their sham, or even perhaps at the pretensions of the audience. '*Red fire. Curtain.*'

However gentle this fairy laughter might be, the gaiety of the wedding guests resembles the joy they obediently assumed when Talbot insisted, at the play's outset, that 'this is really and truly a festive occasion'. The traditional family picture has thus been emptied of meaning or turned against itself in a way that would not have been tolerated in the mid seventies when Gilbert himself drew back from the brink in *Sweethearts* and Byron's *Our Boys* took wing 'through the cloudless sky'. That change becomes still more evident in the nineties, and Gilbert's own critique moves beyond domestic values to poke fun at those of the very home of Empire.

Utopia, Limited, the Savoy Opera of 1893, contains another of Gilbert's gorgons, but Lady Sophy, governess to the daughters of King Paramount, is not outlandish in either her appearance or opinions. Prim rectitude no longer needs to be distorted to seem ludicrous. When she embarks on her first recitative, the grave demeanour of this 'English lady of mature years' is 'extreme' but recognizably true to life as she raises her lecturer's pointer and requests her royal pupils to show how well they have learned the 'course of maiden courtship'.[29] Theirs is not simply a lesson in captivating hypocrisy; the realities of courtship, formerly unspoken, are now accepted facts which must be confronted as nicely and unsentimentally as possible despite the understandable curiosity a man's natural trickery provokes:

> As he gazes,
> Hat he raises,
> Enters into conversation.
> Makes excuses –
> This produces
> Interesting agitation.
> He, with daring,
> Undespairing,
> Gives his card – his rank discloses –
> Little heeding
> This proceeding,
> They turn up their little noses. (pp. 415–16)

Social position and money in the bank do offer more security than a man's smiles but, until she ascertains his firm intentions, a lady demurely demurs and, since 'English girls of well-bred notions, / Shun all unrehearsed emotions', she had better practise in the mirror at home. A woman's knowing participation in love's combat no longer makes her calculatingly heartless or deceptive – at least, no more than her opponent's does; in fact, the ultimate comedy derives from the similarity between the sexes. Should two modern ladies find themselves rivals for the same man (who of course will happily accept either), they settle the matter in sportsmanly English fashion:

> Do they quarrel for his dross?
> Not a bit of it – they toss!

So women are finally seen to be human beings, with passions, faults, and brains. As governess, Lady Sophy is not unattractive, but her insistence on absolute 'Respectability' is: 'there is not a European Monarch who has not implored me, with tears in his eyes, to quit his kingdom, and take my fatal charms elsewhere' (p. 420). Although she can not see the irony of her 'fatal' effect on men, she does know that to expect them to live blameless lives is naively unrealistic yet, comically, she still treasures that adolescent dream:

> For spotless monarchs I became
>> An advertiser:
> But all in vain I searched each land,
> So, kingless, to my native strand
> Returned, a little older, and
>> a good deal wiser!
> I learnt that spotless King and Prince
> Have disappeared some ages since –
> Even Paramount's angelic grace,
>> Ah, me!
> Is but a mask on Nature's face! (p. 450)

In consequence, she shuns the King and moulds his daughters into what she (and Mrs Linton before her) considers 'that blameless type of perfect womanhood' (p. 419) and so (according to the nineties) creates two 'clockwork toys' (p. 414). The old idea of 'maidenly perfection' has become a mechanical pose, as one-dimensionally static as a snap-shot:

KALYBA: To diagnose
  Our modest pose
  The Kodaks do their best:
NEKAYA: If evidence you would possess
  Of what is maiden bashfulness,
  You only need a button press –
KALYBA: And *we* do all the rest. (p. 415)

The princesses must therefore learn to accept their own humanity and, despite 'the inestimable privilege of being educated by a most refined and easily-shocked English lady, on the very strictest English principles', must understand that no English girl could be 'so ridiculously demure':

She is frank, open-hearted, and fearless, and never shows in so favourable a light as when she gives her own blameless impulses full play! (p. 447)

This impulsive freedom is not without its own comedy, but it seems more wholesome than press-the-button primness especially when tempered with intelligence, as it is in the King's eldest daughter, Princess Zara. She has had a modern education, at Girton, and when she returns, the Utopians beg her to explain calculus and to 'teach us, please, / To speak with ease / All languages, / Alive and dead' (p. 422). But Zara is no blue-stocking: her heart already belongs to Captain Fitzbattleaxe 'who has taken, oh! such care of me during the voyage' (p. 423); she also adores fashionable clothes. Nor is she a blushing rose: scandalous articles in the *Palace Peeper* offend her, but only because of their 'ungrammatical twaddle' and their exaggerated cartoons of her father's nose. Yet the men who love her need to worship. The captain wants to express his devotion 'with all the passionate enthusiasm of [his] nature', until Zara reminds him that 'true love does not indulge in declamation' (p. 438). Scaphio, one of two 'Wise Men' who manipulate the King, has spent sixty-six years waiting for 'an ideal – a semi-transparent Being – filled with an inorganic pink jelly' (p. 411). When he sets eyes on Zara, the aging fool is instantly convulsed by that 'extraordinarily – miraculously lovely . . . goddess' (p. 426). Phantis, his colleague, has also been 'palsied with love for this girl' but, to quell the other's inconvenient ardour, now insists that Zara, though 'attractive', is like any other girl: 'perfectly opaque'. The audience would agree with him.

A gentle disillusion colours the entire opera. The old ideals have grown so ridiculously threadbare that Gilbert does not have to wrench them away in order to expose the fact that 'properly considered, everything has its humorous side' (p. 417). King Paramount, whose words those are, laughs at himself and, as author of the *Palace Peeper*, invites others to do the same. His first solo establishes that mood by describing life's 'farce', from birth (when one's parents' 'Every symptom tends to show / You're decidedly *de trop*') to romantic youth and soured old-age:

> Ho! ho! ho! ho! ho! ho! ho! ho!
> Daily driven
>   (Wife as drover)
> Ill you've thriven –
>   Ne'er in clover:
> Lastly, when
> Three-score and ten
> (And not till then),
>   The joke is over!
> Ho! ho! ho! ho! ho! ho! ho! ho!
> Then – and then
>   The joke is over!   (p. 419)

But the King and his courtiers never laugh at England. Gilbert does – by making Englishness the Utopians' ideal – and his laughter is openly satirical. Whereas in *The Mikado*, for example, the demure behaviour of the three little maids from school could be thought quaintly Japanese,[30] the island of Utopia offers no such deflecting surface: the two 'toy' princesses are funny because they emulate an Englishness which has itself become amusingly old fashioned.

As for England's social and political institutions, they too have their 'humorous side' for those who, after fifty-five years of Victoria's rule, have the confidence to admit (slight) imperfection. Zara and the six experts she brings back with her from 'the greatest, the most powerful, the wisest country in the world' (p. 408) have plans to turn her south-sea 'lazyland' into an even more perfect Utopia. Nothing could improve Britain's army before whom 'Europe trembles', or her steamships, or her lawyers who can 'show / That "yes" is but another and a neater form of "no"' (p. 431). The Utopians would also do well to create a Lord Chamberlain to 'cleanse' the royal court or 'purify the Stage' and County Councillors to 'sanitate' each home and 'keep meanwhile a modest eye / On wicked music halls' (p. 432). But one British glory could be refined upon. By the terms of the Joint Stock Company's Act, 'seven men form an Association', declare their capital ('To what extent they mean to pay their debts'), and, when the company fails, cannot be required to pay more than their declared liability. The King sees this as a way to avoid being answerable to his Wise Men's criticisms and so declares his island-realm Utopia, Limited:

> . . . at first sight it strikes us as dishonest,
> But if it's good enough for virtuous England –
> The first commercial country in the world –
> It's good enough for us. (p. 435)

Later he finds other ways to improve the English model: abolish divorce, ensure no lady is presented at Court 'who wouldn't be accepted by the lower-middle classes', award peerages for intellectual merit only (pp. 440–1).

Eventually, though, the islanders come to loathe Zara's six advisors, the Flowers of Progress, because life is now too perfect. Having learned 'the principal causes that have tended to make England the powerful, happy, and blameless country which the consensus of European civilization has declared it to be' (p. 430), the Utopians, each one a limited company, can evade their creditors: 'There is not a christened baby . . . who has not already issued his little Prospectus' (p. 438). But their remodelled Army and Navy have so subdued the Pacific that 'War's impossible'; new sanitary regulations have wiped out disease (and doctors), and the legal system has proved so efficient that 'lawyers starve, and all the jails are let / As model lodgings for the working-classes' (p. 452). The islanders have neglected that limiting and most English of institutions, party politics:

> ZARA: . . . Introduce that great and glorious element – at once the bulwark and foundation of England's greatness – and all will be well! No political measures will endure, because one Party will assuredly undo all that the other party has done . . . Then there will be sickness in plenty, endless lawsuits, crowded jails, interminable confusion in the Army and Navy, and, in short, general and unexampled prosperity!

Gilbert's comedy, however direct and critical, strengthens the values it seems to attack. Great Britain ('to which some add – but others do not – Ireland') may not be Elysium. But, after years of peace and progress, audiences could safely laugh at their own reassuringly English foibles, admit that their nation's triumph might be somewhat bullying, and that the soldiers of Empire – 'In a tunic tight / And a helmet hot / And a breastplate bright' (p. 423) – might not all be 'young Greek god[s]' or selfless and unflinching. How much farther this critique was meant to go is debatable, but as the opera ends, with a paean to England's perfect splendour, Gilbert, with uncanny prescience, hints at the over-confidence which soon would cloud that brightness:

> The proudest nations kneel at her command;
>   She terrifies all foreign-born rapscallions;
> And holds the peace of Europe in her hand
>   With half a score invincible battalions!
> Such, at least, is the tale
>   Which is borne on the gale,
> From the island which dwells in the sea.
>   Let us hope, for her sake,
> That she makes no mistake –
>   That she's all she professes to be!   (p. 453)

With the same ambiguous self-congratulation, audiences could now look kindly on the New English Girl. A trifle hearty (at 'eleven stone two, / And five foot ten in her dancing shoe') and boisterously independent (as she bicycled from Girton), she was infinitely brighter and healthier, in body and mind, than the merry but nervous 'dickey bird' who once illumined home and hearth:

> With a ten mile spin she stretches her limbs,
> She golfs, she punts, she rows, she swims –
> She plays, she sings, she dances, too,
> From ten or eleven till all is blue!

At ball or drum, till small hours come,
  (Chaperon's fan conceals her yawning)
She'll waltz away like a teetotum,
  And never go home till daylight's dawning.
Lawn-tennis may share her favours fair –
  Her eyes a-dance and her cheeks a-glowing –
Down comes her hair, but what does she care?
  It's all her own and it's worth the showing!
    Go search the world and search the sea,
    Then come you home and sing with me
    There's no such gold and no such pearl
    As a bright and beautiful English girl!   (p. 448)

CHAPTER 5

Terrible leanings towards
respectability

SIR RICHARD: Mrs Quesnel, what was the exact nature of Sue's acquaintance
with Lucien?
INEZ: What does it matter? You needn't trouble about Sue. We women know
the value of appearances. We are awful cowards, and have terrible leanings
towards respectability. Sue won't shatter Mr Harabin's family gods on his
family hearth, or burst up Mr Harabin's family boiler with any new-fangled
explosive. And as long as Mr Harabin's family boiler remains intact, why
should you meddle with Sue? I must go and dress. My cloak, please.

Henry Arthur Jones, *The Case of Rebellious Susan* (1894)

Gilbert's career, from the sixties to the nineties, maps out a journey
from silly puns and coy sentiment to genuine wit and a relatively
outspoken critique of the times. Admittedly, the realists tired of his
topsy-turvy fantasy or, on occasion, joined the squeamish in
condemning his characteristic brand of humour: 'Sometimes . . . it is
unpleasant to the point of repulsiveness.'[1] But particularly at the
Savoy, where his satire was provokingly topical yet generalized and
made still more palatable by Sullivan's music and his own impeccable
stage pictures, even a well-bred Miss of fifteen or so, whose
sensibilities had always to be soothed (much to Gilbert's annoyance),[2]
even that little maid might learn a lesson or two.

That the theatre had begun to interest the well-bred of all ages was
due in no small measure to those colourful extravaganzas. In *English
Dramatists of To-day* (1882), William Archer had detected the
faintest stirrings of a new sophistication. Four years later, in his essay
'Are We Advancing?', he could point to the fact that 'almost without
exception the serious magazines take frequent cognizance of the acted
drama'; a first night at Irving's Lyceum 'has grown into a solemn
function . . . [and] . . . two or three other theatres may almost be said to
rival the home of the poetic drama in the matter of social vogue'; the
vulgarities of French *opéra-bouffe* have lost their appeal 'owing to

powerful native competition, . . . those most popular entertainments of the day, the Gilbert–Sullivan operettas':

The victory of Gilbertian extravaganza . . . is the victory of literary and musical grace and humour over rampant vulgarity and meretricious jingle . . .; but the decline of burlesque is still unexplained. I am not optimist enough to attribute it altogether to an improvement in popular taste, but neither do I think it reasonable to deny that it is symptomatic of a certain reaction against mere music-hall imbecility.[3]

It may at first seem strange that Archer could see 'the prosperity of modern melodrama' as further evidence of improving taste. For the spectacular banalities of Robert Buchanan and Augustus Harris he had nothing but contempt: '*A Sailor and his Lass* . . . may be shortly described as the worst of recent Drury Lane melodramas, and to have produced the worst of that sublime series is certainly a distinction.' But in *The Silver King* (1882), and the work of Henry Arthur Jones, he perceived something distinctively 'modern', and the play's popularity convinced him that, in melodrama too, 'the public is beginning to demand more and more imperatively that the dramatist shall be, not indeed a moralist (that may come later on), but an observer, and shall give in his work, not yet a judgment or an ideal, but a painting'.[4]

The Victorian stage had always been pictorial, and melodrama's images in particular were designed to involve the spectator and lift him into a world of high emotion and simplified morality. One suspects that *The Silver King*, as pictured at the Princess's Theatre, offered most of the audiences a thrilling *escape* from the ordinary:

The position of Wilfred Denver, recovered from his drunken stupor, and face to face with a dead body in a lonely room . . . It matters not that the scene is in Hatton Garden, or that the actors occupied in this dire tragedy of existence have returned tipsy from the Derby or wear gauze veils over their battered hats; seldom before had such a sermon been preached against the curse of drunkenness and the mad frenzy of youth.[5]

But to Archer it did matter that the play began in the skittle alley of the Wheatsheaf and that the curtain rose on a group at the bar discovered in mid-conversation about the race at Epsom: '. . . neck and neck the three of 'em till just as they were turning the corner drawing in home . . .'[6] Here was no attention-seeking tableau that brought to life, in breath-taking accuracy, the panorama of Frith's *Derby Day* but a natural picture from the courtyards of London, and the dialogue was no transpontine bombast but recognizably kin to the accents of the streets. When Wilfred Denver stumbled in at the gate, dead drunk (not 'tipsy') and defiant at losing all on the Derby, here was a 'painting' that seemed truly lifelike, just as Bulwer's gambling salon or Tom Robertson's Owl's Roost had seemed at other dawnings of a new drama.

In its black and white morality, *The Silver King* preserves stock formulae, but its style is more subdued than the ravings at Drury Lane or the Adelphi, and its plot – though superconsciously theatrical – seems less ridiculously contrived. Geoffrey Ware comes up to the bar to learn that Bilcher, the bookie, has 'cleaned [Denver] out' and to inform the audience, in melodrama's annunciatory way, of his own rivalry: 'Ruined! Now, Nellie Hathaway, I think I'll show you that you made a slight mistake when you threw me over and married Wilfred Denver.' Then Jaikes, an old and faithful servant, arrives to create sympathy for the wastrel hero: 'anybody might happen to get a bit fresh on Derby Day, you know', and the Denvers, from the old Squire down to his grandson, have always been roisterers; 'Master Will's a chip of the old block. He'll make a man yet.' Patently false as a portrait of natural behaviour, when Denver welcomes ruin yet laments what must happen to his angelic wife and 'innocent children', this first scene – with its petty criminals, inept detective, cockney bragster, and coolly immaculate villain ('The Spider') – does convey the dramatist's observation of life's surface. So does the rest of the play, despite the tear-jerking mechanics of faithful Nellie and her starving children who survive by the good graces of the selfless Jaikes until Denver returns, white-haired and penitent, to redeem his family with the wealth he has gained from America's silver-mines. The most sensational episode does not depend on wondrous stage machinery[7] but on midnight horror, as Denver wakes from the chloroform administered by Ware's actual murderer to find the corpse of the rival he believes he must have killed. Denver's flight from that victim's staring eyes, though redolent of Bill Sikes and Duke Ferdinand (*The Duchess of Malfi*), leads him to people and places that are distinctively contemporary and English. Even the Spider's 'snug crib' is no back-alley warren but a luxuriously middle-class villa in suburban Bromley.

Jones's subsequent career shows how difficult it was for any serious dramatist to depict life's pictures objectively. On the one hand, he was unique amongst his fellow playwrights in that he was neither a published novelist or journalist nor an offspring of the theatre. If the way to a new beginning was to observe the ordinary, Jones had every opportunity to find it. Brought up on a farm in Buckinghamshire, he left school at twelve to work in his uncle's drapery shop in Ramsgate. Although he detested his uncle's rigidity and the shop itself, he could, in later years, see those trials as 'a great advantage. I was able to educate myself in my own way and at my own expense, by keeping up a constant and loving acquaintance with the English classics, and with some of the French and German masterpieces; by a close study of social and political economy; and by extensive foragings among the sciences.'[8] At eighteen he moved to London, away from the restrictive provincialism of his chapel-going uncle, and, for the first time in his life, visited a theatre. The experience filled him with new ambition: 'I used to hurry from the City almost every evening at six to see the same successful play for perhaps a dozen times, till I could take its mechanism to pieces.'[9] Play-making was a science which he could learn by analysing what worked on stage, by studying Shakespeare and the Elizabethans, by acting in amateur productions, and by devouring every play in Samuel French's catalogue. But play-making was also box-office, and when one of his scripts was finally presented at Exeter (after he had agreed to pay for half the dress-circle), he attracted the notice of Wilson Barrett, the actor-manager, who knew exactly what would 'go' with the public.[10] Such, then, were the designs to which life had to be shaped for the stage. The success of *The Silver King*, under Barrett's aegis, re-emphasized their efficacy. Yet even as Jones tried to break from those formulae, his own experience and personality naturally affected his vision of things. Self-educated, hard-working, eager to succeed as he toiled at his writing in whatever spare time he had as a commercial traveller, he was never completely free from his puritan upbringing.

Jones admitted to some of those distorting filters when he looked back, with much embarrassment, at his next play, *Breaking a Butterfly* (1884): 'When I came up to London sixteen years ago, to try for a place among English playwrights, a rough translation from the German version of [A] *Doll's House* was put into my hands, and I was told that if it could be turned into a sympathic play, a ready opening would be found for it . . . I knew nothing of Ibsen, but I knew a great deal of Robertson and H.J. Byron.'[11] He also knew melodrama, for he turned the plot into an intense clash between thwarted lover, heroic husband, and terrrified wife who, by the end of the play, has taken an equally heroic stand. What he could not see was the way his alterations were also dictated by his own middle-class sympathies.

Ibsen's Nora did not appear in London for another five years when she added to the furore over what Mr Punch was cheekily to call Ibsenity. Jones's simplified version presents an irresponsible child who has none of her counterpart's manipulative cunning. She is indeed a Robertsonian Miss, but Ibsen's plot requires a Mrs, so (to make such an irresponsible wife credible) Flora has been married four years (instead of eight) and has no children. Her husband treats her with kind patience and, unlike Torvald Helmer, never indulges her kittenish ways. When he finds out that Flora has forged her father's signature, he instantly protects her by confessing to have copied it himself: 'Now do your worst to me. You shall not touch a hair of her head!' (p. 62)[12] The motives behind this brave act (and monstrous travesty) are not entirely theatrical. Humphrey Goddard is deeply sincere, and Jones intends him to earn an audience's uncritical admiration:

My dear Flossie, did I not argue that with you last night, over and over again? You must let me judge what is best. I know you better than you know yourself. You have not strength to endure the excitement, the public disgrace, which would fall upon you if I allowed you to take the consequences. It would kill you – my poor, frail, little Flossie!   (III, p. 64)

Touched by her wise guardian's sacrifice, 'You are a thousand times too good for me' (p. 65), Flora becomes the woman she should have been on her wedding day. Four years' privation on a second clerk's salary, her husband's nearly fatal illness, her father's death have affected her not at all. But when she perceives Humphrey's broken heart, now that his reputation will be 'blackened before all men', Flossie acts as only a good wife can – her suicide will save him. A hurried note to clear Humphrey's name for his employer, a further message to her 'dear, noble husband', and then, with thoughts of death upon her, she muses over its effect upon her New Year's guests:

Ah! the party! They will come to-night to dance, and they will be so full of life and spirits, and I shall be dead, dead! Yes, what a surprise it will be for everybody when they come laughing up to the door in their ball clothes and ask for me, to find that I am dead! I can fancy how they will look, and what they will say! And I shall not care or trouble myself, but lie quite still. (*laughing hysterically*) Ha! I feel I am dead already. How strange it is. (*shutting her eyes*) So cold – no life, no feeling; but I am happy! Yes, I don't mind it. And they are all crying over me.
(p. 72)

The psychology grows even stranger during her last confrontation with the vengeful Mr Dunkley. Now fully a woman, she upbraids him with maternal fury ('you . . . are mad – mad to think I would let you lay so much as a little finger upon my darling') and hurls a final curse: 'You shall never have one moment's peace from this time forth. I will haunt you, and make your life a misery to you' (pp. 73–4).

Wearily operatic and infused with conventional and idealized piety about marriage, the play nevertheless has its genuine facets, not least in its obsessive concern for public reputation and in the Englishness of its secondary characters. Ibsen's Dr Rank, tainted by inherited disease, transmutes into Dan Birdseye, a hale and breezy Tommy Traddles whose devil-may-care attitude to his job in St Petersburg ('I didn't like the climate, and I didn't like the people') permits a xenophobic smile and a topical joke about newspapers which encourage 'Correspondents to give full rein to their fancy and imagination' (I, p. 14). A cheery foil to Humphrey's solid worth, rather than an ironic parallel to Flossie's unsteadiness, Dan reacts to Dunkley's importunity with a boyish 'By Jove, yes, I can kick the fellow downstairs' (II, p. 40). Agnes, Humphrey's widowed sister, is as 'wise and sad' as Flora is all 'gaiety and lightheartedness'. Modest and womanly, she agrees to 'repay' Dan (if he can recover the promissory note from Dunkley) by saying 'yes', at last. But before she becomes a mere device, Agnes has a certain individuality. Her conversation with her mother at the beginning of the play, despite its false notes, captures each lady's concern for the master of the house and their true affection for the unsatisfactory Flora:

MRS G: (*concerned, dropping her sewing*) My dear, you make me quite uncomfortable . . . I shall tell Humphrey what we have seen and what we suspect.
AGNES: But what *do* we suspect? Flora is giddy and thoughtless, but surely she is not wicked.
MRS G: I think not – I hope not.
AGNES: It seems such a shame to worry Humphrey with our suspicions – now, when at last he is happy and comfortable . . .
MRS G: I shall put Humphrey on his guard.
AGNES: I don't think he'll listen to you.
MRS G: He must do as he pleases. Forewarned – fore-armed. (pp. 6–7)

Mrs Goddard has least connection with the melodrama. Fussing over the jellies for the New Year's Party, anxious to reserve the good wine for 'the better people' instead of wasting it on the Jenningses, she shows what Jones could do when he painted from life rather than from novels or playbooks.

But although he was just beginning to be accepted as a dramatist, Jones was already thirty-three, and his view of life had been coloured

by writers like Arnold, Ruskin, and Morris as well as by the
vocabulary of the theatre and the circumstances of his past. Inspired
by Arnold's challenge to 'organize' the drama, he embarked on a life-
long crusade for an art that would 'strictly follow Nature' and so 'be
put in connection with all that is vital and preservative and
honourable in English life'.[13] His quest for vitality set him against
theatrical trumpery:

A dramatist will never draw characters of vital force and lastingness except they
belong to the actual life that he has known and studied and loved – his own
village, his own city, his own country. Without this knowledge of life and men,
. . . his characters will never be more than bloodless phantoms of his fancy, or at
best stage-puppets, reeking of the theatre.[14]

But his conviction that Nature was 'preservative and honourable' put
him at odds with Archer's commonplace realism:

As Ruskin says: 'You can paint a cat or a fiddle so that it may be mistaken for real
life, but you cannot paint the Alps in such a manner.' So it is with the human
passions . . .
    And unless it is touched with this sense of eternity, wrapped round with the
splendour of heroism, and imbedded in what is primary and of everlasting
import, the mere reproduction on the stage of the commonplace details of
everyday life must always be barren, worthless, and evanescent. Because a thing
has happened in real, everyday life, is no reason for putting it on the stage.
Humdrum is one of the infinities. Nothing is so untrue and so unreal as
ultra-realism.[15]

And so he restored Ibsen's Torvald Helmer to Victorian standards
and proclaimed, in all his plays, the importance of being honourable.
    Yet Jones knew, from experience, how commonplace souls could
easily masquerade as honourable men in a society that placed high
value on outward appearances. Remembering his Uncle Thomas,
draper and deacon of the baptist chapel, he determined to portray 'the
curious and grotesque inconsistencies of religious profession and
conduct' in *Saints and Sinners* (1884).[16] On the first night, the play
was hissed by sections of the audience who objected to the way the
characters quoted (and misquoted) the Bible. A debate ensued, in
letters to the newspapers, as to whether religion ought to be discussed
on stage, and Jones publicly defended the right of a dramatist to
choose any aspect of daily life for his subject:

so eager have we been to exclude everything that might be offensive or tedious or
incomprehensible to any possible spectator, that by a process of continual
exhaustion and humble deference to everybody's prejudices we have banished

from the stage all treatment of grave subjects but what is commonplace and cursory and conventional. The course of the drama has been diverted and hopelessly cut off from the main current of modern intellectual life.[17]

In that context, the play was indeed revolutionary; assisted by controversy, it enjoyed a lengthy run.

Its first Act captures the rhythms of a provincial community with such assurance that the action almost completely disguises the playwright's shaping hand. Jones broke more new ground by presenting tradespeople and their servants as individuals in their own right:

Ordinarily the man of business is simply a peg to hang jokes upon. He invariably drops his H's and puts in superfluous aspirates. He is everlastingly making blunders upon his introduction into what passes upon the stage for *polite* society. And these blunders are so dwelt upon and exaggerated that any pit or gallery spectator can instantly detect them and pride himself upon his superior breeding ... And when the good-hearted tradesman makes these blunders, the aristocratic people on the stage at once call attention to them, and correct them with an utter absence not merely of the forms but of the spirit of good breeding. And this type of business-man has made the fortune of many modern comedies.[18]

Each detail in Act One shows how heavily money weighs on the characters' minds: the chapel's diminishing pew-rents, the Minister's generosity, the disapproval of his housekeeper, 'working off my fingers to keep us all decent on less than eighty pounds a year' (I, p. 2). It is her thrift that Lot Burden, 'a plain common little fellow', most admires, and that reality, added to the lady's brusque responses, motivates and enlivens the comedy of his sighs and loving glances: neither character is patronized. Their skirmish immediately establishes a competitive world in which one needs to use one's wits ('we ought to be as wise as serpents in this generation, Miss Lydia'), as does the next episode between Jacob Fletcher and one of the least respectable of his flock. Old Greenacre tries to ingratiate himself ('I'm a monument of grace, Muster Fletcher'), but the Minister cheerfully accepts him as 'a monument of gin and water' (p. 4). Unimpressed by the old soak's cringing bows, yet without the slightest sanctimony, Jacob tells his housekeeper to find the man some food: 'he's spent all his parish pay, . . . and we can't let him starve, can we?' Jacob is equally alert to the wiles of Samuel Hoggard, tanner and deacon of Bethel Chapel, but in their encounter the stakes are higher. Hoggard 'pays twenty pounds a year pew-rent' and thus pressures Jacob not to interfere with his plan to cheat his partner's widow of her share in the tannery. Each of these episodes impresses as a study of character; there is no striving for effect and little story-telling. Hoggard's gestures tell of his power and success; his phrasing is less frank until he finds the Minister unyielding and then abandons unctuous pleasantry. Jones has a thesis, but he allows the action to speak for itself. When Letty Fletcher urges her father to berate the deacon, the Minister has no tirade to give: 'My dear, he isn't worth it' (p. 13). Understatement vitalizes the entire Act.

After that extaordinary beginning, the rest of *Saints and Sinners* sinks back into the standard repertoire. Letty Fletcher must choose between George Kingsmill, a worthy farmer, and Captain Eustace Fanshawe, whose very name suggests unscrupulous and aristocratic trickery. Swept off to perdition, Letty is rescued by her father and, in ministering to the sick, redeems herself. And so, paradoxically, Jones sustains the Victorian fetish for respectability that he had set out to castigate.[19] Championing the freedom to bring contemporary life onto the stage, he was himself imprisoned by all that he considered permanent and valuable in Nature. Yet this was not simply reactionary conservatism but part of his mission to create a drama which would take its place with the other arts and save the nation. An article he wrote for *To-Day*, during the run of *Saints and Sinners*, sets out his artistic programme; its banner is an epigraph from Ruskin: 'The highest thing that art can do is to set before you the true image of the presence of a noble human being.'[20]

Jones begins by inviting his readers to share a view from his study window on to 'one of the prettiest and most old-fashioned of Buckinghamshire villages ... The whole scene is typical of the greater part of English life fifty years ago.' But, 'at our present rate of progress', such scenes will be rare in the years to come.

What can be more striking than the difference between the average Englishman of two generations ago . . . and the probable average Englishman of two generations to come, the typical Englishman we are menaced with, when railways and steam tram-cars shall have done their perfect work, and having provided us with means of going everywhere at a moment's notice, shall have left us no longer any place worth going to or stopping at? . . .

While the bulk of English lives are petty and suburban, so too must remain the bulk of modern English plays.   (pp. 149–51)

A dramatist might escape from that into 'some fairy world', but imaginative flight is at best 'a temporary way out of the difficulty'. Instead, he must turn to 'England and the nineteenth century' and 'resolutely' search for 'that secret aspect of beauty and those admonitions of faith' which lie hidden in 'almost every human life'.

The seduction of Letty Fletcher illustrates this battle for 'sanity and wholesomeness'[21] in an ugly, philistine society. In expressing her distaste for Steepleford, she is perhaps right to complain that everyone is 'so respectable' since the chief representative of that propriety, Deacon Hoggard, only pays lip-service to the old values: 'Lovely scenery, Rodimore Woods. I've a great eye for natural beauty myself. I'm going out that way to see if I can get a bit of land for a new tanyard' (p. 9). But George Kingsmill offers a new, undesecrated future, won by the sweat of his brow, and Letty rejects him. She has always been different from the chapel folk, 'very gay and worldly' (p. 3) like her mother's people, and that makes her susceptible to Captain Fanshawe. However, Jacob orders him from the house: 'My daughter and I are not of your class; we do not desire your acquaintance' (p. 23). Concerned for his daughter's well-being, he decides to tell her of the aunt she was named after: 'she came back to die in our arms, her heart broken, her beauty and innocence gone' (p. 24). Letty sees her own foolishness and agrees to accept the 'good man [who] asked me for my love this morning'.

Had the play ended there, Jones would have made his point through a delicate clash of personalities. But when he magnifies that conflict into an elemental war between evil and good, Letty ceases to act her interior drama and becomes the puppet of external forces, many of which are distinctly contemporary. Lured from a Sunday School outing, Letty arrives at Ousebridge Junction where Fanshawe promises to put her on the train for Steepleford. It happens that the up-express to London has been delayed. When it arrives, Fanshawe tricks Letty into believing it will take her homewards. Instead, the express hurries her to ruin. No horse could carry her father quickly enough to save her; there is no other train till morning; the telegraph-office is closed; so the city enfolds her. Weeks later, in Fanshawe's villa at Torquay, she discovers why he puts off marrying her: he already has a wife. Having brought shame upon her father, she can either leave, 'nameless and dishonoured', or go with Fanshawe to India. Loathing herself, she embraces evil:

Ah, you have me in your power, and you know it. Very well, I will do as you bid me. I will dare to be as bad as you wish me. Make me like yourself. (*Throws herself into his arms.*)
(III, p. 67)

The heroism Jones looked for in an industrial age now takes centre stage, in the drawing-room of Fanshawe's seaside villa. Jacob's love has led him in search of his daughter, and he arrives to wrestle for her soul. But although parental care is both natural and universal, Letty's sin was not against Nature; she has violated the social code of nineteenth-century England. Jones was too much the product of that society to realize the difference. Jacob forgives Letty, but natural love does not wash away her sin for either of them. When he first learns of her disappearance, his cries preserve the national code: 'her good name is gone. I shall never hold up my head again' (II, p. 48). Beseeching Lot never to 'mention this to anybody', he is honourable enough to tell George, but only in the language of propriety:

GEORGE: You have bad news. What is it? Tell me; I can bear it. Ah! She is dead!
JACOB: Would God she were. (*Rises*)
GEORGE: Worse than death! There is but one thing worse than death. Is it *that*?
JACOB: You have said it.   (pp. 49–50)

Words are a means of covering over forbidden facts. Jacob would rather feel that he 'can bear it best alone' than acknowledge his terror of scandal. So he becomes a whited sepulchre, like Hoggard and his cronies who pay their dues on a Sunday in order to tidy over their everyday rapaciousness. And Jacob's heroic forgiveness seems less beautiful or true when he persuades George to spare Captain Fanshawe; 'for her sake, George, it must not be known – it must be hushed up, for her sake' (III, p. 74).

Jones recognized part of that hypocrisy, painting his hero's human failings before allowing him his sainthood. Jacob's attempt to cover over Letty's sin and preserve her good name places him in Hoggard's power. Having set a private detective on the trail from London to Torquay, the deacon finally has the lever he needs. Jacob must either abandon Mrs Bristow's claim to a fair share of the tannery or Hoggard will tell all. Both father and daughter then see that their fear of public disgrace would bind them forever to the merciless deacon. Together they decide to 'stand upon the truth' (IV, p. 91). However, when Jacob appears before his congregation he takes no stand at all. He succumbs to their prejudices because he shares them.

Although he knows 'how bitterly she has repented', he proclaims his daughter's shame and his own infection. Just as she shrank away from him in Torquay, begging him not to touch her, so Jacob turns from his pulpit: 'I dare not stand up in that place as an example any more' (p. 93). In that way, *Saints and Sinners* preserves the narrow-minded respectability it seeks to challenge. Father and daughter suffer hunger and disgrace. Jacob has the opportunity to forgive Hoggard when he offers him their last crust and hides him from the angry mob he has defrauded. Letty earns back the respect of Steepleford by nursing the victims of a fever epidemic 'in them courts and alleys, week after week, night and day, with scarcely any rest' (v, p. 97). At last they are accepted back into the respectable circle, but only because the new minister has found a more prosperous congregation and the wicked Captain Fanshawe is dead and buried. Even Lydia has agreed to marry Lot Burden 'for the sake of propriety' (p. 101) so that they can provide a proper home for the Fletchers. How one wishes she meant what she says after pledging her troth: 'What fools women are!' (p. 102). For Jones cannot forgive Letty's sin, despite the beauty she sheds on urban squalor. That simply earns her a deathbed reunion with George who has 'come all across the world only to see your face' (p. 112).[22] Steepleford will continue to be 'so respectable'.

Jones's serious plays are unactable today because of their intense idealism. They are cluttered with incident and emotive rhetoric because Jones aspired to write 'Gothic cathedrals . . . dealing with great masses and volumes of human life and character and emotion'.[23] Hoping to win audiences from contemporary barbarism, he determined to woo them by degrees from within the system:

English playgoers . . . like their sympathies to be strongly roused and definitely centred. They relish an appeal to their feelings rather than an appeal to their judgment. And in all matters connected with the feelings, in all questions of conduct and emotion, the instinct of a popular audience is invariably right. And this keen sympathetic instinct is most valuable to the dramatist who knows how to seize it and guide it aright.[24]

For a time, therefore, he returned to melodrama and Wilson Barrett but, since the latter's idea of theatre constantly negated Jones's aesthetic reforms, he eventually joined forces with E. S. Willard at the Shaftesbury. His first success there, *The Middleman* (1889), presents another example of modern heroism. Cyrus Blenkarn sacrifices everything to rediscover the formula for a fine chinaware that used to be made at Tatlow in the previous century. Both his genius and his livelihood are threatened by the representatives of 'that great commercial spirit of the age which . . . has covered . . . the land with . . . railways and factories and mines – and chimneys and steam-engines'.[25] That conflict involves yet another seduction-drama whose morality is again questionable, but Jones sees no irony in a convention whereby marriage instantly restores the good name of seducer and seduced. In his view, the theatre was neither a debating chamber nor a lecture hall. Drama should not preach, but it could teach by indirection through a story which captured the emotions. '*The drama cannot directly and explicitly affirm or teach or solve or prove anything.*' In the nineties, that was his answer to 'all the childish nonsense that has recently been written about so-called "problem" plays.'[26]

Judah (1890) is his indirect defence of idealism itself, and Judah Llewellyn reflects Jones's own Welsh antecedents and pastoral upbringing, but magnified into a burning sincerity: he has 'a wonderful power . . . over the people . . . it's born in him'.[27] Here, however, Jones does place his hero's charismatic enthusiasm in a provocative light, for the young ladies of the chapel feel slighted by the young minister's belief in Vashti Dethic and her healing powers. Miracles cannot happen in modern England, and the presence of Professor Jopp ('keen, alert, intellectual . . . genial Voltaire type of face') injects a philosophical scepticism into the opening conversation. The difference between his beliefs and Judah's becomes plain when the two men meet: the professor's 'last lecture was on tadpoles and lizards'; Judah's was about 'the unseen world' (I, p. 209). Jopp can root up facts or explain 'miracles', but Judah wonders why he cannot feel the miraculous in everyday facts:

Explain? Explain to the mother the mystery of the love that gives a living child to her arms! Explain to the husband what hand snatches back his wife from the gates of death! Explain? They do not need it. They hold their dear ones to their hearts – safe. They do not question – they love. (p. 211)

Such reliance on the heart echoes Jones's own appeal to the 'keen sympathetic instinct' of the average playgoer. Yet, for a time, feeling is held in check by a situation which does raise questions. Vashti cures the sick, but her ability to do so depends, to some extent, on her special mystery, 'a kind of trance' she achieves after several weeks' fasting. However, this is simply a performance directed by her father, an experienced confidence-trickster, who uses its effect to extort money from the superstitious. Is Vashti's power due solely to a fraudulent charade or does she indeed have 'some sort of magnetic influence'? When Judah discovers the sham, will he be completely disillusioned or will he recognize in Vashti herself a genuine power which, though mundane, is worthy of the people's faith? The key scene, in which Judah learns of the fraud, exemplifies the way Jones prefers emotion to argument. Judah and Vashti are passionately in love. Although he sees her father secretly bringing food, he rescues her from the sceptics and dishonour by swearing he has seen nothing. So the play avoids issues and vindicates Judah's heart rather than his judgement.

Judah is an idealist in a doubting world. Like an Arthurian knight, he tended his father's sheep alone on the hills until he was almost twenty; spirit voices speak to him. Vashti is his first love, and he worships her although she begs him to see her human flaws. The discovery scene begins with a soliloquy whose lyricism aims to convey the power and beauty of Judah's love even if it is as yet misdirected, and it is that strength of feeling which enables him to withstand the shock to his ideals and discover a woman who is perhaps more lovely now he sees her clearly: 'I thought you out of my reach, up there amongst the stars . . . I'm glad you are what you are, for I can make you mine now' (II, p. 250). When he lies in order to protect her reputation, Judah forfeits his own, and that burns at his conscience. Eventually he resigns his ministry, but this hero's final stand is a matter of conscience rather than social repute. He and Vashti decide to stay on in the town, convinced that the integrity of their life together will win respect: 'Yes, we will build our new church with our lives, and its foundation shall be the truth' (III, p. 278).

The emotion is pitched too high, but Jones also means to persuade through contrast. He surrounds Judah's idealism with varying shades of doubt. Vashti knows her own flaws yet she yearns to believe in her healing power and to deserve Judah's worship. Lord Asgarby's attitude also creates sympathy for Judah and the ways of the heart. Terrified of losing his last, adored child, he recognizes Dethic's roguery yet sees that Vashti has an extraordinary effect on the ailing Lady Eve. No explanation of that power can shake his belief in its quality. Dr Jopp believes in explanations, yet Jones respected science, and his professor is not an entirely unsympathetic character. Jones ridicules him when he steps beyond his province, as in his article on 'The Scientific Conception of Truth' (p. 204), but he allows him compassion. Jopp urges Vashti to abandon her dangerous fast and, when he has finally sifted the facts, responds to Lord Asgarby's appeal to uphold Lady Eve's faith in her. Jones reserves his sharpest barbs for the sort of realist who reduces life to facts and figures with an ill-mannered and insensitive assertiveness. Juxon Prall 'knows everything' and, to contrast Judah's muscular radiance, Jones visualizes him with 'spectacles, sharp features ... [and] ... a peculiar finicking trick of speaking with the tips of the fingers of one hand playing on the tips of the other' (p. 206). Juxon is a modern barbarian: jeeringly contemptuous of his parents, unprincipled, and without a jot of sentiment.

That portrait shows how an appeal to the playgoer's instinct might pamper middle-class prejudice. Jones caricatures this flower of progress and allies him with a female equivalent, the New Woman. A more strident figure than the lively Girl of the Period, she personifies the fear of those who saw the Woman's Rights movement and the reforms which had been won since the seventies as blows to the foundation of society. Jones's stage-direction reveals his hatred:

Enter Sophie Jopp at window, in outdoor dress; a dogmatic, supercilious, incisive young lady, with eye-glass and short hair. She speaks in a metallic, confident voice; a girl who could never blush. (I, p. 206)

He sneers at her pedantic intellect and lack of grace, but the pair's indirect function is to illumine Judah's inner grandeur with their own contrasting pettiness. Judah may be too much the dreamer at first, but he can feel the beauty of the world around him which is made even more radiant by his love for Vashti: 'All the world is transfigured because you are in it. When I walk along the streets, all the men and women seem to be smitten with your beauty' (II, pp. 231–2). His soul shines all the brighter when Juxon 'somehow gets [Sophie's] hand', and the two begin anatomizing love:

JUXON: ... You'll permit me to speak frankly?
SOPHIE: Do so; I wish it.
JUXON: In approaching the really momentous subject of marriage – (*After a pause.*) Have I made it plain to you that I am about to suggest that we should become united for life?
SOPHIE: (*unembarrassed*). I gathered as much.
JUXON: Thank you. I have considered the matter very carefully, and – you fully understand, do you not, that I am now making you a definitive offer of marriage?
SOPHIE: (*quite unembarrassed*). Oh, yes. And I may say frankly, I am disposed to accept you – under certain conditions.
JUXON: Pecuniary, I suppose? You are aware I am quite dependent upon my father. I cannot truthfully affirm that my poor father is of the slightest use in the world, and yet, so far as I can judge, there is very little prospect of his immediately retiring from it. Not that I wish him to do so; still, it would simplify matters. However, as I am one of his only two children, I suppose he will make some provision for me.

145

THE NEW WOMAN.

"You 're not leaving us, Jack ? Tea will be here directly !"
"Oh, I 'm going for a Cup of Tea in the Servants' Hall. I can't get on without Female Society, you know !"

5 The New Woman

SOPHIE: My objections were not pecuniary, but physiological.
JUXON: Very necessary! Extremely necessary! How sensible of you! The neglect of the simplest physiological laws is simply deplorable. But, my dear Miss Jopp, my physical development, though somewhat retarded by my great mental exertions, is in the most satisfying state.
SOPHIE: You had a bad cough last winter. (pp. 235–6)

Jones's antipathy to modern gracelessness affects other elements of *Judah*. Unlike the play's realists who classify everything – 'genus, cheat; species, religious; variety, bogus-miracle business' (p. 213) – Jones describes the diseases Vashti cures with deliberate reticence. Lady Eve's illness is never named; it must be conveyed by her 'sudden alternate fits of languor and restless energy' (p. 203). Benjamin Bandy's lameness and 'various disorders' represent all the other 'marvellous manifestations' Vashti has achieved. Mr Prall brings the man's crutches onto the stage, but Jones makes them objects of humour in that they depict Prall's enthusiastic gullibility and, since Bandy has a reputation for swearing, they suggest to the Professor that 'Miss Dethic has set free an alarming quantity of bad language to perambulate the country' (p. 209). In Jones's opinion, disease had no business at stage centre, for Nature was essentially life-giving. He loathed 'the Pentonville-Omnibus and lobworm symbolic school of drama'.[28] The prominence of syphilis and other maladies in the plays of Ibsen and Zola was one more symptom of society's degeneration:

The present epidemic of physical horror and disease which has very slightly attacked the English stage is a town-bred mental disease arising, I believe, from the nausea of town-life, an insanity that to escape from its own self-weariness and self-disgust plunges its nose more deeply into the fumes and the mire of its own creating.[29]

Resisting that attack, Jones set the play in the tapestry-room at Asgarby Castle and on the moonlit terrace below its Norman keep. Since action on stage, however truthfully realized, could not possibly reproduce life itself, Jones considered the drawing-rooms or squalid kitchens of the new realism to be no more truthful to nineteenth-century life than any other setting:

I cannot imagine why those who wish for sordid and mean and disgusting details of life to be shown upon the stage in their naked and ugly truth – I repeat that I cannot for the life of me imagine why they want a stage or a theatre at all, when already every detail is being acted in the outside world, and can be seen all around them without the payment of a single shilling.[30]

The Gothic proportions of the set do not represent his retreat from 'the nausea of town-life'. They provide a symbolically appropriate milieu for those 'great qualities, beauty, mystery, passion, imagination', which Zolaesque naturalism 'sets itself to deride . . . and brags that it does not possess'.[31] The colour and size of the tapestries, and the solid tradition they present, dwarf those characters who resist life's splendour and expose the narrow limits of their drab, factual minds. The Asgarbys and the Jopps act out that symbolism. Lady Eve sees 'this world is all for the strong. To do something, and then to die'; and even death is action, 'a kiss from an unknown lover' (p. 205). Lord Asgarby also allies himself with action when he informs the mayor that he will 'bear the entire cost' of the city's new library, and he fights as much for tradition as for his daughter's life: she is 'the last of us! The end of our race' (pp. 203–5). To that lament, Jopp can only offer 'no-creed' comfort, 'your family . . . has lived its life, a long and honoured one . . . why rebel because the night has come . . . ?' (pp. 205–6), and his own daughter's rebelliousness perverts Nature. Accordingly, the moonlit terrace of Act Two becomes a sounding-board for Judah and Vashti's fervent acceptance of love's mystery, a rapture which a villa's snug portico could not have sustained.

Jones valued science, but he saw drama as a way for the newly educated to rise above 'mere technical knowledge and skill' to arrive at 'the science of living'.[32] The theatre could burn that lesson on the brain: 'how it isolates, how it vivifies, how it enlarges, how it inflames!' Yet the dramatist's message was simple and as old as Eden:

> The man who in the midst of all the tangled threads and rank growths of our latter-day commercialism knows, and knows surely, that honesty is the best policy; the woman who knows, and knows surely, that her virtue means health and strength to the next generation – this man and this woman are in possession of the profoundest truths, the deepest secrets of national prosperity and well-being, compared with which all other education is secondary, auxiliary, and illustrative.

In Jones's plays, honesty and virtue are intertwined with sexuality. A woman's good name (her social virtue) tends to be synonymous with her bodily virtue, and if she loses her virginity she can only re-enter society as a legally recognized wife. *Saints and Sinners* showed how little a woman's reputation depends on her good deeds. Fanshawe is already married, and Letty can never recover her maiden innocence. Her father upholds her good name but cannot forget her lost virginity, and that anomaly corrodes his own honesty. Letty wins back her neighbours' respect, but it is Fanshawe's death which allows them to accept her – as her father's bereft daughter. In *Judah*, Vashti Dethic's maidenhood is not at issue, and the play is correspondingly less irksome, but Judah's honesty collides with his sexual desire. The puritan in Jones sees Judah's struggle as all the more heroic because of the force of that passion.

Vashti is not actually a temptress, 'not willingly wicked, only weak', yet Jones imagines the discovery scene as if her crime *were* sexual. Judah, for example, thrusts her aside as she kneels before him: 'God forgive me – if I listen to you I shall be ready to sell my eternal peace, my very soul, at your bidding' (p. 248). He can 'forgive' her weakness, but he still feels betrayed. As he turns away coldly, she seizes his hand and kisses it; Judah is 'fired' by that kiss. Visually, the rest of the scene presents a fallen woman who (like Letty Fletcher to her father) recoils from his embrace as if she were physically tainted. After Judah has lied to save her from disgrace, he takes on her sin and, throwing away 'all the world' for the woman he now wants to 'protect', embraces evil gladly: 'I will be your mate. If you are evil, I will be evil too . . . and keep your soul side by side with mine for ever!' (p. 259). The feverous sensuality of their scenes together evaporates only in the play's final episode. Vashti and Judah have agreed (off stage) to tell the truth about her pretended fasting. She enters, 'trembling, ashamed', and he whispers encouragement. Judah still claims her 'guilt' as his, but now the crime is plain dishonesty. After their confession, Jopp urges them to 'stay here, live down your fault, amongst the people whom you have deceived', and together they 'dare' to face those who now know them for what they truly are.

Jones never seems to have realized how his finely tuned conscience and his crusade for an heroic drama could 'magnify' his characters' moral crises beyond all due proportion. In *Michael and His Lost Angel* (1896), the minister's severe love of truth makes him a self-righteous prude, and his sense of sin, after he has fallen from that pedestal, is well-nigh masochistic. Yet Jones felt no need to examine the workings of Michael Feversham's soul and the pleasure he takes in castigating others or lacerating his own desire:

> I know what you [his assistant's fallen daughter, forced to a public confession] have suffered this morning. I would willingly have borne it for you, but that would not have made reparation to those whom you have deceived, or given you peace in your own soul. (*She continues sobbing.*) Hush! Hush! All the bitterness is past! Look only to the future! Think of the happy newness and whiteness of your life from this moment! Think of the delight of waking in the morning and knowing that you have nothing to hide! Be sure you have done right to own your sin. There won't be a softer pillow in England to-night than the one your head rests upon. (*She becomes quieter. Michael turns to the Sister.*) Watch over her very carefully. Keep her from brooding. Let her be occupied constantly with work.
>
> (p. 9)

Jones simply places him between a good angel and a bad. Inspired by the purity of his mother (whose portrait beatifies his soul), Michael is drawn away by the magnetic Audrie Lesden, a neurotically restless sophisticate who, bored by her life of pleasure, finds an amusing challenge and a promise of peace in the minister's fierce chastity. A combination of design and accident leads to a night of love, and Michael is man enough to have no regrets, despite the subterfuge required to save both their reputations. But when he discovers that Audrie's husband is still living, his anguish drives him to the altar steps and public confession. This conflict between the soul and the flesh relates curiously to the church that Michael has worked so hard to restore:

> MICHAEL (*alone*):   One thing more and all is done. (*Looking round the church.*) And I must give you up! Never enter your doors, never lead my people through you in chariots of fire, never make you the very presence-chamber of God to my soul and their souls who were committed to me! Oh, if I had been worthy!
>
> (p. 69)

Like Judah Llewellyn, who was also offered a monument to his good name, Michael cannot enter that temple because of his 'deadly sin'. Audrie's anonymous donations have facilitated the Minster's restoration, just as Vashti's miracle has caused Lord Asgarby to found a church for Judah. Love opens the gates to glory but sex closes them, and the tainted lovers must expiate their sin by painful labour or, as in Audrie's case, by death. Looking back at his heroes' fervid passion, towards the end of his life, Jones conceded that their struggle might 'be called exalted and spiritual, or exaggerated and ridiculous, according to the temperament of the critic', but nothing would shake his conviction as to 'the actuality and permanent truth of such heightened love . . .'.[33]

For the modern reader, there is far more actuality in the comedies Jones wrote for Charles Wyndham in the nineties. Comedy needs no heroes, just men and women who learn good sense by adjusting to society's tattered rules of conduct. From that lower standpoint, Jones focusses on the tatters, and characters who seek to discard those frail remnants of honesty and virtue confront no fiery 'thou shalt not' but a gentler and more pragmatic 'it won't work'. What does work, according to Jones, is the natural law which distinguishes male from female.

Yet Jones was aware how bitter that comic resolution could be for a worldly woman. In *The Case of Rebellious Susan* (1894), Lady Susan Harabin discovers that her husband has been unfaithful and is determined 'to pay him back in his own coin' (I, p. 109).[34] Her friends urge her to overlook the matter, and while their need to hush things up may be hypocritical, it is perhaps necessary in a society nearing collapse. Lady Darby, Susan's aunt, describes James Harabin as 'a gentleman in every sense of the word', and so his indiscretion 'can't be a very bad case'. Her logic is laughable, but only because society has accepted all types as 'gentlemen'. From Jones's point of view, no true gentleman would allow his wife to feel neglected, just as no true lady would forget her femininity by seeking a 'romance' of her own. When Susan finally returns to Harabin, the pathos behind that reconciliation results from the fact that James has shown himself incapable of truly cherishing his wife. He wants her back because her absence has affected 'all his little home comforts' (II, p. 136) and exposed him to 'the treachery, the extravagance, and the heartlessness of womankind' (p. 139) when he followed his natural inclinations after her departure. In his wounded vanity, he can appreciate her for the moment and ply her with Bond Street's jewels, but that solicitude will probably soon pass. To those who scorn the double standard, Susan's decision 'to be a good wife' (III, p. 161) represents a betrayal of her true self. To Jones, Harabin's inadequacy betrays Susan's fémininity since he will never understand the mysteries of woman's nature: 'treasures of faithfulness, treasures of devotion, of self-sacrifice, of courage, of comradeship, of loyalty. And above all, treasures of deceit – loving, honourable deceit, and secrecy and treachery' (II, p. 125).

Jones had originally intended that his 'tragedy dressed up as comedy' should show a more provocative lie than the 'loving, honourable deceit' (to save her family) which Susan's oldest friend, Inez, allows a woman. By giving herself entirely to the new permissiveness, Lady Susan would have had to lie to save her own honour. But Wyndham was distressed by the unequivocal allusion to Susan's affair with Lucien Edensor in Cairo and asked Jones to alter several key lines, particularly Susan's fear that Lucien might have 'boasted' about his conquest since his return from Egypt. How could 'an author, a clean living, clear-minded man, [wish] to extract laughter from an audience on the score of a woman's impurity'?[35] The changes allowed audiences to believe that Susan and Edensor had not in fact been lovers. A vague, romantic attachment is hardly less dishonourable, but as long as nothing could be proved against her, Susan's friends (on both sides of the footlights) could acquiesce in the lies she tells to extricate herself. Jones meant to prove that 'what is sauce for the goose will never be sauce for the gander' (p. 112) because a love affair must involve Susan in unnatural and unfeminine deceit. The alterations blur that and involve everyone in a scramble to maintain appearances.

As a preface to the printed version of the script, Jones appended an open letter addressed to Mrs Grundy,[36] the Victorian goddess of propriety, in which he reminded her that 'Nature has ten thousand various morals, all of them as shocking as truth itself' (p. 107). But Jones's own theory of Nature is conveniently and prettily uphol- stered. The female mates for life; the male mates whenever he can although, to reward her loyalty, he will especially cherish his formal partner. That cosy formula differentiates Harabin's uncaring indis- cretions from those of the other men in the play. Sir Richard Kato, Susan's uncle and the play's chief *raisonneur*, has had his sexual adventures, and Inez does not expect a man of 'say forty-five' to have behaved differently. They can laugh together as he reels off the 'whole catalogue', because Kato has already told her of his one redeeming love:

I've thought myself in love scores of times, but I've really loved once, and that was – (*longish pause with great feeling*) – I won't tell you. It's too sacred. I did love that woman with all my heart and soul. And she loved me. (III, p. 149)

On the other hand, when Inez jokingly suggests that she might have 'had vagrant fancies for' a similarly vague list of men, though 'no woman's case ever is as bad as a man's', Kato is shocked and Inez hastens to reassure him. Constancy can be no more than 'a dream' for sophisticated people, so they agree to 'draw a veil' over the particulars of Kato's past; he would refuse to supply her with 'further details' anyway. He may have 'drunk the wine and broken the bread with sluts', but he has 'loved once' and that purifies him just as Inez's devotion to her husband's memory dignifies her. Their banter shows their mutual understanding and implies that, one day soon, the lady will agree to be his second love.

Susan's other uncle, Admiral Darby, falls somewhere between Kato and Harabin in Jones's sympathies. As an old sea-dog, he too 'has his little failings' but he cannot think them reason enough for his wife to take offence. Women are such forgiving angels: 'What a comfort it is to have a wife of the good old-fashioned sort like you, Victoria' (p. 139). To spare Lady Darby's feelings, he prefers to cover over that part of his life, though he boasts remorsefully to his men friends:

(*getting very confidential, and a little maudlin*) You wouldn't believe me, Jim, (*pawing* HARABIN *affectionately*) if I were to tell you half of the particulars of my – my unfortunate history. (*crying a little*) Of course, in these matters (*turning to* SIR RICHARD, *and taking him in*) we must all make great allowances for men (SIR RICHARD *acquiesces.*), especially for sailors. How do you account for it, Jim, (*suddenly brightening into great joviality and pride*) that the best Englishmen have always been such devils amongst the women? Always! I wouldn't give a damn for a soldier or a sailor that wasn't, eh? How is it, Jim? (II, p. 138)

Yet beneath his comic contradictions, the Admiral does value his wife: 'when a man has a good wife it's a rascally shame to forget her' (p. 136). Lady Darby understands, for 'men are men, and they are led away, and the rest of it' (p. 110), and she has the consolation of the Admiral's genuine affection: 'You never seem to appreciate me so much as you do the week before you leave me, and the week after you return [from sea]' (p. 136). But in spite of these fine distinctions, all three men would react in precisely the same way if they thought their ladies indiscreet. As Lady Susan remarks to her husband, 'My dear Jim, you don't feel anything like so much remorse for your own transgressions as you do for mine' (p. 158).

Jones draws a veil of laughter over his characters' town-bred imperfections but he rigorously defends the way society traditionally operates. He allows each playgoer to turn away from the hypocrisies of the double standard when Inez remarks that, however surprising the human heart might be, 'God has put everything there', and Kato, kissing her hand 'very tenderly', suggests they 'leave these problems and go in to dinner' (p. 161). But before that final tableau, Jones insists that marriage is also God-given. His spokesman is Sir Richard Kato, QC, an impartial observer of worldly folly 'after twenty-five years' constant practice in the Divorce Court' (p. 113). Early in the play he establishes its battle front: 'marriage is a perfect institution . . . worked by imperfect creatures. So it's like a good ship manned by a mutinous crew.'

In her rebellion, Susan does more than unsex herself; she fails to distinguish between romance and marriage. Romance admits no imperfection. Susan could not see James's faults at the time of their engagement; had they been pointed out to her, she 'would have been shocked and grieved' but would finally 'have forgiven him' (p. 114). In marriage, she ought to forgive knowingly. But James's expectations are equally confused: 'Well – married life, even with the best and sweetest of wives, does grow confoundedly unromantic at times' (p. 115). Susan's retaliatory affair with Edensor is designed to show the justice of Kato's remarks: 'Married life isn't very romantic anywhere, with anybody, and it ought not to be. When it is, it gets into the Divorce Court. You ought to have finished with romance long ago, both of you' (pp. 115–16). Susan has to learn that romance deludes and that its temporary glamour cannot outshine the security of marriage. Perceiving how Susan's romantic notions endanger her reputation, Kato packs Lucien off to New Zealand, but not before that young man has sworn undying love. On the voyage out, his gloom attracts the sympathy of the Jacomb ladies and the sporting instincts of the men. Having discovered the cause of his despair, they bet he will soon recover and marry their Annie. As Mr Jacomb tells it, there was some doubt about his fifty pounds, for Lucien remained inconsolable for over three weeks. Hearing this story, Susan perceives its bitter irony and is wounded still further when she unwraps the piece of wedding cake Jacomb has brought her and discovers the ring she had given Lucien at his departure. And so she accepts the reasonable alternative by agreeing to 'let things shake down' as her other (sea-faring) uncle has always advised:

Oh, yes. I allow every married couple twelve months for what I call the shaking-down process, that is, to learn each other's tempers, to learn the give and take of married life. In all well-regulated households, for the woman to learn that she has got a master. In all ill-regulated households, for the man to learn that he has got a master. The first year of our married life Lady Darby and I lived a thorough cat and dog life. (*a roar of reminiscent laughter*) We had a battle-royal, I assure you, every day of our life. Ho! Ho! Ho! But we shook down comfortably after that – God bless her! God bless her! (I, p. 117)

Jones never reconciles that 'give and take' with the fact that women must do most of the giving nor does he question why men should be masters if their natural frailties make them more susceptible to temporary romance. He defends the double standard by presenting the ill-regulated present to his audience's instinctive antipathy. Susan's unbeautiful rebellion vindicates Lady Darby's sensible, old-fashioned submissiveness: 'You see, dear, we poor women cannot retaliate' (p. 160). And the exploits of Kato's ward, Elaine Shrimpton, also present their awful warning to those who would break with tradition.

Pressed by the spectre of the New Woman, Jones abandons his comic detachment and heaps punishment on Elaine's assertive head. According to her beleaguered guardian, she 'is a rather ignorant, impulsive girl, with a smattering of pseudo-scientific knowledge, chiefly picked up from unwholesome feminine novels' (p. 122).[37] When she insists on marrying in spite of his disapproval, Kato agrees to allow her the same income as her prospective husband, Mr Pybus, but Elaine scorns such equality: "You will hold back my money! It's cowardly! But so like a man! Brute force! – brute force!— never anything but brute force!' (p. 121). Yet even this sloganeering termagant has her illusions, romantic and political. Mr Pybus is 'a genius', and together they will break through society's 'worm-eaten conventionalities': 'Why should we dwarf and stunt ourselves physically, morally, intellectually, for the sake of propping up a society that is decrepit and moribund to its core?' Pybus, however, is an aesthete. To discuss money at all 'seems like a crime. I want my wife to be a fairy creature, incessantly, perpetually, a fairy creature' (p. 120). He regrets the Harabins' *contretemps*: 'It affects me like a wrong note in music, like a . . . faulty dash of colour in a picture – it distresses me' (p. 118). All Kato can do for such heady extremists is to offer realistic advice: Elaine should take cooking lessons and Pybus ought to choose something 'lucrative' when he finally selects a way to 'stamp [him]self upon the age'. He also warns them of what lies ahead:

> you will have to face the coarse and brutal bread-and-cheese realities of life. You'll find that you have tempers to train and subdue, whims and obstinacies of your own to check, whims and obstinacies of your partner to indulge. There will be the need of daily, hourly, forbearance and kindliness, a constant overlooking of each other's faults and imperfections. (p. 122)

But Pybus wants Elaine to devote herself to his 'divine afflatus', and she too has 'a message for this age' (p. 123).

Jones deposits them in Clapham, an appropriately blighted arena for their unequal sparring-match, and the message they actually give is clear and crude.[38] Only a namby-pamby fool would allow his wife to neglect her domestic duties and organize a Boadicean Society for the Inculcation of the New Morality, and Pybus is punished for his weakness when an irate neighbour assaults him. Elaine, who so hates men's brutality, becomes a bully herself, inciting the telegraph girls to go on strike and destroying public property. She 'never will understand the Woman question'. Because of her ferocious need for martyrdom, she has no real principles, only an urge to tear the social fabric in any way she can, and her unfocussed energies provoke Jones into a direct plea for sanity and retrenchment:

> KATO: There is an immense future for women as wives and mothers, and a very limited future for them in any other capacity. While you ladies without passions – or with distorted and defeated passions – are raving and trumpeting all over the country, that wise, grim, old grandmother of us all, Dame Nature, is simply laughing up her sleeve and snapping her fingers at you and your new epochs and new movements ... Go home! Go home! Nature's darling woman is a stay-at-home woman, a woman who wants to be a good wife and a good mother, and cares very little for anything else. (pp. 153–4)

Although Kato dismisses 'this tiresome sexual business', Jones could not, and his comedies grew darker. Lady Susan snaps her fingers at James and walks out,[39] but her uncle refuses to countenance such a dismissal and steers her back to sanity and duty. In *The Liars* (1897), however, ill-regulated behaviour appears to be the norm amongst the well-to-do. Lady Rosamund Tatton is no caricatured firebrand; she simply treats her husband with charmingly witty contempt. And Freddie deserves it because he always gives in to her:

ROSAMUND: I wish he wouldn't. I really believe I should love and respect him a little if he were to take me and give me a good shaking, or do something to make me feel that he's my master. But (*Sighs.*) he never will! He'll only go on asking everybody's advice how to manage me – and never find out. As if it weren't the easiest thing in the world to manage a woman – if men only knew.[40]

(I, p. 169)

Her sister, Lady Jessica Nepean, uses the same sarcastic wit to smooth away her own husband's rough ill-temper, and Dolly Coke, their cousin, does what she can to survive her partner's irritating uxoriousness. Real concern and sympathy might save these marriages, too, but the old panacea (good dinners for the men, jewels for the ladies) seems less effective than ever. Restless and dissatisfied, these women crave excitement: a little more outrageous chatter, a little less innocent flirtation, anything to stretch their bonds. Because they know there must come a breaking-point, the risks they take are exciting in themselves.

Lady Jessica does push perilously near to that limit, and her friends scurry to the rescue. As their lies pile up, their story becomes less credible. Finally, to satisfy her raging husband, Captain Falkner responds to Lady Jessica's request to tell him the truth:

I asked her to come to me at Shepperford last evening. She came. Your brother saw us and left us. The next moment Lady Rosamund came, and she had scarcely gone when the maid came with your telegram and took Lady Jessica back to town. If you think there was anything more on your wife's side than a passing folly and amusement at my expense, you will wrong her. If you think there is anything less on my side than the deepest, deepest, deepest love and worship, you will wrong me. Understand this. She is guiltless. Be sure of that. And now you've got the truth, and be damned to *you*.   (III, p. 209)

But when that brave, old-fashioned speech moves Jessica to leave her brutish husband, Jones makes it clear that Falkner's romantic worship will 'make [her] miserable for life'. Should she dare to sacrifice her reputation (her 'terrible leanings towards respectability' as Inez had called it), her defiance 'won't work'. After the 'dirty business of the divorce court', they would no longer be received in society. They could retire to the country, 'with no single occupation except to nag and rag each other to pieces from morning to night', or they could go abroad, 'rubbing shoulders with all the blackguards and demimondaines of Europe' (p. 215). Jones raises the emotional odds, for Gilbert Nepean has been 'a terror' and Ned Falkner has 'behaved splendidly', but, to survive, Jessica must step back from the sentimental promptings of wounded pride:

Go to [Gilbert], and do, once for all, have done with this other folly. Do believe me, my dear Ned, my dear Lady Jessica, before it is too late, do believe me, it won't work, it won't work, it won't work! (IV, p. 216)

As he chastens his socialites' frivolity, Jones offers a way out from a world which women seek to dominate. There are, after all, more important ways to maintain a reputation. When Colonel Deering cautions Lady Jessica, he voices deep concern for Falkner's good name. He and Ned are old campaigners; in the three years they spent together in Africa, he has come to know him as 'the very soul of honour'. Falkner seems out of place in high society. The clever Mrs Crespin smiles at his reputation, 'the one cruel fact about heroes is that they are made of flesh and blood' (p. 166), and his first entrance emasculates him. Playing Hercules to Jessica's Omphale, he scrambles out of the Thames, clutching her 'ten-and-sixpenny brooch' (p. 169). The 'poor dear, foolish fellow' makes an amusing spectacle but he had been too 'demonstrative' in begging the lady 'for some little souvenir', and so she tossed it in the river. Should he remain her toy soldier, Falkner would abandon a higher duty, for only he and Deering can quell the slave-traders: 'He's at the height of his career, with a great and honourable task in front of him' (p. 216). Africa would not suit Lady Jessica who blossoms in her sister's river-side marquee, but there is one woman fit for the tents of war. Beatrice Ebernoe, the widow of Deering's oldest friend, has been on past campaigns, and Jones makes her a quiet but telling presence until the play's fourth Act when the Colonel declares his love for her.[41] He has no time to play the wooer, as he hurriedly packs his kit, and she is too serious a person to require that. She does hesitate, in deference to her memories, but then responds to his soldierly request: 'Once give me your promise, and it will give me the pluck of fifty men!' (p. 210). If they marry at once, she can take her place by his side, for 'there will be some nursing and other woman's work out there' (p. 211). Falkner is also ignited by Deering's challenge: 'There's work in front of you, and fame and honour! And I must take you out and bring you back with flying colours!' (p. 218). As the others return to their listless games, Deering stands firm with his arms around his 'two comrades', assured of a glorious 'tomorrow' (p. 219).

Duty, hard work, the traditional relationship between the sexes, mutual tolerance in the 'shake down' of marriage: these were the defences Jones built against the permissiveness of the nineties. Yet there was one pregnable gate in that barricade. He repels those who only appear to be virtuous but collaborates with his characters' need to preserve appearances. He can lash at the dangerous game Lady Jessica plays with her marriage and at the lies it leads to, but he joins in the conspiracy to save her reputation when Colonel Deering, in the name of honour, agrees to help concoct an alibi. The cloak of respectability gave free entrance to the Castle of Morality; without it, no person, however worthy, could pass through. And Jones knowingly condoned that injustice, as is apparent from a conversation between Lady Eastney and Sir Daniel Carteret in *Mrs Dane's Defence* (1900).[42]

After Lucy Dane's scandalous past has been exposed, Lady Eastney wonders why she must now 'pretend that I can't know her'. What right has she to feel superior to someone who, as a young girl, was seduced by her employer?

LADY EASTNEY: I wasn't in her place – I didn't meet with her temptations – and if I had, I should have been cold-hearted enough, or cunning enough, to resist.

SIR DANIEL: Very well. That's all a man can ask; the temperament – call it virtue or cunning – that resists.

Lady Eastney suggests that men are Pharisees, to condemn women for a sin in which they too are partners, and that women of so-called virtue are either cowards (because they dared not sin) or hypocrites (because their sin has not been found out). On being told that those are 'the rules' which 'will never be altered', she protests their injustice. Why should they come between Sir Daniel's adopted son and Lucy Dane who love each other dearly?

SIR DANIEL: If he were your son, would you wish him to marry her? Would you wish all his after-life to be poisoned by the thought that . . . she had belonged to another man, and that man and his child still living? Do, for heaven's sake, let us get rid of all this sentimental cant and sophistry about this woman business. (*Unconsciously getting very heated.*) A man demands the treasure of a woman's purest love. It's what he buys and pays for with the strength of his arm and the sweat of his brow. It's the condition on which he makes her his wife and fights the world for her and his children. It's his fiercest instinct, and he does well to guard it; for it's the very mainspring of a nation's health and soundness. And whatever I've done, whatever I've been myself, I'm quite resolved my son shan't marry another man's mistress. There's the plain sense of the whole matter, so let us have no more talk about patching up things that ought not to be patched up, that can't be patched up, and that shan't be patched up if I can stop them from being patched up!

The rising passion of this speech and its insistent conclusion suggest the dramatist's own rear-guard action against the 'sentimental cant' of the reformers. Jones does give ground a little by allowing 'this woman business' to be voiced by the attractive and sympathetic Lady Eastney. He also makes Lucy Dane a thoroughly pleasant woman who has gained their genuine affection: Lady Eastney will continue to receive her, and Sir Daniel offers his friendship and financial assistance. Nevertheless, however hypocritical and unfair the double standard may appear to be, Lucy's respectability cannot, should not be 'patched up'.

Sir Daniel's passionate certitude accords with Jones's view of his own role as the dramatist of Nature whose strict adherence to eternal rules connects his art 'with all that is vital and preservative and honourable in English life'. That banner, unfurled against 'the Mob' in 1883, stands, at century's end, against misguided liberalism, but the fight to preserve 'a nation's health and soundness' is no less manly ('the strength of his arm and the sweat of his brow') and instinctive. The unalterable law whereby 'A man demands the treasure of a woman's purest love' has nothing to do with Sir Daniel's own impure adventures; it has nothing to do with any individual circumstance. In defending Nature's tenets, Sir Daniel (in Jones's view) is no hypocrite whereas the personal animosity of the local scandal-monger, Mrs Bulsom-Porter, represents the spiteful Grundyism Jones despised. Consequently, to protect Lucy's reputation from vicious self-righteousness, Lady Eastney does lie to Mrs Bulsom-Porter and extracts a signed apology from that lady into the bargain:

LADY EASTNEY: Mrs Bulsom-Porter won't dare attack your reputation now.
MRS DANE: Reputation? Reputation isn't much, is it, when love has gone? Don't think I'm ungrateful to you (*tearing up the apology*), but I shan't trouble to defend my reputation. Good-bye, Sir Daniel. Don't you think the world is very hard on a woman?
SIR DANIEL: It isn't the world that's hard. It isn't men and women. Am I hard? Call on me at any time, and you shall find me the truest friend to you and yours. Is Lady Eastney hard? She has been fighting all the week to save you.
MRS DANE: Then who is it, what is it, drives me out?
SIR DANIEL: The law, the hard law that we didn't make, that we would break if we could, for we are all sinners at heart – the law that is above us all, made for us all, that we can't escape from, that we must keep or perish. (pp. 271–2)

Jones meant the disinterested logic of this to speak louder than Mrs Dane's private irony: 'we mustn't get found out. I'm afraid I've broken that part of the law.' Convinced that Lal Carteret would recover from his thwarted love affair when set to building the Empire's railways and exposed to the restorative purity of Lady Eastney's niece – 'throw him into young society, and trust to time and his healthy instincts to bring him round' (p. 267) – he did not see that his play in fact justifies Lady Eastney's 'sophistry' about 'one set of rules to admonish our neighbours, and another to guide our own conduct' (p. 259).

To protect the ragged tatters of morality, Jones fought long and valiantly against the narrow prudery of mean-hearted Mrs Grundy but allied himself with the goddess, Reputation, in all her guises. So, oddly enough, did many of his liberal opponents. The plays of Oscar Wilde, for instance, mock at Grundyism but derive their passion from the awe Wilde felt towards those of spotless repute. Jones had 'never liked' Wilde but 'was very fond of quoting [his] three rules for writing plays. "The first rule is not to write like Henry Arthur Jones, the second and third rules are the same!" '[43] His vision of modern heroism was just the sort of idealized logic which Wilde sought to corrode with thought-provoking epigrams. As Lord Illingworth teasingly suggests, in *A Woman of No Importance*, 'all thought is immoral. Its very essence is destructive.' Jones stood firmly against contemporary barbarism whereas Wilde pretended that 'taking sides is the beginning of sincerity, and earnestness follows shortly afterwards'. Yet Wilde's plays do side with Reputation. Lord Illingworth, for example, may smile at the thought that 'good women have such limited views of life, their horizon is so small, their interests are so petty', but he eventually bows low (with his cynicism barely intact) before Mrs Arbuthnot's fierce purity. The virtuous woman who inspires and worships becomes, in Wilde's plays, a truly terrifying figure because no man can defeat her or live up to her idealism however naughtily he tweaks at her old-fashioned garb.

But ironically, Wilde's apparent insolence gave ammunition to Mrs Grundy. In 1895, the fracas about Ibsenity became a war against decadence when Wilde's own scandal rocked the nation: his name was erased from theatre billboards, but audiences ceased to patronize *An Ideal Husband* and *The Importance of Being Earnest*. Other dramatists suffered by association, and even the conservers of Nature's ideal, like Henry Arthur Jones, were under siege. In the following year, *Michael and his Lost Angel* was hooted and booed for showing a religious service on stage, and the play closed after eleven performances. The theatre-going public had fallen into 'one of its periodical panics of morality' and, as Jones lamented, the leading dramatists stood, 'for the moment, defeated and discredited before their countrymen. But the movement is not killed. It is only scotched.'[44] Yet, in the years after that, Jones needed no prompting from Charles Wyndham to ensure the inoffensive bounds of Lady Jessica's rebellion and, since needs must, he abandoned indirection, in *Mrs Dane's Defence*, to teach – explicitly and insistently – the hard law of respectability.

CHAPTER 6

Shades of goodness

AUBREY: . . . Oh, of course! To you, Cayley, all women who have been roughly treated, and who dare to survive by borrowing a little of our philosophy, are alike. You see in the crowd of the Ill-used only one pattern; you can't detect the shades of goodness, intelligence, even nobility there. Well, well, how should you? The crowd is dimly lighted! And, besides, yours is the way of the world.
DRUMMLE: My dear Aubrey, I *live* in the world.
AUBREY: The name we give our little parish of St James's.

Arthur Wing Pinero, *The Second Mrs Tanqueray* (1893)

The failure of *Michael and his Lost Angel* in 1896 brought Jones a commiserating letter from his friend, Arthur Pinero, and it too acknowledged the public's nervous reaction to intelligent drama: 'You will have accepted the matter philosophically, I feel sure – recognising that the theatres are in for a silly period.'[1] Pinero had written in the same vein to Archer, some days before, ruefully accepting the fact that the success of Wilson Barrett's religious melodrama, *The Sign of the Cross*, gave cheer to the old guard: 'It comes to them as a sign that the good old crusted "British Drama" is still "going strong" . . . *We* are in, if I mistake not, for a silly period – but it will pass. There is no finality, thank God, in any theatrical fashion.'[2] In for it they were! Almost immediately, Sydney Grundy, whose own serious work had gone down to defeat, abandoned the cause: the new drama never had, and never would attract, an audience. Archer took issue with that 'Crack of Doom',[3] but the next two years seemed to prove Grundy's point: 'In what has . . . the tremendous forward movement of psychology resulted? In the popular triumph of *The Prisoner of Zenda*, *Under the Red Robe*, *Trilby*, and *The Little Minister*. I have nothing that is not good to say of these entertainments, and I rejoice that an estranged audience has returned with gusto to the theatre; but do these financial phenomena represent an advance in popular taste, do they indicate a raising of the theatrical standard . . .?'[4]

162

Yet although the new drama had, in Jones's analysis, become unjustly 'entangled with another movement, got caught in the skirts of the sexual-pessimistic blizzard sweeping over North Europe, was confounded with it, and was execrated and condemned',[5] that stigma was, in a sense, a badge of honour. Like Jones, Pinero was no Ibsenite, but he too had felt the blizzard from the North and, unlike his colleague, had not raged against it. Instead, that stubborn wind had blown him in a direction that would not have seemed possible a mere ten years before when his farces won him fame and popular success.

From early boyhood, when he watched from the pit at Sadler's Wells, Pinero loved the stage. He was ten when he left school to help shore up his father's law practice and, in his spare time, began to frequent the newly opened Prince of Wales's. At nineteen he joined the company at the Theatre Royal, Edinburgh; two years later, he made his London debut in Wilkie Collins's *Miss Gwilt* (1876). Irving was impressed enough to offer him a place at the Lyceum and, during his five years there, Pinero began to write plays, three of which Irving produced as curtain-raisers. His first full-length play, *The Money-Spinner* (1881), was presented by the Kendals and John Hare at the St James's; in the same year, Pinero moved to the Bancrofts' company at the Haymarket. Those theatrical alliances determined his career after he gave up acting to become a professional dramatist. Joining forces with John Clayton and Arthur Cecil, managers at the Court Theatre, he directed his own play, just as Robertson had done at the Prince of Wales's, and brought his experience as an actor and as an observer of the methods of Irving and the Bancrofts to the staging of his first big success, *The Magistrate* (1885). Now, though, the actors each had a printed copy of the entire script, and Pinero drilled them to the precise movements he had visualized when writing the play. He also supervised its American premiere because, as he told Augustin Daly, 'the play is produced here under my sole direction and is animated with the life and character I have instilled into it, [and] I think it of vital moment that the same spirit should be infused into the New York production'.[6] Pinero never went to America again, but he sent detailed instructions or a substitute director who knew precisely how each new play had been 'animated' on the London stage by a cast that had been selected and advised by the author himself.[7]

Details of intonation or movement and the exact placement of each character within the general ensemble, these were crucial to the texture and meaning of Pinero's plays. His methods were those of the cup-and-saucer drama, but he injected them with renewed energy at a time when they seemed to have had their say. In 1885, the Bancrofts retired from the stage. No dramatist had brought them the success that Robertson had, and at the Haymarket they had relied on the classics and Parisian adaptations between revivals of their characteristic repertoire. Pinero's *Lords and Commons* (1883) was the Bancrofts' last production of a new play before they bowed out with their prestige glowingly intact. And as they did so, Pinero took up the torch by applying their principles to a new brand of comedy. Experience had taught him that audiences were essentially sentimental and, to evoke their sympathies, he created a type of farce whose intricate plot exploded out of his characters' attractive vulnerability.[8] Unlike the selfish figures in Gilbert's farces, Pinero's dignitaries are led to disaster by goodheartedness. Despite their well-meaning common sense, they cannot defend themselves against the eccentric demands of those for whom they feel responsible. So Aeneas Posket, in *The Magistrate*, almost comes to trial in his own courtroom; Miss Dyott's academy for young ladies, in *The Schoolmistress* (1886), goes up in flames; the Very Reverend Dean of St Marvells, in *Dandy Dick* (1887), finds himself accused of poisoning a race horse. By allowing character to motivate action, Pinero ensured that his farces had 'as substantial and reasonable a backbone as a serious play'.[9]

The logic of these personalities makes the escalating impossibilities of each play seem probable, and Pinero's sympathetic treatment assures a cordial response to such unseemly events as the arrest of a magistrate, a wife's rebellion, or a clergyman's 'flutter' at the racetrack. *The Schoolmistress*, for example, takes a veiled look at the Woman Question, although Volumnia College is presented as a convenient repository for the daughters of divorcees and Colonial administrators rather than the exemplum of a modern education. By play's end, the audience delights in the wives' revolt against their husbands and relishes Miss Dyott's metamorphosis from respectable headmistress to liberated actress. Lured by Pinero's careful strategy into the licence of farce, playgoers who would not accept Nora Helmer's awakening rocked with laughter as Miss Dyott shattered their proprieties.

The Schoolmistress begins by championing propriety. Miss Dyott's 'rigid austerity' and 'the precious confidence reposed in [her] by the parents and relations of twenty-seven innocent pupils'[10] are emphasized long before the lady's own entrance. The servants wonder how the headmistress can leave 'a lot of foolish young gals for a month or six weeks', why she has dismissed the cook and the parlourmaid, and how she can travel without her husband whose name remains 'a Mystery' (I, p. 19). But the opening duologue also suggests the riot which might break loose in authority's absence. Dinah Rankling, the Admiral's daughter from across the road, has 'been fallin' in love or something, and has got to be locked up'; the Mystery 'is kicking his 'eels about the 'ouse, and giving himself the airs of the 'aughty'; Tyler, the servant boy, has a propensity for fireworks, although 'there ain't much danger unless anybody lunges at me. Friction is the risk I run' (p. 20). All the characters share Tyler's self-importance, and much of their dignity will be rubbed away by the 'friction' of the schoolgirls' behaviour which, from the outset, shows its explosive potential when they physically assault the boy for not attending to his duties. Everything that happens at Volumnia College arises from the girls' romantic desire to restore Dinah to Reggie Paulover with whom she was 'secretly united at the Registry Office' three weeks before, so the deflation of the Honourable Vere Queckett, Miss Dyott's mysterious spouse, and the taming of Admiral Rankling result from a series of schoolgirl pranks.

Having established this spirit of benevolent mischief, Pinero takes pains to show that the two husbands deserve their come-uppance. Queckett, a 'breezy, dapper little gentleman', with curls, a waxed moustache, 'and a simple boyish manner', has expensive tastes and very little else to recommend him. But Miss Dyott adores his 'birth, blood, and breeding', and, as a mere commoner, readily assumes the 'noble task' of supplying his 'elaborate necessities'. Although she would 'drop flat on the pavement' were she to see her name on the play-bills, the schoolmistress prepares to earn some extra money during the Christmas holidays by appearing as Queen Honorine in a comic opera. Her 'only consolation' is that its music comes from the composer's new Oratorio, but Queckett must not know of her disgraceful venture. As 'a gentleman', he would insist on accompanying her and, as an expert dancer, he would find 'a common chord of sympathy' with the *coryphées*: 'Oh, there is so much variety in Vere's character' (pp. 25–7). Admiral Rankling, on the other hand, bristles with sustained rage. Returning from four years' service in Malta, he mistakes Peggy Hesslerigge, the inky orphan who earns her keep as Miss Dyott's assistant, for his recalcitrant daughter and gives the 'good-for-nothing girl' a good shaking. Earlier, his peremptory telegram, a monosyllabic 'Bosh!' to Dinah's announced affections, had led to her secret marriage for, though 'the telegraphic rate from Malta necessitates abruptness, [she] can never forgive the choice of such a phrase' (p. 22). But it is Mrs Rankling who bears the brunt of his tyranny, and she too is an adoring slave despite the fact that everything she does rankles the Admiral's apoplectic sensibility. And thus Pinero lays the foundations for Act Two in which Queckett's soirée for Jack Mallory and 'two or three good fellows' becomes ludicrously entangled with the girls' unsophisticated wedding-breakfast and the Admiral, an unwitting guest at that celebration, gives the couple his bibulous blessing and takes a more than paternal interest in the charms of Dinah's schoolfellows. The gentlemen's downfall is effected in the absence of their wives and so avoids unwomanly rebellion. Their adventure ends when Tyler and his fireworks go 'off bang in the kitchen', at which point a flamboyant *opéra-bouffe* Queen appears at the balcony window to bring her husband down the firemen's ladder to a denouement which depicts the ladies' happy transformation.

As Constance Delaporte, queen of the stage, Miss Dyott had received a rapturous ovation, having forced herself to sing and dance for Vere's sake. But, 'the moment I dragged you down that ladder last night and left behind me the smouldering ruins of Volumnia College, I became an altered woman' (p. 69). She revels in her new identity. Queen Connie will no longer pamper the bankrupt charms of the Honourable Vere nor need she underestimate herself as a lowly schoolmistress: 'You *did* marry a lady! But scratch the lady and you find a hardworking comic actress!' From that new view of herself, she urges Mrs Rankling also to take stock of her own 'true character'. Both ladies have been 'undervalued' by unworthy men:

MISS DYOTT: Now – looking at him microscopically – is there much to love and to honour in Admiral Rankling?
MRS RANKLING: He is a genial after-dinner speaker.
MISS DYOTT: Hah!
MRS RANKLING: It is true he is rather austere.
MISS DYOTT: An austere sailor! All bows abroad and stern at home. Well then – knowing what occurred last night – is there anything to love and to honour in Mr Queckett?
MRS RANKLING: Nothing whatever. (III, p. 63)

And so, holding up a broken portrait-bust of herself, Mrs Rankling upbraids her husband with the wreckage of her former self, before she was 'worried and fretted' by his constant 'ill-humour' (p. 66). The Admiral may think the shattered bust proves she has 'completely lost [her] head', but his wife insists on Dinah's happiness and, thanks to the events of the night before, there is nothing he can do except become his 'dear old self again' and allow their daughter to meet Reggie once a quarter, 'in the presence of Admiral Rankling and a policeman' (p. 70), until the two are old enough to be man and wife. And now that Constance Delaporte knows how her husband squandered the servants' wages, the rent money, and the school itself on champagne, cigars, and a party for his 'nieces', she 'will dance more wildly, more demonstratively than ever!' (p. 69). She does, however, allow him a private box while she is at the theatre; it 'will be our lodgings, where he will remain under lock and key' (p. 71).

A woman's self-discovery and the way life's experiences affect her personality are themes which Pinero would often return to, but here he treats them lightheartedly and objectively. The conventional strictures of rank and sex provide an unstated norm against which each character's erratic behaviour is measured, so that when Vere plunges 'into the vortex of these festivities' the comedy rises from the contradiction between what should happen at an evening with 'two or three good fellows' and the girls' spontaneous version of a party. The characters themselves, though, are not judged by convention but by the propriety of their own particular needs. Miss Dyott's participation in 'a nightly entertainment of a volatile description' is neither a social gaffe nor a betrayal of her sex; it raises her in her own and the audience's estimation. Farce permits a temporary respite from society's polite regulations. The rules still lurk behind the action but, for an hour or two, they can be mocked or overthrown. And the characters break free from class and sex to be applauded or reviled as individuals. Those liberties also allow Pinero to discriminate between one shade of goodness and another. Peggy Hesslerigge, the arch manipulator of the first two Acts, would indeed seem to be the 'Gorgon' she threatens Vere with were she judged by prescribed convention. Her catch-phrase, 'I am only a girl', draws attention to her unladylike manner but it also provides an excuse for her unscrupulous energy. Eventually the audience sees beyond Peggy's frowsy exterior to appreciate her human gaucherie, as Jack Mallory does: 'I love that girl!' (p. 61).

Pinero's own view of these plays was a craftsman's. Their success had shown a way to 'raise' farce above the 'low pantomime level'.[11]

Airy trifle though it was, *The Magistrate* was transported to Germany and frequently produced there, 'it seems always with success'.[12] Pinero could claim it as the first homegrown drama to make an impact on Europe. Gilbert and Sullivan's operas had the benefit of music's 'universal language'; Robertson's *David Garrick* had been adapted from a French original; *The Magistrate* was 'purely English':

> I hope the time will come – is coming – when the Englishman, like the Frenchman, will write his plays for all nations. The consciousness, when a man is writing a play, that he is working for the amusement of a few thousand middle-class English people, is not favourable to the development of Dramatic Art. That's why this German business seems of some importance – if the English writer's reach spreads, his thoughts might run out with his arm.

Pinero's greatest success, *Sweet Lavender* (1888), ran for almost seven hundred performances at Terry's Theatre, and it, too, was adapted for the German States and Austria.[13] But its sentimental domesticity did not stretch the reach of 'Dramatic Art' nor did it test the limits of Victorian convention.

The play in fact looks back to Robertson, through Dickens's spectacles, for its contrasted heroines (the one a delicate child-woman, the other a Wiltonesque tease) and its familiarly romantic theme: a modest daughter of the working class can, in her natural womanliness, become the pupil-bride of her patient and loving superior. The minor characters are particularly Dickensian. Dr Delaney, for example, repeatedly asserts his hard heart – 'it's no business of mine' – but every deed proclaims his kindness. Even Dick Phenyl, the play's comic and sentimental showpiece, combines that eccentric genius, Newman Noggs, with the self-consciously disreputable Mr Eccles. Pinero concedes to modernity by making Minnie Gilfillian's persistent suitor an American tourist, and he organizes these ingredients into an expertly modulated first Act. But when Ruth Rolt perceives a photograph of Mr Wedderburn, the man who seduced and abandoned her, she determines that her daughter shall never marry his adopted son, Clement Hale, and the remainder of the play falls victim to the weary story of a wronged woman's struggle to ensure that her child should never know her shameful past. Pinero's individuality shows most when Mrs Gilfillian loses her fortune, doffs her curls and furbelows, and becomes her natural self: 'Now I've lost all my money . . . but somehow I've felt in a kinder temper the last week than I have for years. So I think, Mr Phenyl, to some natures even bankruptcy may be a blessing.'[14] Nevertheless, her brother, Mr

Wedderburn, need not go down to ruin, thanks to Phenyl's generosity, and Lavender does become his daughter (by marriage), though she never discovers he is her actual father. By remaining true to her, Clement shows himself 'wiser, better, braver' than his guardian had been to Mrs Rolt; Lavender's sweet love has taught him 'that the only rank which elevates a woman is that which a gentle spirit bestows upon her' (pp. 174–5).

The Court farces and *Sweet Lavender* brought prosperity, and Pinero could insist on their artistic merit and international repute. But he also knew that greater things were expected by critics like Archer who, by the mid eighties, had proclaimed him 'the most original and remarkable of living English playwrights, with a possible exception in favour of Mr Gilbert'.[15] In *The Weaker Sex*, written in 1884 but not produced in London for another five years, and *The Hobby Horse* (1886), Pinero satirized (blandly and sentimentally) such contemporary issues as women's rights and social philanthropy. He never argued publicly, as Jones did, for a 'dramatic literature', but private letters reveal his increasing purposefulness. The commercial success of his 'serviceable' plays did not blunt a desire 'to yield unresistingly to the higher impress of truth'. By 1887 he had completed *The Profligate* and offered the play to John Hare who reacted nervously to its unrelenting seriousness. Negotiations dragged on for over a year, and in 1889 Hare presented it as his first production at the new Garrick Theatre with a changed ending which, as Pinero himself explained, would not distress 'the audience by sacrificing the life of a character whose sufferings were intended to win sympathy'.[16] As originally conceived, Dunstan Renshaw, haunted by the fact that his spotless wife has discovered his sensual past and will never forget it (*'she knows you!'*), takes poison and dies before he can hear her redeeming words: 'We are one and we will make atonement for the past together.'[17] At the Garrick, Dunstan dashed the poison from his lips to avoid a 'blacker [crime] than that sin for which I suffer' (p. vii) and, on his knees, begged God for strength. Leslie Renshaw returned to bear 'the burden of the sin you have committed' and, though she could not forget, promised to 'be your wife, not your judge. Let us from this moment begin the new life you spoke of' (p. viii). In a final tableau, Dunstan called down blessings on her head (and forgiveness on his) as the pair knelt together, side by side: 'Wife! Ah, God bless you' . . . 'Oh, my husband!' (p. ix).

Both endings throb to the earnest theatrics of the entire play, and yet, by following the lead of Jones's *Saints and Sinners* (1884) while confronting the sexual double-standard with far less compromise, Pinero seemed to project new force into the theatre. *The Profligate* was rapturously welcomed by those who had 'been led to expect such a play from [Pinero] . . . and believe[d he could] produce something out of the beaten track of stagecraft'.[18] But despite the play's unyielding seriousness and provocative theme, set down portentously in a versified programme-note, Pinero's stagecraft still depends, reassuringly and conventionally, on black or white characters whose conflicts are arranged into a series of persuasive images which manipulate the emotions but avoid the issues raised by the plot. Act Three, 'The End of the Honeymoon', presents the most compelling of those pictures. Janet Preece has refused to marry Wilfrid Brudenell. Overwhelmed by Leslie's goodness, she explains why she rejected her brother: 'the time has been when I was one of the tempted and not one of the strong' (p. 90). Leslie quells her instinctive horror and, raising up her friend, determines to protect her. As they leave the villa, for Wilfrid must also be protected, Janet stops on the garden steps and tries to pull Leslie back: 'It's the man – the man!' (p. 92). The audience already knows the identity of Janet's betrayer, but Leslie, in her innocence, assumes the girl refers to Lord Dangars who is soon to marry Irene Stonehay, at the urging of the despicable Mrs Stonehay, and who now arrives at the villa with Dunstan Renshaw. Leslie decides to use Janet's confession to save Irene from the dissolute Lord, but Dangars protests his innocence and, as Leslie 'turns to stone' realizing that 'the man' in question is her own beloved husband, Janet runs wildly from the room: 'Ah! What have I done to you! I'd have died to save you from this. God forgive me! I'm not fit to live! Kill me! Kill me! Ah!' (p. 102).

Unlike the characters in Pinero's farces, these puppets have no individuality. They move to the idealized rhythms of romantic 'tragedy'. There is no irony in the fact that Dunstan, since his marriage, has been exactly the man his adoring wife thought he was nor does their confrontation explore the limitations of a schoolgirl's *naïveté*. The theme is Ibsenesque in that Dunstan's shameful past returns to destroy him, but each episode is unthinkingly melodramatic. And so *The Profligate* impressed the advocates of modernism and seemed strong stuff to those who thrilled to its dark excitements:

(*The mandolin begins to play – Leslie shudders and tries to leave*)
DUNSTAN: Help me to begin a new life! I'm young . . . I won't die till I've done
some good act to make you proud of me! Oh, give me hope!

LESLIE (*As if in a dream*):   Deny it! . . . Deny it.
DUNSTAN: I can't deny it!
LESLIE: Go!
(*After a moment he goes quietly away, then she falls to the ground in a swoon. The voice of the singer rises in the distance*)

CURTAIN   (p. 104)

The Profligate was 'a complete success', but Pinero saw it as a precarious achievement, for the play was 'not altogether well acted', despite a carefully selected cast, and that incompetence reaffirmed 'the enormous difficulties in the way of getting the piece played with absolute conviction & reality', so he doubted whether the play could succeed outside London. Its acclaim was also a burden: 'only the best work is looked for from me'.[19] Then, two months later, *A Doll's House* was produced by Janet Achurch and Charles Charrington at the Novelty, and, as Archer put it, Ibsen became 'the most famous man in the English literary world'.[20] In 1891, *Rosmersholm, Hedda Gabler*, and the Independent Theatre Society's production of *Ghosts*, in particular, made Ibsen infamous with more conservative critics: 'This disgusting representation . . . Absolutely loathsome and fetid . . . Crapulous stuff . . . As foul and filthy a concoction as has ever been allowed to disgrace the boards of an English theatre.' In that same year, Pinero himself made a little theatrical history when, under the new copyright laws, he arranged for the printed edition of his latest play, *The Times*, to be sold at Terry's Theatre. Such 'documentary evidence . . . would always apportion fairly to actor and author their just shares of credit or of blame. It would also offer conclusive testimony as to the condition of theatrical work in this country.'[21]

But that 'condition' now weighed down upon him as Archer, whom he respected as a critic and friend, pressed for greater realism. Pinero felt 'that in your earnest, persistent search for one object you run the risk of missing all others, and that you and the school you have created are perhaps too inclined to accept the latest formula in art, whatever that formula may be, as the only true one.'[22] He defended his past achievements as 'my attempt to purge the popular comic play of something worse than mere vulgarity' and politely objected to the fact that this 'serviceable' work had brought him 'blame for not having done something else. However I hope I shall by and by turn out work which may take rank on a different platform.' In the back of his mind he was soon shaping 'something else'. At the beginning of 1892 he began work on *The Second Mrs Tanqueray*, 'and in February or March [he] read the first act to Hare'.[23]

171

As he worked on the play, he could not escape the thought that Ibsen had altered his world. The serious critics were no longer satisfied with his past efforts, and yet Northern realism was turning audiences away to mindless entertainments:

A few years ago the native authors were working with a distinct and sound aim and with every prospect of popularising a rational, observant home-grown play. Then came the Scandinavian drama, held up by the New Critics as the Perfect drama and used by them as a means of discrediting native produce. Just for the present everything is knocked askew; the English dramatist has little influence and the public, urged to witness *A Doll's House*, patronises the Empire Theatre of Varieties![24]

Pinero could not ignore Ibsen, whether he would have preferred to or not, and he responded to the challenge by discarding soliloquies, minimizing asides, and concentrating his powers of characterization. That autumn, when *Mrs Tanqueray* was completed, Hare refused to produce it. Pinero turned to George Alexander of the St James's, who was then presenting *Lady Windermere's Fan*, and managed to get him to agree to a series of afternoon performances. But the play was 'risky', and Pinero was determined to secure the best cast possible; this meant further delay, although 'the fittest time to begin rehearsing a play [was], in [Pinero's] opinion, the day after it is finished'.[25] Even minor characters worried their creator: 'Are you sure Fanny Coleman is a little like Mrs Cortelyon? Keep on telling me she is or I shall doubt it. Miss C. is so like a cook we once had.'[26] And what actress could portray the complexity of Paula Tanqueray? Eventually Pinero noticed Mrs Patrick Campbell in an Adelphi melodrama, 'a very interesting actress', and, at the St James's, R.C. Carton's *Liberty Hall*, which had followed Wilde's play, began to falter. In May 1893, *Mrs Tanqueray* was ready to replace it on the evening bill. Pinero invited William Heinemann (his publisher), George Meredith, Henry James, and Edmund Gosse, whose *Studies in the Literature of Northern Europe* (1879) had introduced Ibsen to the public: 'It is not my habit to ask folks to witness my work . . . but this play is a play for grown-up people, and you are amongst the few grown-up people whose word I care for.'[27] On that opening night, much to Archer's delight, Victorian drama came of age:

Well now, Mr Pinero and Mr Alexander, whatever your box-office returns may say . . . don't you feel that you have done a fine thing, a thing really worth doing, worth suffering for if need be, a thing that enhances your self-respect . . .? Now that the thing is done – and not in a tentative, apologetic, afternoon fashion, but with straightforward courage and confidence – don't you feel that if art is not virile it is childish, and that virile art alone is really worth living for? . . . It is the astonishing advance in philosophical insight and technical skill which places the new play in a new category.[28]

Victorian drama turns 'virile' and 'new' once Paula arrives at Aubrey Tanqueray's apartment during the closing moments of Act One. In the episodes which lead to that, Pinero masks the suspense with dialogue that sounds authentic and uncontrived, although the exposition is not without its clumsiness. Three middle-aged men sit round the dinner-table in Aubrey Tanqueray's 'luxuriously furnished' chambers at the Albany; a fourth chair proclaims the absence of another invited guest. Pinero's stagecraft begins to obtrude when Aubrey moves away to 'scribble a couple of notes now while I think of them' (p. 79)[29] and so allows his friends to whisper their astonished reaction to the unconventional marriage he plans to embark on. The arrival of Cayley Drummle, 'a neat little man . . . bright, airy, debonair', quickens the tempo but does not entirely disguise this artifice. In his embarrassment, he understandably exaggerates the woes of Lady Orreyed which delayed him but, as he expands his story, it seems unlikely that Aubrey should turn again to his letters, for George Orreyed's marriage to the notorious Miss Hervey matches his own circumstance. Pinero makes him listen with increasing irritation to Cayley's waspish account of the 'social Dead Sea', which has swallowed up Lord George, and then hurries him out of the room in order that the friends can relate the necessary facts. After that contrivance, the conversation runs naturally, controlled by Cayley's cynical gaiety and by his concern for Aubrey whose first marriage, to a saintly 'iceberg', proved disastrous: 'I believe she kept a thermometer in her stays and always registered ten degrees below zero' (p. 83). The final detail falls into place when Cayley tells them about Aubrey's daughter who has been brought up in a convent, in accord with her dead mother's wishes, and whose determination to become a nun has left her father desperately 'alone'. On that suggestive word, Aubrey returns, and Dr Jayne and Mr Misquith go out into the night. They never appear again, and their absence underscores the change in Tanqueray's social life after he marries Paula.

The subsequent dialogue between Cayley and Aubrey sheds important light on the latter's character and motives; it also explores the lady's unfortunate past. At first Aubrey refuses to explain anything but, when Cayley appeals to their friendship, he reacts with deliberate frankness in order to prove that his alliance with Paula Ray (alias Mrs Jarman, alias Mrs Dartry, and so forth) is not the usual 'case of a blind man entrapped by an artful woman' (p. 86). Aubrey is, after all, 'alone'; his marriage may lose him 'the esteem' of his friends, but he intends to re-open his house in the country; no one else will be harmed by his plunge into the Dead Sea. The precise nature of his present relationship with Paula is side-stepped discreetly; Aubrey feels 'a temperate, honourable affection' for her and is moved by her unhappiness: 'She has never met a man who has treated her well – I intend to treat her well' (p. 87). His plans for their future may be idealistic, but they sound reasonable, and Cayley heartily supports his resolve 'to rear a life of happiness, of good repute, on a – miserable foundation'. The two friends shake hands with regret, on Aubrey's part, that they 'have spoken too freely of – of Mrs Jarman' and with a promise from Cayley that 'when we next meet I shall remember nothing but my respect for the lady who bears your name'. At that, Aubrey's manservant enters to announce Mrs Jarman, and the New Order begins.

From then on, the relationships between the characters evolve by implication (what we now call sub-text) rather than through statement and picture-making. How apt, then, that a man called Morse should signal the new style. Flustered by Paula's unorthodox visit to a gentleman's rooms at a quarter to eleven at night, Morse 'clos[es] the door behind him carefully' and announces her arrival to his master 'in an undertone'. Aubrey assumes she must be 'at the lodge in her carriage' and is visibly rattled when he learns otherwise. Then, in a revealing piece of by-play, Morse mentions the 'nice fire' in the room beyond and glances at the bedroom door, much to Aubrey's embarrassment. But in Cayley's presence he must suppress his annoyance at Paula's indiscretion and its effect on his servant, and the text itself gives no hint as to whether his friend has perceived these undercurrents. Pinero depends here on the actor who must convey Cayley's awareness, or lack of it, through the way he looks at his watch, puts on his hat and coat, and, with too much brightness, takes his leave. Once he has gone, Morse brings in some 'unopened letters', which remain on the mantelpiece until the end of the Act, and 'hesitatingly' offers to retire for the night now that the caterers have departed. Aubrey brusquely cuts off that suggestion; Morse leaves, and his master opens the door to Paula.

Paula's radiant entrance challenges the audience. She is 'about twenty-seven: beautiful, fresh, innocent-looking' and dresses superbly, yet she could not be received in respectable society, and her unconventional behaviour affirms that. Laughing away the lateness of her visit, she teases Aubrey for caring about what the servants will think and notices the remains of his 'snug little dinner'. Pinero presents her as an individual, worldly and irresponsible but also vulnerable when she assumes that the dinner-party was not exclusively masculine. Aubrey and Paula have colours which constantly surprise, and that unpredictability appears at the very beginning of Pinero's first exchange between, and for, grown-ups:

PAULA: I haven't dined, Aubrey dear.
AUBREY: My poor girl! Why?
PAULA: In the first place, I forgot to order any dinner, and my cook, who has always loathed me, thought he'd pay me out before he departed.
AUBREY: The beast!
PAULA: That's precisely what I –
AUBREY: No, Paula!
PAULA: What I told my maid to call him. What next will you think of me?
AUBREY: Forgive me. You must be starved.
PAULA: (*eating fruit*) I didn't care. As there was nothing to eat, I sat in my best frock with my toes on the dining-room fender, and dreamt, oh, such a lovely dinner-party.
AUBREY: Dear lonely little woman! (pp. 88–9)

It is ironic, yet human, that Aubrey should automatically label her as the sort of woman who would trade insults with her cook. He had spoken up for Mabel Hervey, insisting that his friends did not 'really know anything' about the new Lady Orreyed, and had argued with Cayley about the 'shades of goodness' that ought to distinguish Mabel Orreyed from Paula Ray, but he cannot fight down his prejudice towards the woman he cares about. And Paula does lead a rackety life, yet her ravenous delight ('I love fruit when it's expensive') and her childlike dream of respectability reveal the inner need of this fast, disorganized woman and explain why the well-bred Aubrey should reach out to her in his own loneliness.

But the sequence also contains their future. Controlled more or less by social convention, they are both driven by their individual personalities and see the world from their own points of view. Paula has always taken risks, tearing at life just as she tears at the fruit, and is now prepared to stake everything on Aubrey's reaction to a letter in which she has spelled out each detail of her former life: 'It may save discussion by and by, don't you think?' That defensive humour is also in character. Used to insults, and over-quick to find them, she would rather be the first to mock the weight of her accusing history: 'I wonder if it would go for a penny.' But she is dissatisfied, as well as world-weary, and the fact that someone like Aubrey should want to marry her has allowed her to dream of a future with 'the sort of men and women that can't be imitated'. The risk she takes is a calculated one: Aubrey must surely do the gentlemanly thing and refuse to read the letter. But she feels hurt nonetheless when he silently destroys it, for he might have acknowledged the sacrifice she was prepared to make. These shades of character suggest that she possibly might carry out her threat to kill herself were 'anything serious' to come between herself and Aubrey, though he would like her always to 'think of something bright'. In the past, she *had* inured herself to love's failure and life's mayhem in that way; now her love for Aubrey and her longing for the life he offers make her newly vulnerable. That irony points to certain weaknesses behind Aubrey's confident optimism. As the misunderstanding over the cook illustrates, Aubrey is not as open-minded as he thinks he is. If only Paula would not talk so freely about her shabby past, he could help her sweep it aside, for it pleases him to do good things for his 'dear baby'. But when Paula goes to fetch her cloak, he opens one of the letters on the mantelpiece, and suddenly the future looks less easy. Ellean has been touched by her father's loneliness and by her mother's guiding spirit: 'I am ready to take my place by you' (p. 91). Distracted by that news, he stares blankly at Paula and now finds it difficult to respond to her bright hopes for 'To-morrow.' Poor Aubrey lacks her sense of humour.

In the next Act and a half, Pinero explores the relationship between Paula, Aubrey, and Ellean with impressive objectivity. The trio are trapped in their own personalities. Snubbed by the neighbours and so condemned to a monotonous routine, Paula feels she will wither away 'from sheer, solitary respectability' (p. 94) and, in reaction to that boredom, goads Aubrey to the verge of despair. She knows her behaviour hurts him, yet his aggrieved patience provokes her still farther. In consequence, he cannot help but judge her or compare her to the saintly Ellean, and that tortures Paula. If she could make a friend of the girl, she might think better of herself and earn Aubrey's respect, but Ellean will not respond to her as she does to her father. Paula's restless frustration, her jealous and destructive wit are much like Hedda Gabler's and, for the moment, Pinero examines those moods, resisting the blanket judgement her husband casts upon them. For all his good will, Aubrey is shocked by 'poor Paula's light, careless nature' (p. 98). He no longer sees her as an individual; her every word and action types her as the sort whose 'maimed' womanhood endangers his daughter: 'there's hardly a subject you can broach on which poor Paula hasn't some strange, out-of-the-way thought to give utterance to; some curious, warped notion'. Listening to his friend's distress, Cayley does not tell him to consider 'poor Paula's' situation but he does criticize his overprotective attitude to his angel: 'I am sure there are many women upon earth who are almost divinely innocent; but being on earth, they must send their robes to the laundry occasionally.' Ellean cannot hide from the world for ever, and a knowledge of its ways might bring her understanding: 'it is only one step from toleration to forgiveness' (p. 99). Both men assume that Paula needs forgiveness; however, Cayley's remarks allow the audience to understand her as her own (rather than Ellean's) worst enemy, to see the turmoil below her outrageous behaviour and so react with less shock and more compassion than Aubrey can.

This is particularly the case when Paula confronts Mrs Cortelyon, an intimate of the first Mrs Tanqueray, whom Cayley has persuaded to unbend and help Aubrey by taking Ellean away for the Season in Paris and London (II, pp. 100–3). For the past two months, this nearest of neighbours has refused to acknowledge the Tanquerays, so Paula, *whose manner now alternates between deliberate insolence and assumed sweetness*, takes glorious revenge by pretending not to know the lady ('I have quite a wretched memory') and by offering her sympathy since a prolonged illness must have kept her away ('You look dreadfully pulled down'). Mrs Cortelyon fights back her anger as Paula feigns innocence ('Aubrey, tell Mrs Cortelyon how stupid and thoughtless I always am!'), snipes at her age, and forces her to humble herself. But Paula does not enjoy that victory for long. She notices Ellean's warm response to her mother's friend and is cut to the quick when she learns the purpose of the lady's visit. The bond of good breeding defeats her after all and, suspecting the gentlemen's complicity, she turns her back on them to stare through the window of the imprisoning morning-room. This episode points specifically to Paula's qualities: her intelligence, courage, resistance. Aubrey only sees a generalized 'good woman' whose *past* will not allow him 'to make happy and contented' (p. 98); Pinero stands back from that to show how her particular character and circumstances create her *present* misery. And, once the Orreyeds arrive on the scene, 'the shades of goodness' between one scarlet woman and another are clear to us if not to Mr Tanqueray. Lady Mabel's shaky grammar, petty snobbery, slangy manners, and vacant beauty illumine Paula's brave individuality. Excluded by her unconventional past and her disruptive personality from Aubrey's orderly circle, she is too much a lady to ally herself with Mabel and the ghastly Lord George. Caught between two worlds, she is frantically jealous of Ellean's repose yet nauseated by the Orreyeds' shoddiness: 'I've outgrown these people. This woman – I used to think her "jolly!" – sickens me. I can't breathe when she's near me: the whiff of her handkerchief turns me faint!' (III, p. 108).

Ultimately, however, Pinero's own restrictive and conventional idea of womanhood determines Paula's fate. The signs are there under the play's apparent objectivity in that no male character is able to see Paula in her own right; even Cayley classifies her as 'mad', like 'all jealous women' (II, p. 103), after her encounter with Mrs Cortelyon. That the gentlemen voice their creator's *theory* of womanhood becomes evident at the moment in Act Three when Aubrey urges Paula to take stock of herself. With unwavering confidence ('I have no curiosity – I know what you were at Ellean's age'), he tells her to think back to a time, not so many years before, when 'you hadn't an impulse that didn't tend towards good, you never harboured a notion you couldn't have gossiped about to a parcel of children' (p. 111). Because she is a woman of a certain education, her girlhood *must* have been as pure as Ellean's, but the 'cruel life' she has led since then has tainted that feminine essence: 'Every belief that a young, pure-minded girl holds sacred – that you once held sacred – you now make a target for a jest, a sneer, a paltry cynicism. I tell you, you're not mistress any longer of your thoughts or your tongue.' Paula reacts angrily but is not allowed to question his assumption. In fact, once she recovers from the hurt, she subscribes to that archetypal picture of herself: 'A few – years ago! (*She walks slowly towards the door, then suddenly drops upon the ottoman in a paroxysm of weeping.*) O God! A few years ago!' Pinero, too, has shaped her character to that imposed pattern, saying nothing about her upbringing, her parentage, and the particular circumstances that could have led to her disreputable career. Mabel Orreyed has a mother who 'has stuck to [her] through everything – well, you know!' (IV, p. 121) and that may account for her comparative tawdriness; but, having shown the difference between them, Pinero now sees Paula as if she were like 'all women who have been roughly treated, and who dare to survive by borrowing a little of [men's] philosophy' (p. 86). So Paula is finally judged by the rules of 'our little parish of St James's' rather than the demands of her own personality.

Paula's resilient sarcasm, her courage and resourcefulness need not necessarily lead to suicide even though that destiny is foreshadowed when she declares she would kill herself if 'anything serious happened to [her]' (p. 90) and when she cries out against her respectable prison: 'You'll kill me with this life!' (p. 93). Pinero's idealized concept of her sex proves stronger than his understanding of her individual psychology. He believes, with Aubrey, that she 'is really and truly a good woman' (p. 98) who, sensitive enough to acknowledge her lost innocence, can beg for 'another chance' (p. 112). When Ellean returns suddenly from Paris, joyfully in love with Captain Ardale, it seems Paula might become a confidante if she could curb her waywardness. But Ellean's boyish suitor had once 'kept house' with Paula and, unlike the heroic captain, the lady refuses to lie her way out of trouble. There *is* no way to escape the past for, as Ellean furiously asserts, it shows in her face. Paula is good enough to acknowledge that, too. Her prettiness may mask the taint but, even if she and Aubrey went abroad to 'begin afresh', her past would inevitably show itself. Aubrey's memory of what occurred in Surrey would be 'an everlasting nightmare' (p. 128) and that tarnish would become increasingly apparent:

You'll see me then, at last, with other people's eyes; you'll see me just as your daughter does now, as all wholesome folks see women like me. And I shall have no weapon to fight with – not one serviceable little bit of prettiness left me to defend myself with! A worn out creature – broken up, very likely, some time before I ought to be – my hair bright, my eyes dull, my body too thin or too stout, my cheeks raddled and ruddled – a ghost, a wreck, a caricature, a candle that gutters, call such an end what you like! (p. 129)

Paula dies because she (and Pinero) believe in this inescapable pattern and, though the play protests against the double standard, the past adventures of men like Hugh Ardale or of Aubrey himself do not show in their faces. Paula rails against the fact that Ellean could forgive Ardale, because of his military heroism, but Pinero ultimately implies that the code of St James's reflects the law of Nature.

The Second Mrs Tanqueray is revolutionary in the degree to which the characters' minds and personalities propel the action's twists and turns. Their feelings often move between the lines of dialogue and are finely shaded. Despite her past, Paula is allowed an independent stature and is presented with discriminating sympathy; but, as a fallen woman, she has coarsened herself, and the consequences of that lie beyond her individual control. Any woman who betrays her femininity goes against Nature. This principle, engraved on Pinero's psyche, restricts his vision both before and after he discovered his artistic freedom.

The 'gentlemanly women' in *The Weaker Sex* (1884)[30] who plan to further their 'Advancement . . . from the Rear to the Van' at a 'monster' rally are crudely drawn grotesques in dowdy clothes and short, straight hair. Attempting to be 'strong, self-reliant, fine-minded' (p. 14), they have become narrow and rigid. They can, however, return to physical and mental health if, like Lady Vivash, they obey the promptings of their sex: 'A woman's only battles should be those of her husband, the intellects she should develop are those of her children' (p. 31). In *The Times* (1891), that masculine prejudice appears with more finesse. Miss Cazalet, proprietress of the *Morning Message*, is allowed a 'well-preserved and richly attired' vivacity (p. 28). After her father's death, 'she wrote realistic novels' which 'alienated' and 'shocked' the lending libraries (p. 33). Since then she has traded on her looks, and a 'dear good friend in the City, who believes in me', has given her the *Morning Message* as a birthday present (p. 31). But she is not an efficient nurse to her 'rickety baby': she has 'such trouble' with its editors and, as someone who always 'tired of a new toy after a fortnight', is amazed to have kept 'this influential journal for a whole month!' (pp. 73–4). Her actual child, whom she introduces as 'my little niece', has none of her worldly 'coarseness' (p. 31). She is pale, sad-looking, bespectacled, and shabby: 'Poor Lucy has broken down wofully at Newnham. Her feminine intellect has drawn the line at Latin Prose, and left her rubbing menthol into her brows from morning till night' (p. 29). The futility of women who unsex themselves also pervades the genial farce Pinero wrote for the Court Theatre while waiting to rehearse *Mrs Tanqueray*. Once Lady Castlejordan of *The Amazons* (1893) discovers that her daughters have romantic inclinations, despite their manly upbringing ('If we're boys, we must have pals!'), she renounces her fantastic regime and orders them into their frocks ('And never, never, never come out of them!'): a transformation that satisfies the longings of the confused Noel(ine), Wil(helmina) and Thom(asin).[31]

When Pinero addressed the Woman Question seriously, in *The*

Notorious Mrs Ebbsmith (1895), his conservatism continued to shackle his imagination. Like *The Profligate*, *Mrs Ebbsmith* is essentially a problem play and, despite the sophistication of his dialogue and characterization, Pinero cannot explore the issues he raises in complete freedom. To a certain extent, he does comprehend the tyranny women endure in marriage but he will not open himself to every possible alternative. Consequently, he depicts marital injustice from each character's point of view but shies away from the sort of political and social rebellion that situation might lead to. Unable to make this imaginative leap, he understands the mind of Agnes Ebbsmith less well than the tainted Paula's.

Perhaps because of her unnatural character, Pinero has to document the past which turned Agnes into a 'lean witch', whereas Paula's type needs no such explanation. Like her, Agnes at nineteen 'was as simple – ay, in my heart as devout – as any girl in a parsonage'.[32] Her father's atheistic socialism and her mother's ill-temper did not infect her: away from her unhappy home, 'the air blew away uncertainty and scepticism; I seemed only to have to take a long, deep breath to be full of hope and faith'. Determined to avoid the 'choked-up, seething pit' of marriage, she nonetheless succumbed to the attractiveness of her very first suitor. Eight years of married hell 'changed' her; once widowed, she became 'an out-and-out child of [her] father', preaching revolution: 'Oh, and I was fond, too, of warning women' (I, p. 231). The rest of her story illustrates Pinero's thesis. In deciding to create a passionless and illicit union with Lucas Cleeve, she shows herself to be as 'mad' and deluded as she was when she wore herself out in the public arena. But as soon as she concedes to femininity, Pinero can respond to her knowing and magnificent self-sacrifice. The egotistic Lucas will quickly tire of her, but nothing matters except the 'one supreme hour' that comes to every woman (III, p. 317). Even when she discovers her partner's utter selfishness, she willingly yields to his ambition. That clear-eyed devotion proves stronger than his worthlessness or her friends' attempt to save her from shame. Only Mrs Cleeve, recognizing a fellow victim and refusing to 'accept the service of this wretched woman' (IV, p. 358), can free her to pursue a life of prayer and good works in her friends' Yorkshire rectory.

As Archer noticed when reviewing the play, Pinero imposes a particular 'view' about womanliness onto Agnes Ebbsmith 'and "views", like knotty window-panes, are fatal to observation'.[33]

Convinced that all young girls are devout by nature, he takes that as the essential element in her character to which she will return, at play's end, to find peace and restoration. In his view, unconditional devotion is woman's supreme quality. A youthful infatuation swept Agnes into marriage, but devotion gave her strength to endure eight miserable years, just as Mrs Cleeve learned to bear her husband's failings. Gertrude Thorpe's marriage had also been vile but she, too, 'came through it', resisting the other man she 'couldn't help loving' (III, p. 331). Agnes had been wrong to think that, after one disaster, 'you don't begin to believe all over again' (I, p. 231). Her devotion to Lucas during his illness has already stirred her feelings; when she ceases to fight them ('My sex has found me out'), she achieves her greatest victory:

Nothing matters now . . . He's mine. He would have died but for me. I gave him life. He is my child, my husband, my lover, my bread, my daylight – all – everything. Mine, mine.   (III, p. 316)

Before that return to noble feeling, Pinero can only regard her as a monster. He recreates the external image of such a creature but can find no way into her brain. Agnes voices *his* opinions when she describes her childhood ('The other thing hadn't soaked into me') or her father's philosophy: 'He believed in nothing that people who go to church are credited with believing in, Mrs Thorpe' (I, pp. 229–30). These are not the words of someone who now promotes that 'thing' and is herself fiercely anti-religious. When she 'Trafalgar Square[s]' the Duke of St Olpherts, her harangue has no internal energy since its slogans sound literary: 'Those who would strip the robes from a dummy aristrocracy and cast the broken dolls into the limbo of a nation's discarded toys' (II, p. 270). At the end of the play, a woman once more, she looks back at her mad schemes with a detachment that is just as stilted even if her self-consciousness is now more appropriate:

I – *I* was to lead women! *I* was to show them, in your company, how laws – laws made and laws that are natural – may be set aside or slighted; how men and women may live independent and noble lives without rule, or guidance, or sacrament. *I* was to be the example – the figure set up for others to observe and imitate. But the figure was made of wax – it fell awry at the first hot breath that touched it! You and I! What a partnership it has been! How base and gross and wicked almost from the very beginning!   (IV, pp. 360–1)

Pinero fails to animate this transgressor against Nature but he responds sympathetically to feminine self-sacrifice. The pathos of that division between unnatural will and a devoted heart gives his plot a convincing dynamism. At the outset, Agnes has already com- promised her austere principles. She did not proclaim the truth after Lucas introduced her to their friends as his wife, and her relationship with him is physical although she would rather 'passion had no share in it' (I, p. 243). She still believes they could go their separate ways if 'one of [them] was making the other unhappy' (p. 234), but Lucas has grown more demanding. He needs the 'subtle sympathy which a sacrificing, unselfish woman alone possesses' (p. 241) and urges her to love him so that he can forget 'the lost opportunities' of his former career. Social disgrace is more real to him now he has left his sick-bed, and his nurse's 'slovenliness' displeases him. He orders her a fashionable gown like Lady Heytesbury's, the woman whose letter he has not destroyed along with the others that begged him to return to England and who, presumably, was the first to offer 'subtle sympathy' when his wife withdrew hers. Agnes refuses to wear 'rags of that kind' (II, p. 252), but the arrival of the Duke of St Olpherts in Venice, and its effect on his nephew, makes her 'fear lest, after all my beliefs and protestations, I should eventually find myself loving Lucas in the helpless, common way of women' (p. 260). Intending to convince the Duke that she is not 'some poor, feeble ballet-girl', she is faced, instead, with his version of the real Lucas Cleeve and recognizes its truth. Putting on the gown and femininity, she fights to keep Lucas and to show herself and others that, with a soul-mate such as she, he can conquer his weak and sensual egoism. Ironically, the more she tries to prove his worth, the more she perceives his contempt for her individuality. Gaping there before her lies the 'seething pit': in the first year of her marriage, she had been treated 'like a woman in a harem, for the rest of the time like a beast of burden' (I, p. 230), and the past begins to repeat itself. Delighted with his new creation, Lucas persuades her to renounce 'that crazy plan of ours':

AGNES: (*After a pause*) I – I will never be mad again.
LUCAS: (*Triumphantly*) Hah! ha, ha! (*She deliberately removes the shawl from about her shoulders and, putting her arms around his neck, draws him to her.*) Ah, my dear girl.
AGNES: (*In a whisper with her head on his breast*) Lucas.
LUCAS: Yes.
AGNES: Isn't *this* madness?
LUCAS: I don't think so.
AGNES: Oh! oh! oh!. I believe, to be a woman is to be mad.
LUCAS: No, to be a woman trying not to be a woman – *that* is to be mad.

(III, pp. 299–300)

As this sequence shows, Pinero's version of woman's predicament is fundamentally patronizing. He presents Agnes as the helpless victim of a man's absorbing selfishness yet sides with Lucas in condemning her particular brand of independence. To be the sort of woman Pinero can feel for, Agnes must remain submissive and entirely self-sacrificing. Such a figure cannot save herself, even from a man who would install her in some suburban villa while his wife agrees to maintain appearances in a compromise 'strictly à la mode' (III, pp. 318–19). To limit such boundless devotion, Pinero must eventually supply external agents: first, the Bible Gertrude and her brother leave for Agnes which she flings into the fire and then retrieves in terror; then, when she again submits to Mrs Cleeve's 'arrangement', the compassion of that fellow victim which releases her. So her situation is resolved by two contrived and theatrically attractive coups, and Agnes, who *has* spirit and desires of her own, retreats to rural pietism. The courageous individualism of types like Agnes and Paula resists the sort of 'tenderness' Pinero is prepared to award them. They do not deserve his benevolent chastisement.

The women who do seem free to be themselves, in Pinero's mature plays, are those whose lives and personalities conform exactly to his prescribed view of womanhood. Theophila Fraser in *The Benefit of the Doubt* (1895), though less exciting than her predecessors, is a more coherent character-study because her actions accord with Pinero's judgement of her worth. He introduces her through her family's comments and behaviour as they wait to learn the outcome of a plea for legal separation that involves her. By the time she arrives home from the divorce court, her milieu has been shown in telling detail. Her mother's prettiness is 'carefully preserved' by dye and paint; a martyr to her nerves, she reclines on the settee with a bottle of smelling-salts. Mrs Emptage is not the sort to guide her children, as her elder daughter's racy smartness indicates. At twenty-nine, Justina's chums-together manner seems 'passé' and she worries that her younger sister's trouble might spoil her chances: 'suppose I got left!'[34] As she reminds Kitty Twelves, 'we three musketeers' have been 'just a *leetle* rapid in our time'. So no more slang or 'swears, no more smokes with the men after dinner, no more cycling at the club in knickers!' (p. 12). Claude Emptage, an 'insignificant' young drifter, sees himself as the major victim: 'The brother of the witness in the box! Every eye upon me' (p. 15). The lesson he has drawn from the proceedings flatters his heroic sense of self; perhaps he should visit his

II   I

6   Scenes from Pinero's play, *The Benefit of the Doubt*, at the Comedy Theatre. Act I: Mrs Fraser's return from the Divorce Court. Act II: Mrs Fraser (Miss Winifred Emery) and Mr Allingham (Mr J.G. Grahame).

pretty, married friends less often: 'how easy it is for a fellow to imperil a woman's reputation!' Their uncle feels quite satisfied with his good name. A well-meaning fool, he is rich enough to have bought a knighthood and, full of his own importance, explains how his imposing presence influenced the day's outcome. Then Sir Fletcher's sister, Mrs Cloys, swoops down upon them. She has evidently been wise to have 'washed her hands' of her relations ten years before; however, there is more to this daunting lady than might at first appear. Her sister's 'cheerful method of training her children' disgusts her, but a genuine concern has brought her back to Regent's Park and she rejoices tearfully when it appears that Theo's name has not been sullied. Nevertheless, on hearing the details of her niece's indiscretion, seen by the rest of the family as the usual form between 'pals', she wonders how her sister 'like[s] seeing [her] children dabbling their hands in this – this pig-pail' (p. 47). Pinero's sprightly comedy of manners (or no manners) prepares the way for Theo who, like her aunt, has a number of hidden depths.

From the first, she is not quite the empty-headed rattle one might expect. Allingham versus Allingham has given her an unpleasing look at herself for, as she waited to give evidence, a distinctly shoddy creature, 'a patchouli business waiting to come on after us' (p. 52), sat down beside her in exactly the same bonnet; the fact that 'it' looked about the same age and could have had the same complexion as Theo's has not escaped her. She can wash away that cheap scent which clings to her clothes and person, but the judge's verdict on her friendship with Jack Allingham has sullied her. Mrs Allingham's lawyers proved nothing against Theo, yet her conduct has hardly been that 'of a woman who is properly watchful of her own and her husband's reputation – honour' (p. 59). By giving her 'the benefit of the doubt', the judge simply underscores the doubt Society will now cast upon her. Even her family, retreating from the shame her news brings down on them, harbours a suspicion that she may have drawn the boundaries of propriety 'rather zigzag'. Feeling 'like a woman caught with bare shoulders in daylight' (p. 67), Theo turns dejectedly to her husband for support and pardon but, though she tries to be considerate, Alec's sober defensiveness makes her prattle out her grievances. Under the surface of this comic exchange, the hollow confines of Theo's little soul begin to reverberate as she remembers 'the solemn, stupid stateliness' of her husband's Scottish mansion with its eternal pipers and kilts; after jolly times in London, life in the Highlands gave her the shudders (pp. 71–4). However, a certain integrity lurks below her silly chatter and that comes to the fore when she discovers that her husband refuses to help her brave out the scandal because he, too, has doubts about her relationship with Jack. Genuine hurt as well as habitual wilfulness send her rushing off to Epsom to borrow money from her sympathetic friend so that she can go abroad alone. In the play's climactic scene, Pinero pits Theo's heedlessness against her sensitive potential until, worn out by the strain of her whole situation, she downs two tumblers of champagne and loses all control.

The facets of her personality account for her subsequent decisions. Mrs Allingham has overheard her hysterical outburst which, ironically, proves that Theo's feelings for Jack are innocent. But, remembering the drunken way she challenged 'the world, your wife, my husband . . ., with my finger to my nose like a cheeky urchin' (pp. 210–11), Theo refuses to excuse her own vulgarity by suggesting she was ill or 'not myself'. The previous evening's dreams of a life 't'other side of the Channel' took her beyond the 'bad form' of an ill-regulated upbringing, 'flirting, and giggling, and dodging mother, and getting lost in conservatories and gardens' (p. 244); they have shown her 'the dregs of myself'. Always a 'poor, tawdry little thing', she had her pride nonetheless, and it kept her 'square and honest' (pp. 245–6). That intrinsic honesty gave her the right to ask Alec to stand by her after the trial; now it makes her ashamed, and she cannot accept her husband's renewed support since he could only be granting a favour. For the same reason she declines to let Mrs Allingham restore her to Society and, when the latter suggests she is over-reacting like a sentimental schoolgirl, she holds her ground: 'Well, ninety-nine women out of a hundred are kept fresh and sweet by nothing better than mere sentiment' (p. 259). There is something of Aunt Cloys in that downright remark, and when that lady, after summoning her ancient husband from St Olpherts, announces her intention to acquire a house in London 'for the season – sufficiently large for the dear bishop, myself, and Theophila' (p. 283), her solution seems an appropriate one. Only Mrs Cloys has shown unceasing concern for Theo's plight; envying her sister, Mrs Emptage, she would 'have given the world if Theo had been mine' (p. 96). And Theo's awakening sensibility has brought her to the point where she could well benefit from her aunt's frankness as well as her respectability. Pinero detonates any lingering sanctimoniousness, for his play is after all a comedy, by making her mother declare that 'in less than twelve months, if I know my girl, she will have grown heartily sick of her solemn surroundings' (p. 286). After a moment's anger, Mrs Cloys retaliates: even if she should bore her niece, 'good will result even from *that* if it sends her back to her husband'. Their sparring match ends amusingly as Mrs Emptage refuses to upbraid Theo for almost breaking her heart, 'I'm only your mother', and, with envy of her own, whispers 'mind you see that we visit you constantly in London and St Olpherts!' (p. 289).

Whereas Mrs Thorpe's Yorkshire refuge appears to cripple Agnes Ebbsmith's vitality,[35] Mrs Cloys' household may well be the making of Theophila. Sinner she is not, but the crucial difference between Theo and her flawed predecessors lies in her nature which, under an unladylike exterior, *is* conventional. Agnes and Paula's return to convention seems thrust upon them; little Mrs Fraser journeys bravely towards her actual self. The other characters in *The Benefit of the Doubt* are sketched with the same sure hand; as stereotypes, they

are far more delicately observed than the crude, pun-laden caricatures of earlier plays, like *The Weaker Sex*, and together they create a
vivid picture of ill-mannered affluence that nicely differentiates the
girls' 'bad form' at Regent's Park from the chaps' easy camaraderie at
Jack's cottage near the race-course. The exposition unfurls with a
convincing naturalness as characters arrive with news of the trial; Mrs
Cloys dampens things, but the family rapturously welcome Theo's
return only to shrink into their own woes when they hear how the
judge 'was rather rough' on her. Despite the dated contrivances and
unintended silliness of Act Two in which Pinero goes to great lengths
to ensure the audience knows that anyone in the 'library' can hear
what is said on stage and then manoeuvres Jack into letting Olive
listen to his interview with Theo, the rest of the comedy remains
effective and acerbic. Even Olive Allingham, whose alternate bursts
of jealousy and contrition sound artificial during the long sequence
when she and Jack are alone, eventually blends into the bustling
action and assumes a more human dimension. For all the palaver
about poor Theo's social repute, the characters' behaviour exemplifies the 'shabby little circle' in which they are all so happy to belong.

Because of inadequate acting, the play closed after ten weeks.
Looking back over the year's productions, at the end of 1895, Archer
focussed on that relatively short run in order to press his pet scheme
for a repertory system which would free thought-provoking writers
from the make-or-break philosophy of the commercial theatre. He
insisted that 'the Public is a myth'. Theatregoers had divers tastes;
the crowds which flocked to *Trilby* or the latest musical extravaganza
could not be expected to patronize *The Benefit of the Doubt*. A national
theatre which mounted classical revivals along with the best
contemporary drama would have allowed the play to be seen 'again
next season, re-studied, and, we might not unreasonably hope, with
the mistakes of the first cast corrected'.[36] Box-office receipts were not
the only bothersome factor. On the one hand, writers like Grundy
complained that Pinero's sombre plays were driving audiences to
trivial entertainments; on the other, critics like Shaw wrote scornfully
of his conservative attitudes and falsified characters. Even supporters
like Archer suggested that *Mrs Tanqueray* and *Mrs Ebbsmith* revealed
'a certain depressing negativeness – I had almost said aridity'[37] and
that *The Benefit of the Doubt*, 'the truest, firmest, finest thing Mr
Pinero has yet done', lacked 'a touch of the ideal'.[38] Considering his
situation, and the 'silly period' he predicted for the months ahead,

Pinero turned from storm-wracked women and vulgar socialites to depict the sophisticated follies of two middle-aged, upper-class people who, trying to beat back the years, seem for a time to be drawn to each other but settle eventually for partners half their age. Despite its more kindly satire, *The Princess and the Butterfly* (1897) was withdrawn after three months.

Like the Princess Pannonia and Sir George Lamorant, Pinero had himself turned forty, and his whimsical account of two hearts, grown older but no wiser, reflects a man at a crucial turning-point of his own. But his next play, *Trelawny of the 'Wells'* (1898), represents something more than a retreat to a reassuring past: the players at Sadler's Wells, his own progress as an actor, the brave novelties of Tom Robertson and Marie Wilton. Chided from both sides, either for being too advanced or insufficiently progressive, Pinero turns back to his apprenticeship in order to defend his artistic achievements while commiserating with those who feel threatened by change and urging tolerance in those for whom change comes too slowly. That stance is implicit in 'A Direction to the Stage Manager' which accompanies his text. Sets and costumes 'should follow, to the closest detail, the mode of the early sixties . . . [in order] to reproduce, perhaps to accentuate, any feature which may now seem particularly quaint and bizarre'.[39] On the one hand, the estranging grotesquerie of the action proclaims the advances that have occurred in the intervening years and yet its outmodedness also suggests that the revolutions of the present will seem just as quaint in another thirty years. Like Rose Trelawny's 'beauty [which] fades assuredly in its own time, [and] may appear to succeeding generations not to have been beauty at all' (p. 135), the protests of Grundy or Shaw and the sympathetic strictures of Archer will one day seem equally outmoded, and the play reminds both its creator and his critics, friendly or ferocious, to view the theatrical storms of the nineties in just such a humbling perspective.

The play begins in 'a sitting-room on the first floor of a respectable lodging-house', defined by the sort of detail that was once fostered at the Prince of Wales's. A large black trunk with the faded legend, 'Miss Violet Sylvester, Theatre Royal, Drury Lane', and 'two or three pairs of ladies' satin shoes, much the worse for wear', some 'dog-eared playbooks' or 'a wig-block with a man's wig upon it' all announce the lives of the room's present occupants in the same way that Robertson sketched those of the Eccles sisters in the first scene of

Caste. Ironically, the tenants of this room, Mr and Mrs Telfer of Bagnigge-Wells Theatre, are about to be swept aside by the sort of scripts that required such domestic realism, a point which Pinero expands upon in Act Two when Tom Wrench, prophet of the new drama, walks into the sombre drawing room in Cavendish Square and, in Robertsonian ecstasy, exclaims '*This* is the kind of chamber I want for the second act of my comedy . . . Windows on the one side (*pointing to the right*) doors on the other – just where they should be, architecturally. And locks on the doors, *real locks*, to work; and handles – to turn! (*rubbing his hands together gleefully*) Ha, ha! you wait! wait – !' (p. 165).[40] Pinero allies himself to Robertson stylistically, as well, by the cards-on-the-table quality of his opening sequence which sets out the plot with naive directness, unlike the disguising chatter that begins *The Benefit of the Doubt.* Mr Ablett, a local greengrocer, having volunteered his services as waiter, enquires of Mrs Mossop whether the room he has entered belongs to the Telfers and, taking his cue from the landlady – 'You let fall the word "ceremony", ma'am' (p. 137) – helps to establish that Rose Trelawny, 'juvenile-lady' at the Wells, has fallen in love with 'A non-professional gentleman.' The 'farewell cold collation' is to honour her departure from the stage, although before Vice-Chancellor Sir William Gower can agree to his grandson's marriage, 'Miss Trelawny is to make her home in Cavendish Square for a short term – "short-term" is the Gower family's own expression – in order to habituate herself to the West End.'

This rapid exposition seems unsophisticated but it was once a style that subverted an older, declamatory drama, and the implication that the greater sophistication of Pinero's own time must one day seem equally passé is made plain at the beginning of Act Four when the Telfers react with bewilderment to Tom Wrench's play. Poor Mrs Telfer, relegated from tragedy-queen to wardrobe-mistress, sits dejectedly in a throne-chair on an empty stage. Her husband hurries in from the Green-room, since his 'part is confined to the latter 'alf of the second act' (p. 187). The new style has no big speeches, 'so line-y, Violet; so very line-y', so Telfer doubts whether he can 'get near' his character: 'An old, stagey, out-of-date actor.' Pinero draws pathos from the Telfers' failure to relate their sort of theatre to the realities of their personal drama:

TELFER: Let us both go home.
MRS TELFER: (*restraining him*) No, let us remain. We've been idle six months,

and I can't bear to see you without your watch and all your comforts about you.

TELFER: (*pointing towards the Green-room*) And so this new-fangled stuff, and these dandified people, are to push us, and such as us, from our stools!

MRS TELFER: Yes, James, just as some other new fashion will, in course of time, push *them* from their stools. (p. 188)

That conversation also sets a context for Pinero's affectionate parody of Robertson as the actors rehearse their new parts in 'Life, a comedy, by Thomas Wrench'. Its domestic and insouciant charm must appear faded and contrived to modern eyes yet if Pinero's own play (itself a deliberate return to pleasing sentiment) seems to abandon Northern realism, the champions of that latest style should learn humility from changing fashion that now makes *Life* so quaint:

THE GENTLEMAN: 'Your bravura has just arrived from London. Lady McArchie wishes you to try it over.'

IMOGEN: (*taking his arm*) 'Delighted, Lord Parracourt. Miss Harrington, bring your work indoors and hear me squall.' (p. 196)

Viewed in that way, Pinero's seemingly escapist comedietta is actually an oblique problem play which questions the growing sophistication of Victorian drama and, through the efficient grace of his own art, Pinero's contribution to that development. Extending sympathy to the old school's rigid theatricality while challenging the critical rigour of the new, *Trelawny* also dramatizes the changing status of the acting profession itself. The Telfers' sonorous tones and dropped aitches are comically unrefined; so is the boisterous good-nature of their colleagues – the low comedian, the soubrette, the flashy juvenile-lead – who seem even rougher when they visit Rose in Cavendish Square. But that, too, is a matter of changing perspective since these roustabouts from the Wells have displaced the vagabond Kean, still glorious in old Sir William's memory, and are in turn supplanted by other gypsies, 'though of a different order from the old order which is departing' (p. 199). Those actors, gathered on the stage of the Pantheon, behave with refinement yet, as their vociferous stage-manager, O'Dwyer, illustrates, they are less naturally polite than the colleagues of Sir Henry Irving and Sir Squire Bancroft would be, thirty years later.

Such changing manners are personified in Rose herself, whose character animates and extends Pinero's thesis. Compared to her colleagues at the Wells, she has an in-born refinement which persuades us that she could attract young Arthur Gower. She 'looks divine'; her modesty springs from her mother's lessons on the transience of beauty and fame; her reputation is blameless: 'Mrs Telfer has kept an eye on me all through. Not that it was necessary, brought up as I was' (p. 146). Yet that idealized portrait admits coarse brush strokes. Her vanity flutters when '*The* Miss Parrott, of the Olympic' condescends to return 'from the West to see me make my exit from Brydon Crescent' and when Arthur 'forgets everything but the parts *I* play, and the pieces *I* play in' (p. 144). Her idea of love is tuppence-coloured: 'Fate ordains that I shall be a well-to-do fashionable lady' and Arthur will 'grow manly in time, and have moustaches, and whiskers out to here, he says' (p. 145). Charged diction and a sentimental fondness for *The Pedlar of Marseilles*, in which 'I got leave to introduce a song . . . "Ever of thee I'm fondly dreaming",' tinsel her intrinsic worth. In Cavendish Square, Rose withers. The stifling propriety of Sir William and his sister, Miss Trafalgar, make her see that West End society is not the romantic idyll she imagined, although she responds to the Gowers' tyranny with her usual theatricality: 'They are killing me – like Agnes in *The Spectre of St Ives*. She expires, in the fourth act, as I shall die in Cavendish Square, painfully, of no recognised disorder' (p. 157). Her predicament is a comic version of Paula Tanqueray's. Bored to distraction by polite restriction, Rose behaves provocatively, but her past life no longer satisfies her.

However, unlike Paula, Rose has never abandoned womanliness, and so Pinero can treat her as an individual whose consequent history evolves from her inner self rather than inevitable precept. Rose is never as tawdry as Theo Fraser, but, like her, she discovers her true nature, and the fact that it is ladylike and disenchanted with the theatre's picture of life exemplifies Pinero's theme: the theatre and life become one – whatever the prevailing fashion – when art speaks of reality. It is this which reconciles Rose and Sir William as together they remember Edmund Kean whose gestures caught the true essence rather than the details of a character. It is this which buzzes in Sir William's head as he responds to Tom Wrench's scaled-down drama 'which contains a character resembling a member of my family – a *late* member of my family. I don't relish being reminded of late members of my family in this way, and being kept awake at night, thinking –' (pp. 192–3).

Pinero's vested interest in the theatre community's current respectability colours the way Rose escapes from 'stagey postures, and . . . sayings out of rubbishy plays' (p. 174). Her good-breeding appears long before experience of a larger world makes her 'genteel', and Arthur Gower wins her by adapting his gentility to the stage rather than by raising her to his own rank. Sophy Fullgarney, of *The Gay Lord Quex* (1899), needs no such romantic grace-notes. As a member of the 'vulgar' class, she is no better than she should be, yet (once one accepts the premise that a bailiff's daughter could be foster-sister to Muriel Eden of the landed gentry) her character develops with a subtlety which moves beyond stereotype. Pinero does have 'views' about the manners of her class but takes a comic delight in her individuality. Sophy must find her niche in life and so clings to the shades of goodness which distinguish one working-girl from another, and they, rather than the exigencies of the play's well-made theatrics, determine her behaviour. The proprietress of a manicure establishment in New Bond Street, this 'pretty, elegant, innocently vulgar, fascinating young woman of six-and-twenty'[41] has risen from '*very small beginnings*' (p. 37) and is consequently anxious to distance herself from her employees while encouraging their claim to a refinement which will accentuate hers. As Miss Huddle explains to a gentleman client, next time 'you'd better ask for Miss Hud-delle; I fancy Miss Fullgarney is going to alter me to that' (p. 32). Sophy's snobberies are as petty and human as those of her next-door neighbour, Valma the fortune teller, whose showy clothes and commonplace good-looks have captured her sentimental heart but whose earnest fastidiousness – 'Pardon me for the liberty I have taken in again crossing the leads' (p. 34) – makes her tremble for her own. When Valma asks her to 'accord me permission to pay you my addresses' (p. 37), Sophy plays 'perfectly straight' and tells him how, as 'a self-willed, independent sort of a girl', she started out – 'you'd hardly believe it!' – as a nursery-maid, 'rose to be Useful Maid, and then Maid' before becoming a hairdresser at 'Dundas's opposite, . . . that's an extremely refined position, I needn't say':

Nobody can breathe a word against my respectability. All the same, I am quite aware that it mightn't be over-pleasant for a gentleman to remember that his wife was once – well, a servant. (p. 38)

Valma, however, worries about her present eminence; he would happily see her 'glide about your rooms, superintending your young ladies! But I hate the idea of your sitting here, or there, holding some man's hand in yours!' (p. 39). Sophy retorts that a fortune teller must hold women's hands in his, and her encouraging show of jealousy prompts Valma to his own confession: he was until recently a solicitor's clerk and his real name is Frank Toleman Pollitt. Social equals once more, Sophy sinks into the arms of her Frank: 'Oh, no, no! always Valma to me – [*dreamily*] my Valma' (p. 41).

Sophy's sentimental imagination makes her a party to Miss Eden's assignations with Captain Bastling and rouses her prejudice against Lord Quex, the middle-aged roué whom the title-conscious Edens have tentatively approved as Muriel's fiancé. Determined to rescue her 'own darling' from 'the wickedest man in London', Sophy behaves as no lady could, and Pinero makes her all the more attractive and spirited because of the way she lies, tricks, and listens at keyholes. The climactic duel of wits in the Duchess of Strood's bedroom impels Sophy to sacrifice her tender proprieties in order to save Muriel, whereupon Lord Quex, admiring her fierce loyalty, delivers his own future happiness into her hands. Sophy may be vulgar but she is far more honest than the Duchess, who clothes adultery in romantic disguise, or even Muriel, 'the typical, creamy English girl' (p. 57), who is eager to profit from Sophy's shocking tricks and who plays with fire herself. Similarly, Lord Quex, despite his wicked past, genuinely adores Muriel, unlike his womanizing chum, Chick Frayne, or the unscrupulous fortune-hunter, Captain Bastling:

It isn't the scamp, the roué, a girl shies at; it's the *old* scamp, the *old* roué. She'll take the young one, the blackguard with a smooth skin and a bright eye, directly he raises a hand – take him without a murmur, money-hunter though he may be.

(pp. 206–7)

Lord Quex forgives Muriel's indiscretion: 'she is not much more than a girl' and she has, after all, stepped back from calamity. But though Sophy is the same age, she is, in Quex's view, 'a woman' with experience, 'upstairs and downstairs, boudoir and kitchen': 'you own you have encouraged her in this, made her clandestine meetings with this penniless beggar possible. You –! you deserve to be whipped, Miss Fullgarney – whipped!' (p. 206). Pinero allows us to see more clearly than that by tracing the quirks of character which led to such romantic meddling.

Despite his personal reaction to Sophy's individuality, Lord Quex finally judges her as a type. Pinero observes her much more closely but he, too, eventually takes refuge in unarguable social, moral and, above all, sexual rules which subvert an otherwise objective account of life-as-it-is. The uneasy conjunction of two worlds – New Bond

Street and Fauncey Court – in *The Gay Lord Quex* exemplifies
Pinero's divided self. Reacting to the rhythms of Sophy's workplace,
he pinpoints (in an unconventional and revolutionary way) the
snobberies of the working class and the hypocrisies of the gentry. At
Fauncey Court, though, he reduces Sophy to an uppity and theatrical
servant-girl whose propriety reflects her superiors' tiresome, and
dated, obeisance to reputation. As a demographer of Victorian
manners, Pinero has no equal: one only has to compare Sophy with
Shaw's Louka (*Arms and the Man*, 1894) to discover the fine shades of
personality which distinguish the soul of *his* shopgirl. But always he
drew back whenever manners touched morality,[42] so that his open-
minded attitude to the flawed behaviour of Theo Fraser, Rose
Trelawny, and Sophy Fullgarney is very different from his purblind
view of Paula Tanqueray's sensual past (which limits his sense of her
independent personality) and his inability to come to grips with the
aggressively feminist (in his view, unfeminine) monster in Agnes
Ebbsmith. Enraptured by womanly women, however warped by
circumstance, Pinero reacted sympathetically to their volatile desires:
'When they talk, I listen to them; when they act, I watch them.'[43] But
whenever those women stepped beyond the limits of middle-class
morality, he could no longer treat them as individuals.

CHAPTER 7

A middle-class education

> LORD DARLINGTON: Oh! she doesn't love me. She is a good woman. She is the only good woman I have ever met in my life . . .
> CECIL GRAHAM (*lighting a cigarette*): Well, you are a lucky fellow! Why, I have met hundreds of good women. I never seem to meet any but good women. The world is perfectly packed with good women. To know them is a middle-class education.
>
> *Lady Windermere's Fan* (1892)

Like Henry Arthur Jones, whose earnestness amused him,[1] Oscar Wilde was an idealist. Jones, the disciple of Arnold, organized drama against the petty and suburban; Wilde, the disciple of Pater, marshalled his own personality against the drab and doctrinaire. Neither man cared much for reality. As a moral idealist, Jones looked at modern barbarism and found it unnatural; as an aesthetic idealist, Wilde, the spectator of his personal drama, considered actuality less interesting than his own thoughts about it:

From the high tower of Thought we can look out at the world. Calm, and self-centred, and complete, the aesthetic critic contemplates life, and no arrow drawn at a venture can pierce between the joints of his harness. He at least is safe. He has discovered how to live.[2]

Wilde's intellect, shaped by artists and thinkers of all ages, allowed a comic detachment from himself and his times; his impressionable soul, whirling from one gem-like flame to the next, made him the slave of hedonism. A paradox himself, Wilde opened Victorian drama to playfully subversive, contradictory ideas yet, in his worship of the beautiful, he was also content to decorate old clichés. In consequence, his plays exhibit a disjointed, even naive critique of life whenever gadfly and butterfly pull against each other; but when provocateur and poseur unite in a sustained, provocative pose, Wilde's artifice distils the reality it feeds on: 'the more strongly this personality enters into the interpretation the more real the interpretation becomes, the more satisfying, the more convincing, and the more true' ('The Critic as Artist', p. 373).

196

Initially, Wilde fired the public's imagination as a mere poseur. Nevertheless, he invented himself out of the imagery of the aesthetic movement with such self-conscious calculation and conviction that he became a living artifact, caricatured by cartoonists (particularly by George du Maurier in *Punch*) and burlesqued by actors and playwrights. After Richard D'Oyly Carte invited him to New York (to explicate the languid cult lampooned in Gilbert and Sullivan's *Patience*, 1882) and Wilde charmed or enraged America with his studied, yet courageous individualism, 'Oscar' emerged as spokesman–guardian of taste, a provoking phenomenon at home and abroad. Wilde's early plays were also concocted from borrowed remnants, but they remained lifeless postures because their design was lyrical and painterly.

The impetus behind *Vera, or The Nihilists* (1880) may have been personal: a young Irishman courting success in London might, on the face of things, cause a stir with a play about the enemies of tyranny.[3] Yet fame mattered more than republican sentiment, and Sardou more than Tolstoy, so Wilde adopted the theatre's 'moving' pictures, applied them to a hazy concept of contemporary Russian politics, arranged a private printing, and sent his book to such luminaries as Ellen Terry with pretty compliments and apologies for his own poor pen: 'Perhaps some day I shall be fortunate enough to write something worthy of your playing.'[4] To Mr Pigott, Examiner of Plays for the Lord Chamberlain, he was frank about his quest for fame, coy about his achievement (what looked poor on paper might shine out on stage), and disarmingly eager to profit from revered authority: 'any suggestion, any helpful advice, your experience and very brilliant critical powers can give me I shall thank you very much for'.[5] Ellen Terry did not take the hint and, though Mrs Bernard Beere agreed to play Vera, discreet pressure from Pigott's office ended that arrangement (1881): Alexander II had been assassinated that Spring, and the new Czarina was the Prince of Wales's sister-in-law. Preparing for his journey to America, Wilde forwarded his 'new and original drama' to another actress, Clara Morris, because 'the character of the heroine is drawn in all those varying moods and notes of passion which you can so well touch'. London had frowned on Republicanism: 'with you there is more freedom, and though democracy is the note through which the play is expressed, yet the tragedy is an entirely human one'.[6]

Wilde's concept of human tragedy reflects the naive dramatics of the early eighties (before Jones and Pinero) in that his plot is simply a thread on which to hang contrasted passions: staged effects which, as he told another American correspondent, 'a study of Sarah Bernhardt could suggest'.[7] Those contrasts animate the Prologue, appended to explain the political background through a series of emotive images. For instance, 'Russia' is established by a '*Large door opening on snowy landscape at back of stage*',[8] by names like Nicolas, Michael, Dmitri, and by the fact that Vera, who can read, has 'got too many ideas' whereas her father, Peter Sabouroff, endures his fated lot: 'I didn't make the world – let God or the Czar look to it' (p. 376). The arrival of chained and ragged prisoners – 'I heard this was to be the new road to Siberia' (p. 377) – brings unexpected custom since the Colonel, later to appear as a General, retires with his aide-de-camp to 'good dried venison' and rye whisky while Vera, moved by the prisoners' unjust punishment, sells 'her peasant's necklace' in order to give them food. These contrasts build in rapid succession to an affecting finale. Vera discovers her long-lost brother amongst the nihilists; the Colonel moves them on; Peter recognizes his son and flings away the money he had welcomed; Vera picks up a note her brother drops and, renouncing feminine pity, responds passionately to his cause.

Yet Wilde was not an unthinking imitator. When the play was finally produced in New York (1883), he wrote to Marie Prescott, his Vera, in order to expound his aesthetics: 'Success is a science; if you have the conditions, you get the result. Art is the mathematical result of the emotional desire for beauty. If it is not thought out, it is nothing.'[9] That his mathematics depend entirely on his play's *external* appeal to an audience's sensibilities becomes apparent from the way he describes the psychology of contrasts:

Never be afraid that by raising a laugh you destroy tragedy. On the contrary, you intensify it. The canons of each art depend on what they appeal to. Painting appeals to the eye, and is founded on the science of optics. Music appeals to the ear and is founded on the science of acoustics. The drama appeals to human nature, and must have as its ultimate basis the science of psychology and physiology. Now, one of the facts of physiology is the desire of any very intensified emotion to be relieved by some emotion that is its opposite. Nature's example of dramatic effect is the laughter of hysteria or the tears of joy.

Psychology, then, is not the internal and social logic of the characters themselves but the effect of their orchestrated and conflicting emotions (however unmotivated) upon the observer.

Accordingly, Act One brings the nihilists together in pleasing coloured masks; their mystery is intensified by their ritual passwords at the midnight hour and by the presence of an enigmatic medical student who has delicate hands and features and knows the layout of the Czar's palace. Vera, presented now as a she-wolf, 'and twice as dangerous', is torn between her pledge to unsex herself and her tremulous feelings for the unknown student: 'Oh, fool, fool, fool! False to your oath! Weak as water! Have done! Remember what you are – a Nihilist, a Nihilist!' (p. 387). Martial law is about to fall on Moscow ('It means the strangling of a whole nation') and that fills Vera with Elizabethan anguish: 'But now methinks the brood of men is dead and the dull earth grown sick of childbearing, else would no crowned dog pollute God's air by living' (p. 385). She also faces the wrath of Michael, her admirer in the Prologue and now a hardened nihilist who, having followed the student to the Czar's palace, denounces him as a traitor. Vera rushes to defend the boy; she needs no explanations: 'He is the noblest heart amongst us' (p. 388). These passions resolve at the entrance of the General, determined to arrest this illegal gathering. Unimpressed by their claim to be gypsies, he is about to unmask Vera (whom he would remember from the Prologue) but is stopped by the student who (after all those dark hints) now reveals himself as the Czarevitch, Alexis. One last thrill awaits the audience when the General talks of Vera, 'the most dangerous [woman] in all Europe', whom he has hunted for the past eighteen months. Unknowingly, he begs to see the gypsy girl's face, 'she has such fine eyes through her mask', then, as a man of the world, gives way to her princely admirer:

> *Exit* GENERAL *and the soldiers.*
> VERA (*throwing off her mask*):   Saved! and by you!
> ALEXIS (*clasping her hand*):   Brothers, you trust me now?
> TABLEAU   (p. 391)

In his maturity, Wilde would arrive at a less scientific definition of Art and Beauty: 'A work of art is the unique result of a unique temperament. Its beauty comes from the fact that the author is what he is.'[10] In *Vera*, the emotional colours, arranged so mathematically, come neither from the speakers' personalities nor, with one exception, from the author's. At the time, as he told Miss Prescott, Wilde thought dialogue also should aim at contrast; it 'should give the effect of its being made by the reaction of the personages on one another. It should never seem to be ready made by the author, . . .' Wilde broke that rule in creating Prince Paul Maraloffski, endowing him with aspects of the persona he had already created for 'Oscar'. Although the unscrupulous Prime Minister of Russia's aphorisms appear increasingly unlikely as events explode around him, they do bear the stamp of Wilde's deliberate eccentricity: 'To make a good salad is to be a brilliant diplomatist – the problem is so entirely the same in both cases. To know exactly how much oil one must put with one's vinegar' (p. 393). The dialogue of the Czar, however, veers with ludicrous abruptness between paranoid terror and abject dependency. Then, for no other purpose than Act Two's climactic tableau, this puppet strides out to the palace balcony and his assassination.

As uninterested as his contemporaries in self-motivated characters or social realism, Wilde responds to the theatre of the early eighties as a poet of sensation. His philosophy of exquisite contrasts is Pateresque; his word-music is Keats/Swinburne. In the final Act, Vera must honour the nihilists' oath and avenge her brother's misery by killing the man she loves. Alexis has accepted the crown of Russia, but only to offer that supreme gift to his beloved. As her companions wait in the street below, Vera enters the new Czar's bedchamber: she must fling her bloody dagger down to them by midnight or the conspirators will storm the palace. In an ecstasy of love, she stabs herself and so saves Russia and Alexis with her own blood:

VERA: Our wedding night! Oh, let me drink my fill of love to-night! Nay, sweet, not yet, not yet. How still it is, and yet methinks the air is full of music. It is some nightingale who, wearying of the south, has come to sing in this bleak north to lovers such as we. It is the nightingale. Dost thou not hear it?

(p. 420)

This rhapsodic *liebestod* has exactly the colour of Wilde's own style, away from the theatre, whenever he thought of Art and Beauty:

For we might bow before the same marble goddess, and with hymns not dissimilar fill the reeds of her flutes: the gold of the night-time, and the silver of the dawn, should pass into perfection for us: and from each string that is touched by the fingers of the player, from each bird that is rapturous in brake or covert, from each hill-flower that blossoms on the hill, we might draw into our hearts the same sense of beauty, and in the House of Beauty meet and join hands.[11]

Stage-pictures also enticed Wilde's sensibility. Writing to Miss Prescott as the production drew nearer, he was 'very much pleased to know that my directions as regards scenery and costume have been carried out. The yellow satin council-chamber is sure to be a most artistic scene, and as you have been unable to match in New York the vermilion silk of which I sent you a pattern, I hope you will allow me to bring you over a piece large enough for your dress in the last act.'[12] He would also bring a samovar donated by Madame Sarah. Alas, these objects, though more aesthetic than a pump and washtubs, did not attract the 'appreciative audiences' he expected in New York. *The Tribune* called the play 'a foolish, highly-peppered story of love, intrigue and politics'; *The Herald* damned it as 'long-drawn dramatic rot'.

Wilde's second play, *The Duchess of Padua* (1883), is even more 'highly-peppered'. Lured into blank verse by the Renaissance setting, he creates a mosaic of images and phrases out of Shakespeare and the darker Jacobeans. Dramatic action is reduced to *coups de théâtre* and, between those strategic moments, the characters display their passions in jewel-encrusted dialogue of great weight and very little substance. Such grandeur harks back to Bulwer, but Wilde had no Macready to tailor his decorated fustian for the stage, and so this five-act tragedy is simply word-music and pictorial splendour: beauties for beauty's sake. Each character strikes an attitude which is sounded at some length against a second, contrasted attitude or played in harmony until an abrupt turn of events sends one voice against the other. In Act Two, for instance, Guido declares his love for the ill-used Duchess. The two talk *at* each other – fire-bright ideals from him, pretty hesitations from her – until the ghost-like appearance of Count Moranzone, come to deliver the dagger (wrapped in vermilion silk) with which Guido must dispatch the Duke, his father's murderer. Harmony turns to dissonance. Guido, like the nihilists before him, remembers his destiny and renounces love; the Duchess, knowing nothing of that mission, cannot understand why he should suddenly reject her. Faced with her husband's cruelty and Moranzone's implacable cry of 'Revenge!', the Duchess steels herself (with hints from *Macbeth*) to the night world of toads, owls, and bats that must herald her self-murder.

Empty and silly though all this is, Wilde had such confidence in the science of orchestrated contrasts that he unhesitatingly assured Mary Anderson, for whom he had completed the script, 'that it is the masterpiece of all my literary work, the *chef-d'oeuvre* of my youth'.[13] Tragedy, he observed, must allow its audience moments of comic relief and, in Act Two, the Duke's comedy 'which is bitter' was entirely different from the Duchess's reluctance to admit her love for Guido 'which is the comedy of Viola, and Rosalind; the comedy in which joy smiles through a mask of beauty'. The radiant appearance of the Duchess herself would be so impressive that she could pass across the stage, at the end of Act One, without a word:

but it is not enough to make her stir the artistic sensibility of the audience, so in Act II she appears as the image of pity, and mercy: she comes with the poor about her: she stirs the sympathy of the gallery and pit. I do not know how it is in New York, but in London, where the misery is terrible among the poor, and where the sympathy for them is growing every day, such speeches as the one about the children dying in the lanes, or the people sleeping under the arches of the bridges, cannot fail to bring down the house: they will not expect to find in an Italian tragedy modern life: but *the essence of art is to produce the modern idea under an antique form.*

Intellectual sympathy would also be roused by a number of other devices which temper and strengthen an emotional response to the play's aesthetic beauty. Audiences would recognize themselves in the Duchess's plight – *'her cue is "we women" always'* – and, surprised by the sudden twists of plot, would vacillate between compassion and moral antipathy when the Duchess murders her husband for Guido's love then denounces her lover after he recoils in horror from the bloody deed:

An audience longs to be first out of sympathy, and ultimately in sympathy, with a character they have loved: they desire it; they demand it; without it they are not contented; but *this sympathy must not be merely emotional, it must have its intellectual basis*, above all it must be summed up for them briefly in the form of thought: audiences are well meaning but very stupid: they must have things told them clearly: they are nice children who need to have their vague emotions crystallised and expressed for them.

Thus the ambiguities of the Duchess's passion are made plain in speeches which deliberately set her crime against the love which caused it, and Wilde congratulated himself on pushing beyond the simple emotion of the genre:

This intellectual idea is the *health* of art, as the emotional idea is the *heart* of art: such a play for instance as *La Dame aux Camélias* is unhealthy: *Why?* Not because sympathy is asked for a fallen woman, but because it is only played on one string, an emotional string merely: so that in the last act the sympathy of the audience naturally excited for a woman who is dying young (and has a dreadful cough!) has no real intellectual basis: . . .

So much for theory. In practice, *The Duchess* is distinguished by love scenes whose self-indulgent glitter halts the action and by comic business from the citizens which reads like a wicked parody of Shakespeare's mechanicals but which, as contrasting music, becomes unintentionally ludicrous. Miss Anderson, ignoring those *longeurs* and gaucheries, rejected the play as barbarously Italianate: 'in its present form, I fear, [it] would no more please the public of today than would *Venice Preserved* or *Lucretia Borgia*'. Another American actor, Lawrence Barrett, who had been interested in *The Duchess* from its inception, finally offered to produce the play and, in 1891, it opened in New York as *Guido Ferranti*. Wilde's name was not on the playbill but, after a favourable first night, his authorship was consequently acknowledged and the piece ran for about three weeks. On the strength of that 'immense success', Wilde wrote to *The Daily Telegraph* and to a number of English actor-managers telling them of the 'crowded houses' his play had attracted.[14]

That he continued to promote the *chef-d'oeuvre* of his youth when, as the author of *The Picture of Dorian Gray* (1890), he had become a renowned sophisticate is not as surprising as it might appear. Though Wilde's outlook had changed considerably in the intervening years, he always admired the sort of acting whose good taste and personality (like his own lectures and essays) might educate the sensibility of the middle classes. Irving had long been one of his heroes,[15] and it was to him he appealed in 1891: 'The public as a class don't read poetry, but you have made them listen to it'.[16] Embracing a new socialism which would release Man's individuality and creative freedom, Wilde saw Irving's "style that has really a true colour-element in it, [and] his extraordinary power, not over mere mimicry but over imaginative and intellectual creation', as the blazon of a man who, in a commodity-ruled society, had refused to compromise 'his own perfection as an artist' by pandering to the public's second-rate standards. '*The work of art is to dominate the spectator: the spectator is not to dominate the work of art*. The spectator is to be receptive. He is to be the violin on which the master is to play' ('The Soul of Man under Socialism', pp. 278–9). *The Duchess*, especially when shaped and cut to emphasize Guido, had the sort of music the master could play. But Irving declined, as had George Alexander before him, although the latter did commission a modern comedy, and Wilde, finding himself in difficulties with that idiom ('I can't get a grip of the play yet: I can't get my people real'[17]), concurrently pursued the heroic and artistic Ideal. The music that now possessed him was the insistent rhythm of the perverse. In Paris, later that year, while wrestling with his vision of a woman who dances for the blood of the man she craves, he asked the gypsy orchestra at the Grand Café to interpret those thoughts: 'And Rigo played such wild and terrible music that those who were there stopped talking and looked at each other with blanched faces. Then I went back and finished *Salomé*.'[18]

That play abandons realistic portraiture entirely. Hypnotized by desire, the Young Syrian, Salomé, and Herod seem to move in a dream that weaves inevitably towards the Baptist's severed head. The rhythms, colours, and imagery of this prose poem are established in its very first lines, as is a mood of fatal yearning. The Syrian sees nothing but the beautiful Princess and, though the Page of Herodias urges him to look at the moon ('She is like a dead woman. You would fancy she was looking for dead things'), the Syrian's reply, ostensibly about the moon, is coloured by his obsession so that those two pale hunters, moon and princess, unite in symbolic correspondence.

THE YOUNG SYRIAN: She has a strange look. She is like a little princess who
  wears a yellow veil, and whose feet are of silver. She is like a princess who has
  little white doves for feet. You would fancy she was dancing.
THE PAGE OF HERODIAS: She is like a woman who is dead. She moves very
  slowly.   (p. 269)

These images surround the silent princess with a mythic power which keeps the Syrian spellbound, despite the chatter of the soldiers and the warnings of his friend: 'Do not look at her. I pray you not to look at her.' From the depth of a cistern in the shadows of the courtyard, the prophet, Jokanaan, proclaims the coming of 'another mightier than I'. Jokanaan 'was very terrible to look upon', and Herod has forbidden anyone to see him. In the banquet hall, the princess hides her face with her fan then rises 'like a silver flower' to escape the Tetrarch's 'mole's eyes' and the feast's oppressive clamour. Her words to the moon echo the Syrian ('you would think she was a little silver flower'), then, hearing the prophet's voice, she too becomes enslaved.

Writing in French, Wilde creates a network of repeating motifs in the manner of the Symbolists, but his rhythms are those of The Song of Solomon, as is evident in the English version where the plain sentences build out of each other in a liturgical way. Their simplicity keeps the mounting emotion in check until Salomé asks for Jokanaan's head; at that, the repetitive phrasing explodes into panic as Herod fights against disaster:

What desirest thou more than this, Salomé? Tell me the thing that thou desirest, and I will give it thee. All that thou asked I will give thee save one thing. I will give thee all that is mine, save one life. I will give thee the mantle of the high priest. I will give thee the veil of the sanctuary.   (p. 291)

Reiterating patterns of dialogue and imagery bind the major characters into a compulsive ritual whose suppressing rhythms are far more effective than the sharp contrasts of the earlier tragedies. The minor characters, however, show that Wilde remained true to his former theories. The soldiers' conflicting superstitions and the Jews' ridiculous disputations are intended to loosen the tension, but those everyday arguments sound perilously banal when phrased liturgically and, more dangerously, that prattle turns the Tetrarch's court into an historic reality as opposed to the timeless arena the obsessive atmosphere demands. When they fall silent, the play regains its epic stature.

Salomé is as lyric and pictorial as Wilde's other romantic tragedies, but the archetypal passions of its fabled antagonists support that structure; in fact, the ornate design gives added import to those archetypes. The Syrian's enchantment by the pale princess sets out the pattern. Salomé ignores Herod's request to return to the banquet and disobeys him further by demanding to see Jokanaan. When the terrified soldiers refuse her, she tempts the Syrian with 'a little green flower' she will drop 'when I pass in my litter beneath the gateway of the idol-sellers'. He resists, so the chaste goddess smiles and promises that 'when I pass in my litter by the bridge of the idol-buyers, I will look at you through the muslin veils, I will look at you, Narraboth, it may be I will smile at you. Look at me, Narraboth, look at me' (p. 274). The Syrian gives in, and the fatality of that and his helpless obsession is underscored by a return of the moon motif:

THE PAGE OF HERODIAS: Oh! How strange the moon looks. You would think it was the hand of a dead woman who is seeking to cover herself with a shroud.
THE YOUNG SYRIAN: She has a strange look! She is like a little princess, whose eyes are eyes of amber. Through the clouds of muslin she is smiling like a little princess.

For Salomé, the prophet's eyes are terrible, 'like black lakes troubled by fantastic moons', and his pale wasted body 'is like an image of silver. I am sure he is chaste as the moon is' (p. 275). Hypnotized, she stares 'with her golden eyes, under her gilded eyelids' at Jokanaan. Twice he repulses her as she moves to touch his body then his hair; the third time she gazes at his mouth, and nothing will deflect her: 'I will kiss thy mouth, Jokanaan.' The prophet had heard 'the beatings of the wings of the angel of death' when Salomé began to tempt him; now the Syrian, horrified by her desire, kills himself at her feet, but neither that portent nor Jokanaan's fury quells her longing:

SALOMÉ: I will kiss thy mouth, Jokanaan.
JOKANAAN: I do not wish to look at thee. I will not look at thee, thou art accursed. Salomé, thou art accursed.
He goes down into the cistern.
SALOMÉ: I will kiss thy mouth, Jokanaan. I will kiss thy mouth.   (p. 278)

Because those elements of design also control and shape the play's central episode, the story as sketched in the Bible seems to unfold as the inevitable result of Jokanaan's curse. Like the Syrian before him, Herod is entranced by the princess who colours his perception of the moon: 'Has she not a strange look? She is like a mad woman, a mad woman who is seeking everywhere for lovers.' His stepdaughter's silence through much of the episode effectively suggests her ferocious concentration on the forbidden, but Herod cannot take his eyes off her, to the fury of Herodias: 'You must not look at her! You are always looking at her!' Yet although Herod reacts with alarm when he slips on the blood of the dead Syrian or when he seems to feel a cold wind and hear 'the beating of vast wings', his daughter's fascination, and the terse way she refuses to eat and drink with him, lure him onward. Herodias is driven, too, by the prophet's accusing voice and by her consort's lust which sends him reeling in that icy wind or burning, just as suddenly, with choking heat:

It is my garland that hurts me, my garland of roses. The flowers are like fire. They have burned my forehead. (*He tears the wreath from his head* . . .) Ah! I can breathe now. How red those petals are! They are like stains of blood on the cloth. That does not matter. You must not find symbols in everything you see. It makes life impossible.   (pp. 286–7)

Aesthetically, though, this tight pattern of symbols substantiates the notorious moment when the princess dances. The white flutterings that charmed the Syrian, and which Herod expects to see, turn deadly: 'Your little feet will be like white doves. They will be like little white flowers that dance upon the trees . . . No, no, she is going to dance on blood. There is blood spilt on the ground.' While the princess readies herself, the moon turns red, as Jokanaan had prophesied. These symbols also give logic to Wilde's own alterations to the fable and protect its lurid climax from incipient melodrama. The Tetrarch's court seems by this time so fantastical that Salomé's obsession as she listens greedily for the sword to fall is as well attuned to that atmosphere as are Jokanaan's silence when he meets his death and the 'huge black arm' which rises up from the cistern to display the head on a silver shield. This is not mere grand guignol.

Some of the legends Wilde considered as he wrote *Salomé* see the prophet's execution as so terrible that the princess, instrument of her mother's hatred for her accuser, takes on a monstrous sanctity. One such version makes her an exile in the desert who, meeting Jesus, recalls the Baptist's prophecies and journeys into far countries to proclaim Him. Calling the names of Jesus and John, she too is decapitated when she falls through a frozen lake, and the silvery ice bears up her severed head crowned with a ruby diadem.[19] In Wilde's play, Salomé demands Jokanaan's head so that she can kiss his lips and triumph over one who reviled her 'as a harlot, as a wanton'. But that victory is also her defeat. Imagining how she will bite that mouth 'with my teeth as one bites a ripe fruit' (p. 292), she cannot stir the dead to respond as Herod had when he saw 'in a fruit the mark of thy little teeth' (p. 280). The eyes that refused to look at her will not open in death, despite her cries that 'the mystery of love is greater than the mystery of death. Love only should one consider' (p. 293). Like the Duchess of Padua, Salomé destroys the lover who rejected her. But unlike the Duchess who then perceives her lover's goodness and is moved to futile, but redeeming self-sacrifice, Salomé sees only pale skin, dark hair, red lips: sensual pleasures which turn 'bitter' at the moment she achieves them. As a 'great black cloud crosses the moon' to plunge the terrace in darkness, Salomé kisses that mouth at last and discovers 'love hath a bitter taste'. Desire is as evanescent as the moon whose equivocal beam wraps her in sudden light or as fleeting as Herod's which turns to cold disgust as he orders his soldiers to crush her with their shields: 'Kill that woman!'

Pursuing the sensual at any cost, Salomé is another Dorian Gray. Both discover its bitter aftertaste and both react to that discovery in an enigmatic way. Dorian, by slashing his loathsome portrait, kills himself in maddened protest; Salomé, tasting blood-stained lips, fights against their acrid lesson: 'But what of that? What of that? I have kissed thy mouth, Jokanaan.' Neither is illumined by desire, though both are destroyed by it. Yet the possibility of the *monstre sacré* whose terrible pleasures would eventually refine the soul continued to intrigue Wilde's imagination, just as the aesthetic journey to refinement had possessed his younger self. In 'Pen, Pencil and Poison' (1889), Wilde had described the criminal energies which, he mockingly suggested, give an artist the completeness he might otherwise lack. Thomas Wainewright was 'not merely a poet and a painter, ... and a dilettante of things delightful, but also a forger of no mean or ordinary capabilities, and as a subtle and secret poisoner almost without rival in this or any age'.[20] Wilde projected him as a fellow spirit for whom 'Life itself is an art' and conjectured that his crimes 'had an important effect upon his art. They gave a strong personality to his style, ... One can fancy an intense personality being created out of sin.' Salomé's sin intensifies her personality which, reflected in the moon, dominates the entire structure of the play: Wilde had himself photographed in the guise of the Princess reaching out for a severed head.[21]

Redeeming sin occurs in two short plays begun in 1894. *La Sainte Courtisane* takes place beside a hermit's cave in the Egyptian desert. Its style and structure imitate *Salomé*'s though its colours take their key from a sky of lapis lazuli as opposed to a bronze-green cistern. Myrrhina, the courtesan, worships the sensual and the power it gives her over kings and princes. Curious to see 'the beautiful young hermit who will not look on the face of woman' (p. 442), she urges him to join her: 'I will smear your body with myrrh and pour spikenard on your hair. I will clothe you in hyacinth and put honey in your mouth' (p. 445). For Honorius, no love can equal God's: the body is vile and corrupt; 'The beauty of the soul increases till it can see God.' However (after a break in the manuscript), Honorius returns a changed man: 'Take me to Alexandria and let me taste of the seven sins.' A last fragment shows Myrrhina cursing her body and the harm it has done to the man who has revealed God to her. Yet God ordained this meeting in the desert so that she might know Him and so Honorius might 'see Sin in its painted mask and look on Death in its robe of Shame'. This suggests that his life of abnegation was no victory at all and that, cleansed by desire, his soul may shine the brighter. Similarly, *A Florentine Tragedy* shows how murder changes an otherwise suppressed personality into a fiery libertarian and, perversely, makes a woman seem more lovely. Here Wilde slips back into Bardics which are singularly inappropriate for a merchant who talks of 'dim towers / Like shadows silvered by the wandering moon' (p. 425) yet whose commercial soul apparently sees neither his wife's beauty nor the Young Lord's interest in her. These stylistic absurdities do, however, lead to a last wayward twist that suggests Simone has been using his wife to lure Guido's custom and, in seeming humility, vent his hatred on an unjust world until the moment he can strike against those who take what is rightfully his. By strangling Guido, Simone gives voice to the resentments of his class then, thinking to destroy his wife, he finds himself transfigured in her eyes and she in his by murder and treachery. The two embrace.

Wilde never finished those two plays, but they reveal a disregard for form as he explores the borders of his own temperament. *Salomé* is the one tragedy in which structure and theme support each other to convey Wilde's personality, and when Sarah Bernhardt asked for the play he acquired the artist whose extraordinary presence could interpret his.[22] But the censor refused to allow biblical figures to appear on stage and, though Wilde railed against a system which 'panders to the vulgarity and hypocrisy of the English people, by licensing every low farce and vulgar melodrama',[23] the production was cancelled; the text, however, was printed the following year (1893). Wilde had other ways to educate public taste. *Lady Windermere's Fan*, the comedy George Alexander had commissioned, was playing to large audiences at the St James's.

'All art is quite useless', said the preface to *Dorian Gray* and, in one of his letters, Wilde expanded that aphorism. 'Art is useless because its aim is simply to create a mood. It is not meant to instruct, or to influence action in any way. It is superbly sterile, and the note of its pleasure is sterility . . . A work of art is useless as a flower is useless. A flower blossoms for its own joy. We gain a moment of joy by looking at it.'[24] In *Lady Windermere's Fan* (1892) Wilde aimed at that pleasurable sterility. If the play was instructive at all, its message was 'sheer individualism. It is not for anyone to censure what anyone else does, and everyone should go his own way, to whatever place he chooses, in exactly the way that he chooses.'[25] Wilde also would choose his own way as a dramatist, regardless of new realism. He had admired Elizabeth Robins's 'great performance' as Hedda Gabler, 'a real masterpiece of art', but he also noticed that Hedda's search 'for scarlet sensations in a drab-coloured existence' attracted just as dreary an audience: 'the pit full of sad vegetarians, and the stalls occupied by men in mackintoshes and women in knitted shawls of red wool'.[26] Wilde's stance in itself is somewhat contradictory: the detached and independent artist who would prefer not to waste his brilliance on a drab collection of seedy intellectuals. The actual play shows a more radical contradiction. Wilde does indeed champion individualism (and rather blatantly) through a plot which reaffirms the moral prejudice he supposedly deplores. This is not a cynical attempt to gain large audiences, those 'well meaning but very stupid . . . nice children'. Would that it were. Wilde's intellect produces flowers that are a joy to experience, but his emotion draws him to conventional blooms that are sentimental or theatrical and so the play's wit pampers the vulgar by enfolding tawdry melodrama in a 'mood' of attractive, and slightly wicked modernity.

Lord Darlington illustrates that schism between head and heart. In Lady Windermere's morning-room, his clever and extravagant compliments seem to be those of a man who, knowing that life is 'too complex a thing to be settled by these hard and fast rules', can never take anything seriously. There is a warmth behind that flippancy as he teases Lady Margaret for 'mak[ing] badness of such extraordinary importance' (p. 78) or plays the suave amoralist to titillate the Duchess of Berwick's self-satisfaction. But behind his attractive playfulness, he also appears to be toying with Margaret's naive certainties by hinting that her husband is unfaithful. Maurice Barrymore played him that way in the American production so that his scene with Lady Windermere in Act Two, after she has been forced to receive the woman she thinks is her husband's mistress, snared Margaret with a calculated appeal to the clichés of affronted virtue. His hollow dialogue thus became a corrosive attack on self-righteous purity and the sort of drama that upholds it:

What sort of life would you have with him? You would feel that he was lying to you every moment of the day. You would feel that the look in his eyes was false, his voice false, his touch false, his passion false. He would come to you when he was weary of others; you would have to comfort him. He would come to you when he was devoted to others; you would have to charm him. You would have to be to him the mask of his real life, the cloak to hide his secret.   (p. 96)

But, as Wilde pointed out when he heard about that interpretation, those sentiments are meant to be entirely sincere: 'His appeal is not to the weakness, but to the strength of her character . . . he really loves her.'[27] So Darlington is actually a man of feeling who assumes a mask in order to hide his emotional susceptibility. He is also the man who makes us question Lady Windermere's black or white morality and then subscribes to it himself. Yet Wilde means us to sympathize with Darlington's romantic despair when, in Act Three, he idealizes the 'purity and goodness' of a woman whose conventionality has failed to cope with life's complexity.

Mrs Erlynne is just as inconsistent. Through her, Wilde means to test the label 'wicked'. Adulteress, blackmailer, adventuress, she nevertheless risks everything for her daughter's happiness. In one of the play's more convincing moments, she laughs off the pain of that sudden return of maternal feeling:

I suppose, Windermere, you would like me to retire into a convent, or become a hospital nurse, or something of that kind, as people do in silly modern novels . . . Repentance is quite out of date. And besides, if a woman really repents, she has to go to a bad dressmaker, otherwise no one believes in her. And nothing in the world would induce me to do that. (p. 121)

Unrepentant, and successfully so, she inveigles Lord Augustus Lorton into marrying her, despite the events of the night before, and leaves with a dowry from Lord Windermere and her daughter's admiration. Yet she is not actually unscrupulous. She describes her own past with as much loathing as any puritan would feel, and her emotion enforces that narrow view of wickedness Wilde claims to deny. Her fall from grace twenty years before has stained her for ever:

One pays for one's sin, and then one pays again, and all one's life one pays. You must never know that. – As for me, if suffering be an expiation, then at this moment I have expiated all my faults, whatever they have been; for to-night you have made a heart in one who had it not, made it and broken it. – But let that pass. I may have wrecked my own life, but I will not let you wreck yours.

(pp. 106–7)

Her pathos as a mother figure is just as intense, despite her disclaimers. Desperate to stop Lady Windermere from repeating her own mistake, she appeals to her daughter with all the tremor of a guilty conscience:

You have a child, Lady Windermere. Go back to that child who even now, in pain or in joy, may be calling to you. God gave you that child. He will require from you that you make his life fine, that you watch over him. What answer will you make to God if his life is ruined through you? (p. 107)

And the ending of the play affirms that image, for Mrs Erlynne also takes with her a picture of her daughter and little grandson – 'I like to think of you as a mother' (p. 123) – and the fan which 'will always remind me of you' (p. 124). The hard-bitten adventuress is really the Lost One stained but redeemed by maternal sacrifice.

The pragmatic intellect which sustains the taunting pose of Wilde's essays and dialogues succumbs to the theatre's romantic idealism. *Lady Windermere* veers erratically between provocative thought and windy rhetoric: aiming at tolerance, it encourages prejudice; attacking delusion, it recommends pretence. 'Ideals are dangerous things. Realities are better. They wound, but they're better', says Mrs Erlynne (p. 122). Yet, moments later, she determines to protect Lady Windermere's picturesque illusion of the mother who 'died a few months after I was born' and the father who 'really died of a broken heart' (p. 123). Lady Windermere's complacent rectitude has been shaken. She no longer believes 'that people can be divided into the

good and the bad as though they were two separate races or creations'
(pp. 116–17). Her mother's decision to conceal the truth robs her of
the chance to put that lesson to the test. So her changed attitude to
Mrs Erlynne has no substance and is yet another pretty fantasy: a
despised woman has sacrificed all chance of respectability to save a
stranger from the same disgrace. Nor will Mrs Erlynne allow her to
test her husband's love by admitting her folly with Lord Darlington:
one wonders how Arthur would react to that reality. But none of this
can be taken seriously except by those who think that *any* woman who
leaves her husband and child or who visits a man's apartments at the
dead of night is indeed wicked. In real terms, the blackmail Lord
Arthur submits to and the misunderstanding he courts in order to
protect his pure young wife from her disreputable mother are as
nonsensical as the tremulous soliloquies and impassioned duets
which animate those mechanics. There is also a discomforting
emptiness about the ending which returns the Windermeres to their
rose garden at Selby with their innocence intact.

'How hard good women are!', says Lord Windermere to his wife,
but that verdict more accurately applies to Mrs Arbuthnot in *A
Woman of No Importance* (1893). Wilde wrote the play for Beerbohm
Tree while recovering from the debacle of *Salomé* and, under the
guise of comedy, he re-explored that clash of mighty opposites. Mrs
Arbuthnot has the unflinching purity of Jokanaan, but through the
secular saint Wilde shows how righteousness contains its own defeat.
Mrs Arbuthnot is taunted, sneered at, and dismissed by a sensual
aristocrat, Lord Illingworth, but is brought to her knees by the son
she has reared so respectably and by the affronted puritanism of his
American admirer. However, in Act Four, the situation is curiously
reversed. Rachel Arbuthnot becomes the Salomé of legend, that
sacred monster who, through lamentation and good works, comes to
glory. For the sins of her flesh, Rachel lacerates herself and embraces
the ongoing pain of all mothers who sacrifice themselves for their
children's well-being. Now the puritan sees her as a holy icon – 'in her
all womanhood is martyred' – and her son 'need[s] no second parent'.
Loved and accepted, she again confronts Lord Illingworth and puts
an end to his callous insults. There is something pathological in the
excess of self-loathing and guilt which burns Rachel's spirit into
radiance. Wilde was with Bosie when he finished the script: the
anguish and ecstasy of its peculiar last Act surely reflects his own
passion.[28]

In the first three Acts, however, Wilde discovered how to stamp his personality on comedy. Throughout Act One and much of Act Two the dialogue delights in itself: 'useless as a flower is useless'. Those blossoms are too tightly packed and are plucked by some unlikely characters, but this mood piece on the lawn at Lady Hunstanton's affords Wilde opportunity to distil his table-talk, although the jokes about America are not as fresh as the Australian ones that sprang from the Duchess of Berwick's pursuit of Mr Hopper: 'dear Agatha and I are so much interested in Australia. It must be so pretty with all the dear little kangaroos flying about' (*Lady Windermere's Fan*, p. 90). With fine effrontery,[29] Wilde extends that banter into Act Two where it eventually provokes the American, Hester Worsley, into angry frankness: 'of the unseen beauty of a higher life, you know nothing. You have lost life's secret. Oh, your English society seems to me shallow, selfish, foolish. It has blinded its eyes, and stopped its ears' (p. 149). That leads on to sexual decadence, and Mrs Arbuthnot arrives in the drawing-room to hear her proclaim the injustice that brands a woman, but lets a man go free: 'if a man and woman have sinned, let them both go forth into the desert to love or loathe each other there' (p. 150). Irony also circumscribes the scene between Rachel and Lord Illingworth. A genuine and complacent cynic, Lord Illingworth turns aside her bitterness with assured calm. The past must be buried; Rachel should think of their son's future instead of her own indignation:

What a typical woman you are! You talk sentimentally and you are thoroughly selfish the whole time. But don't let us have a scene. Rachel, I want you to look at this matter from the common-sense point of view, from the point of view of what is best for our son, leaving you and me out of the question . . . simply because it turns out that I am the boy's own father and he my own son, you propose practically to ruin his career. That is to say, if I were a perfect stranger, you would allow Gerald to go away with me, but as he is my own flesh and blood you won't. How utterly illogical you are! (p. 157)

Wilde uses Illingworth's self-serving logic to explore the motives behind Rachel's proud defiance. Detaching himself from the Victorian cliché, he delivers a body blow to the sacred image of motherhood and sustains that critique to the end of the sequence where Illingworth curtly dismisses Rachel's sentimental plea: 'There is nothing more to be said on the subject' (p. 158).

In Act Three, when Rachel appeals to her son, Wilde exploits the sentiment in order to subvert one of the theatre's most touching pictures. Just as he used to 'when [he was] a little boy, [his] mother's own boy', Gerald sits beside her as she strokes his hair and tells him of a girl who 'was very young, and – and ignorant of what life really is' (p. 171). Her story creates a genre painting of ruined innocence and its consequences: 'Nothing can heal her! no anodyne can give her sleep! no poppies forgetfulness! She is lost! She is a lost soul!' But in obedience to that same convention, Gerald has been educated in the paths of righteousness and so his reaction is naturally (and devastatingly) respectable:

My dear mother, it all sounds very tragic, of course. But I dare say the girl was just as much to blame as Lord Illingworth was. – After all, would a really nice girl, a girl with any nice feelings at all, go away from her home with a man to whom she was not married, and live with him as his wife? No nice girl would.
(pp. 171–2)

Whereupon another girl runs in terror from Lord Illingworth's embrace. Taking up the challenge of his verbal sparring partner, Mrs Allonby, Illingworth has dared to kiss Hester. Gerald's attitude is suddenly very different and, with unconscious irony, he rushes to her defence: 'Lord Illingworth, you have insulted the purest thing on God's earth, a thing as pure as my own mother. You have insulted the woman I love most in the world with my own mother.' The final tableau snaps the strings of the over-wrought trio: 'Stop, Gerald, stop! He is your own father!' Gerald 'clutches his mother's hands and looks into her face'; Rachel sinks to the floor 'in shame'; Hester 'steals' away from the tainted woman. After a lengthy pause, Gerald raises his mother and, with his arms around her, takes her from the room and Lord Illingworth: Virtue Rewarded.

Act Four begins with the same ironic control as Mrs Allonby and Lady Hunstanton enter the sitting-room of Mrs Arbuthnot's rural retreat. Their conversation further diminishes the histrionics: 'Ah, I am afraid the heat was too much for her last night. I think there must have been thunder in the air' (p. 173). The old-fashioned room is 'quite the happy English home', and Mrs Arbuthnot's arrival after dinner had given 'quite an atmosphere of respectability to the party' (p. 174). 'Ah', purrs Mrs Allonby, 'that must have been what you thought was thunder in the air.' When they leave, Gerald determines to force Illingworth to marry Rachel, and she refuses. The reversal is comically incongruous, but Wilde no longer distances himself from Gerald's earnestness and Rachel's eager shame. Fired by the enigma of redemptive sin, he builds Rachel into love's martyr, outcast and ashamed, yet clinging to that sin:

And you thought I spent too much of my time in going to Church, and in Church duties. But where else could I turn? God's house is the only house where sinners are made welcome, and you were always in my heart, Gerald, too much in my heart. For, though day after day, at morn or evensong, I have knelt in God's house, I have never repented of my sin. How could I repent of my sin when you, my love, were its fruit. Even now that you are bitter to me I cannot repent. I do not. (p. 179)

The dialogue is over-pitched and the reconciliation of the purified is flooded with sentiment. Nor does the final confrontation drain that away. Unable to attain his son, Lord Illingworth contents himself with one last sneer: 'you gave yourself to me like a flower, to do anything I liked with. You were the prettiest of playthings, the most fascinating of small romances' (pp. 184–5). Mrs Arbuthnot picks up his glove and strikes him across the face. Defeated, he leaves the house: 'A man of no importance.'

Illingworth's importance to the play itself derives from the surface he presents to the world around him: Wilde does not explore him in depth. As with all of Lady Hunstanton's circle, 'what is interesting about people in good society . . . is the mask that each one of them wears, not the reality that lies behind the mask'.[30] Similarly, their paradoxical talk fractures the certitude of commonplace ideas without probing further. In *An Ideal Husband* (1895), however, Wilde does push below the surface. In the person of Sir Robert Chiltern, he examines ideas like goodness, ambition, honour in a more complex, personal way. The deceptive blandness of that persona, so unlike Wilde's usual façade, allows him that freedom. 'Man is least like himself when he talks in his own person. Give him a mask, and he will tell you the truth' ('The Critic as Artist', p. 389). Whether or not Wilde consciously built that disguise when writing the play in 1893, he certainly recognized his hidden self as he prepared the stage-directions for publication (1899) after his own disgrace. His description of Sir Robert moves beyond exteriors:

One feels that he is conscious of the success he has made in life . . . The firmly-chiselled mouth and chin contrast strikingly with the romantic expression in the deep-set eyes. The variance is suggestive of an almost complete separation of passion and intellect, as though thought and emotion were each isolated in its own sphere through some violence of will-power. (p. 192)

As the action reveals, Sir Robert's intellect persuades him that the unsavoury aspects of his passionate ambition all work to the good. Wilde understands the power and frailty of that delusion and, through Sir Robert's conflict, sheds new light on old conventions.

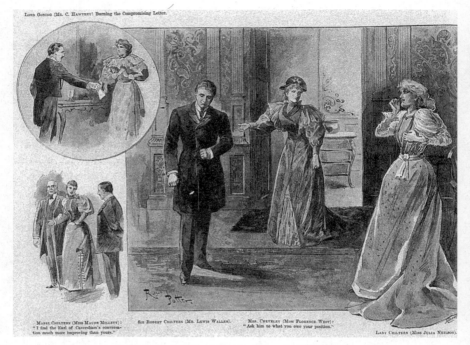

Lord Goring (Mr. C. Hawtrey) Burning the Compromising Letter.

Mabel Chiltern (Miss Maude Millett):
"I find the Earl of Caversham's conversation much more improving than yours."

Sir Robert Chiltern (Mr. Lewis Waller).

Mrs. Cheveley (Miss Florence West):
"Ask him to what you owe your position."

Lady Chiltern (Miss Julia Neilson).

7   Oscar Wilde's *An Ideal Husband* at the Haymarket Theatre

Chiltern is an honourable man in his own eyes and the public's. When he gives in to blackmail by agreeing to throw his official support behind the fraudulent investment scheme he had previously attacked, he explains that 'public and private life are different things' and that, due to 'certain obligations', he has opted 'to compromise'. His wife idolizes his probity and insists that 'circumstances should never alter principles': were he like other men 'who treat life simply as a sordid speculation', she could not love him (pp. 209–10). In Act Two, Wilde subjects that womanly ideal to the world's realities. Chiltern can be franker with Lord Goring and, though he begins with spurious self-justification, the more he convinces himself, the more he reveals his actual character. He admits that at the beginning of his career he sold financial information: 'I suppose most men would call [that] shameful and dishonourable' (p. 213). But those men do just the same: 'Private information is practically the source of every large modern fortune . . . Is it fair that the folly, the sin of one's youth, if men choose to call it a sin, should wreck a life like mine?' He has simply fought the world with its own weapons: 'The God of this century is wealth . . . At all costs one must have wealth.' Recalling the 'subtle and refined intellect' of Baron Arnheim whose seductive luxuries were simply a means to the one thing worth having – 'power over other men' – Chiltern becomes dazzled by the 'freedom' success brought him and by the 'courage' it took to seize that opportunity: 'To stake all one's life on a single moment, to risk everything on one throw, whether the stake be power or pleasure, I care not – there is no weakness in that' (p. 215). Thus Chiltern is convinced he never sold himself; he 'bought success at a great price' and has since donated twice that sum to charity. In the scene between the Chilterns, after she discovers his dishonesty, Wilde smashes the holy tablets of Victorian marriage as Sir Robert justifies himself. By urging her husband to an honourable decision, Lady Chiltern has brought him to ruin; the unscrupulous Mrs Cheveley, by bribing him with an incriminating letter, 'offered security, peace, stability':

Why can't you women love us, faults and all? Why do you place us on monstrous pedestals? We have all feet of clay, women as well as men; . . . Let women make no more ideals of men! let them not put them on altars and bow before them or they may ruin other lives as completely as you – you whom I have so wildly loved – have ruined mine! (pp. 231–2)

Chiltern has told Lord Goring of the panic he feels as he faces the scandal his wife's ideals have forced him to – 'It is as if a hand of ice were laid upon one's heart' (p. 217) – so his outburst, despite its misrepresentation, turns her virtue into a terrifying burden.

Yet Gertrude Chiltern is neither a prude (like Lady Windermere) nor a zealot (like Mrs Arbuthnot). Wilde emphasizes her 'grave Greek beauty' as she receives her guests at an evening party. Above her hangs a tapestry, the Triumph of Love; around her are luxuries and influential people. She is at home in those surroundings: an elegant woman of 'serious purpose' (p. 189) who likes listening to politics, belongs to the Woman's Liberal Association, and concerns herself with 'dull, useful, delightful things' like Factory Acts and Parliamentary Franchise (p. 219). Her intelligence and experience have not dimmed her idealism and, ironically, her husband 'worships' her for that; she is an attribute to his career and the standard he would like to think he lives by. Lord Goring tries to warn her that 'in every nature there are elements of weakness' (p. 221), but her heart tells her otherwise. She, too, has a divided personality. When her world collapses, she shrinks in horror from her fallen idol, but Wilde presents that sympathetically when, still ruled by her heart, she wishes Robert would lie to her, as he has deceived the world, by denying Mrs Cheveley's story or when she instinctively rushes towards him as he storms out of the room. Both the Chilterns are 'nice' people, and that makes Wilde's critique all the more effective. His empathy also mirrors his theme: 'life cannot be understood without much charity, cannot be lived without much charity'.

Wilde's genial *raisonneur*, Lord Goring, 'plays with life, and is on perfectly good terms with the world' (p. 195). The mask he presents is an extension of his private self. 'A flawless dandy' who does nothing but amuse himself and others, he sees through the Chilterns' self-deception but, with friendly concern, tries to make them acknowledge that 'in practical life' there is something 'unscrupulous always' about ambition and success (p. 221). His own ambition is simply to enjoy himself and give pleasure to others, so he plays the irresponsible son for his father, who loves to grumble, and thus avoids the practical life Lord Caversham would choose for him. He continually urges the Chilterns to speak truly to each other, and his levity with Mabel Chiltern, who shares his 'modern' cleverness, allows them both to talk honestly without resort to 'moral' principles. By trivializing words like 'ideal' and 'serious', they show a flexibility of mind and character which frees them from society's deluding earnestness. Miss Mabel is perfectly serious as she dashes off to rehearse for a Charity Benefit – 'I have got to stand on my head in some tableaux' (p. 224) – since by turning things upside down she sees her upright world in comic perspective. Thus she 'delights' in Goring's 'bad qualities' and, accepting him completely, will be 'a real wife' to him. And Goring adores her irreverence because the conventional idea of a 'thoroughly sensible wife would reduce me to a condition of absolute idiocy in less than six months' (p. 252). Here Wilde's subversive wit has a buoyant charm which radiates good-feeling (as it did in his actual conversation) and offers a salutary contrast to the purposeful Chilterns. It is no longer a decorative veneer.

Mrs Cheveley's unscrupulous cleverness also gives the *boulevard* intrigue a certain humanity. Going beyond the type, Wilde takes an unsentimental look at a woman whose past has taught her how to manipulate more successfully. Unlike Pinero, he has no set view of maidenly innocence: Mrs Cheveley has been a liar and a thief since her schooldays. Nor does he envision the sort of taint that must inevitably destroy Paula Tanqueray. Mrs Cheveley's beauty is somewhat raffish – 'A work of art, on the whole, but showing the influence of too many schools' (p. 191) – but the 'experience' and wealth she has accrued from men like Baron Arnheim enhance her style. And cigarettes, that trademark of the 'fast' and loose, are not for Mrs Cheveley: 'My dressmaker wouldn't like it, and a woman's first duty in life is to her dressmaker, isn't it?' (pp. 243–4). Entirely without conscience – her 'memory is under admirable control' (p. 196) – she recognizes her own ambition and dishonesty in Chiltern and so decides to use him. Her animus against Gertrude Chiltern's rectitude – 'She always got the good conduct prize' (p. 193) – motivates the other devices of the plot, though it cannot hide their contrivance. Wilde uses her astuteness to throw a less kindly light on moral rigidity and the politics of power. At the end of Act Three, he takes her out of the play in seeming triumph: her spite would disrupt the festive conclusion and she is not the type for last-minute contrition.

An Ideal Husband is the most unified and graceful of Wilde's three comedies. Having exposed the hypocrisy and terror of the ideal, in the home and in society at large, he returns his characters to a less demanding norm. At heart he, too, could not break free from the Victorian dream. And so Lord Goring steps out of character to lecture Lady Chiltern on little women:

> A man's life is of more value than a woman's. It has larger issues, wider scope, greater ambitions. A woman's life revolves in curves of emotions. It is upon lines of intellect that a man's life progresses. (p. 261)

Sir Robert is allowed his cabinet post and a forgiving wife he can worship once more. Wilde lets that pass, but he does plant one last irony. Having been restored to honour and position by Lord Goring, Chiltern has to deny him Mabel's hand in marriage. He is right to protect his sister from a known philanderer but, when the evidence against Lord Goring turns out to be nothing of the sort, he does not see the fragility of all certitudes. Sir Robert has learned little about life's complexity, a fact which undermines the happy confidence of Gertrude's last speech: 'For both of us a new life is beginning.' The general *bonhomie*, as each couple joins hands, does not quite absolve Sir Robert.

Characteristically, Wilde's most realistic treatment of London Society proclaims the uncertainty behind nearly all its prized realities. A slogan like The Higher Education of Woman, which the Chilterns both subscribe to, loses its capital letters and changes meaning when Lord Goring offers his own brand of education and Mrs Cheveley hers: 'The higher education of men is what I should like to see. Men need it so sadly' (p. 226). Lady Markby says more than she means by assenting to that: 'I don't think man has much capacity for development.' *The Importance of Being Earnest* (1895) raises that idea to farcical proportions. In that play, nobody learns anything except that Mr Worthing is Ernest John Moncrieff, and even those names mean different things to different people. In Lady Bracknell's words, 'Fortunately in England, at any rate, education produces no effect whatsoever. If it did, it would prove a serious danger to the upper classes, and probably lead to acts of violence in Grosvenor Square' (as it had at the Chilterns' house). All the characters (except Worthing) believe superbly in their social masks, and that egoism allows them utter confidence: mask and face become one and the same. For them, reality seems solid and simple as they ride roughshod over all facts and ideas that might disturb their view of the world. Whereas *An Ideal Husband* revealed the hypocrisy and inadequacy of the upright through the somersaults of the nimble, *The Importance* looks at the way life's complex contradictions are rapidly absorbed by a self-confidence which makes the characters impermeable to change or doubt. This is not only the prerogative of wealth and position, though Lady Bracknell's imposing personality has made her the paradigm of upper-class self-satisfaction. Even Algy, who 'has nothing but his debts to depend upon', presents himself with an assurance which smooths away fiscal details as deftly as it flattens other inconveniences:

JACK: Yes, but you said yourself that a severe chill was not hereditary.
ALGERNON: It usen't to be, I know – but I dare say it is now. Science is always making wonderful improvements in things.   (p. 60)

Lower down the social scale, Canon Chasuble ingests the accidental into his own invulnerable order with similar efficiency: 'My sermon on the meaning of the manna in the wilderness can be adapted to almost any occasion, joyful, or, as in the present case, distressing. I have preached it at harvest celebrations, christenings, confirmations, on days of humiliation and festal days' (p. 44). What looks like supple adaptability is actually the determination of a steam-roller.

Into the middle of this steps Mr Worthing who has one mask for town and another for the country. He does not know he is Ernest John so, when he projects himself as one or the other, his behaviour is peculiarly erratic even before both masks disintegrate. As Ernest, he can seriously enjoy a life of pleasure: at ease with Algy's style, irresistibly fascinating to Gwendolen, and resilient enough to recover from Lady Bracknell's scrutiny. But he also has an earnestness which makes him critical of Algy and vulnerable to Lady Bracknell, a John-like propriety which, for Gwendolen, suggests uxoriousness: 'any woman . . . married to a man called John . . . would probably never be allowed to know the entrancing pleasure of a single moment's solitude' (p. 29). As 'Uncle Jack', his domesticity endears him to Cecily, especially when he talks of wicked Ernest, yet to Dr Chasuble and Miss Prism he is Mr John Worthing, JP. They are deeply impressed when he appears in full mourning (for his reprobate self), but Cecily thinks his sombre clothes are 'horrid'. When his town life invades the country, he tries on each frail mask in desperation until Miss Prism recounts 'the plain facts' about the hand-bag. His identity secured, he too can sweep the inopportune aside:

JACK (*embracing her*): Yes . . . mother!
MISS PRISM (*recoiling in indignant astonishment*): Mr Worthing, I am unmarried!
JACK: Unmarried! I do not deny that is a serious blow. But after all, who has the right to cast a stone against one who has suffered? Cannot repentance wipe out an act of folly? Why should there be one law for men, and another for women? Mother, I forgive you. (*Tries to embrace her again.*)   (p. 71)

In this version of the divided self, Mr Worthing can recover his position in the family and society, thanks to Aunt Augusta and the Army Lists, and so eradicate the lies of the past. Should 'speaking nothing but the truth' disturb him, Gwendolen assures him he is 'sure to change'. Once he becomes thoroughly secure as Ernest John, truth will give way to the vital importance of being earnest.

In Wilde's original four-Act script, Algy's progress was less smooth than it is now. Arriving in the country as Ernest, he was accosted by Mr Gribsby, of Parker and Gribsby, Solicitors, Chancery Lane, who delivered 'a writ of attachment for 20 days against [him] at the suit of the Savoy Hotel Co. Limited, for £762.14.2.'[31] Plain truth seems to threaten, though 'the truth is rarely plain and never simple' since Ernest's debts are actually Mr Worthing's who is delighted to embarrass Algy. But Algy will not be embarrassed. As a confirmed Bunburyist, he is as sure of himself in Hertfordshire as he is in London or Shropshire. Gribsby threatens him with Holloway Gaol; Worthing refuses to save his 'brother'; Chasuble and Miss Prism urge retribution: 'As a man sows so let him reap. This proposed incarceration might be most salutary. It is to be regretted that it is only for 20 days!' (p. 121). None of this makes Algy admit his fraudulence: Jack ought to be brotherly, and the law is 'nonsensical' for seeking to imprison him 'in the suburbs for having dined in the West End' (p. 122). Funny though it is, that protracted wrangle ties Algy too closely to the mundane. By cutting this and other passages of argument and explanation, Wilde underlined each character's dogmatic will and, perceiving that, added idiosyncratic grace notes, like Miss Prism's 'temperance beverage'. In the original, Prism told her story then resigned, since her pupil had outshone her 'in the very difficult accomplishment of getting married' (p. 185). Taking the hint at last, Chasuble thrust aside the celibate rule of the Primitive Church: 'Corrupt readings seem to have crept into the text' (p. 186). An extended sequence then delayed the pressing question of Worthing's Christian name and brought the action back to earth with details like Lady Brancaster's coachman, her advice to Chasuble, her arrangements for Cecily to go to Upper Grosvenor Street. Without all that, the realities of the outside world pale in contrast to the characters' blazing egoism. Within their impregnable circle, Worthing tries to dislodge Algy, arranges a hurried christening, frantically hunts for the hand-bag upstairs, fumbles through the Army Lists, and becomes like the others at last. His final euphoria sends Chasuble and Prism into each other's arms with comic, but appropriate suddenness for they, too, absorb life's arbitrariness into their ordered selves.

Mr Worthing's farcical search for himself ridicules the way names and words impose their own authority on life, especially for those who hide behind them. That solidity is, of course, deceptive, for the other characters can make words mean whatever they want them to. Lady Bracknell is expert at that, but even Cecily turns a christening into a 'fearful ordeal' and, twisting set phrases to her own advantage, endows her beloved with a 'physical courage of which we women know absolutely nothing' (p. 62). In ordinary farce, the characters suffer increasingly ludicrous embarrassments as they try to maintain their equipoise: Worthing becomes like that in Act Three, but first he tries to fight off panic with words. The others mould everyday language – and cliché in particular – into a fantasy of their own. Because of that, their personalities, rather than their actions, escalate into farce without quite losing touch with the world they transcend. Like superlative cartoons, they attain a reality which alters our perception of their real-life counterparts: dictatorial matrons, suitable bachelors, inexperienced young girls can never seem the same again.

Wilde described the play, in an interview he concocted with a friend, as 'exquisitely trivial, a delicate bubble of fancy' for which 'Realism is only a background.'[32] On the first night, the critics saw the delicate bubble but missed the reality behind it. Shaw, for example, thought Cecily and Gwendolen's meeting in Act Two 'was quite in the literary style of Mr Gilbert, and almost inhuman enough to have been written by him'.[33] He was presumably thinking of the two rival ladies in *Engaged* and wanted to deflate Wilde's 'modern' triviality by suggesting that the play was at least ten years out of date. But Wilde *is* attacking his contemporaries' ineducable complacency and he does so with warm humanity. In *Engaged*, Gilbert satirized the theatre's sentimentality by making his characters do mercenary and unfeeling things while acting out the stock emotions and situations of the playhouse. So Angus sells Maggie for 'twa pound' while his 'bonnie blue een' fill with tears and he swears that all the gold in the world cannot part him from his heart's treasure. In *The Importance*, reality and fantasy are fused together. Even at their most ridiculous, the characters remain intensely human and delicately true to the habits of their class or occupation. Shaw may have been misled by the actors' inadequate performances, but when, a few years later, he wrote to Janet Achurch, explaining how she should play Lady Cecily in *Captain Brassbound's Conversion*, he made exactly the point about the English 'great lady' that Wilde makes with Lady Bracknell: 'She would hardly ever shew real excitement, or lose her distinction and immense self-conceit & habit of patronage . . . in everything external she would be distinguished from the middle-class woman, who lives her whole life under suspicion & shortness of cash.'[34] Max Beerbohm, whose own satiric caricatures caught the human and fantastic elements of Wilde himself and whose name appears as Maxbohm in Mr Worthing's Army Lists, understood how the play's humour rises out of the characters' personalities as well as from the words they manipulate.[35] For example, when Miss Prism examines the hand- bag, the precise way she recalls its tell-tale features transforms this parody of a recognition-scene into a poignant revelation of her whole self-centred history even as she calmly re-adjusts events to suit her:

It seems to be mine. Yes, here is the injury it received through the upsetting of a Gower Street omnibus in younger and happier days. Here is the stain on the lining caused by the explosion of a temperance beverage, an incident that occurred at Leamington. And here, on the lock, are my initials. I had forgotten that in an extravagant mood I had had them placed there. The bag is undoubtedly mine. I am delighted to have it so unexpectedly restored to me. It has been a great inconvenience being without it all these years.   (p. 70)

Each detail carries the savour of Miss Prism's individuality while the pedantic, self-satisfied tone of the speech links her to all Victorian governesses.

For Wilde, Art was 'a veil, rather than a mirror. She has flowers that no forests know of, birds that no woodland possesses . . . Hers are the "forms more real than living man", and hers the great archetypes of which things that have existence are but unfinished copies' ('The Decay of Lying', p. 306). The archetypal Victorians in *The Importance* are also able to transform the world about them into their idea of what should be. In a sense, they are artists without the objectivity of form and style which allowed Wilde to create his own imagined pictures of the self-possessed and (in *Salomé*) the obsessed. Ironically, in his everyday life, Wilde was very like the characters in *The Importance* who believe so intensely in themselves that 'plain facts' evaporate into fantasy. It was that persuasive self which made him sue the Marquess of Queensberry and then, at his own trial, courageously defend the 'Love that dare not speak its name.' Yet however convinced he was that 'feasting with panthers' was an intellectual affection between an elder and a younger man, the evidence against him – some of which was hysterically fanciful – would not disappear. In exile, after his two-year prison sentence, Wilde came to terms with the degrading nightmare of Reading Gaol and tried to write plays, but he had lost the imaginative drive: 'Something is killed in me.' Nevertheless there was one scenario, from the time he was writing *The Importance*, which he sold to various producers and actor-managers for 'ready money'. He also half-heartedly agreed to write a first Act for Frank Harris, the editor and novelist, who would work on the other three. When Harris sent him that script, Wilde reacted angrily: 'You have not only stolen my play, you have spoiled it.'[36] Harris then wrote his own first Act and, in *Mr and Mrs Daventry*, he turned Wilde's idea into a *mirror* of upper-middle-class life.

The first half of the play reflects the empty soullessness of the leisured. While the men-folk are off shooting pheasant in the West Wood at Wadham, the Daventrys' country house, five women move listlessly about the morning-room. They have nothing to talk about except marriage and dressmakers. Lady Solway takes a perfunctory glance at a Rossetti drawing; Lady Hallingdon makes risqué remarks and sarcastic asides; Mrs Willie Powell flutters from one to the other: 'I love talking to men or to women; talking to women is more interesting, but talking to men is more exciting' (p. 51). After her guests drift off in search of ways to fill their morning, Mrs Daventry completes the day's orders to her housekeeper, glad 'to have things to do that prevent one thinking' (p. 55). Her mother returns for the 'little talk' she had not been able to have during her visit. Are the Daventrys 'get[ting] on better'? What a pity there are no children! 'We women are meant to be patient' (p. 57). Unable to understand her daughter's misery, poor Mrs Buxton grows tearful and has to be humoured with compliments about her new hat. Delightedly she reminisces about the bargains to be had at sales, the joy of window-shopping, the silk remnant she bought at Peter Robinson's: 'It must have been in '80. Yes, it was in '80 . . . I have it yet and it will come to some use at last, I know it will. Keep a thing for twenty years, all of a sudden you want it – and – there it is!' (p. 59). Her chatter and the awe she feels for 'all you very clever people' who, like her late husband, tend to be 'so impatient' open up yet another desert vista. But in Mr Daventry's opinion his wife 'ought to invent or create an occupation for [her]self'. As he tells her at the beginning of the play, she looks 'a little pale'; she should 'brisk about' more or 'amuse' herself with young Ashurst or Solway, who both obviously admire her. 'I've given you the best advice I can, and if you don't take it, that's your look-out' (pp. 47–8).

Dick Daventry is not intentionally cruel: 'It's what he is, not what he does, that matters' (p. 57). A coarse man without a jot of sensitivity or imagination, he has his dogs and horses, a set of comfortable friends to entertain and play billiards with, and women who are more responsive than his wife is. Such tastes, particularly the latter, are apt to be expensive so he borrows on the sly from Ashurst who, for Hilda's sake, would not want him arraigned for debt. Harris himself was a notorious womanizer, but he analyses Daventry with remarkable objectivity and turns the big 'discovery scene' into a squalid scuffle between Dick and his mistress which epitomizes the indignities of Hilda's marriage. That scene is also the moment Dick's life starts to unravel, and the last two Acts show him trying to behave generously despite his innate crassness. The cool scorn with which Hilda saved him from scandal has touched his vanity, and he wants to prove he is not the brute she knows he is. Appealing to Ashurst as a friend who wants what is best for Hilda, he asks him to persuade her to return home because 'she's good – straight as a line' (p. 92), the sort who 'couldn't stand a life of disdain' if she ran off with some other man. But to remain at her mother's would surely bore her; 'if I behave decently, which is the better life?' (p. 94). In arguing that, he shows how impossible his 'reformation' would be: 'Women are made to live with one man, just as men are made to run after a number of women' (p. 95). When Hilda goes abroad with Ashurst, Dick feels doubly betrayed so, in his own view, he is being even more magnanimous in offering to take her back. Again his nature defeats him. If he cannot have her, then no one shall and, if he kills Hilda's lover, perhaps she will come back to him. Desperate to do right by her, he bristles with masculine pride. So his eventual suicide may be a peculiar generosity, as Hilda seems to think, for it frees her to marry Ashurst and thus avoid 'disdain'. Or it may be the result of his despair when he learns that Hilda is pregnant and so would never return to him – or it may be animal fury. Whatever the motive, his death effectively threatens Hilda's future happiness.

Daventry is no stage villain nor is Hilda the conventional 'good woman'. When Lady Hallingdon warns her that people will think she has left Dick for another man and that, even if she stays with her mother, 'the world will punish you', Hilda simply feels 'how good it is to be free again, to possess one's own soul in peace, to breathe without fear' (pp. 84–5). With Ashurst she is singularly open about the way Dick has degraded her body and soul 'without realising what he was doing'. Having learned to despise men, she immediately assumes her friend sides with her husband. Yet Ashurst is her one chance to prove that tenderness exists. Admitting she knows he loves her, she decides to trust him: 'The world is more charitable than it used to be, I think. People are beginning to see that no single mistake – not even marriage – should be allowed to ruin a whole life. We have a sort of second chance now and most of us need it' (p. 100). Their relationship restores her ideals, and nothing can shake them. Rather than beg Ashurst to refuse the duel, she allows him his outmoded honour – 'What lies all these masculine conventions are!' (p. 105) – since she is 'absolutely sure' her love will protect him. And that conviction makes her rage against her husband's jealous stupidity: God would never allow him to win. 'If you could kill [Ashurst], life would be a hell. Goodness would have no meaning; evil would triumph everywhere; our souls would die; the world would be a murder-den. It is impossible' (p. 113).

Frank Harris saw Wilde's scenario with the eyes of a novelist and, to be entirely convincing, his account of Hilda's strength needs more scope than the theatre allows. As a social document, the play has the impact and the limitations of a photograph; the novel's dimensions might have given it a living permanence. Wilde's own concept of the Daventrys and his critique of Harris's script reveal his skill and idiosyncrasy. For him, all literature 'require[d] distinction, charm, beauty, and imaginative power' ('The Decay of Lying', p. 296). Rather than reproduce the emptiness behind society's façade, he concentrates on the façade itself in order to disclose, through that veil, the malice and hypocrisy of an age of surfaces. He planned Act One to show the mannered talk of 'fashionable *fin-de-siècle*' people and their rudeness to Mrs Daventry, 'a lady – but simple and ignorant of fashionable life', whom they consider 'dowdy and dull'.[37] Gerald Lancing's sympathy for her heightens the contrast between those two worlds. The love scene in Act Two between Daventry and Mrs Preston is sophisticated and takes place in the drawing-room after the others have retired. Wilde envisions its theatrical potential as Mrs Daventry, who has overheard everything, unlocks the door to admit George Preston, and coolly saves the situation. He also sees it as a way to involve Gerald in the conflict so that his disgust at Daventry's behaviour accentuates his love for Mrs Daventry and makes his situation particularly awkward when Daventry asks for his help in Act Three. Ignoring that scheme, Harris ended his second Act in anti-climax and revealed Gerald's feelings through a clumsy solilo-quy in the middle of Act Three: Wilde noted that drop in energy and told him soliloquies were 'absolutely outmoded'.

Wilde planned Act Three as his turning-point. Whereas the episodes in Harris's version remain separate, adding little to the forward movement of the Act, Wilde uses each sequence to put added pressure on Gerald. At first, he and Mrs Daventry decide to go away together. Then Daventry arrives to ask him to use his influence: the 'husband is a gross sentimental materialist'. Despite his disgust, Gerald feels he ought to do the right thing and, alone again with Mrs Daventry, tells her to go back to her husband. Here Wilde re-examines self-sacrifice which Gerald, in a conventional way, appeals to in order to gain sympathy and to display the terrible cost of his honourable actions. Whereupon the good wife turns on him: '"You have no right to hand my life over to anyone else. All this self-sacrifice is wrong, we are meant to live. That is the meaning of life." Etc.' In the final Act, Wilde deploys that personal freedom against the theatrical conventions he exploits in the earlier 'discovery scene'. Mrs Daventry is reading Act Four of *Frou Frou* in which an errant wife returns, dying and repentant, to the child she has not been allowed to see because of her terrible sin. In contrast, Wilde's play would proclaim the triumph of love:

No morbid self-sacrifice. No renunciation. A sheer flame of love between a man and a woman. That is what the play is to rise to – from the social chatter of Act I, through the theatrical effectiveness of Act II, up to the psychology with its great *dénouement* in Act III, till love dominates Act IV and accepts the death of the husband as in a way its proper right, leaving love its tragedy, and so making it a still greater passion.

That summary bears a remarkable resemblance to his descriptions of *Vera* and *The Duchess of Padua*: the excitement and tragedy of love's flame, the effectiveness of big theatrical moments, his concern for contrast and structure (even in a dashed-off letter). But self-sacrifice, which once seemed noble, is now 'morbid', and the psychology of the characters themselves now motivates the theatre's coloured contrivances even to the point where they subvert them. The good woman remains at the centre of Wilde's imagination. No longer forced to subdue her feelings, she breaks the bonds of the marriage market and of men's honourable conventions despite the patronizing sneers of the worldly-wise. Yet Wilde was too much the sentimentalist to let her break entirely free. Mr Daventry has to die, and Wilde eventually made George Preston kill him. That would give added point to Daventry's philandering and would also make Mrs Daventry less controversial. Wilde aimed, in either case, to show the complexity which cannot be contained by rigid rules of conduct just as his own creative imagination would not submit to a supposedly solid world of impersonal facts:

As the inevitable result of this substitution of an imitative for a creative medium, this surrender of an imaginative form, we have the modern English melodrama. The characters in these plays talk on the stage exactly as they would talk off it; they have neither aspirations nor aspirates; they are taken directly from life and reproduce its vulgarity down to the smallest detail; they present the gait, manner, costume, and accent of real people; they would pass unnoticed in a third-class railway carriage. And yet how wearisome the plays are! They do not succeed in producing even that impression of reality at which they aim, and which is their only reason for existing. As a method, realism is a complete failure.

('The Decay of Lying', p. 303)

CHAPTER 8

Vigilant open-mindedness

There can be no question as to the effect likely to be produced on an individual by his conversion from the ordinary acceptance of current ideals as safe standards of conduct, to the vigilant open-mindedness of Ibsen ... What Ibsen insists on is that there is no golden rule – that conduct must justify itself by its effect upon happiness and not by its conformity to any rule or ideal. And since happiness consists in the fulfilment of the will, which is constantly growing, ... he claims afresh the old Protestant right of private judgment in questions of conduct as against all institutions, the so-called Protestant Churches themselves included.

The Quintessence of Ibsenism (1891)

When the French text of *Salomé* appeared in February 1893, Wilde sent a copy to Bernard Shaw with a note acknowledging his wise and witty fight against 'the ridiculous institution' of stage-censorship:

your little book on Ibsenism and Ibsen is such a delight to me that I constantly take it up, and always find it stimulating and refreshing: England is the land of intellectual fogs but you have done much to clear the air: we are both Celtic, and I like to think that we are friends.[1]

Shaw's reply was just as gracious but, despite national and professional ties, the two Dubliners were never more than wary acquaintances. Wilde thought censorship fettered the creative spirit, a degradation which, like the 'Tyranny of want', denied men the right to live imaginatively: 'the man who is poor is in himself absolutely of no importance. He is merely the infinitesimal atom of a force that, so far from regarding him, crushes him: indeed, prefers him crushed, as in that case he is far more obedient' (*The Soul of Man under Socialism*, p. 257). Shaw, whose speeches to the Fabian Society had restructured Wilde's aesthetic socialism, maintained that any kind of censorship denied man's right to question social, economic, and political conventions. His 'little book on Ibsenism' aimed at bringing that debate onto the Victorian stage by proclaiming the freedom of each individual to create himself and his society anew.

Ibsen was Shaw's mirror image, a vindication of the philosophy he had built against Irish squalor and adolescent loneliness. Forced in upon himself, Shaw had conquered his painful reticence and, in the process, discovered a congenial home in the rough-and-tumble of London's socialist debating societies. Told to read Karl Marx, Shaw wrestled with the first volume of *Das Kapital* in French: '[Marx] opened my eyes to the facts of history and civilization, gave me an entirely fresh conception of the universe, provided me with a purpose and a mission in life.'[2] In 1884 he stumbled across the Fabian Society, his spiritual family thereafter, and, at the instigation of William Archer (a neighbour in the Reading Room at the British Museum), earned a few pounds as book reviewer for the *Pall Mall Gazette* and art critic for the *World* while writing novels no one would publish. Art was ever the expression of society, as it was for Ruskin and Morris, so Shaw retained his social conscience midst the banalities of minor novelists and sentimental painters. 'At least three times every week he would abscond from literature and art, go down among the Fabians and, like a man bathing himself, "talk seriously on serious subjects to serious people".'[3] One evening in Bloomsbury, Marx's daughter, Eleanor, played Nora Helmer to Shaw's Krogstad, but Archer, at work on his translation, thought Shaw had very little notion of what Ibsen was about. In 1889, on his first trip abroad, Shaw attended a Dutch production of *A Doll's House* and, that June, saw the first London performance at the Novelty Theatre. Walter Besant wrote a sequel that brought Nora to her knees; Shaw answered with a broadside which his friends declared was 'slosh, rubbish, dull dreary Philistine stuff', a reaction that fuelled the fires of Ibsenism: 'Anyhow, there will be discussion, and repetition of Doll's House Doll's House Doll's House here, there & everywhere, which is the desideratum.'[4] To further this debate, Shaw lectured on Ibsen to the Fabian Society 'in the most provocative terms' (1890) and, after the furore over *Ghosts*, developed his essay into *The Quintessence of Ibsenism* (1891): 'the controversialists . . . by no means made clear what they were abusing, or apologizing for, or going into ecstasies about; and I came to the conclusion that my explanation might as well be placed in the field until a better could be found'.[5]

Shaw's reaction to Ibsen's mind was more important than his account of the plays themselves. He had seen six of them on stage and knew others in outline, so he used their plots as practical examples of the way individual behaviour must be judged by particular circumstances and not by predetermined rules of conduct. *The Quintessence* is not a literary critique but a political manifesto in which, under the banner of Ibsenism, Shaw joins the ranks of European savants. The first three chapters, in particular, strike at society's most honoured ideals: devotion to duty, the family unit, the womanly woman. They begin with an image of two 'pioneers of the march to the plains of heaven (so to speak)': the one (with eyes in the back of his head) declares that it is not necessarily right to do something because it has always been an acceptable thing to do; the other ('whose eyes are very longsighted') maintains that it can sometimes be right to do things that have always been considered 'infamous'. Having recruited the admired Bunyan to his cause, Shaw suggests that the farsighted pilgrim (like Ibsen) will always evoke most hatred because 'the guilty conscience of the middle class' (p. 3) regards any deviation from the accepted code as an inflammatory incitement to anti-social behaviour. Yet the history of man's progress has always meant the overthrow of sacred beliefs: the age of Faith gave way to the age of Reason which must now submit to Individualism. Casting himself as Mr Evangelist, Shaw depicts a change from serving what one fears (the God of Wrath) to serving what one loves (social altruism) until that, too, becomes enslaving if the competitive struggle for wealth and position crushes fellow feeling. The courageous pilgrim should then realize that he owes duty to the spirit within himself: 'And when this sense is fully grown, which it hardly is yet, the tyranny of duty is broken; for now the man's God is himself; and he, self-satisfied at last, ceases to be selfish' (p. 18). This paradox was meant to disturb those socialists who, in putting society's needs above all else, clung to ideals which the next two chapters would show to be sentimental and restrictive.

Ibsen's plays question marriage, and Shaw, having had to defend himself from his own parents' unsatisfactory union, had no illusions about that sacred image. With concise logic, he uses the conventional family to explore the ideal and the real. Taking a representative group of 1,000, he conjectures that 700 will feel quite satisfied with 'the British family arrangement' whereas 299 will know from personal experience that it is possible to detest one's partner, one's parents, or one's children. But, since the majority believe otherwise, the 299 hide their discoveries guiltily beneath 'fancy' pictures (ideals) and, to convince themselves, proclaim 'the ideal in fiction, poetry, pulpit and platform oratory, and serious private conversation' until the placid 700 (the Philistines) wonder why the idealists make such 'crack-brained fuss about nothing' (p. 24). Only the odd man out, the realist, has the courage to face facts and tear away the fancy pictures. In consequence, the idealists, terrified by thoughts of actuality, appeal against him to the Philistine majority (idealized as 'Society'). Shaw deftly turns the Philistine hordes (so feared by Arnold) into relatively harmless creatures and makes society's educated leaders the realist's deadly enemies. This is particularly true of the Woman Question, for it is the cultured who proclaim the womanly woman and declare that those who fail to live by that picture are not 'true' women at all. And women subscribe to that idealistic conspiracy rather than admit to selling themselves in the marriage market for a man's sexual gratification. When they do wake to those unromantic facts, the lucky ones may be able to regain their self-respect as home-makers and mothers. Yet the home is no more natural a place for women than a cage is for parrots, and most women are no fonder of their children than are most men 'who nevertheless do not consider that their proper sphere is the nursery' (p. 43). It therefore behoves women to abjure womanly self-sacrifice and find emancipation, as men must too, in the duty they owe to themselves which 'is no duty at all, since a debt is cancelled when the debtor and creditor are the same person' (pp. 44–5). Shaw admits to the 'clatter and breakage' which will follow the repudiation of duty and consoles those who scream 'anathema' at Ibsen with the fact that each old ideal is always replaced by a new which 'is less of an illusion than the one it has supplanted; so that the destroyer of ideals, though denounced as an enemy of society, is in fact sweeping the world clear of lies' (p. 46).

Shaw's version of Ibsen reflects his own struggle to think freely, with 'conscientious unscrupulousness'.[6] He describes the early verse dramas as groping explorations into the dangers of idealism. Once Ibsen fully understood what he needed to say, he then deliberately projected those ideas onto the lives of ordinary men and women in a series of 'realistic prose plays of modern life'. Each presents idealism from a different angle, for the quintessence of Ibsenism 'is that there is no formula' (p. 141): what may save Nora Helmer has no effect on Gina Ekdal and, certainly, that famous slam of the door does not signal all women to leave their husbands. Each person must obey his or her own will to grow. Tracing Ibsen's progress seems to have been a turning-point for Shaw: he too now understood what had to be done in the theatre. Six years before, he had attempted to dramatize a plot suggested by Archer but had used up that story by the end of Act Two

IBSEN IN BRIXTON.

Mrs. Harris. "YES, WILLIAM, I'VE THOUGHT A DEAL ABOUT IT, AND I FIND I'M NOTHING BUT YOUR DOLL AND DICKEY-BIRD, AND SO I'M GOING!"

8   The Ibsen furore

and could think of no suitable denouement. Ibsen helped him see. Since each character's circumstance is unique in itself, the final Act of a play should investigate that circumstance. Consequently, the exposition, situation, unravelling of a well-made play becomes, in post-Ibsen drama, exposition, situation, and 'discussion'. Shaw returned to his unfinished script and, released from mere plot, completed *Widowers' Houses*. Soon afterwards, J.T. Grein happened to complain about the scarcity of British plays for his Independent Theatre. Shaw submitted his script which was then given two performances at the Royalty in December 1892. Ibsenism and Grein's Independent Theatre offered a forum for real-life issues. Within that tiny arena, Shaw determined to make war against the giants of Victorian idealism: womanly women, manly men, and the politics of wealth.

Act One of *Widowers' Houses* pits the dream of middle-class romance against the facts of sex and money. Harry Trench, a well-meaning if slightly brainless young doctor, has been smitten by the beauty of Blanche Sartorius. His friend, William de Burgh Cokane, knows that a love match needs more enduring attractions. With English 'good taste', he effects an introduction to Blanche and her father by making sure they hear him mention Harry's aunt, Lady Roxdale. Charmed by those credentials, Sartorius joins Cokane in a stroll along the Rhine while Blanche, in the hotel garden, steers Harry's bumbling admiration towards an articulate proposal. From then on, Sartorius allows Harry to prattle blithely about his love for Blanche provided he can 'guarantee' his titled relatives will receive her 'on equal terms'; he even appeals to the young man's idealism, asking him to behave manfully – 'May I depend on you to keep a fair distance?'[7] – until matters have been settled. By these means, Shaw manipulates the audience towards a realistic assessment of Harry among the Philistines. Flushed with romance, Harry leaves them with the actual business of writing to Lady Roxdale. Marriage clearly *is* a business as Sartorius supplies Cokane with 'the best way of wording' the desirable facts about Blanche's wealth and 'breeding' although Cokane, jostling for position against a self-made 'gentleman', finds some of that wording too mercantile: 'dont you think this is rather too much in the style of a prospectus of the young lady? I throw out the suggestion as a matter of taste' (p. 30). And when Harry does behave honourably, by keeping his distance, he risks offending the lady herself and so must plunge deeper into the waters of love: 'Blanche: on my most sacred honour, family or no family, promise or no promise – ' (p. 33). Happily, the idealist does not see how others control his destiny.

In the rest of the play, Shaw makes it harder for the audience to remain superior and detached. Sartorius, whose money comes from renting slums 'by the room or half room – aye, or quarter room' (p. 47), is an intelligent, practical businessman. From his point of view, to repair a dangerous staircase or replace a cistern lid wastes money since his tenants would quickly burn them: 'I do not blame the poor creatures: they need fires, and often have no other way of getting them' (p. 64). He does use his authority as a vestryman to head off complaints from Sanitary Inspectors, but he keeps within the law and can ignore the bluebooks of the Royal Commission on the Housing of the Working Classes: 'My friends dont read them; and I'm neither a Cabinet Minister nor a candidate for Parliament' (p. 80). Fundamentally, that practical attitude to the way things are is no worse than Harry's sentimental righteousness, and a good deal more thoughtful. Hearing how Mr Lickcheese squeezes money from Sartorius's tenants – 'It's a damnable business from beginning to end' – Harry offers no solution: 'I have seen it all among the out-patients at the hospital; and it used to make my blood boil to think that such things couldnt be prevented' (p. 48). Instead, he condemns the poor agent and gallantly refuses to touch Blanche's fortune, only to discover that his own income derives from the same source (so does Lady Roxdale's). As Sartorius explains, they can only lament their powerlessness 'to alter the state of society' (p. 66).

Having deflated his hero and implicated the respectable classes in capitalism's realities, Shaw completes his case by demythologizing the deserving poor. Mr Lickcheese willingly takes money that would buy the tenants bread because he has children of his own to feed, just as Sartorius uses his earnings to support Blanche. By Act Three, Lickcheese has acquired his own fortune and faces his former employer on equal terms: 'It was money that used to be my master, and not you, dont think it' (p. 77). But dog still eats dog, and Lickcheese knows that the County Council plans a road across Sartorius's property. If half the houses were repaired and the rest let out to Lickcheese's new company, both men could claim handsome compensation from the Council; but they need Harry's support in case the road goes elsewhere. Were he to marry Blanche, the situation would solve itself, but her father dislikes the idea of that 'money bargain' – unless disguised as a 'guarantee' or, as Lickcheese puts it, 'what is for Miss Blanche's advantage' (p. 96). Harry, however, stands by his illusions, though he may lose most of his money, by refusing to 'have the relations between Miss Sartorius and myself made part of a bargain' (p. 97). Immune to the pretty phrases of Cupid-Lickcheese and Cokane, his principles succumb instead to sex. Blanche's photograph and her reaction to the way he kisses it bring about their reconciliation and an equally dubious business alliance as the idealist agrees to 'stand in, compensation or no compensation' (p. 101).

The play ends with a disturbing picture of greed and opportunism which challenges the audience either to give in to the persuasiveness of Sartorius and his cheery cohort or to do more than Harry does by trying to change the system. Shaw's first audience closed their eyes to that by damning all the characters as 'unsympathetic, sordid, soulless' (p. 108) or by dismissing the play as 'a Fabian pamphlet' (p. 112). Hoping to puff up that dispute, Shaw wrote letters to the press complaining of his critics' limitations. 'They denounce Sartorius . . . as a monstrous libel on the middle and upper class, . . . But they do not (and cannot) answer his argument as to the impossibility of his acting otherwise under our social system' (p. 116). As for 'bluebook' drama, 'It has long been clear to me that nothing will be done for the theatre until the most able dramatists refuse to write down to the level of that imaginary monster the British Public' (p. 123). But what also obscured the play's reformist theme was the 'hateful' character of Blanche Sartorius.

Shaw wanted her to startle conventional minds. On the one hand, she shows 'that women are human beings just like men' (p. 123): she manipulates Harry, scornfully rejects him when he refuses her fortune, and relieves some of her anger by assaulting her maid. On the other hand, her hypocrisies and limited sympathy illustrate the effects of a ladylike education. Shaw emphasized this when he revised her first scene with Harry to show her annoyance at the genteel code which forces both of them into embarrassing pretence:

(*contemptuously*) . . . Why didnt you speak to my father yourself on the boat? You
were ready enough to speak to me without any introduction.
TRENCH: I didnt particularly want to talk to him.
BLANCHE: It didnt occur to you, I suppose, that you put me in a false position
by that. (*Plays Unpleasant*, p. 10)

In the rest of the episode she is partly caught up in that gentility (sighing 'with false pathos' because she is alone and motherless) and partly impatient with the game she must play until, 'with calculated impulsiveness', she takes Harry's hand:

(*He snatches her into his arms with a cry of relief*). Dear Blanche! I thought I
should never have said it. I believe I should have stood stuttering here all day if
you hadnt helped me out with it.

BLANCHE (*indignantly trying to break loose from him*):   I didnt help you out with
it.

TRENCH (*holding her*):   I dont mean that you did it on purpose, of course. Only
instinctively.   (*Plays Unpleasant*, p. 12)

Taking his cue from Carlyle, Shaw makes the sartorial elegance of
father and daughter an emblem of their apparent respectability. But
Blanche finds it hard to maintain ladylike appearances since, by
nature, she is spirited and wilful; her fashionable education has
warped that vitality into moody ill-temper.

Conventionally, there are things a lady must not know. As a
gentleman, Harry cannot bring himself to explain how her fortune is
tainted: the more delicately he treads around those ill-gotten gains,
the more bewildered and angry Blanche becomes. A womanly woman
might have thrown fortune to the winds and, responding to Harry's
prompts, lived nobly on £700 a year, but Blanche is shrewder than
that: 'I am sure there is something I ought to know' (p. 55). By
keeping her in the dark, Harry courts misunderstanding which, for a
personality like Blanche, leads to recrimination and, in private, a
violent battle with her maid: she 'flies at her . . . seizes her by the throat
. . . shaking her furiously' (pp. 68–9). Eventually enlightened by a
bluebook, instead of a Sardouesque letter, Blanche 'stands up, staring
– terrible – the book hanging in her hands' (p. 83). Then she responds
as only a lady of restricted education would by trying to tear the pages
and refusing to think about such sordid facts:

Oh, I hate the poor. At least, I hate those dirty, drunken, disreputable people
who live like pigs. If they must be provided for, let other people look after them.
How can you expect any one to think well of us when such things are written
about us in that infamous book?   (p. 86)

As Sartorius wistfully remarks, 'I see I have made a real lady of you,
Blanche.' Nevertheless, she is far more knowing and intelligent than
Harry is. She also has sexual urges, but her 'triumph' on seeing Harry
kiss her portrait can only be expressed through an appropriate façade.
Harry has already been shocked by her unfeminine outbursts (not
that he saw her with the maid), but now he realizes her continued
anger is a way of 'making love to him' and he instinctively responds to
her 'animal excitement' (*Plays Unpleasant*, p. 63). Victorious at last,
Harry never knows what he bargained for.

If Blanche makes a disconcerting heroine, Julia Craven of *The*

Philanderer (1893) is an equally unsettling villainess since the 'utterly vile worthless' Lost One of convention is equated with the sort of womanly woman whose lack of self-respect destroys her own freedom and her lover's. Shaw accepts her sexual magnetism in a frank and open-minded way, but he has 'views' about passion's slaves, and Julia is little more than a stalking horse for that particular puritanism. The Charteris/Julia relationship corresponds quite closely to Shaw's own with Jenny Patterson, a widowed friend of his mother's to whom he lost his virginity on his twenty-ninth birthday. For years he tried to break from her, and his anger at her possessiveness (and his own sexual need) appears in an objective way in *The Quintessence*: 'Although romantic idealists generally insist on self-surrender as an indispensable element in true womanly love, its repulsive effect is well known and feared in practice by both sexes. The extreme instance is the reckless self-abandonment seen in the infatuation of passionate sexual desire' (p. 35). *The Philanderer* presents self-abasement as a distinctively feminine affliction. Julia wants to be respected for herself alone, but her emotional behaviour makes her odious. Viewed with detachment, she could be a comic figure caught between contradictory values, and, from her own point of view, she deserves pity as someone who would be free and yet gives in to the easy victories of womanliness. Both those aspects appear in the play but, for most of the time, we see her as Charteris does: predatory and scheming, a farcical virago.

When Julia bursts in on Charteris and Grace Tranfield,[8] there is something immediately theatrical about her 'dark, tragic looking' beauty, a pathos which she quickly sheds as she lunges at her rival and has to be manhandled into some sort of quiet. For the rest of the scene, she veers between wild jealousy and injured submission until Charteris, losing patience and reasoned argument – 'Advanced views, Julia, involve advanced duties' (p. 79) – stalks out of the room. Thrust to the floor, she immediately recovers and listens to his receding footsteps. When she hears him hesitate, 'her face lights up with eager, triumphant cunning' then she sinks back piteously for his return (pp. 82–3). Clever though he is, Charteris has to play his part in her scenario: soothing her, petting her, allowing her to forgive him for the wounds he inflicts. She performs the same dramatics for Grace when they meet next day at the Ibsen Club: kneeling at her feet, she begs her not to 'take him from me. Oh dont – dont be so cruel' (p. 122). Grace is revolted by 'that ridiculous attitude'; only a man could 'be imposed on by this sort of rubbish'. Knowing that Julia has 'calculated to an inch how far [she] could go' in her jealousy, Grace wants to separate herself from the despair that appeals to men's sympathetic gallantry: 'Oh, if you had a scrap of self-respect, their indulgence would make you creep all over' (p. 123). Once she stops acting, Julia triumphantly (and illogically) declares her independence: dozens of men would come crawling at the snap of her fingers, a boast which makes her a courtesan from both the advanced and the traditional point of view. She behaves so contemptibly that even her more lucid moments seem contrived and suspect. Yet Julia yearns for any sort of sympathy, and her old games begin afresh when Dr Paramore looks into her heart and sees its 'sterling reality':

(*looking intently at him, and yet beginning to be derisively sceptical in spite of herself*)
Have you really seen all that in me?
PARAMORE: I have felt it. I have been alone in the world; and I need you, Julia. That is how I have divined that you, also, are alone in the world.
JULIA (*with theatrical pathos*): You are right there. I am indeed alone in the world.
(p. 131)

Shaw said this farcical comedy 'exude[d] brimstone at every pore';[9] his acid caricature of sentimental tyranny adds a touch of sulphur.

Surprisingly, his New Woman is also drawn with a certain bias. Grace is a widow in her early thirties, an experienced adult as opposed to a spoiled child. As the curtain rises, she and Charteris embrace 'affectionately' on her sofa: despite her emotion, everything about her shows 'plenty of determination and self-respect' (p. 69). She admits she loves Leonard and, when he says he likes her, reacts philosophically, taking stock of him as he squirms round the problem of Julia or plays word-games to persuade her they are both free agents: 'Ibsen for ever!' (p. 73). Affronted when he says he wants to marry her to save himself from Julia, pained when he tells her how he and Julia made love, annoyed by his philanderings, she remains detached enough to see past his banter: 'I dont think you like to be loved too much' (p. 74). By Act Two she has made up her mind: 'Nothing could make it worth my while to be exposed to such scenes as last night's. You had much better go back to Julia, and forget me' (p. 100). Her arrival at the Ibsen Club in business-like, fastidiously elegant clothes seems to confirm her independence. Yet she gives in to Leonard's charm, and only when he runs for cover, perceiving her renewed delight, does she steel herself to stand by her principles: she will not marry a man she loves too much, for that would put her in his power. So Charteris has a soul-mate who will not make demands on him, and Grace is the New Woman as men would like her to be. Feminine, responsive, too sensible to marry, she illustrates Shaw's *theories* about the inadequacy of 'the legalized conjugal relation' and the *ideal* he finds in Ibsen's Rebecca West whose passion evolves into a higher and 'more perfect love' (*Quintessence*, pp. 36–8). By remaining true to her own person, Grace sacrifices herself nonetheless. Whereas Julia seizes on a man she does not love, Grace lets the man she rejects know she loves him, and both Dr Paramore and Leonard are delighted: 'They think this a happy ending, Julia, these men: our lords and masters!' (p. 141).

Shaw makes fun of conventional manliness through Colonel Craven (bluff veteran of the Sudan wars) and Joseph Cuthbertson, a theatre critic who (like Clement Scott) relishes 'scenes of suffering nobly endured and sacrifice willingly rendered by womanly women and manly men' (p. 87). Both are shocked by the Ibsen Club where women monopolize the smoking-room and the reading-room's fireside seats beneath the Master's bust. But details like those also turn Ibsen into farce, as does Leonard's philandering. The new freedom gives his games a modish licence. Like Julia, he preaches liberty but wants to conquer. Through him, Shaw laughs at his own contradictions as lover and philosopher: 'it's my business to tell other people the truth; but it's not their business to tell it to me. I dont like it: it hurts' (p. 109). Leonard's jaunty impudence chips away at the old order, but his insouciant ego makes him something of a fraud and, by association, calls the new order into question. He fascinates women by refusing to treat them 'with the respect due to their sex', but his candour is just a clever way to assert his power as, for one glorious moment, Julia realizes: 'Sometimes I wonder at myself for ever caring for you . . . You fraud! You humbug! You miserable little plaster saint! (*He looks delighted*). Oh!' (p. 137). Shaw's ambivalent focus and the way he plays in and out of Ibsenism or raises and drops issues like vegetarianism, modern medicine, vivisection create a restless texture which bewildered his supporters at the Independent Theatre. Grein 'found the play excessively verbose, overloaded with side-issues on bacteria and so on', and refused to produce it.[10]

But Shaw was already working on a way to peel the glamour from the likes of Paula Tanqueray, whose tragedy was the talk of the season, and to show why vice stretched wider than Aubrey's 'little parish'.[11] *Mrs Warren's Profession* (1893) dares to suggest most women must prostitute themselves or starve. The idea is all the more alarming because Kitty Warren, who says she wants the best for her girls like any respectable mother, has neither Sartorius's poise nor Julia's allure: she is 'decidedly vulgar, but, on the whole, a genial and fairly presentable old blackguard of a woman' (p. 184). Arguing with Sir George Crofts, her brutish friend, about her daughter's dubious parentage, she cuts an incongruous figure as Vivie's 'mater'. Nevertheless, Shaw plays those dark tones against her endearing assumption that, being a daughter, Vivie will do as Mother says. He wins her still more sympathy when Vivie, with cold good sense, explains they have separate lives, recommends 'good walks and a little lawn tennis' to attune her sagging flesh, and has no patience with her 'whimpering' (p. 206). Kitty's rage is therefore understandable when Vivie maintains that 'people who get on' either make or find the circumstances for success. Kitty's defence goes beyond her own life-story to represent the plight of women in general and the economics which make her profession both logical and respectable. By the end of her tirade she has earned Vivie's admiration and proved herself as disciplined and self-respecting as any lady graduate.

One of the purposes behind this set-piece is to supply the psychology Pinero left blank in Paula's story and, in the process, to explode the theory of woman's natural innocence. Kitty had two ungainly half-sisters who *were* models of purity whereas she and sister Liz, the offspring of a different, well-fed sire, 'would have half-murdered' that emaciated pair 'if mother hadnt half-murdered us to keep our hands off them' (p. 209). Those two had no alternative but unremitting labour. Jane worked in a whitelead factory for nine shillings a week: 'She only expected to get her hands a little paralyzed; but she died' from lead poisoning. Her sister married a government labourer 'and kept his room and the three children neat and tidy on eighteen shillings a week – until he took to drink'. The accidents of breeding gave Kitty and Liz a superiority which drove them to acquire some formal education 'until Liz went out one night and never came back' (p. 210). None of her teacher's pious warnings could persuade Kitty that the lead factory was less fearsome than a prostitute's watery grave, but she set to work as scullery maid, waitress, barmaid until Liz appeared one night in the bar, 'elegant and comfortable'. Why, she argued, should others profit from good looks and healthy bodies. So the two pooled their resources, went into business, and saved enough to buy a house in Brussels where their girls were treated better than she had been in the bar at Waterloo station or back home in her mother's fried-fish shop by the Mint. The logic of this makes sense if one accepts inevitable injustice, as Kitty does. In the light of that despairing premise, prostitution becomes a practical way to acquire capital if a woman has neither 'a turn for music, or the stage, or newspaper-writing' nor the power 'to catch some rich man's fancy and get the benefit of his money by marrying him' (p. 211). Shaw underlines her middle-class propriety and ignores the disease and exploitation of her trade by having her describe its inconveniences as no more 'digusting' than a nurse's duties: no 'bed of roses' but a fine opportunity for a sensible, good-looking, underprivileged girl who 'can resist temptation' by saving money for the polite retirement Liz has 'in a cathedral town' or the syndicate Kitty creates with her business partners. Tied to the system, Kitty regretfully enforces it: 'I always thought that oughtnt to be. It cant be right, Vivie, that there shouldnt be better opportunities for women. I stick to that: it's wrong. But it's so, right or wrong; and a girl must make the best of it' (p. 212).

Kitty's courage impresses Vivie ('you are stronger than all England'), but an audience must resist the persuasive way she turns black white. To equate prostitution with marriage is an amusing sleight of hand and, in many cases, a bitter truism, but to accept Mrs Warren's picture of herself as a lady who simply wants her girls 'to be good to some man that can afford to be good to [them]' would condone two hypocrisies instead of one. Though she claims to talk 'straight', her phrasing is as 'crooked' as any lady's 'in London society that has daughters' (p. 213). To emphasize that, Shaw makes her admit to being 'a bit of a vulgarian' who, like other women, has 'to pretend' to fine feelings, whereupon she congratulates herself on the way Vivie has grown up 'ladylike, determined' like Aunt Liz: 'such a perfect lady!' Her speech ends in cosy (and comic) domesticity; she is 'proud of how we managed everything so respectably, and never had a word against us, and how the girls were so well taken care of. Some of them did very well: one of them married an ambassador.' Vivie's secure view of things falters. To regain her composure she adopts the ideal Kitty offers, and here Shaw's staging exploits that romanticism. In need of air, Vivie opens the cottage door and is delighted by the harvest moon. Mrs Warren, with philistine self-satisfaction, takes 'a perfunctory glance' and warns her not to catch cold. But Vivie rapturously embraces her, promising to 'be good to [her] poor old mother', and they stand fondly in the moonbeam's glow as Kitty unctuously murmurs 'Blessings on my own dearie darling! a mother's blessing!' Shaw underscores that Victorian primness when Kitty 'instinctively' looks heavenwards as she cradles 'her daughter protectingly' (p. 214). Mrs Warren's respectability is simply moonshine.

Vivie acknowledges that in Act Three. Although the sky above the rectory garden is cloudless, Sir George's presence and his effect on the vicar have sent the latter's wife and daughter scurrying up to town on the 11.13 to avoid receiving Mrs Warren. His son, Frank Gardner, enjoys playing up to Kitty but is shocked by Vivie's daughterly affection: 'Dont it make your flesh creep ever so little? that wicked old devil, up to every villainy under the sun, I'll swear, and Vivie – ugh!' (p. 218). All the characters have bucolic surnames, and Kitty's influence tunnels under the rural idyll; the Reverend Sam is an old flame, and his wastrel son recognizes the 'freemasonry among thoroughly immoral people' even as he teases her: 'This quiet old rectory garden becomes you perfectly' (pp. 219–20). Reality surfaces when Crofts makes his bid for Vivie. Having invested 'in ways that other men have overlooked', he offers position, wealth, and the prospect of a hefty settlement since he is so much older than she is. Vivie stays aloof until she discovers her mother is still in business. Disillusioned, she rejects Crofts's happy picture – a chain of 'really comfortable private hotel[s]' – and learns that the trade touches the aristocracy of Church and State and even sullies her Cambridge scholarship. Crofts's smug justifications bring home to her the reality of exploitation; she now sees 'how helpless nine out of ten young girls would be in the hands of you and my mother! the unmentionable woman and her capitalist bully –' (p. 227). Throughout this episode, the physical menace of Crofts's attitude dramatizes the gathering horror Vivie experiences. Impervious to her outrage and sarcasm, he becomes more and more friendly and confiding, pressing in on her until she lashes him with the truth and he reacts with violent fury. Stopped by Frank's gun, he coolly introduces half-brother to half-sister and, stung to the heart by her mother's amorality, Vivie turns the muzzle on herself. The spectre of incest fades away when Sam Gardner eventually insists he is not Vivie's father. But the mere possibility of that relationship exemplifies the effect of prostitution which, like a disease, pervades all levels of society.

Vivie is a realist's version of Ellean Tanqueray. They are both nun-like, but Vivie has isolated herself in a secular convent, working with measured enthusiasm on 'nothing but mathematics' at Newnham.

Ellean returns from Paris fired by love; Vivie spends three days with 'artistic people in Fitzjohn's Avenue' then escapes to the joys of actuarial calculations in Chancery Lane: 'Outside mathematics, lawn-tennis, eating, sleeping, cycling, and walking, I'm a more ignorant barbarian than any woman could possibly be who hadnt gone in for the tripos' (p. 181). Frank Gardner, a more boyish and less presentable Hugh Ardale, does persuade Vivvums into baby-talk (and how unreal and annoying that is), but she tolerates him as a mildly irritating brother (before Crofts's coup) and knows all about his sexual adventures, his gambling, and his interest in her money. Characteristically, Vivie's emotions burst into passionate disgust at the laws which protect her mother's enterprises. But that momentary passion leads nowhere because, like Ellean, she lacks imaginative sympathy; so she misses a chance to better the lives of all women. Tough-minded, physically strong, interested in Law, she is someone who could change society. Instead she retreats from her mother's money, from love and art and fashionable living, to her columns of figures. As Honoria Fraser's business partner she will study commercial law 'with one eye on the Stock Exchange' to protect her own investments. Shaw saw her as 'a real modern lady of the governing class – not the sort of thing that theatrical and critical authorities imagine such a lady to be'.[12]

The reality of organized prostitution was in itself offensive to theatrical authority: 'I do not think there is the least chance of the play being licensed.'[13] It would therefore be difficult to find a venue for private performances, but Shaw knew who could act the parts and expected the Independent Theatre to take on the challenge. Mrs Theodore Wright, a convinced socialist who had originated the part of Mrs Alving in *Ghosts*, was a possible Kitty Warren. But when Shaw read her the script, she 'declared that not even in her own room could she speak the part to herself, much less in public to a younger woman'; hurrying out to calm her nerves, she 'came back in ten minutes to hear the rest of the play'.[14] Grein responded with similar alarm: the play should not be produced under any circumstances. Shaw 'threw the play aside' but sustained his own pride and the public's interest by insisting to the press that the real obstacle was 'that intolerable social nuisance, the Censorship': he would go down fighting if and when he applied for a licence.[15] In the meantime, he seized the chance to bring everyday truth to popular audiences. Florence Farr, whose avant-garde credentials included Blanche Sartorius and a production of

Rosmersholm, had the backing for a season of new plays at the Avenue Theatre. For his contribution, Shaw turned from social economics and the sensual games of the intelligentsia to the romantic ideals of society at large. In *The Quintessence*, he had pointed to the 'dual aspect' of Ibsen's characters and to the difficulties an actor would find if he tried 'to get back to familiar ground by reducing his part to one of the stage types with which he is familiar, and which he has learnt to present by rule of thumb' (p. 142). In *Arms and the Man* (1894), he would create characters who were neither saints nor sinners and whose contradictory actions shattered familiar theatrical generalizations, blurring the strict division between the ideal and the 'real' as the fantastic 'chivalry of the Balkans' collided with 'the comparative coolness, good sense, efficiency, and social training of the higher civilisation of Western Europe'.[16]

The dualities of Act One, in particular, show the tantalizing interconnection between illusion and reality. The set, which seems to present a contrast between the picturesque and the prosaic, quickly asserts the reality of a distinctive place and time *because* of the way it combines the gorgeous with the mass-produced: 'half rich Bulgarian, half cheap Viennese' (*Plays Pleasant*, p. 4). This is no illusory Ruritania, yet the moonlit balcony, the midnight fugitive, and Raina's stand against the search-party all belong there. Similarly, Raina herself has felt the pull of actuality, but the news that Sergius is 'the hero of the hour' after leading a cavalry charge against the Serbian guns persuades her 'our heroic ideals' are 'anything but dreams' (p. 5). Assured 'that the world is really a glorious world for women who can see its glory and men who can act its romance' (p. 6), she expects to blot out the inglorious slaughter in the streets outside by rolling herself 'up in bed with [her] ears well covered' (p. 7). When Bluntschli clambers into her bedroom, his bedraggled exhaustion and unchivalrous manner, as he snatches her fur wrap in order to embarrass her, simply encourage proud heroism. His determination to survive unsettles her, but the more battle-weary he becomes the more she see herself as a noble saviour like the Count in the opera of *Ernani* whose 'guest is sacred to him' (p. 20). The audience, too, are allowed the colour and excitement of romantic action while Shaw bombards them with an unheroic view of war: all soldiers want to stay alive; nine out of ten are fools, and even the best become nervous wrecks under prolonged fire. From one view, Bluntschli cuts a poor figure as he gobbles Raina's sweets; from another, he prefers energizing chocolate to unreliable bullets. But as one scoffs at Raina's inflated view of glory and her family's importance, one might also consider her suggestion that a 'professional' thinker would have delivered up her enemy even if his gore spattered her ornamental carpet. Beneath this volatile surface runs an energy which moves consistently from nervous self-consciousness to relaxed calm. Raina starts the scene in a romantic flutter then resorts to her 'noble attitude' and 'thrilling voice' until the vulnerability of her efficient antagonist allows her to be 'more and more at her ease' (p. 13). By the end of the Act, Bluntschli has fallen asleep on her bed, and 'the brute' her mother sees is simply a 'poor dear': worn out, child-like, and invitingly human. That discovery points on to Raina's education (and the audience's) in the remainder of the play.

In Act Two, the 'real' and the ideal strive with each other more divisively, just as the washing on the bushes jars against the garden's charming prettiness. This change of key announces Nicola and Louka whose quarrel shows the pragmatist and the dreamer in brusque contrast as he advises tactful servitude and she defies the world. Then Major Petkoff's earthiness ruptures his wife's sense of grandeur and patriotic honour. All this leads to Sergius, the prisoner of conventional ideals. He basks in the ladies' hero-worship and has tasted war's glory during the cavalry charge, but he knows his own behaviour and the ways of the world are seldom so exalted. Too intelligent to ignore that, he regards himself and the common herd with jaundiced 'Byronism'. Love, war, and life itself turn farcical because they nearly always fall below the romantic vision he will not abandon. In practical terms, he has assaulted the enemy with insane bravado; the charge happened to work because the Serbs had the wrong ammunition. Rather than acknowledge that, he sneers at his commanders' pedestrian attitude: '[I] upset their plans, and wounded their self-esteem' (p. 30). Disgusted by a trade which needs efficient men like Bluntschli – 'He was like a commercial traveller in uniform. Bourgeois to his boots!' (p. 32) – he retires from the army and, as a point of honour, will 'never withdraw' that decision. He is just as enslaved by 'higher love', and Shaw uses all his acquired stagecraft to pinpoint this comedy. In operatic ecstasy, Raina places her hands on her idol's 'shoulders as she looks up at him with admiration and worship' (p. 34). Together they breathe the rarefied air of love and honour as Raina wonders whether she will ever be worthy of the 'king' who has proved himself 'on the field of battle' and Sergius

246

swears he has 'gone through the war like a knight in a tournament with his lady looking down at him'. But cracks begin to show when Sergius, adoring 'My lady, and my saint', balks as she returns the compliment, and Raina finds it hard to sustain her intensity in the presence of Louka who comes to clear the breakfast table. Running up the garden stairs, she turns to waft him a kiss with both hands. Fired by that vision in green and gold, crowned with a tinsel cap, Sergius sighs adoringly as she disappears, then, attracted by the workaday Louka, strides towards her in one of his other roles, twirling his moustache with left hand akimbo: an idyll is a 'very fatiguing thing to keep up . . . One feels the need of some relief after it' (p. 35). But Sergius is still not free, for which is his real self amongst the 'half dozen Sergiuses who keep popping in and out of this handsome figure?' Louka also has her grand illusions, despite her 'common clay'. Were their rigid postures less ridiculous, the two might seem sad victims of imprisoning romance.

Raina has felt the stress of that ideal. Even before her chocolate-cream soldier returns, she confesses to 'a longing to do or say something dreadful to [Sergius] – to shock his propriety – to scandalize the five senses out of him' (p. 40). Those chains fall away in the final Act when, in a radiant moment, Bluntschli cuts through her grand manner and 'find[s] it impossible to believe a single word [she] say[s]' (p. 53). Stunned by that, Raina changes 'from the heroic to the familiar' and, with complete frankness, asks 'How did you find me out?' (p. 54). Liberated by his 'instinct, and experience of the world', she warms to 'the first man that has ever taken [her] quite seriously' and, from then on, can be her intelligent and open-minded self. Once his heroine discovers the duty she owes to herself, Shaw returns the play to doubleness. The arch-romantics, Sergius and Louka, lock themselves in unromantic union because he 'will not be a coward and a trifler. If I choose to love you, I dare marry you, in spite of all Bulgaria' (p. 62). Louka's own heroic dream has challenged him to that: 'If I were Empress of Russia, . . . you should see, you should see' (p. 61). Their heroics 'have their practical side after all' (p. 72). And the efficient Bluntschli, who sees immediately how to move three regiments to Philippopolis, admits his 'incurably romantic disposition' since he joined the army instead of his father's business and climbed the Petkoffs' balcony instead of diving 'into the nearest cellar' (p. 73). Intrigued by the photo Raina placed in the coat she lent him, he deludes himself into thinking he is not 'the sort of fellow a young girl falls in love with'. Raina rounds on him with newfound independence, but when her parents remind her suitor of their daughter's 'historical' position and 'comfortable' establishment, Bluntschli can offer 'six palatial establishments, besides two livery stables, a tea gardens and a private house' (p. 75). As the heir of a Swiss hotelier, he ranks above any Emperor: 'I am a free citizen.' He has also freed Raina, and when the pair join hands romantically, they do so for 'real' and unromantic reasons.

The joy and freedom of that meeting of minds escaped Shaw's audience. Archer, for instance, described the play as 'a fantastic, psychological extravaganza, in which drama, farce, and Gilbertian irony keep flashing past the bewildered eye, as in a sort of merry-go-round, . . .'[17] He enjoyed the anti-heroic comedy of the first Act but thought the rest of the play was 'dehumanised by Mr Shaw's peculiar habit of straining all the red corpuscles out of the blood of his personages. They have nothing of human nature except its petti-nesses; they are devoid alike of its spiritual and its sensual instincts.' It was, he maintained, unnatural for a girl to 'transfer her affections (save the mark!)' within a matter of hours to a man she had seen once only; so Shaw pointed out that Raina subconsciously dislikes Sergius, because of 'the strain' of living up to his heroic image, 'and fall[s] in love for the first time with Bluntschli'.[18] Shaw was particularly irritated by the way Archer and others reduced the play's positive energies to Gilbertian fantasy:

My whole secret is that I have got clean through the old categories of good & evil . . . Sergius is ridiculous through the breakdown of his ideals, not odious from his falling short of them. As Gilbert sees, they dont work; but what Gilbert does not see is that there is something else that does work, and that in that something else there is a completely satisfactory asylum for the affections. It is this positive element in my philosophy that makes Arms & The Man a perfectly genuine play about real people, with a happy ending and hope & life in it, . . .

The play succeeded for the wrong reasons. At the end of its run, Shaw publicly took issue with those who judged his characters by the very ideals he wished to explode. All his 'whimsical perversions' came from real life (particularly the memoirs of famous soldiers), and he 'demand[ed] respect, interest, affection for human nature as it is'.[19]

Refusing to write down to 'the British Public', Shaw was prepared to wait for them to come to grips with his progressive ideas while snatching every chance to speed the process. Charles Wyndham had liked *Arms and the Man*, so Shaw read him *The Philanderer* knowing the actor-manager's light touch and popular following might win that play an audience: nothing came of this. When Richard Mansfield, the American actor-manager, bought *Arms and the Man*, Shaw warned that its 'novel flavor . . . involves a certain struggle with the public' and urged him to play Sergius in order to 'lift that flirtation scene with Louka into one of the hits of the play'.[20] Mansfield chose Bluntschli, and once again Shaw was praised 'as a monstrously clever sparkler in the cynical line . . . there is about as much of me in the affair as there is of Shakespere in Garrick's "Katherine and Petruchio" '.[21] Writing to Henry Arthur Jones, he predicted the 'long fight' it would take to reach the paying public:

Now here you will at once detect an enormous assumption on my part that I am a man of genius. But what can I do – on what other assumption am I to proceed if I am to write plays at all? You will detect the further assumption that the public, which will still be the public twenty years hence, will nevertheless see feeling and reality where they see nothing now but mere intellectual swordplay and satire. But that is what always happens.

Shaw understood the economics of the theatre and that actor-managers, as businessmen, *ought* to choose plays with good parts for themselves. Yet the emergence of female characters 'in no sense secondary to the men . . . indeed immeasurably superior in wisdom, courage, and every great quality of heart and mind'[22] had given rise to the sort of hero who, in wishing to keep the new woman 'in her old place', suffered humiliation and defeat, a position which did not appeal to actor-managers: 'it is just such peculiarities that make characteristically modern plays as repugnant to the actor as they are attractive to the actress, . . .' That situation required a new breed of performer as well as receptive audiences, and when Frank Harris offered him the post of drama critic on the *Saturday Review*, Shaw set out to remake the theatre just as he had educated his readers to Wagner during his years as music critic for the *World*.

From January 1895 until his health and patience gave out in May 1898, Shaw campaigned with enthusiastic partiality for his own sort of plays and for the style of acting they needed. Brushing aside the conventional as transparently ridiculous, he branded the fashionable 'advanced' drama as stage trickery and cajoled performers into being more than automatons or tailor's dummies. Battle began with Sydney Grundy's 'new and original' play, *Slaves of the Ring*. Grundy had a 'reputation as a master of stage technique' (Shaw's plays were not considered 'true' drama) and his theme, inadequate marriage laws, was not unfamiliar to readers of *The Quintessence*. Shaw demolished the play's originality and substance with a nod to Wagner, then, having shown its 'mere contrivance', mocked its 'worn-out French stage conventions' by describing their cumbersome absurdity and a finale at which it was 'really impossible to do anything but laugh and fish out one's hat to go'. The actors had turned their emotions on and off to order, when they had anything to act at all, while sets and costumes 'were solidly and expensively Philistine, . . . epitomizing the whole history of plutocracy in England during the expiring century'.[23] In like manner, week after week, he speared the 'mechanical rabbits' of Sardoodledom and the 'boredoms and all the otherdoms' of the theatre's wasteland, nurturing 'the spontaneity, sensitiveness, and touch with the cultivated non-professional world which the latest developments of the drama demand' (I, p. 53). The emptiness of 'galvanic' farces, manicured drawing-rooms, scurrilous skirt dancers, and fashionable actors who 'have only one note, or perhaps, if they are very clever, half a dozen' (I, p. 426), sent him into suicidal paroxysms. What kept him from expiring (like the century and the British theatre) was a sense of mission, beyond the self-serving, and the wicked humour of his impudent pen. Reviewing *Gossip*, a vehicle for Lillie Langtry's dresses and diamonds based on 'several suggestions' from a recent novel, Shaw could 'only say that if [the authors] had made use of several suggestions to be found in these columns, they would not have written the play at all. Oh, that goody-goody Amurrican husband . . . And oh, that young wife who was about to run away from him when she was reminded of her own mother and her own chee-yild! Oh, my goodness! It *was* dull' (I, p. 349). For actors, he unravelled 'the methods of Duse, [whose] emotion exists only to make thought live and move for us, [as opposed to] Sarah Bernhardt and the claptraps which Sardou contrives for her' (I, pp. 121–2). For playwrights and audiences, he paraded Ibsen, Ibsen, Ibsen, and the modernity of Wagner, Nietzsche, Sudermann, Echegaray, and (with nice effrontery) the art of G.B.S.: 'For my own part, I do not endorse all Ibsen's views: I even prefer my own plays to his in some respects' (II, p. 157).

In March 1895, Grein imported Lugné-Poë's company, *L'Oeuvre de Paris*, and Shaw described the 'enchanted mist' of Ibsen's *Rosmersholm* and the 'parochial squabblings' which ought to be 'instantly recognizable in London and Chicago (where Mr Beerbohm Tree, by the way, has just made a remarkable sensation with *An Enemy of the People*)' (I, pp. 55–9). Despite the company's gimcrack budget, here was a subtlety, breadth of vision, psychological truth which annihilated the West End's best efforts; here, too, were the beginnings of a repertory (as challenging and respectable as the classical tradition) to confound those who thought Ibsenism was a passing vogue and hoped it would go away. So Shaw took the opportunity to compare the French Rebecca West with Florence Farr's 'somewhat amateurish attempt to find a new stage method for a new style of play' and with Elizabeth Robins who had 'submerged Rebecca in an ocean of grief'. Ibsen affected everything Shaw wrote about: he 'never presents his play to you as a romance for your entertainment: he says, in effect, "Here is yourself and myself, our society, our civilization"' (I, p. 86). The plays might not be box-office, though 'in legitimate theatrical business Ibsen is as safe and profitable as Beethoven and Wagner in legitimate musical business' (II, p. 155), but the 'artistic experiments' of the European moderns (and Shaw's weekly columns) ought to have such a profound effect upon public taste that managers 'must be very careful not to produce a play which will seem insipid and old-fashioned to playgoers who have seen *The Wild Duck*, even though they may have hissed it' (I, p. 156). Shaw raked the London stage with withering scorn while holding up the palm for those who sought to win his lyrical tribute: 'to look on with horror and pity at a profound tragedy, shaking with laughter all the time at an irresistible comedy; to go out, not from a diversion, but from an experience deeper than real life ever brings to most men, . . .: that is what *The Wild Duck* was like last Monday at the Globe' (II, p. 266). Yet this aesthetic agenda was also aimed at Pinero whose callow smartness usurped the drama of ideas.

Shaw's attack was two-pronged: Pinero's psychology was sham Ibsen and his method genuine Sardou. The publication of *Mrs Tanqueray* drew the first salvo from the battery Shaw had mounted in (the neglected) *Mrs Warren*. He dismissed Pinero as 'a humble and somewhat belated follower of the novelists of the middle of the nineteenth century': to compare his characters with those 'in Robertson's *Caste* would be almost as ridiculous as to compare *Caste* with *A Doll's House*'. His status as a modern dramatist collapsed at the moment Aubrey assumed he knew what his wife had been at Ellean's age and Paula accepted that view of maiden virtue. 'Mr Pinero, then, is no interpreter of character, but simply an adroit describer of people as the ordinary man sees and judges them.' As for his stage-craft: his confidants, supernumaries, multiple doors, 'supplemented by the inevitable "French windows" (two of them); and . . . the activity of the postman', were so much 'dead machinery' (I, pp. 36–40). A month later, Shaw narrowed in on the way Pinero flattered audiences by giving them what they liked 'whilst persuading them that such appreciation was only possible from persons of great culture and intellectual acuteness'. As a thinker, he was merely a character actor who substituted 'disguises and stage tricks' for inner truth. *Mrs Ebbsmith* was a bad play, although the 'personal genius' of Mrs Campbell had created the illusion that 'Clearly there must be a great tragedy somewhere in the immediate neighbourhood.' Pinero, he said, took his ideas from the novels of forty years back, but if he would like to find out what politically active ladies were in real life, Shaw would happily teach him. Refusing to say anything good about a play he so detested, Shaw impishly declared his personal animus and so deflected any possible counterblast: 'And here let me warn the reader to carefully discount my opinion in view of the fact that I write plays myself, and that my school is in violent reaction against that of Mr Pinero. But my criticism has not, I hope, any other fault than the inevitable one of extreme unfairness' (I, pp. 40–7). Shaw brought the two schools into ironic opposition in his next review (on the Independent Theatre) by jovially suggesting that Grein was becoming 'wretchedly respectable' and that his would soon be the only safe refuge in London from 'real wicked Pinerotic theatre' (I, pp. 48–9).

The pun nailed Pinero to the glamorized erotics of pseudo-Ibsenism which Shaw would later stigmatize as 'the ordinary sensuous ritual of the stage become as frankly pornographic as good manners allowed . . . the way is smoothest for those plays and those performers that appeal specially to the Jewish taste'.[24] Shaw left his readers to draw those connections. However, in a hideous letter to Archer, after his review of *Mrs Ebbsmith*, he regretted the rushed deadline that had not allowed him 'to get into a sympathetic, humane mood' but felt his savagery would have been worthwhile if Pinero could retreat back to comedy: 'But he won't do that, because he is a Jew, with the Jew's passion for fame and effect and the Jew's indifference to the reality of the means by which they are produced.'[25] Shaw kept his racist contempt out of the *Saturday Review*, finding weapons enough in Mrs Tanqueray and Mrs Ebbsmith as emblems of pretentious effect. *The Benefit of the Doubt* was worth ten of those ladies put together, for in that play Pinero 'sticks to the Bayswater–Kensington *genre*, of which he is a master' (I, p. 196). But even that was used as ammunition when Shaw reviewed Pinero's preface to *The*

Theatrical 'World' of 1895 in which the latter jokingly described the
way he spent the fortnight after each new play with papers like the
Mining Journal in order to avoid the reviewers. Shaw seized on this
with glee. What else could account for *The Benefit of the Doubt* except
a year's worth of G.B.S. Then he merrily hit at Pinero's intellectual
limitations: 'Why, [he] is one of the most conspicuous of the very,
very few playwrights we have who are more interested in the drama
than in mines' (I, p. 352). *The Princess and the Butterfly* brought
further scorn. Its 'sentimental drawing-room fiction' did not get
going till the middle of Act Three: 'So, though it is true that the man
who goes to the St James's Theatre now at 7.45 will wish he had never
been born, none the less will the man who goes at 9.30 spend a very
pleasant evening' (II, pp. 234–5). Shaw was not sent a ticket to
Trelawny since the Court Theatre felt 'three lines of adverse criticism
were of no use to it'. He was later delighted to inform the Court that its
'low opinion' of the play was unwarranted: '(Will the "Mining
Journal" please copy, as Mr Pinero reads no other paper during the
current fortnight'). He was genuinely moved by *Trelawny*'s delicacy
and charm. The 1860s were home territory: 'That is why Mr Pinero,
as a critic of the advanced guard in modern life, is unendurable to me'
(II, pp. 405–11).

Although the timidity of actor-managers in backing Pinero,
Grundy, and Jones proved that 'those who make half revolutions dig
their own graves' (I, p. 181), Shaw appreciated Henry Arthur's
courageous response to social reality: 'I unhesitatingly class Mr Jones
as first, and eminently first, among the surviving fittest of his own
generation of playwrights' (I, p. 309). In private correspondence,
Shaw frequently chaffed at Jones's idealism and wished his 'first-rate'
satire could break free of that. Reading *The Masqueraders*, he
protested against the heroine's 'allusions to duty [which] elicited a
howl of rage from me. She morally outrages my tenderest sensibilities.'[26] But, in his reviews, Shaw turned his friend into a Dickens
figure, bursting with social outrage, rough-and-ready honesty and
sentiment, in order to goad Pinero who, like the detestable Thack-
eray, had 'no convictions, no views, no general ideas of any kind'.
Pinero observed life 'as a gentleman observes the picturesqueness of a
gypsy' whereas Jones worked 'passionately from the real' despite his
'vulgar habit of bringing persons indiscriminately to the bar of his
convictions as to what is needful for the life and welfare of the real
world' (II, pp. 232–3). Jones had a conventional mind but did not

flatter the plutocracy, and Shaw embraced him as a fellow outcast when *Michael and his Lost Angel* failed so miserably: 'The melancholy truth of the matter is that the English stage got a good play, and was completely and ignominiously beaten by it. Mr Jones has got beyond the penny novelette conventions which are actable in our theatre. I fear there is no future for him except as a dramatic critic' (I, p. 316). By dividing the establishment against itself, there was also the chance that Shaw might conquer.

A major purpose of these reviews was to build G.B.S. into an irreverent and fiendishly clever personality. As a series, they chronicled the wretched comedy of Sisyphus who toiled each week with his heavy stone:

> To the public the tumbling down of the stone is the point of the whole business: they like to see it plunging and bounding and racing in a flying cloud of dust, blackening the eyes of a beautiful actress here and catching an eminent actor-manager in the wind there, flattening out dramatists, demolishing theatres, and generally taking a great deal on itself, considering its size. (II, p. 19)

Regular readers knew his heroes and villains and rejoiced as, with cart and trumpet, he brandished *Widowers' Houses* and *Arms and the Man* in 'the revolt of the working classes against economic, and of the women against idealistic, slavery' (II, p. 299). And nobody was more aware 'of the convenience to an Irishman in England of being able, by an occasional cunning flourish of his nationality, to secure all the privileges of a harmless lunatic without forfeiting the position of a responsible member of society' (I, pp. 328–9). Wilde could have muted that foolery. Reviewing *An Ideal Husband*, Shaw announced 'our only thorough playwright' who, unlike an Englishman, knew how to play 'with wit, with philosophy, with drama, with actors and audience, with the whole theatre'. Shaw, the work-horse, delighted in Wilde as 'an arch-artist . . . colossally lazy . . . He distils the very quintessence, and gets as product plays which are so unapproachably playful that they are the delight of every playgoer with twopenn'orth of brains' (I, p. 12). But when *The Importance* threatened his territory, Shaw was not amused, branding it bloodless and cynically Gilbertian just as *Arms and the Man* had been savaged in the previous season (I, pp. 33–5). After Wilde's public humiliation, Shaw did have the grace to remind readers of his existence and of 'that remarkable scene' in which Chiltern 'reproached his wife with idealizing and worshipping his moral virtues' (I, p. 217). By the end of his tenure, G.B.S. – with his views on vegetarianism, Dr Jaeger, bicycles, the jingoism and smugness of 'The British public' – had pushed the weekly playbill out of centre and was already the voice of the prefaces to Shaw's own plays which were reviewed by Max Beerbohm, his chosen successor, on the day of his angelic farewell.

But G.B.S. had not been able to create a school of actors for those plays. When he joined the *Saturday Review*, Shaw had finished *Candida* and wanted Janet Achurch as his heroine. He tried to interest George Alexander, but the manager would not play Morell and Shaw refused to make Eugene blind in order to disguise the poet's youth. Lewis Waller also rejected the play, so Shaw persuaded Mansfield to produce it in New York. When Achurch arrived with the 'band parts', Mansfield disliked the lady and the play: *Candida* was cancelled. Meanwhile G.B.S. used the occasion of Duse's season at Drury Lane for an essay on modern acting which linked Duse, Ellen Terry, and Janet Achurch, though the latter's good looks and intensity constantly threatened 'the highest distinction in her art' (I, p. 131). Janet would not be disciplined. Shaw, the philanderer, tried to control her morphine, alcohol, and impatient ambition while G.B.S. stormed as 'the only tragic actress of genius we now possess' rampaged like a tigress through Wilkie Collins's *The New Magdalen* (I, p. 221) or made 'Ibsen-and-Wagner pie' out of Shakespeare's Cleopatra (II, p. 215). When she returned to the fold as Nora Helmer, she was still 'far ahead of any living English actress of her generation in this class of work', though there were gains and losses in her performance (II, pp. 258–9). In dismay, Shaw changed allegiance, praising Charrington's productions of Ibsen for the Independent Theatre while his wife, as Cleopatra, was 'generally celebrating her choice between the rare and costly art of being beautifully natural in lifelike human acting, like Duse, and the comparatively common and cheap one of being theatrically beautiful in heroic stage exhibition. Alas for our lost leaders!' (II, p. 275). Shaw allowed the Charringtons to tour *Candida* in the provinces (July 1897), but he would not play 'taskmaster and schoolmaster any longer . . . I held up the mirror in which Janet was beautiful as long as I could, in private and in print: now I've held it up with Janet inarticulate and rowdy.'[27]

Mrs Campbell was as yet a Venus on his horizon, although he could imagine her playing Julia Craven or even Mrs Warren. Elizabeth Robins had intrigued him as Hedda Gabler but she would not respond to his flirtatious blarney; in reaction, he re-invented her as 'St Elizabeth' and teased Archer with his and her respectability.

More and more she came to represent the squeamishness which affected even the 'new' actors who 'recoil from the jar of the peculiarly Ibsenite passages': Miss Robins had cut lines that referred to Hedda's pregnancy and would never find the dedication to slough away her ladylike Americanism.[28] Shaw joked about casting her as the lady in *The Man of Destiny* (1895) – 'It would confirm her worst opinion of me'[29] – and used her as a sentimental foil to set off Janet's genius. His review of *Little Eyolf*, which featured all three actresses, was full of such manoeuvrings, and when Janet was ousted by Mrs Pat, a second review lambasted the Pinerotics of that fashionable speculation: with her feminine fascination 'Mrs Campbell, as Magda, could do nothing with a public spoiled by Duse. I greatly fear she will do even less, as Rita, with a public spoiled by Miss Achurch.' In those circumstances, Miss Robins was promoted to Ibsen's champion, having 'improved greatly on the genteel misery of the first night' (II, pp. 126–7).

Shaw cared passionately for 'fine' acting: a seamless and apparently effortless attention to detail which came from discipline, hard work, psychological insight, and a commitment to life beyond the foot-lights. In Ellen Terry he saw 'the only real New Woman' whose 'ultra-modern talent' radiantly infused the human moments of her 'old-fashioned rhetorical' repertoire and then succumbed to the pic-turesque vacuity of Victorian theatre. 'The most advanced audiences . . . want realistic drama of complete brainy, passional texture all through, and will not have any pictorial stuff' (II, pp. 308–10). In his letters, Shaw wooed her artistry, beseeching his goddess to see she could play the old style with the tip of her little finger which he longed to kiss as he lined the path to a new altar with advice on how to find the human threads within her tattered materials. He also flattered, teased, and coaxed his blessed Ellen to rise up against H.I., 'His Immensity', the Ogre of the Lyceum. In his articles, G.B.S. confessed to the enchantment of her 'quite peculiar and irresistible personal charm' and, on behalf of modernism, set out to reclaim 'its wayward daughter' from a managerial system which confined her to 'plays that date, in feeling if not in actual composition, from the dark ages before the Married Women's Property Act'(I, pp. 130–1). Through her, he attacked 'Slade School' actresses whose surface beauty had none of Ellen's art. Through her, he shook the mighty pedestal of Shakes-peare whose musical genius and comprehensive soul were, like Ellen's, encumbered by the merest fustian and subjugated to Irving's ego. So the knight who ennobled his entire profession was, for

G.B.S., the actor whose mastery of effect betrayed his art (as had Pinero's). In the seventies, Shaw had seen Irving play Digby Grant in *Two Roses* and was fired by a realistic modernity 'which, if applied to an Ibsen play now, would astonish us as much as Miss Achurch's Nora astonished us'. Then Irving ventured into high drama and, after years of struggle, 'mastered the rhetorical style . . . It was a hard-earned and well-deserved triumph.' But had he pursued drama's 'fundamentally serious social function' instead of technical virtuosity, he would have been 'driven by life-or-death necessity to extract from contemporary literature the proper food for the modern side of his talent' and so fostered a new drama (II, pp. 273–4). Irving no longer interpreted a play but re-created it around himself. For G.B.S., 'The history of the Lyceum, with its twenty years' steady cultivation of the actor as a personal force, and its utter neglect of the drama, is the history of the English stage during that period . . . if the actors think they can do without the drama, they are most prodigiously mistaken' (II, pp. 168–9).

In July 1895 Gabrielle Réjane returned to London with Sardou's *Madame Sans-Gêne*: 'I have never seen a French play of which I understood less; and that, for me, is saying a good deal' (I, p. 168). This event had already started Shaw on a curtain-raiser, for it crossed his mind that 'Forbes Robertson ought to play Napoleon in order to forestall Irving' who planned to do an English version of Sardou. Shaw's was 'a perfectly idiotic play . . . but good acting, especially if the woman is a good comedian and very fascinating'.[30] In November, a publicity release from Ellen Terry in America prompted him to mention his little play; she asked to read it and was delighted by it. Shaw asked her to let him know if Irving was seriously interested: 'you are only playing with me. I will go to that beautiful Mrs Patrick Campbell, who won my heart long ago by her pianoforte playing as Mrs Tanqueray, and make her head twirl like a chimney cowl with my blarney.'[31] So he and Ellen began to play at love by post while he and Irving played cat-and-mouse. If G.B.S. could needle H.I. into refusing *The Man of Destiny*, he could prove his case against the Lyceum; as long as H.I. held out the chance of a production, G.B.S. might curb his insults. Shaw cannot seriously have believed the Lyceum would ring with Napoleon's analysis of the typical Englishman: 'His watchword is always Duty; and he never forgets that the nation which lets its duty get on the opposite side to its interests is lost' (p. 201). H.I. offered a retainer which, as an independent critic,

G.B.S. refused, suggesting instead 'that *he* should have a present of it on condition of his instantly producing works by Ibsen'.[32] The game continued into 1897 when Irving broke their agreement: Shaw was finally in a position to show that Sir Henry was no gentleman at all. But he could not deliver that blow: 'were I to let the public see that I have private reasons for destroying him, I never could criticise him again without suspicion of partiality'. He released him, too, for Ellen's sake, even though Irving had 'warmed his wretched hands callously at the embers of nearly twenty of your priceless years; . . . Nevertheless you shall play for me yet; but not with him, not with him, not with him.'[33] Forbes Robertson could not mount the play, so Shaw allowed Murray Carson three nights in Croydon (July 1897): 'Oh Lord, Ellen, I've been to see "The Man of Destiny" . . . Picture to yourself the worst you ever feared for it; raise that worst to nightmare absurdity and horror; multiply it by ten; and then imagine even that result ruined by an attack of utter panic on the part of the company.'[34]

In the meantime, Cyril Maude's company at the Haymarket had run afoul of *You Never Can Tell*. Hoping for a commercial success, Shaw had taken his ingredients from drawing-room comedy: 'fun, fashionable dresses, a little music, and even an exhibition of eating and drinking by people with an expensive air, attended by an if-possible-comic waiter, I was more than willing to shew that the drama can humanize these things as easily as they, in undramatic hands, can dehumanize the drama' (*Plays Pleasant*, p. x). To vivify those materials, Shaw focussed on the manners of three generations: Crampton's insistence that women owe their masters dutiful obedience; Mrs Clandon's militant attachment to Mill's *The Subjection of Women*; Valentine and Gloria's duel of sex which Shaw would later call the Life Force. The scene between the pair, at the end of Act Two, completely defeated Allan Aynesworth, a friend of Maude's who had made his name as Wilde's Algy. After two weeks' rehearsal (April 1897), Shaw chose to withdraw the play rather than rewrite the crucial episode into the standard product scorned by G.B.S.: 'a tailor's advertisement making sentimental remarks to a milliner's advertisement in the middle of an upholsterer's and decorator's advertisement' (II, p. 189). The experience convinced him that the 'walking toffs' preferred by gentlemen-managers were driving genuine talent from the stage, to the detriment of playwrights.[35] Three years later, the play was presented by the Stage Society with Yorke Stephens and James Welch whose careers G.B.S. had encouraged after they created Bluntschli and Lickcheese. This production transferred to the Strand Theatre for six Saturday matinées, but Shaw would not allow it into the evening bill as a summer stop-gap. The Society attracted performers who were eager to experiment, and Shaw was pleased with their individual efforts but would have re-cast certain roles in order to achieve a unified ensemble if the manager had agreed to present the play during the theatre season.

In one of his earliest reviews, G.B.S. had announced his very first visit to Adelphi melodrama. With tongue in cheek, as 'a superior person', he discovered that 'it only needs elaboration to become a masterpiece'. Buoyed up by contrasting types, fast-paced action, and simple fun, melodrama should 'be allegorical, idealistic, full of generalizations and moral lessons'. But the genre was rarely served by able dramatists (1, pp. 72–3). The publication of W.E. Henley and R.L. Stevenson's adaptation of *Macaire* (reviewed June 1895) suggested the heights melodrama could rise to and offered a nice illustration of 'the divorce of the stage from literature' since the witless version Irving used was simple blood-and-thunder (1, p. 124). Some months later, William Terriss of the Adelphi told Shaw he needed a strong play for the company's American tour and reeled off a list of melodrama's stock situations. Like the authors of *Macaire*, Shaw determined to ignore the obligatory love-interest and so created a hero who, in Shavian fashion, obeys his own will despite his father's money, Judith's sentimental adoration, and the army's attempt to ritualize murder into gentlemanly ceremony. Allegorically, when Dick Dudgeon exchanges coats with Anthony Anderson, the rebel becomes a dispassionate martyr and the parson finds his vocation as a fighter. Terriss's tour did not materialize, so Shaw offered *The Devil's Disciple* to Richard Mansfield who had rejected *Candida* because 'a bustling – striving – hustling – pushing – stirring American audience [would not] sit out calmly two hours of deliberate talk . . . You'll have to write a play that a *man* can play and about a woman that heroes fought for and a bit of ribbon that a knight tied to his lance.'[36] Shaw intended his heroine to be conventional (and uninteresting), but Mansfield turned his realist hero into a romantic for audiences who revelled in Dick's patriotism and Burgoyne's critique of inefficient British marksmen. The New York production (October 1897) and subsequent tour established Shaw's name in America; in England the play was not produced until the indefatigable Murray Carson presented it for two weeks in South London (1899). He too sentimentalized Dick Dudgeon. In the following year, when Shaw himself rehearsed Forbes Robertson's company, he found 'only two men . . . who [could] act'.[37] The play toured the provinces for three months, but Shaw would not permit a London season.

By that time, Shaw had 'throw[n] the theatre to the devil' by publishing his plays and doing 'with [his] pen what the actors can't do'.[38] Although he knew there was little demand for printed plays, other than sets of paper-bound West End successes supplied to amateur groups, he had succumbed to Grant Richards's blandishments and his own frustration. Given the economics of the theatre, 'a dramatist like Ibsen, who absolutely disregards the conditions which managers are subject to, and throws himself on the reading public, is taking the only course in which any serious advance is possible, especially if his dramas demand much technical skill from the actors'.[39] Having made that decision, Shaw set out to describe his settings and his characters' appearance and motivation in ways which would capture the imagination of readers who found the usual '*take flowers from table O.P. – exit L.U.E.*' incomprehensible. In addition, his narrative comments were aimed at actors who might otherwise resort to stereotypes. Shaw also deluged Richards with detailed advice about the look of the texts on the page and the price he could reasonably charge for each volume. In all this, Shaw set his sights on a wider public than either the theatre or a publisher's 'season' could garner. He tightened the structure of *Widowers' Houses* (which had sold miserably in the Independent Theatre's edition) and exhumed *The Philanderer* and *Mrs Warren*: although the latter play could not be performed in public, the Censor had licensed a bowdlerized version which secured Shaw's copyright. Yet despite these victories and the plays' innovative format, the 1,200 copies of *Plays Unpleasant* and *Plays Pleasant* (1898) sold so slowly that Shaw offered to pay the cost of *Three Plays for Puritans* (1901), believing time would secure them an audience.

Both the voice in those tangential commentaries and the vision of the plays themselves were out of the ordinary. Consequently, Shaw introduced himself as a man whose oculist said his eyes were normal, like one in ten other cases: 'My mind's eye, like my body's, was "normal": it saw things differently from other people's eyes, and saw them better' (*Plays Unpleasant*, p. vi). Viewing domestic comedy, Sardouesque intrigue, polite farce, and historical drama from his own perspective, he overturned the archetypes of Victorian theatre. The women of the ten plays were meant to be provocative. Those with conventional attitudes, like Kitty Warren and Catherine Petkoff, satirize the norm or, like Judith the house-angel, show the real weakness of adoring dependency when put to the test. In contrast, the Shavian archetype has a will of her own: an unstable temper, a determined sensuality and restless mind which, in the Strange Lady, modulate into charming and effective weapons. Shaw's 'new' women either suppress their sexuality, like Grace, or sublimate it through work, like Vivie and Mrs Clandon. They all explain themselves incessantly – what they are or what they wish to be – yet their behaviour plays havoc with those certainties or they become the agents of imperious Nature, like Blanche and Gloria. Men quail before their energy and instinct. Bluntschli shows Raina how to be herself, but will always be her 'poor dear'; even Caesar, the monster who is human after all, turns Cleopatra into 'what these Romans call a New Woman' (p. 255) who sees him as 'a great baby' because he will 'not behave seriously' (p. 291). Candida knows her husband is a child because he takes himself *too* seriously, and Lady Cicely tells 'little lies for men, and sometimes big ones' because they *will* play with guns or trap themselves in ideal laws and attitudes. These two see through and past men's confident assumptions: enchantingly serene, they are also terrifying. Through Candida, Eugene discovers his strength but flees into the night in order to escape her motherly compassion and find his destiny. Brassbound cannot 'look at any ordinary woman after' Lady Cicely who, with maternal 'cleverness', sees him as 'one of the Idealists – the Impossibilists' (p. 414). For a moment, commander and subordinate gravitate towards each other, knowing that only equals love, until a distant cannonade releases them, and Brassbound frees himself, grateful 'for a man's power and purpose restored and righted' (pp. 416–17).

Uprooting old values, Shaw replaced them with a reality which, in theory, seemed logical and open-minded but which, in practice, reflected his particular psychology. For all their articulate self-confidence, his heroes become deluded boys when they demand rule and right supremacy. His men of destiny, though flattered by the challenge of a vivacious duellist or the worship of a kittenish savage, accept sex, glory, conquest, and possessions as pleasing incidents along the way to self-fulfilment. Dick Dudgeon, the puritan diabolist, shuns those vanities completely, as will Eugene and Brassbound in their chosen exile. But the energetic realism of those heroes entails so much denial that the easy-going pragmatism of Bluntschli and Burgoyne appears more life-affirming. Paradoxically, Shaw's rogues and canny Philistines have a greater humanity than his idealized realists. Readers could relate to, and learn from, Lickcheese, Sartorius, Nicola, Burgess, Giuseppe, and the philosophic Waiter whose lives touched the day-to-day rhythms of the nineties and pushed the theatre beyond the confines of sexual scandal and intrigue.

Shaw's vision of reality did not impress the critics. Unlike Ibsen, who portrayed the actual world objectively, Shaw created a fantastic realm of his own. For Archer, his claim to 'normal' eyesight was perverse: 'He looks at life through an exceedingly abnormal temperament, and has convinced himself that it is the one absolutely normal temperament in the world.'[40] As an Ibsenite himself, Archer deplored 'the baseness of *The Philanderer*' and the unstructured tedium of *You Never Can Tell*, 'this formless and empty farce'. Ibsen plumbed his characters' souls whereas Shaw (in Ibsen's name) 'scarcely ever touches a higher emotional pitch than anger, ill-temper, shrewishness. His ideal of dramatic effect is a quarrel, often a slanging-match.' Yet *Mrs Warren* was 'not only intellectually but dramatically one of the very ablest plays of our time' and *Candida* was 'a work of rare genius'. There the characters had internal lives, and Archer delighted in Candida's 'radiant beauty and sanity' and Eugene's romantic idealism which made 'him really and convincingly a poet'. If Shaw could curb his intransigent ego, 'he would be a pillar of fire to our dramatic movement, instead of an irresponsible jack o' lantern'. But all too often his creations had 'the imperturbable temper of the practised debater, and the stoicism of the man who cares more for the intellectual than for the emotional side of life'. It was nonsensical of Shaw to set himself up as the one true rationalist: 'when he . . . makes out that the serious drama, poetic and realistic, lives, or seeks to live, by stimulating the erotic instincts, his contention is monstrously and fantastically wide of the truth'.[41] Less concerned with the progress of realism, A.B. Walkley of *The Times* was happy to allow Shaw his fantasies: 'His method of travestying life is to eliminate from it everything but the pure intelligence.'[42] However much he claimed to be a realist, Shaw was simply a Gilbertian ironist who, by suppressing the unconscious and 'representing life in general and love in particular as based upon ratiocination, . . . obtains most amusing results'. With their 'brilliant dialectic', the plays ought to delight intelligent actors: 'they are never called upon to open their mouths without saying something worth saying'. Max Beerbohm thought the early plays were flawed by Shaw's 'desire to Ibsenise the English stage from footlights to flies'.[43] As a would-be realist, Shaw worked against his born talent for penetrating satire. To a dramatist who took no interest in human complexity *per se*, 'moral purpose [was] a disaster; it forces him to burden himself and his puppets with a load which they cannot bear, a load without which they might be quite agile, effective and amusing . . . When Mr Shaw is not morally purposeful, he is fantastic and frivolous, and it is then that his plays are good.' If he could always be true to himself, he would have 'a great future in English drama'. *Three Plays for Puritans* confirmed that. Perceiving their 'large, loose scale' and 'that Mr Shaw has got clean away from the Ibsen formula', Max accepted him – with some uneasiness – as 'a jester with serious interludes, not an occasionally jocular seer'.[44]

By the turn of the century, Shaw's plays were known in England to few beyond the inner circles of 'advanced' drama. To those *cognoscenti*, they had shown the theatre's potential as a forum for lively, unconventional ideas which proved that serious playwrights, like Jones and Pinero, were either too orthodox or insufficiently rigorous critics of life as it is lived. In revolutionizing the way plays could be presented to the ordinary reader, Shaw had opened doors for other writers with knowledge and experience of social, political, and economic realities to pass beyond the established literature of the Victorian theatre. And Shaw had freed his own texts from managers' commercial interests, actors' limitations, and audiences' ingrained prejudices: readers could explore them under his guidance. 'The theatre is my battering ram as much as the [political] platform or the press', he once told Ellen Terry; 'that is why I want to drag it to the front. My capers are part of a bigger design than you think: Shakspere, for instance, is to me one of the towers of the Bastille, and down he must come.'[45] As G.B.S., he had cracked the foundations of that tower, the emblem of emotional display and romantic picture-making. Other towers stood firm: censorship, walking toffs, drawing-room Pinerotics. By fighting under Ibsen's banner, Shaw brought down on himself the opposition of critics who attacked him for not being a disciplined realist or an observer of the soul, and allied himself with actresses who disappointed him or were prisoners of the system. Even a persistent and ingenious batterer like Shaw needed actor-managers (like Mansfield and Carson) who, for whatever mistaken reasons, helped him dent the wall. The ultimate breakthrough was still to be, and Shaw had not entirely abandoned Ibsen or seen that his own gifts led to the *play* of realistic ideas through plots and dialogue which were openly theatrical. But he knew his time would come. 'The contemporary playgoer doesnt want me, and I dont want him (or her); and there are terrible things still to be said'; 'My next play will be a Don Juan – an immense play, but not for the stage of this generation.'[46] Unaccepted and scoffed at, Shaw had turned the Victorian sideshow into a sacred pulpit which, for a new generation of writers, would 'interest people of divers ages, classes, and temperaments by some generally momentous subject of thought, as the politicians and preachers do, . . .'[47]

Notes

1 Breaking through the darkness

1 Henry Arthur Jones, preface to *Saints and Sinners* (London, 1891), p. viii. For Jones, popular entertainment proclaimed 'the mere impatience of intellectual exertion in a theatre on the part of both entertained and entertainers'.

2 Richard Mansfield's hilariously naive and foolish letter is reprinted in Bernard Shaw's *Collected Letters*, ed. Dan H. Laurence (New York, 1965), vol. I, pp. 523–4.

3 Joseph Farington's Diary, quoted in Linda Kelly, *The Kemble Era* (London, 1980), p. 182.

4 Percy Fitzgerald, *A New History of the English Stage* (London, 1882), vol. II, p. 351.

5 Sir Frederick Pollock (ed.), *Macready's Reminiscences* (London, 1876), p. 442.

6 George Rowell, *The Victorian Theatre: 1792–1914* (Cambridge, 1978), p. 10.

7 Leigh Hunt, *Autobiography*, ed. R. Ingpen (London, 1903), vol. I, p. 152.

8 *Macready's Reminiscences*, p. 655.

9 Viscount Esher (ed.), *The Girlhood of Queen Victoria* (London, 1912), vol. I, p. 114.

10 Ibid., p. 149.

11 Ibid., p. 148.

12 Royal Archives, Windsor Castle, Queen Victoria's Journal (cited as RA: QVJ), 6 March 1838.

13 RA: QVJ, 9 March 1839.

14 Esher, *Girlhood*, vol. I, p. 147.

15 RA: QVJ, 10 April 1840.

16 RA; QVJ, 10 January 1839.

17 RA: QVJ, 1 February 1839.
18 Quoted in Margaret Webster, *The Same Only Different: Five Generations of a Great Theatre Family* (New York, 1969), pp. 52–3.
19 Quoted in George Rowell, *Queen Victoria Goes to the Theatre* (London, 1978), p. 46.
20 *The Court Theatre and Royal Dramatic Record of Performances at Windsor* (London, 1849), pp. 1 and 38.
21 RA: QVJ, 26 March 1851.
22 RA: QVJ, 31 March 1851.
23 RA: QVJ, 14 June 1852.
24 RA: QVJ, 21 June 1852.
25 RA: QVJ, 5 February 1861.
26 For several Buckstone stories see W. Macqueen-Pope, *Haymarket: Theatre of Perfection* (London, 1948), p. 308.
27 The London *Times* quoted in Cyril Pearl, *The Girl with the Swansdown Seat* (London, 1955), p. 107.
28 Quoted in Christopher Hibbert, *Edward VII: A Portrait* (London, 1976), p. 109.
29 Ibid., p. 133.
30 The London *Times* quoted ibid., p. 138.
31 Charles Wyndham quoted in Percy Hutchison, *Masquerade* (London, 1936), p. 58.
32 Quoted in A.E. Wilson, *Edwardian Theatre* (London, 1951), p. 12.
33 Thomas Dibdin, *Reminiscences* (London, 1827), vol. I, p. 199.
34 George Odell, *Shakespeare from Betterton to Irving* (New York, 1920), vol. II, p. 96. 'What a noble beautiful Play it is', wrote Queen Victoria of *King John*, '& what glorious language! One could see it a 1000 times over, & it would ever remain new.' RA: QVJ, 21 June 1852.
35 James Robinson Planché, *Recollections and Reflections* (London, 1872), vol. I, pp. 56–7.
36 Charles Dickens, jun. (ed.), *The Life of Charles James Mathews* (London, 1879), vol. II, p. 76. For details of the Vestris innovations at the Olympic see also Charles Pearce, *Madame Vestris and her Times* (New York, 1969), pp. 220–6.
37 Dion Boucicault, 'The Debut of a Dramatist', *North American Review* (April 1889), p. 457.
38 William Appleton, *Madame Vestris and the London Stage* (New York, 1974), pp. 136–41.
39 *Theatrical Journal*, 13 March 1841 quoted in James L. Smith (ed.), *London Assurance* (London, 1984), p. xxxv.
40 Lester Wallack, *Memories of Fifty Years* (New York, 1889), p. 175.
41 The London *Times* quoted in Alan S. Downer, *The Eminent Tragedian: William Charles Macready* (Harvard, 1966), p. 217.

42 Ibid., p. 229.
43 Lady Pollock, *Macready as I Knew Him* (London, 1885), p. 84.
44 RA: QVJ, 28 February 1852.
45 Rowell, *Victorian Theatre*, p. 21.
46 Macqueen-Pope, *Haymarket*, p. 281.
47 Ibid., pp. 316–18.
48 The London *Daily News* quoted in Madeleine Bingham, *The Great Lover: The Life and Art of Herbert Beerbohm Tree* (New York, 1979), p. 38.
49 The *Saturday Review*, 1 May 1897.
50 Bingham, *Beerbohm Tree*, p. 90.
51 *Pickwick Papers* (Nelson's edn, n.d.), p. 37.
52 Webster, *Same Only Different*, pp. 82–3.
53 Pearce, *Vestris and her Times*, p. 103.
54 Appleton, *Vestris and London Stage*, p. 21.
55 Charles Dickens, jun. (ed.), *Mathews*, vol. II, p. 76.
56 Esher, *Girlhood*, vol. I, p. 149.
57 RA: QVJ, 4 October 1881.
58 The Queen whispered this to her granddaughter, Marie, who with some embarrassment had obeyed a request to explain the plot of *Carmen*. See Rowell, *Queen Victoria*, pp. 108–9. The Queen's impressions of de Lussan are from RA: QVJ, 3 December 1892.
59 RA: QVJ, 27 June 1893.
60 RA: QVJ, 26 April 1889, 17 March 1891, 16 September 1895.
61 Michael Sanderson, *From Irving to Olivier (The Social History of the Acting Profession in England: 1880–1983)* (London, 1984), p. 13.
62 Ibid., pp. 136–7.
63 Seymour Hicks, *Twenty-Four Years of an Actor's Life* (London, 1910), p. 11.
64 Laurence Irving, *Henry Irving: The Actor and His World* (London, 1951), pp. 410–12.
65 George Rowell, *Theatre in the Age of Irving* (Oxford, 1981), p. 38.
66 Tom Prideaux, *Love or Nothing: The Life and Times of Ellen Terry* (New York, 1975), p. 156.
67 Charles Dickens, *Nicholas Nickleby* (Everyman edn, London, 1957), pp. 288–9.
68 *Macready's Reminiscences*, p. 492.
69 Preface to *Quid Pro Quo* (Mrs Gore's winning play) quoted in Michael R. Booth, *English Plays of the Nineteenth Century* (Oxford, 1973), vol. III, p. 16.
70 Letter to the New York *Tribune*, 23 October 1873 quoted in Richard Fawkes, *Dion Boucicault: A Biography* (London, 1979), p. 68.
71 Ibid., p. 57.

72 Ibid., p. 49.
73 Ibid., p. 83.
74 Ibid., p. 50.
75 Peter Thomson (ed.), *Plays by Dion Boucicault* (Cambridge, 1984), p. 163.
76 Quoted in Townsend Walsh, *The Career of Dion Boucicault* (New York, 1915), p. 96.
77 Thomson (ed.), *Plays*, pp. 101–32.
78 *The Drama of Yesterday and To-Day* (London, 1899), vol. II, p. 396.
79 The play that withered under Archer's analysis was H.J. Byron's *Our Boys*. See chapter 4.
80 'The Drama of the Reign', *The Theatrical 'World' of 1897* (London, 1898), pp. 183–5.
81 'Robert Louis Stevenson as a Dramatist', reprinted in *Papers on Playmaking*, ed. Brander Matthews (New York, 1957), p. 57.
82 V. Sackville-West, 'The Women Poets of the 'Seventies', *The Eighteen-Seventies*, ed. Harley Granville-Barker (Cambridge, 1929), p. 113.

2 The grandeur of Nature

1 *The Diaries of William Charles Macready*, ed. William Toynbee (New York, 1912), vol. I, p. 197. Bulwer added his mother's maiden name (to become Bulwer-Lytton) when he inherited her property in 1843.
2 This interview between Bulwer and Macready is documented in Charles H. Shattuck, *Bulwer and Macready* (Urbana, 1958), pp. 18–20.
3 Every reference to Bulwer's plays is taken from his *Dramatic Works* (London, 1873), and for all substantial quotation Act, scene, and page are noted in my text.
4 George Henry Lewes, *On Actors and the Art of Acting* (Leipzig, 1875), p. 122.
5 William Archer, *The Old Drama and the New* (Boston, 1923), pp. 249–50.
6 The Earl of Lytton, *The Life of Edward Bulwer* (London, 1913), vol. I, p. 561.
7 Ibid., p. 557.
8 Edward Bulwer-Lytton, *The Last Days of Pompeii* (Dent edn, London, 1973), p. 54.
9 Alan S. Downer, *The Eminent Tragedian* (Harvard, 1966), p. 143.
10 Bulwer's letter to Macready, 22 March 1838, Shattuck, *Bulwer*, p. 76.
11 26 November 1838, ibid., p. 96.
12 Nancy Mitford, *The Sun King* (New York, 1966), p. 26.
13 For this and other contemporary reactions see Shattuck, *Bulwer*, p. 51.
14 William IV's conception of constitutional monarchy led him into constant battles with reformist ministers, Bulwer's colleagues. This

particular attack was brought on by the government's instructions to Lord Gosford, the newly nominated Governor of Canada, which in the King's view were directed towards that colony's self-government. Philip Ziegler, *King William IV* (London, 1971), p. 274.

15 *Dramatic Works*, p. 106.

16 Edward Bulwer-Lytton, *England and the English*, ed. Standish Meacham (Chicago, 1970), pp. 85–6.

17 Ibid., p. 87.

18 Bulwer dashed off the play's first four Acts in just over three weeks so that, apart from plotting the final Act, his correspondence with Macready for this play concerned particularities like costuming and the suitability or availability of individual actors. The three quotations are from letters dated 20 December 1837, 2 January 1838, early February 1838, Shattuck, *Bulwer*, pp. 58, 60 and 70.

19 *The Life of Edward Bulwer*, p. 538.

20 *On Actors*, p. 48.

21 Lady Blessington and Count d'Orsay's salon at Gore House in Kensington was a mecca for fashionable men of letters; the two had long been friends and admirers of Bulwer. Lady Blessington's letter is in Lytton, *The Life of Edward Bulwer*, pp. 536–7 and Shattuck, *Bulwer*, pp. 71–2. Macready's opinion of Bulwer's style was somewhat less passionate: 'he writes too hastily, he does not do himself justice', Shattuck, *Bulwer*, p. 61.

22 *England and the English*, pp. 286–9.

23 For this and other contemporary reactions see Shattuck, *Bulwer*, pp. 70–4.

24 Ibid., pp. 81–6.

25 Ibid., pp. 89–90, 94, and 109.

26 RA: QVJ, 26 April 1889. The Queen thought 'Macready as Richelieu acted beautifully . . . The only fault in [his] acting was his being somewhat too weak and tottering in his walk . . . We came home at 20 m.p. 10, and I was much amused.' RA: QVJ, 9 March 1839.

27 Shattuck, *Bulwer*, p. 121.

28 Ibid., pp. 132–4.

29 Macready to Bulwer, 9 September 1838, ibid., p. 82.

30 Ibid., pp. 152–5.

31 Ibid., p. 173.

32 *The Life of Edward Bulwer*, p. 553.

33 A certain element of society would not care whether Evelyn won or lost. To suggest their self-centred isolation, Bulwer includes an old gentleman in the first club scene (III, 6) who keeps repeating 'Waiter! – the snuff-box' and remains completely oblivious of the escalating tension around him.

34 Bulwer had his own experiences of the hustings to draw on, but his Grog/ in/hole owes something to Dickens's Eatanswill (eat and swill) in *Pickwick Papers* (1836–7). The novel's extraordinary popularity obviously convinced him that a satirical election campaign would work well on stage, too.

35 *The Life of Edward Bulwer*, p. 554.

36 In the intervening years, Bulwer had sketched out a number of plays for Macready including a comedy which contained a Mr Formal who seems to have been tailored to the actor's personality: 'Very methodical & precise – severe outwardly – but full of the milk of human nature.' Macready was not amused. Bulwer also thought of reworking his Cromwell play and dabbled with classical themes. In 1846 he completed a version of *Oedipus Rex* but Macready thought 'it would not be attractive if performed'. The actor was more concerned with saving money for his retirement and was not receptive to risky ventures. Cf. Shattuck, *Bulwer*, pp. 189–93 and 232. After Macready retired in 1851, he and Bulwer continued to correspond, though not very frequently, until illness and old age put a stop to their letters.

37 RA: QVJ, 16 May 1851.

38 Cf. Bulwer's own Mr Warm, 'a most respectable man; he pays his bills regularly – he subscribes to six public charities – he goes to church with all his family on a Sunday – he is in bed at twelve o'clock. Well, well, all that's very proper; but is Mr Warm a good father, a good friend . . . is he not avaricious . . . *is not his heart cold*, is he not vindictive, is he not unjust, is he not unfeeling? Lord, sir, I believe he *may* be all that; but what then? *every body allows Mr Warm is a most respectable man.' England and the English*, p. 76.

39 That alarming thought explains the popularity of *The Corsican Brothers*, *The Lyons Mail*, and *The Only Way* in which two characters of seemingly opposite virtues were played by the same actor. Still more disturbing were the two distinctive personalities of a single character such as Svengali or Mathias of *The Bells*.

3 Domestic and commonplace

1 *The Principal Dramatic Works of Thomas William Robertson*, with a memoir by his son (London, 1889), vol. I, p. 189. This volume also contains *David Garrick* and *M.P.*

2 The script calls for both the Rittmeister Harfthal and his son, Rudolf, to be played by the same actor (Alfred Wigan). The device seems to have been simply a theatrical 'effect', engineered to stimulate the audience's wonderment, since the exit of one character always precedes the entrance of his other self by a matter of seconds. At one point, Rudolf watches a

sword fight between his father (now played by a double) and the Earl of Mount-Forestcourt who cross the rear of the stage silhouetted by flashes of blue lightning.

3 This couplet had been something of a refrain in *Caste* (1867) as D'Alroy and Hawtree argue the relative merits of character and social position. Robertson elevates work and brains as ways to achieve acceptance in society.

4 Edward Bulwer Lytton (ed.), *Speeches of Edward Lord Lytton* (London, 1874), vol. I, pp. 101–2.

5 *Dame Madge Kendal by Herself* (London, 1933), p. 7.

6 Memoir of Robertson, p. xxxviii.

7 Mr and Mrs Bancroft, *On and Off the Stage* (London, 1891), pp. 3–4.

8 Ibid., pp. 5–6 and 38.

9 Quoted in Maynard Savin, *Thomas William Robertson: His Plays and Stagecraft* (Providence, 1950), pp. 78–9.

10 *On and Off the Stage*, pp. 86–9. The pair tell their story in such a respectably upholstered way, from the heights of their public image as retired theatrical grandees, that it is easy to forget they were only in their mid twenties when they threw down the gauntlet at Tottenham Street.

11 The Bancrofts, *Recollections of Sixty Years* (London, 1911), p. 101.

12 William Tydeman (ed.), *Plays by Tom Robertson* (Cambridge, 1982), p. 42. This edition contains *Society*, *Ours*, *Caste*, and *School*; all citations in parentheses refer to those texts.

13 Quoted by T. Edgar Pemberton (ed.), *Society and Caste* (Boston, 1905), p. xxvi.

14 *Pall Mall Gazette*, 17 November 1865.

15 The Bancrofts, *Recollections*, p. 102.

16 *The Principal Dramatic Works*, vol. II, Act I, p. 750. All citations to *War* refer to this volume.

17 Quoted by Pemberton, *Society*, p. xxxi.

18 *On and Off the Stage*, p. 110.

19 Robertson habitually protected himself from cliché – here the idealized lady of a man's dreams – by making his characters consciously play up to the convention. His most extended parodies come from the mouth of Jack Randall, a playwright himself, who satirizes the old style of acting and writing in *Birth*. *Dramatic Works*, vol. I, pp. 11 ff.

20 The Bancrofts, *Recollections*, p. 113.

21 Robertson's characters can sometimes be overtly emblematic. At the final moments of *Progress* (1869) Lord Mompesson, representing tradition, and John Ferne, the new breed of hard-working, educated, young technician, walk on either side of the frail Eva who, by that time, has become a sort of Britannia.

22 *On and Off the Stage*, p. 118.

23 Quoted in Savin, *Robertson*, p. 86.
24 *On and Off the Stage*, pp. 392–3.
25 Augustin Filon, *The English Stage* (London, 1897), p. 127.
26 *On and Off the Stage*, p. 393.
27 Cecilia's handbook is a pale reflection of John Stuart Mill's *The Subjection of Women* published in the previous year, 1869. As in Robertson's paraphrase, Mill identifies 'the peculiar character of the modern world' as the right of all individuals 'to achieve the lot which may appear to them most desirable': 'if the principle is true, we ought to act as if we believed it, and not to ordain that to be born a girl instead of a boy, any more than to be born black instead of white, or a commoner instead of a nobleman, shall decide the person's position through all life . . . the disabilities of women are the only case, save one, in which laws and institutions take persons at their birth, and ordain that they shall never in all their lives be allowed to compete for certain things. The one exception is that of royalty.' Stanton Coit (ed.), London, 1909, pp. 44–6.
28 Cecilia's determination to do whatever is necessary for the man she loves looks forward to *A Doll's House* (1879):

HELMER: . . . You must have *some* moral sense. Or am I wrong? Perhaps you haven't.

NORA: . . . All I know is that I think quite differently from you about things; and now I find that the law is quite different from what I thought, and I simply can't convince myself that the law is right. That a woman shouldn't have the right to spare her old father on his deathbed, or to save her husband's life! I can't believe things like that.

    (Act III, trans. Peter Watts, *Ibsen Plays* (Harmondsworth, 1965), p. 228)

After Ibsen's play was finally produced 'for seven performances only' at the Novelty Theatre in June 1889, the shock that rippled from the stage rocked the nation's presses and gave momentum to women's political struggle in the nineties.
29 The Bancrofts, *Recollections*, pp. 95–6.

4 Critics of the hearth

1 *Saturday Review*, 14 March 1868, pp. 339–40. The comic weeklies were as satirical about the old breed as they were of the new. *Judy* ran a series on 'Young Ladies of the Period'. Number five, the 'Domestic' young lady, likens her to 'home-made bread – wholesome, but heavy. In this respect is she the direct opposite of the "Fashionably-Fast" Young Lady. One touch of Nature . . . makes both species akin, *i.e.*, the desire to land the biggest fish in the matrimonial market; but the bait each uses for the same prey is very, very different.' 2 September 1874, p. 199.
2 *Punch*, 14 January 1871, p. 12.

3 *Punch*, 16 April 1870, p. 153. Imagining college rules for the newly established Girton, *Punch* suggested that 'The Sub-mistress and tutorial staff will be happy to furnish Students with the names and addresses of dress-makers and milliners, who are prepared to study economy in combination with elegance, . . . Arrangements have been made with Circulating Libraries of repute for a regular supply of sound and wholesome light literature . . . (N.B. – Reading in bed is strictly prohibited)'. 1 November 1873, p. 173.

4 Quoted in Lynton Hudson, *The English Stage: 1850–1950* (London, 1951), p. 57.

5 Quoted by Jim Davis, *Plays by H.J. Byron* (Cambridge, 1984), p. 20.

6 *Illustrated London News*, 23 January 1875. Act and page numbers of *Our Boys* refer to Davis's edition.

7 Gilbert wrote this fragment of autobiography for the *Theatre* magazine. See Sidney Dark and Rowland Grey, *W.S. Gilbert: His Life and Letters* (London, 1923), p. 5.

8 Hesketh Pearson, *Gilbert: His Life and Strife* (London, 1957), p. 17. In his letters, Gilbert frequently caricatured himself as bad-tempered. Leslie Baily reproduces one of these drawings surrounded by such scribbles as 'I am an ill-tempered pig, & I glory in it . . . I hate my fellow-man.' *Gilbert and Sullivan and their World* (London, 1973), p. 87.

9 James Ellis (ed.), *The Bab Ballads* (Harvard, 1970), pp. 129–31. All further quotation is from this edition.

10 In a semi-serious letter 'On Pantomimic Unities' to *Fun*, 20 February 1864, Gilbert had explored ways of integrating a pantomime's plot with its obligatory Harlequinade. The letter and its illustrations are reprinted by Dark and Grey, *W.S. Gilbert*, pp. 18–21.

11 Quoted in Dark and Grey, *W.S. Gilbert*, p. 44.

12 'On Pantomimic Unities', *Fun*, 20 February 1864.

13 W.S. Gilbert, *Original Plays* (London, 1924), vol. IV, pp. 455–6.

14 Pearson, *Life and Strife*, p. 85.

15 Subtitled 'A Trial by Jury', Gilbert's satire appears in *Foggerty's Fairy and Other Tales* (London, 1890), pp. 215–36.

16 George Rowell (ed.), *Plays by W.S. Gilbert* (Cambridge, 1982), p. 29. Act and page numbers refer to this edition.

17 Ibid., p. 74. All quotation is from this edition.

18 *Figaro*, 10 October 1877. Reprinted by Michael R. Booth in the appendix to his edition of *Engaged. English Plays of the Nineteenth Century* (Oxford, 1973), vol. III, pp. 391–2.

19 The text is from Rowell's edition.

20 In 'How to write an Irish Drama', published in *Fun*, 1 December 1866, Bab–Gilbert's recipe requires a whole list of stale ingredients and a final watery grave:

> Take, oh take some lads and lasses,
>   Take a dreary moonlight glen, . . .
> Take the village bells a-ringing, –
>   Take and pitch 'em in the Thames.
>
> (Ellis, *Bab Ballads*, p. 93)

21 *Hornet*, 10 October 1877. See Booth, *English Plays*, p. 390.

22 In his review of *Earnest*, George Bernard Shaw remarked that parts of the play were 'quite in the literary style of Mr Gilbert', and teasingly suggested that Wilde had refurbished one of his early plays 'for practical commercial use', *Saturday Review*, 23 February 1895, p. 249. Lynton Hudson was the first to explore the specific elements of Wilde's indebtedness, *The English Stage*, pp. 102–5. However, the essential difference between the plays lies in the fact that Gilbert's characters have no driving purpose whereas Wilde's have consistent ambitions which they mean to fulfil, come what may.

23 Most Victorian playwrights, when they satirized the lower and middle classes, tended to take their cue from Dickens whose caricatured 'humours' suited the demonstrative and pictorial aims of the theatre. But Gilbert, in particular, shared Dickens's exuberant and fantastical attitude towards social, theatrical, or amorous pretension.

24 *Foggerty's Fairy* was originally a short story, published in *Temple Bar*, March 1880. In re-shaping it for the stage, Gilbert altered the entire plot, turning it into a satire on middle-class greed, and changed the characters into familiar stage types like Malvina, the tragedy queen, and Jenny, the romantic idealist. In the earlier version, Rebecca, the over-worked chorine, was merely an anonymous cake-decoration from the window of Foggerty's confectioner's shop.

25 *Original Plays*, vol. III, p. 32. Act and page numbers refer to this edition.

26 Fearsome ladies of mature years and romantic inclinations were a trademark of Gilbert's imagination. Sullivan grew increasingly revolted by such figures and finally balked at the scenario for *Utopia, Limited* and Lady Sophy: 'If there is to be an old or middleaged woman at all in the piece, is it necessary that she should be very old, ugly, raddled, and perhaps grotesque, and still more is it necessary that she should be seething with love and passion (requited or unrequited) . . .', Pearson, *Gilbert*, pp. 171–2. Delia Spiff's sudden arrival from Melbourne amusingly reverses the journey of Victorian drama's inconvenient characters who were often shipped off to the Colonies by the last Act.

27 Love potions and magic elixirs bedevilled Gilbert's relationship with Sullivan from *The Sorcerer* (1877) onwards.

28 Breach of promise cases, and the legal complications they raised, filled the newspapers in the eighties.

29 *Original Plays*, vol. III, p. 415. Act and page numbers refer to this edition.

30 The camouflage was all the more effective because the principals 'wore genuine Japanese costumes of ancient date' and the ladies were taught deportment by geishas from the Japanese Exhibition then in London. See Baily, *Gilbert and Sullivan*, pp. 83–6. *Utopia, Limited* ran for eight months but was not revived by the D'Oyly Carte Company until the middle of this century. Its music is not Sullivan's best, and subsequent events made Gilbert's thrusts at Empire increasingly less palatable. Rowell, however, detects 'failing inspiration' in the libretto and 'a return to the political and theatrical Aunt Sallies of Victorian burlesque', *Plays*, p. 18.

5 Terrible leanings towards respectability

1 William Archer, *About the Theatre* (London, 1886), p. 33.
2 Gilbert complained to the *Daily News* that 'Young girls are not allowed to read Novels, and yet are taken to the Theatre. This accounts for the weakness of many English plays.' For the apostles of English Drama, 'the young lady of fifteen' became a rallying cry; at the time, though, *Punch* thought W.S.G. should have known the sort of novels young girls read:

> She read OUIDA? Oh! never! never!
> (So says GILBERT, and he is clever)
> If she does, it is on the sly.
> But she comes with her glassy eye,
> Sits and stares from a private box,
> Power, or passion, or aught that 'shocks'
> Palsying out of the playwright's soul.
> ('That Tyrant Girl', 31 January 1885, p. 50.)

The mechanically modest princesses of *Utopia, Limited* 'are twins, about fifteen years old'.
3 *About the Theatre*, pp. 6, 4, 21–2.
4 Ibid., pp. 26, 99–100.
5 Clement Scott, *The Drama of Yesterday and To-day* (London, 1899), vol. II, p. 390.
6 Russell Jackson (ed.), *Plays by Henry Arthur Jones* (Cambridge, 1982), pp. 37–102. 'Although he was collaborating with Barrett and with a co-author, Henry Herman (who later disputed his part in the undertaking), Jones appears to have been responsible for the overall treatment of the story, as well as for most of the actual writing', Jackson, *Plays*, p. 5. The controversy over both Barrett's and Herman's contribution is documented in Doris Arthur Jones, *The Life and Letters of Henry Arthur Jones* (London, 1930), pp. 66–74.
7 After his Hatton Garden nightmare, Denver evades the police by jumping from a train which later crashes into a goods wagon 'loaded with

petroleum'. Nothing of this is shown on stage; Denver simply reads a newspaper report which lists him among 'the ill-fated passengers'. Archer makes an amusing comment about Denver's thanks to God for his escape: 'Neither he, the author, nor the audience, bestows a single thought on the carbonized passengers, slowly roasted in order to aid the escape of a drunkard who has by the merest chance missed becoming a murderer.' *About the Theatre*, p. 88.

8 *Life and Letters*, p. 31.

9 Ibid., p. 34.

10 Barrett was a particularly energetic collaborator: 'dramatic authors are mistaken in finishing off a play and expecting to direct its entire production themselves, without reference to scenic effect and many other things which go to make the success of a stage-play . . . I think that people who do the work of the production can often help the author very much after he has invented his motive or mainspring.' *Daily News*, 16 February 1885.

11 Jones's apology, after Ibsen had conquered, disingenuously suggests a very young (as well as inexperienced) neophyte. Introduction to Augustin Filon, *The English Stage* (London, 1897), p. 13.

12 Act and page numbers refer to the privately printed text of 1884. Henry Herman was again co-author and presumably was responsible for the 'rough translation' from the German.

13 'The Theatre and the Mob', reprinted from the *Nineteenth Century Review*, September 1883, in *The Renascence of the English Drama* (London, 1895), p. 23. Arnold's dictum, 'The Theatre is irresistible; organize the theatre!', appeared in his article on 'The French Play in London' for the *Nineteenth Century*, August 1879.

14 From a short article written for a London newspaper in 1884. Quoted in *Life and Letters*, p. 84.

15 'The Dramatic Outlook', an inaugural address to the Playgoers' Club, 7 October 1884, reprinted in *Renascence*, pp. 166–7.

16 Jones published the play immediately the American Copyright Bill passed into law, and his preface rejoices in the fact that plays could once again be read as literature. Act and page numbers refer to that edition, printed in London, 1891.

17 'Religion and the Stage', reprinted from the *Nineteenth Century*, January 1885, as an appendix to the text, pp. 119–20.

18 Ibid., p. 121.

19 Jones included Arnold's congratulatory note in his preface: 'The piece is full of good and telling things, and one cannot watch the audience without seeing that by strokes of this kind faith in the middle-class fetish is weakened . . .' But Jones did not hearken to his mentor's added stricture: 'I dislike seduction-dramas (even in *Faust* the feeling tells with me)', *Saints and Sinners*, pp. xxiv–v.

20 'A Playwright's Grumble', December 1884, reprinted in *Renascence*, p. 146.

21 In his preface to *Renascence*, Jones listed the things he had 'fought for during the last ten years': '3rd. I have fought for sanity and wholesomeness, for largeness and breadth of view. I have fought against the cramping and deadening influences of modern pessimistic realism, its littleness, its ugliness, its narrowness, its parochial aims', pp. vii–ix.

22 *Saints and Sinners* puzzled and discomforted the Margate audience during a pre-London try out: 'A lot of folks going into a little chapel!' (xx). Because 'the public is pliable and teachable within very considerable limits' (xiii), Jones 'accepted a kind suggestion from a well-known critic [Clement Scott], and changed the last scene into a happy union between Letty and George' (xxiii). Ironically, in making that change, Jones allowed the audience to forgive Letty's sin. However, 'the marriage of the heroine with her farmer [did] not please' Arnold (xxv), and the published text restored the original ending. The helpful critic is identified by Richard A. Cordell, *Henry Arthur Jones and the Modern Drama* (New York, 1932), p. 68.

23 'On Playmaking', an address to the National Sunday League, February 1891, reprinted in *Renascence*, p. 242.

24 'On Being Rightly Amused at the Theatre', November 1887, reprinted in *Renascence*, p. 209.

25 Clayton Hamilton, *Representative Plays by Henry Arthur Jones* (London, 1926), vol. I, p. 117.

26 'Relations of the Drama to Education', City of London College, October 1893; the comment about 'problem' plays appears as an added footnote in *Renascence*, pp. 302–3.

27 Act and page numbers refer to Hamilton, *Plays*, vol. I.

28 Cordell, *Jones*, p. 56. Variations of this phrase thread through Jones's articles and speeches in *Renascence*.

29 '. . . Education' (1893), *Renascence*, pp. 294–5.

30 'On Playmaking' (1891), *Renascence*, p. 245.

31 Preface to *Renascence*, p. x. Jones concludes with a death knell for Realism: 'The dark places of the earth are full of cruelties and abominations. So are the dark places of the soul. We know that well enough. But the epitaph – it is already written – on all this realistic business will be – "It does not matter what happens in kitchen-middens"', p. xi.

32 '. . . Education' (1893), *Renascence*, pp. 291–3.

33 In his comments (1922) on a thesis about his plays by Aubrey Goodenough: quoted in Cordell, *Jones*, p. 83. *Michael and His Lost Angel* is included in Hamilton, *Plays*, vol. III.

34 Act and page numbers refer to Jackson's edition.

35 *Life and Letters*, p. 164. Wyndham wondered what would 'induce

married men to bring their wives to a theatre to learn the lesson that their wives can descend to such nastiness, as giving themselves up for one evening of adulterous pleasure and then return safely to their husband's arms, provided they are clever enough, low enough, and dishonest enough to avoid being found out', p. 165.

36 Mrs Grundy made her debut (off stage) in Thomas Morton's *Speed the Plough* (1800) and so pre-dates the Victorian prudery she came to symbolize. In the letter, Jones is determined to disassociate himself from 'the lobworm-symbolic school' while assuring Mrs Grundy that the moral of his comedy, if she must insist on one, is somewhat shocking: 'as women cannot retaliate openly, they may retaliate secretly – and *lie*!' Consequently his 'comedy isn't a comedy at all. It's a tragedy dressed up as a comedy.' Jackson feels that the letter is also aimed at 'Wyndham's insistence on changes in the text', *Plays*, p. 105.

37 Kato refers to a contemporary 'group of popular writers dubbed "the New Woman novelists" [who] created a sensation with their highly polemical, and often lurid, feminist fiction'. Cf. Gail Cunningham, *The New Woman and the Victorian Novel* (London, 1978), p. 3.

38 Clapham was always a paradigm of modern barbarism for Jones: 'But the poor modern vamper-up of plays, searching for a definite heroic idea and heroic persons to embody it, finds himself able to seize nothing better than a steady, persistent glorification of money-making . . . so the Victorian drama reeks of the spirit of successful tradesmen and is relative to the age of Clapham Junction'. *Renascence*, p. 15.

39 Kato's refusal to let Susan walk away from him is another hit against the lobworm school. In his old age, Jones joked that any revival of *A Doll's House* should end, after the famous door bang, with Helmer pouring 'himself a stiff glass of whiskey and water, and lifting it reverently toward heaven [he] should exclaim: "Thank God, I'm well rid of her"'. Cordell, *Jones*, p. 80.

40 Act and page numbers refer to Jackson's edition.

41 Mrs Ebernoe's contrasting presence at the riverside party in Act One depended for much of its effect on Charles Wyndham's style. A piano is heard off stage (167); Mrs Crespin asks, 'Is that Mrs Ebernoe?', and Wyndham's 'Yes' conveyed such feeling and regard that the audience understood her special quality before she had entered the scene. '. . . his voice created an illusion round the woman he was in love with in the play and marked her as his goddess', Irene Vanbrugh, *To Tell My Story* (London, 1948), p. 37. Wyndham's 'Yes' was praised in William Archer's review, *The Theatrical 'World' of 1897* (London, 1898), p. 283.

42 Hamilton, *Plays*, vol. III, pp. 259–61. Lady Eastney smilingly defers to Sir Daniel; his loss of temper shows 'that if I marry you, you'd be my master'.

43 Despite their opposed moral stance, it was rumoured that *The Liars* was really by Wilde and that Jones 'had put his name to it because of the scandal attaching to Wilde'. *Life and Letters*, p. 187.

44 Introduction to Filon's *English Stage*, pp. 16, 29. Jones always blamed the failure of *Michael*, his favourite play, on Forbes Robertson's timidity and on the machinations of Mrs Patrick Campbell who, he suspected, continued to denigrate the play after she had withdrawn from the part of Audrie some days before opening night. Controversy had helped *Saints and Sinners* in 1884; it destroyed *Michael*, especially since 'lost angel' was a well-known euphemism for prostitute. *Life and Letters*, pp. 172–80.

6 Shades of goodness

1 26 January 1896, *The Collected Letters of Sir Arthur Pinero*, ed. J.P. Wearing (Minneapolis, 1974), p. 170.

2 16 January 1896, *Letters*, pp. 169–70. Pinero wrote from Paris where 'even the frank indelicacy' of the plays he saw was 'preferable to the Clapham-and-Brixton morality of our home-made article'. *The Sign of the Cross* opened at the Lyric, 4 January 1896, and, as Barrett's epic drew ever-admiring crowds, Archer constantly lambasted it: 'criticism could only stand aghast, and protest . . . this brutal and vulgar spectacle', *The Theatrical 'World' of 1897* (London, 1898), p. 23. Clement Scott, however, classed it with other 'aggressive stage sermons', like Pinero's *Mrs Tanqueray*, whose bleakness illustrated 'the danger of coquetting with dramatic wickedness', *The Drama of Yesterday and To-day* (London, 1899), vol. II, pp. 334–5. But see Mrs Scott's account in *Old Days in Bohemian London* (London, n.d.), pp. 128–9: 'Wilson Barrett was heart and soul in accord with Clement Scott for the clean, human and wholesome school of plays.'

3 'Mr Grundy's Crack of Doom', *The Theatrical 'World' of 1896* (London, 1897), pp. 41–58. Pinero furnished Archer with detailed accounts of the receipts for the run of *Mrs Ebbsmith* to help him disprove Grundy's pessimistic verdict and to discourage his concern with box-office success: 'leave off solving problems of thoughtlessness and vulgarity, and apply yourself once more, in honourable and cordial rivalry with your fellows, to the creation of rational and human works of art', p. 52.

4 Introduction to *The Theatrical 'World' of 1897*, p. xv. Grundy's preference for well-made structures and adaptations from the French had long displeased Archer. That same *'World'* contends that 'Mr Sydney Grundy remains an ardent and militant apostle of the gospel according to Scribe, but has shown himself capable of throwing a strong individuality into the forms imposed by his religion', p. 183. In his introduction to Archer's collected reviews, Grundy defends himself as a

realistic business man: 'Can it be marvelled that an insignificant dramatic author, who long ago abandoned all idea of setting this naughty world to rights, is unable to regard his vocation seriously? . . . I have been original more often than is remembered; but I am not sufficiently conceited to foist on play-goers an article they do not require', pp. xvi–xvii.

5 Henry Arthur Jones, introduction to Augustin Filon's *The English Stage* (London, 1897), p. 17.

6 7 April 1885, *Letters*, p. 80. In the previous year, *Low Water* had been so badly mounted at the Globe that Pinero wrote to Clement Scott asking him to inform readers of the *Theatre* that 'all my endeavours to prevent its performance, under conditions which I knew would result in the complete obscuring of the meaning of my work, were of no avail'. 13 January 1884, *Letters*, p. 70.

7 Pinero eventually clashed with George Alexander, actor-manager at the St James's, because 'frankly, dear Alec, I don't think that you and I go well together in harness'. After *The Princess and the Butterfly* (1897), Pinero refused Alexander's overtures and did not relent until 1906 when *His House in Order* brought both of them renewed success: 'there is not room for two autocrats in one small kingdom; and in every detail, however slight, that pertains to my work – though I avail myself gratefully of any assistance that is afforded me – I take to myself the right of dictation and veto'. 10 August 1899, *Letters*, p. 181.

8 Pinero's decision to blend sentiment with laughter recalls Boucicault's advice to Marie Wilton in the early days of the Prince of Wales's: 'The public pretend they want pure comedy; this is not so. What they want is *domestic drama*, treated with broad comic character. A sentimental, pathetic play, comically rendered'. Quoted by the Bancrofts, *On and Off the Stage* (London, 1889), p. 118.

9 Pinero, interviewed by the New York *Times*, 26 September 1885, p. 5.

10 George Rowell (ed.), *Plays by A.W. Pinero* (Cambridge, 1986), p. 26. Act and page numbers refer to this edition.

11 New York *Times*, 26 September 1885, p. 5.

12 To Clement Scott, 16 December 1887, *Letters*, pp. 98–9.

13 Pinero would soon take a different attitude to his serious plays. As he told Jones, the Germans 'may adapt *Sweet Lavender* till it is sage and onions for all I care; but *The Profligate* I have stipulated shall be merely translated . . . I think you'll agree with me it is far better to be associated with a good play which the Germans *can't* understand than with a bad one which they can.' 15 October 1889, *Letters*, p. 113.

14 *Sweet Lavender* (London, 1893), Act III, p. 132.

15 William Archer, *About the Theatre* (London, 1886), p. 58.

16 Pinero, letter to the *Theatre* (June 1889), pp. 324–5.

17 *The Profligate* (Boston, 1892), p. 123. Page numbers refer to this edition

which includes the amended finale in Malcolm C. Salaman's introduction.

18 14 May 1889, *Letters*, p. 107.

19 To Augustin Daly, 15 May and 10 June 1889, *Letters*, pp. 108, 112.

20 William Archer, 'Ibsen and English Criticism', *Fortnightly Review*, July 1889. During the row over *Ghosts*, Archer compiled an Anthology of Abuse from the hysterical comments of his colleagues; '*Ghosts* and Gibberings', *Pall Mall Gazette*, 8 April 1891. Both essays are reprinted in *William Archer on Ibsen*, ed. Thomas Postlewait (Westport, Connecticut, 1984), pp. 13–27.

21 'Introductory Note' to *The Times* (London, 1891), pp. vii–viii.

22 To William Archer, 25 October 1891, *Letters*, p. 129.

23 Pinero furnished Archer with a chronology of the play's composition after Clement Scott had publicly suggested that *Mrs Tanqueray* had been based on a German original, Paul Lindau's *Der Schatten*. 24 August 1893, *Letters*, p. 149.

24 To William Archer, 25 May 1892, *Letters*, p. 135. At about this time, Pinero 'went down on [his] knees to Irving, begging him to do *Hedda Gabler* at the Lyceum with himself and Ellen Terry as Lövborg and Hedda. That would have been a fight in the open, and no mistake; but unfortunately it was not to be.' To William Archer, 27 November 1907, *Letters*, p. 209.

25 To George Alexander, 21 December 1892, *Letters*, p. 138. Archer had advised him 'to let the Stage Society, or whatever the side-show of that period was, do [*Mrs Tanqueray*]. I replied that I would rather throw the manuscript on the fire . . . what I thought then I still hold to – that the only victory worth gaining in the theatre is a victory, by high aim and artistic means, over the great public.' To William Archer, 27 November 1907, *Letters*, pp. 208–9.

26 To George Alexander, 26 April 1893. The comment about Mrs Campbell was hedged with doubts since the Adelphi play, *The Black Domino*, was so poor that it was 'difficult to form an estimate of her powers'. Perhaps at the St James's and under Alexander's 'good influences . . ., she could rid herself of a certain artificiality of style', 10 April 1893, *Letters*, p. 142.

27 To Edmund Gosse, 2 May 1893, *Letters*, p. 144.

28 Archer's review, 31 May 1893, is reprinted in *The Theatrical 'World' for 1893* (London, 1894), pp. 125–37.

29 Act and page numbers refer to Rowell's edition.

30 *The Weaker Sex* (Boston, 1894). Page numbers refer to this edition.

31 *The Amazons* (Boston, 1895), pp. 182–3.

32 Clayton Hamilton (ed.), *The Social Plays of Arthur Wing Pinero* (New York, 1917), vol. I, p. 230. Act and page numbers refer to this edition.

33 21 March 1895, reprinted in *The Theatrical 'World' of 1895* (London, 1896), pp. 75–85. This essay is searchingly critical and constructively sympathetic, as is its companion piece, 27 March (pp. 86–94). By taking Pinero's stereotype seriously and comparing her to the actual 'new woman', Archer shows that Agnes 'is a very true and fascinating woman, though an unconvincing Socialist and Secularist', p. 92.

34 *The Benefit of the Doubt* (London, 1895), p. 12. Page numbers refer to this edition.

35 To regard Mrs Ebbsmith's end as forced upon her is not simply a modern reaction. Mrs Pat, her originator, felt 'inspired' by the character's 'nobility': 'but the last act broke my heart. I knew that such an Agnes in life could not have drifted into the Bible-reading inertia of the woman she became in the last act: for her earlier vitality, with its mental and emotional activity, gave the lie to it – I felt she would have arisen a phoenix from the ashes.' Mrs Patrick Campbell, *My Life and some Letters* (London, 1922), p. 98.

36 'Epilogue' to Archer's *Theatrical 'World' of 1895*, p. 394.

37 Ibid., p. 93.

38 Ibid., pp. 315 and 321. In a 'Prefatory Letter' to Archer's volume, written at the close of 1895, Pinero reminisced about his early days as an actor and jokingly explained his 'Instinct for Detecting the Presence of Adverse Criticism' which, he asserted, had its flaws. 'I am compelled, by my system, wholly to abstain from studying those articles upon dramatic matters contributed to a well-known journal by your friend Mr George Bernard Shaw . . .' (xxxiv). Shaw began to write for the *Saturday Review* in January 1895 and had lambasted *Mrs Tanqueray*, in retrospect, and *Mrs Ebbsmith*, in performance. Clement Scott, guardian of the wholesome, after having accused Pinero of plagiarism, made desperate amends by praising *Mrs Ebbsmith*, a turn of events which 'filled [Pinero] with as much disgust as [Scott's] dishonesty and misrepresentation have done in the past'. *Letters*, p. 166.

39 Page numbers refer to Rowell's edition.

40 At the very beginning of his flurry with psychological realism, before he was battered by the critics, Pinero had the same hopeful perspective: 'The play [*Mrs Tanqueray*] is a risky one and, at best, must offend many people. But it will be all right in the end – a long time hence, I mean – when we all settle down and review matters calmly and pleasantly.' To Joseph Hatton, 24 May 1893, *Letters*, p. 145.

41 Clayton Hamilton (ed.), *The Social Plays of Arthur Wing Pinero* (New York, 1918), vol. II, p. 34. All references are to this edition.

42 Pinero, with some daring, demonstrates the self-indulgent weakness and generosity of Iris (1901), but when she and Laurence Trenwith part, she begs him to forget he ever made love to her so that, when they meet again,

she can be a stranger to him. On his return from Canada, Laurence does forget the past and his knowledge of her personality, condemning her for giving in to Frederick Maldonado. Similarly, Zoe Blundell's misadventures lead to defeat in *Mid-Channel* (1909). Yet, whenever a woman's sexual repute is not in question, Pinero was free to concentrate, in a remarkably acute way, on social manners and behaviour: cf. *His House in Order* (1906) and *The Thunderbolt* (1908).

43 Hamilton, *Plays*, vol. I, p. 29.

7 A middle-class education

1 Writing to congratulate George Alexander on a speech he gave in Birmingham about English dramatists, Wilde pretended never to have heard of Henry Arthur: 'I know and admire Pinero's work, but *who is Jones*? Perhaps the name as reported in the London papers was a misprint for something else. I have never heard of Jones. Have you?', *The Letters of Oscar Wilde*, ed. Rupert Hart-Davis (London, 1962), p. 376. Jones's plays appear among a list of 'subjects of little or of no importance' in 'The Critic as Artist', in *The Artist as Critic: Critical Writings of Oscar Wilde*, ed. Richard Ellmann (New York, 1969), p. 364.

2 'The Critic as Artist', p. 385.

3 Cf. Richard Ellmann, *Oscar Wilde* (London, 1987), p. 115.

4 *Letters*, p. 70.

5 *More Letters of Oscar Wilde*, ed. Rupert Hart-Davis (London, 1985), p. 32.

6 *Letters*, pp. 70–1.

7 Letter in Ellmann, *Wilde*, p. 147.

8 *Complete Plays of Oscar Wilde* (London, 1954), p. 375. Quotation from all Wilde's plays is from this edition (Collins).

9 *Letters*, p. 143.

10 'The Soul of Man under Socialism', *Critical Writings*, p. 270.

11 To R.H. Sherard, 17 May 1883, *Letters*, p. 147.

12 *Letters*, p. 149. The editor's note gives a selection from the New York reviews. Vermilion was something of an obsession of Wilde's; his mother had worn a similar dress when, as 'Speranza', she stirred the Irish with her nationalistic poems against the English in 1848.

13 23 March 1883, *Letters*, pp. 135–42. Wilde had planned to publish the play in February 1895 (*Letters*, p. 365), but, in his exile, he concluded it was 'unfit for publication – the only one of my works that comes under that category. But there are some good lines in it.' *Letters*, p. 757.

14 Mary Anderson's verdict appears in *Letters*, p. 142, note 1. For Wilde's missives to George Alexander, Edward Lawson (editor of *The Daily Telegraph*), and Charles Cartwright see *Letters*, pp. 282–3, 285.

15 Bored by reporters during his American tour, Wilde 'turned the conversation on three of my heroes, Whistler, Labouchere, and Irving, and on the adored and adorable Lily' Langtry. To Mrs George Lewis, 20 March 1882, *Letters*, p. 105.

16 *Letters*, pp. 285–6.

17 To George Alexander, 2 February 1891, *Letters*, p. 282.

18 Quoted by Ellmann, *Wilde*, p. 324. 'The principal engenderer of the story was an account in the fifth chapter of [Joris-Karl] Huysman's *A Rebours* of two paintings of Salomé by Gustave Moreau, and in the fourteenth chapter of the same book a quotation from [Stephane] Mallarmé's "Herodiade"', Ellmann, *Wilde*, p. 321.

19 Ellmann, *Wilde*, p. 325.

20 *Critical Writings*, pp. 321, 324, 338.

21 Reproduced in Ellmann, *Wilde*, opposite p. 371.

22 Wilde saw Bernhardt's Lady Macbeth in Paris in 1884 (*Letters*, p. 156). In an interview for the *Morning News*, 10 June 1884, he maintained 'There is nothing like it on our stage, and it is her finest creation. I say her creation deliberately . . . Shakespeare is only one of the parties. The second is the artiste through whose mind it passes . . . She brings all her fine intelligence to the part, all her instinctive and acquired knowledge of the stage.' Quoted by Ellmann, *Wilde*, p. 236. Sarah began rehearsals in June 1892; they were cancelled two weeks later. She never did play Salomé, refusing to buy the rights to the play when Wilde was in prison (*Letters*, p. 392), but, to the end of his life, Wilde said 'the only person in the world who could act Salomé is Sarah Bernhardt, that "serpent of old Nile", older than the Pyramids'. To Leonard Smithers, 2 September 1900, *Letters*, p. 834.

23 To William Rothenstein, early July 1892, *Letters*, p. 316. The ban was even more infuriating because a licence had been granted to *The Poet and the Puppets*, Charles Brookfield's travesty of Wilde and *Lady Windermere's Fan*. Archer protested to the *Pall Mall Gazette*, 1 July 1892: 'the record of the Censorship presents nothing quainter than the present conjuncture. A serious work of art, accepted, studied, and rehearsed by the greatest actress of our time, is peremptorily suppressed, at the very moment when the personality of its author is being held up to ridicule . . . on the public stage, with the full sanction and approval of statutory Infallibility.' See *Letters*, p. 317, note 1.

24 To R. Clegg, April 1891, *Letters*, p. 292.

25 A report of Wilde's speech to the Royal General Theatrical Fund, 26 May 1892, George Alexander in the chair. Wilde seemed confused over his role as a suddenly popular dramatist: 'Whatever form of literature is created, the stage will be ready to embody it, and to give it a wonderful visible colour and presentation of life. But if we are to have a real drama in

England, I feel quite sure it will only be on condition that we wean ourselves from the trammelling conventions which have always been a peril to the theatre. I do not think it makes the smallest difference what a play is if an actor has genius and power. Nor do I consider the British public to be of the slightest importance.' Quoted by Ellmann, *Wilde*, pp. 347–8.

26 Telegram to Elizabeth Robins, 23 April 1891, *Letters*, p. 291. To Mrs W.H. Grenfell, late April 1891, *More Letters of Oscar Wilde*, ed. Rupert Hart-Davis (London, 1985), pp. 95–6.

27 To Elizabeth Marbury (Wilde's agent in New York), February 1893, Hart-Davis (ed.), *More Letters*, p. 119.

28 Lord Alfred Douglas stayed at Wilde's rented house in Cromer for ten days (*Letters*, p. 320) and his 'persistent grasp on [Wilde's] life grew stronger and stronger' from that time onwards: *Letters*, pp. 427–8. Wilde told Beerbohm Tree that Lord Illingworth 'is certainly not natural. He is a figure of art. Indeed, if you can bear the truth, he is MYSELF.' Hesketh Pearson, *Beerbohm Tree: His Life and Laughter* (London, 1956), p. 65.

29 Archer put the play 'on the very highest plane of modern English drama, and furthermore . . . it stands alone on that plane'. He revised that opinion one month later when *Mrs Tanqueray* opened at the St James's. Despite his praise, he complained that Wilde ignored dramatic action until the middle of Act Two: 'he amuses himself by lying on his back and blowing soap-bubbles for half an evening'. Also, Archer saw no irony at the end of Act Three: 'It would be a just retribution if Mr Wilde were presently to be confronted with this tableau, in all the horrors of chromolithography, on every hoarding in London, with the legend, "Stay, Gerald! He is your father!" in crinkly letters in the corner.' *The Theatrical 'World' for 1893*, pp. 105–8.

30 'The Decay of Lying', *Critical Writings*, p. 297.

31 *The Definitive Four-Act Version of The Importance of Being Earnest*, ed. Ruth Berggren (New York, 1987), p. 119. Page numbers refer to this edition. Wilde sent the play to George Alexander in October 1894: 'Of course, the play is not suitable to you at all: you are a romantic actor: the people it wants are actors like Wyndham and Hawtrey.' *Letters*, pp. 375–6. Needing a replacement at the St James's, Alexander bought the rights from Wyndham and, together with Wilde, reshaped the play to make Jack Worthing more central. Though Wilde fought to retain the Gribsby episode, the cuts show an unerring eye for inessentials and dropped tempi.

32 'Mr Oscar Wilde on Mr Oscar Wilde: An Interview', *St James's Gazette*, 18 January 1895. Collaborating with Robert Ross in this mocking self-parody, Wilde is asked if he has 'heard it said that all the characters in your play talk as you do'. He lights a cigarette and remarks blandly that

'rumours of that kind have reached me from time to time . . . it is only in the last few years that the dramatic critic has had the opportunity of seeing plays written by anyone who has a mastery of style . . . the work of art, to be a work of art, must be dominated by the artist'. Shakespeare, Ibsen, Dumas 'dominate their works. My works are dominated by myself.' *More Letters*, Appendix A, pp. 189–96.

33 Commenting on the way other critics found the play 'a strained effort of Mr Wilde's at ultra-modernity' under the influence of *Arms and the Man*, Shaw 'confess[ed] to a chuckle'. He was less happy with *The Importance* since its jokes 'could only have been raised from the farcical plane by making them occur to characters who had, like Don Quixote, convinced us of their reality and obtained some hold on our sympathy'. He also thought the acting suffered 'from a devastating consciousness of Mr Wilde's reputation'. *Dramatic Opinions and Essays of Bernard Shaw* (New York, 1907), vol. I, pp. 33–4. For Archer, too, 'Mr Wilde [was] least fortunate where he drops into Mr Gilbert's Palace-of-Truth mannerism.' *The Theatrical 'World' of 1895*, p. 59.

34 To Janet Achurch, 25 December 1900, in Dan H. Laurence (ed.), *Bernard Shaw: Collected Letters* (London, 1972), vol. II, pp. 206–8.

35 In an article (December 1900) marking Wilde's death, Beerbohm praised him 'as a thinker, a weaver of ideas, and as a wit, and as the master of a literary style'. *More Theatres* (London, 1969), pp. 333–4. He continually championed *The Importance*, calling it 'a classic farce . . . the finest, the most inalienably his own . . . a perfect fusion of manner and form'. *Last Theatres* (London, 1970), pp. 508–11.

36 *Mr and Mrs Daventry*, introduction by H. Montgomery Hyde (London, 1956), p. 18. All page numbers refer to this edition. Harris's Act One was originally more epigrammatic; he re-wrote it after the fiftieth performance. Nearly all the critics damned the play. Clement Scott called it 'drama of the dust-bin'; A.B. Walkley thought the 'discovery scene' was 'as near to indecency as anything we remember on the contemporary stage'. J.T. Grein, however, thought Mrs Daventry 'the truest woman in [Mrs Campbell's] gallery, truer than Magda, greater than Paula Tanqueray'. For those reactions and the tangled history of Wilde's scenario, see Hyde's introduction. A review by Max Beerbohm appears in *More Theatres*, pp. 310–14.

37 Wilde originally sketched the scenario for George Alexander in August 1894: 'Of course I have only scribbled this off. I only thought of the plot this morning, but I send it to you. I see great things in it . . .' *Letters*, pp. 360–2.

8 Vigilant open-mindedness

1 *The Letters of Oscar Wilde*, p. 332. 'Salomé is still wandering in her purple raiment in search of me', Shaw replied: '. . . I hope soon to send you my play *Widowers' Houses* which you will find tolerably amusing.' On receipt of that play, Wilde thanked Shaw 'for Op. 2 of the great Celtic School' and added gallantly, 'I admire the horrible flesh and blood of your creatures, and your preface is a masterpiece.' *Letters*, p. 339.

2 Hesketh Pearson, *Bernard Shaw: His Life and Personality* (London, 1961), p. 68.

3 Michael Holroyd, *Bernard Shaw: The Search for Love* (London, 1988), p. 145.

4 To Charles Charrington, 28 January 1890, *Collected Letters* (New York, 1965), vol. I, pp. 239–40.

5 Bernard Shaw, *The Quintessence of Ibsenism* (New York, 1908), p. vii. Page numbers refer to Brentano's reprint of the first London edition, 1891.

6 'Meeting Ibsen in Denmark in 1887, Archer had observed that he "is essentially a kindred spirit with Shaw – a paradoxist, a sort of Devil's Advocate, who goes about picking holes in every 'well-known fact' ".' Holroyd, p. 198.

7 Bernard Shaw, *Widowers' Houses* (London, 1893), p. 22. Page numbers refer to this first volume in the Independent Theatre series. The revised text appears in *Plays Unpleasant* (London, 1898). That two-volume edition also contains *The Philanderer, Mrs Warren's Profession* and (in *Plays Pleasant*) *Arms and the Man, Candida, The Man of Destiny*, and *You Never Can Tell*. For *Three Plays for Puritans* see Bodley Head *Collected Plays*, vol. II (London, 1971). For the way the plays work into or against theatrical conventions, see Martin Meisel, *Shaw and the Nineteenth-Century Theater* (Princeton, 1963).

8 This reflects the actual events of 4 February 1893. 'There was a most shocking scene, [Jenny Patterson] being violent and using atrocious language. At last I sent [Florence Farr] out of the room, having to restrain JP by force from attacking her. I was two hours getting her out of the house.' Holroyd, *Shaw*, p. 260.

9 To Richard Mansfield, October 1894, *Collected Letters*, vol. I, p. 458.

10 Cf. Holroyd, *Shaw*, p. 289.

11 'I have finished the first act of my new play in which I have skilfully blended the plot of The Second Mrs Tanqueray with that of The Cenci. It will be just the thing for the I.T.' To William Archer, 30 August 1893, *Collected Letters*, vol. I, p. 403. Wondering who should play Mrs Warren at the Independent Theatre, Shaw told Grein 'I should be content, myself, with Mrs Patrick Campbell.' Ibid., p. 412.

12 30 April 1898, *Daily Chronicle*. Quoted in *Collected Letters*, vol. I, p. 404.

13 To J.T. Grein, 12 December 1893, *Collected Letters*, vol. I, p. 413.

14 Holroyd, *Shaw*, p. 296.

15 28 April 1894, *To-day*. Reprinted in Bodley Head *Collected Plays*, ed. Dan H. Laurence (London, 1970), vol. I, p. 484.

16 14 April 1894, *The Star*. Reprinted ibid., p. 477.

17 William Archer, *The Theatrical 'World' of 1894*, p. 110.

18 To William Archer, 23 April 1894, *Collected Letters*, vol. I, pp. 427–9.

19 'A Dramatic Realist to His Critics', July 1894, *The New Review*. Reprinted Bodley Head, vol. I, pp. 508–9. Shaw had hoped the article would appear during the run of the play, but delays robbed him of that publicity.

20 To Richard Mansfield, 9 June 1894, *Collected Letters*, vol. I, p. 442.

21 To Henry Arthur Jones, 2 December 1894, *Collected Letters*, vol. I, pp. 462–3.

22 Bernard Shaw, preface to Archer's *The Theatrical 'World' of 1894*. Reprinted by E.J. West (ed.), *Shaw on Theatre* (New York, 1958), pp. 49–51.

23 Bernard Shaw, *Dramatic Opinions and Essays* (New York, 1906), vol. I, pp. 1–7. Volume and page numbers refer to this collection.

24 Preface to *Three Plays for Puritans* in Bodley Head, vol. II, pp. 14–18.

25 To William Archer, 18 March 1895, *Collected Letters*, vol. I, pp. 500–1.

26 To Henry Arthur Jones, 11 June 1894, *Collected Letters*, vol. I, p. 443.

27 To Janet Achurch, 9 December 1897, *Collected Letters*, vol. I, p. 828.

28 To William Archer, 23 April 1891, *Collected Letters*, vol. I, p. 295. When Archer and Robins founded the New Century Theatre, Shaw jibed at their moral realism: 'I cant make an American George Eliot understand the twentieth century ... her American scheme of ethics exactly fits your Sir Walter Scottish social consciousness, and your stupendous ignorance of English life and character.' 24 January 1900, *Collected Letters*, vol. II, pp. 136–7.

29 To Janet Achurch, 31 August 1895, *Collected Letters*, vol. I, p. 554.

30 To Janet Achurch, 8 July 1895, *Collected Letters*, vol. I, p. 539.

31 To Ellen Terry, 9 March 1896, *Collected Letters*, vol. I, p. 610.

32 To Ellen Terry, c. 20–26 August 1896, *Collected Letters*, vol. I, p. 641.

33 To Ellen Terry, 13 May 1897, *Collected Letters*, vol. I, pp. 762–3.

34 To Ellen Terry, 4 July 1897, *Collected Letters*, vol. I, pp. 778–9.

35 'The half-amateurs are at the West End theatres walking through the smart plays, whilst the skilled temperamental professionals are playing for the Stage Society, ostensibly for honour & glory alone ... an excellent view of the English stage during the toffification period which culminated in the knighting of Irving.' To William Archer, 7 September 1903, *Collected Letters*, vol. II, pp. 364–5.

36 Mansfield's letter is quoted in *Collected Letters*, vol. I, pp. 523–4.

37 To Ellen Terry, 10 July 1900, *Collected Letters*, vol. II, p. 179.

38 Complaining that popular actors were themselves in every part, Shaw wrote to Henry Arthur Jones: 'If you will write a comedy in which all the characters are merely our actors in disguise and then have the luck to find the originals disengaged for casting, I'll go out and see them eagerly. But not on any other terms. It will end in your having to do what I am doing', writing for readers. 12 October 1897, *Collected Letters*, vol. I, p. 812.

39 To R. Golding Bright, 7 May 1897, *Collected Letters*, vol. I, p. 754.

40 William Archer, *Study and Stage* (London, 1899), pp. 1–22, reprints the reviews which appeared in the *Daily Chronicle*, 19 and 21 April 1898.

41 Archer's remarks are quoted in *Collected Letters*, vol. II, p. 217.

42 A.B. Walkley, *Drama and Life* (New York, 1908), pp. 214–17.

43 Max Beerbohm, *More Theatres: 1898–1903* (London, 1969), pp. 21–5.

44 Max Beerbohm, *Around Theatres* (London, 1953), p. 120.

45 To Ellen Terry, 27 January 1897, *Collected Letters*, vol. I, p. 722.

46 To Mrs Richard Mansfield, 7 January and 12 June 1900, *Collected Letters*, vol. II, pp. 133 and 174.

47 Preface to *Three Plays for Puritans*, p. 15.

Index

Index

Index

Wordsworth, William 37, 50
World 230, 249, 253
Worth, Charles Frederick 12
Wright, Mrs Theodore 244
Wyndham, Charles 27, 150, 151, 161,
  248, 277/8n35, 278n36, n41, 285n31
Wyndham's Theatre 12

Yellow Dwarf, The (Planché) 7
You Never Can Tell (Shaw) 258–9, 261,
  262
Young Actress, The (Boucicault) 24–5

Zampa (Hérald) 34
Zola, Emil 147